OXFORD TEXTUAL PERSPECTIVES

Shakespeare and the Making of English Whoredom

Shakespeare and the Making of English Whoredom

STEPHEN SPIESS

OXFORD
UNIVERSITY PRESS

OXFORD
UNIVERSITY PRESS

Great Clarendon Street, Oxford, OX2 6DP,
United Kingdom

Oxford University Press is a department of the University of Oxford.
It furthers the University's objective of excellence in research, scholarship,
and education by publishing worldwide. Oxford is a registered trade mark of
Oxford University Press in the UK and in certain other countries.

Published in the United States of America by Oxford University Press
546 Fifth Avenue, New York, NY 10036, United States of America

British Library Cataloguing in Publication Data
Data available

Library of Congress Control Number: 2026936831

ISBN 9780198813217 (hbk)
ISBN 9780198813224 (pbk)

DOI: 10.1093/9780191851223.001.0001

The manufacturer's authorized representative in the EU for product safety is
Oxford University Press España S.A. of Parque Empresarial San Fernando de Henares,
Avenida de Castilla, 2 – 28830 Madrid (www.oup.es/en or product.safety@oup.com).
OUP España S.A. also acts as importer into Spain of products made by the manufacturer.

For
Barbara, Lynda, and Valerie

SERIES EDITORS' PREFACE

Oxford Textual Perspectives is a series of informative and provocative studies focused upon texts (conceived of in the broadest sense of that term) and the technologies, cultures, and communities that produce, inform, and receive them. It provides fresh interpretations of fundamental works, images, and artefacts, and of the vital and challenging issues emerging in English literary studies. By engaging with the contexts and materiality of the text, its production, transmission, and reception history, and by frequently testing and exploring the boundaries of the notions of text and meaning themselves, the volumes in the series question conventional frameworks and provide innovative interpretations of both canonical and less well-known works. These books will offer new perspectives, and challenge familiar ones, both on and through texts and textual communities. While they focus on specific authors, periods, and issues, they nonetheless scan wider horizons, addressing themes and provoking questions that have a more general application to literary studies and cultural history as a whole. Each is designed to be as accessible to the non-specialist reader as it is fresh and rewarding for the specialist, combining an informative orientation in a landscape with detailed analysis of the territory and suggestions for further travel.

Elaine Treharne and Greg Walker

ACKNOWLEDGEMENTS

It is fitting to begin a book about knowledge relations by expressing my gratitude to the many individuals who have informed my thinking, challenged my assumptions, and been willing to linger with me in sites where knowledge breaks down. Preeminent among these is Valerie Traub, who directed the dissertation upon which this study stands and whose capaciousness of thought, intellectual precision, and professional integrity remain both sources of inspiration and standards towards which one can only hope to aspire. To think with Valerie, as her friends and colleagues have long recognized, is a gift of incalculable value. I thank her for bringing me into the room.

I incurred many additional debts at the University of Michigan, including to the other members of my dissertation committee: Steven Mullaney, whose unflagging support and incisive feedback were hallmarks of my time in Ann Arbor; Elizabeth Wingrove, whose breathtaking acuity kept me on my toes and sharpened the contours of my project; and the late Barbara Hodgdon, whose contributions to my life and thinking are as ineffable as my grief at her passing. She is dearly missed. So too is Mike Schoenfeldt, whose erudition was matched only by the warmth, curiosity, and intellectual generosity that he so fully embodied, and which I strive to emulate in my own teaching and scholarship. I am grateful as well to Gregg Crane, Anne Curzan, Adela Pinch, Meg Sweeney, and Doug Trevor for their teaching and mentorship, and to the many other members of the English, Classical Studies, and Women's and Gender Studies faculty at Michigan from whom I received support and encouragement. In graduate school as elsewhere, I have been exceedingly fortunate in my friends. This includes the fabulous cohort of scholars with whom I navigated the program, and whose conviviality, compassion, and brilliance sustained me through its the most challenging of moments: Chris Barnes, Andrew Bozio, Katie Brokaw, Lauren Eriks Cline, Sarah Ehlers, Rachel Feder, Asynith Palmer, and Katie Will. In the years since, it has been a privilege to forge bonds with other Michigan alumni, among whom Amanda Bailey, Gina Bloom, Hannah Bredar, Amrita Dhar, Holly Dugan, Gavin Hollis, Amy Rodgers, and Laura Williamson deserve special mention. I am especially indebted to Ari Friedlander, Joey Gamble, and Marjorie Rubright, each of whom brought their considerable energies and talents to bear on this manuscript, and whose camaraderie, wit, and intellectual radiance continue to illuminate my life beyond it.

Upon leaving Michigan, I was exceptionally fortunate to spend three years as a Thinking Matters postdoctoral fellow at Stanford University. I thank Ellen Woods, Parna Sengupta, and Russell Berman for their invitation to join the program and for the sage counsel they provided in the years which followed; Cari Costanzo, Robert Pogue Harrison, Adam Johnson, David Lummus, Sarah Ogilvie, Kathryn Starkey, Elaine Treharne, Abraham Verghese, Blakey Vermeule, Tobias Wolff, and Lee Yearley for their generous mentorship and inspiring erudition; and the extraordinary fellows with whom I passed those halcyon days, including Risa Cromer, Kjerstin Gruys, Lauren Hirshberg, Kara McCormack, Peter Mohanty, Kate Norako, Sarah Perkins, and Bronwen Tate. During this period, I was also afforded a unique opportunity to return to Ann Arbor as part of a month-long research seminar on 'Theatre and Conversion in Early Modern Europe'. Led by Paul Yachnin and Steven Mullaney, it was this seminar that first turned my attention to repentant whore narratives, catalysing a line of inquiry that would culminate in this book's third and fourth chapters. The seminar also introduced me to J. F. Bernard, Alison Searle, and Lieke Stelling, whose friendship and feedback enlivened my work and life, and to the many vibrant scholars who collectively constituted the Early Modern Conversions project. Among this latter group, I am especially grateful to Patsy Badir, Peggy McCracken, Carla Nappi, Kathleen Perry Long, Benjamin Schmidt, Bronwen Wilson, and Stephen Wittek for their inspired work and instructive feedback.

Research for this project was conducted at the Folger Shakespeare Library, the Huntington Library, the Stanford University Library Special Collections, and the William L. Clements Library at the University of Michigan. I am grateful to the librarians and staff at each of these institutions for their expertise and kindness. This project has also benefited from institutional support that not only funded my writing and research but brought me into contact with scholars whose questions and insights informed my thinking in ways impossible to fully tabulate. For their financial support, I thank the English Department, Women's and Gender

Studies Department, Rackham Graduate School, and the Institute for Research on Women and Gender at the University of Michigan; the Making Publics project and the Early Modern Conversions project, both funded by the Social Sciences and Humanities Research Council of Canada and housed at McGill University; the Thinking Matters program at Stanford University; and the Babson Faculty Research Fund, which provided enormous support during the final stages of the publication process.

Undoubtedly, my argument has been sharpened by questions asked and feedback garnered at a variety of conferences, seminars, and symposia. These include the annual meetings of the Renaissance Society of America and the Shakespeare Association of America, which remain staples of my professional life, as well as presentations at Columbia University, McGill University, Queen's University, the University of California-Merced, the University of Michigan, the University of Toronto, the Center for Medieval and Early Modern Studies at Stanford University, the Kinney Center for Interdisciplinary Renaissance Studies at the University of Massachusetts-Amherst, and the Shakespearean Studies and Women, Gender, & Culture in the Early Modern World seminars at the Mahindra Humanities Center at Harvard University. For their thoughtful engagement with my work at these and other venues, I thank Abdulhamit Arvas, Kristen Abbott Bennett, Erika Boeckeler, Beatrice Bradley, James Bromley, Bill Carroll, Supriya Chaudhuri, Mary Crane, Jane Degenhardt, Mario DiGangi, Jennifer Feather, Will Fisher, Liz Fox, Jack Halberstam, Diana Henderson, Coppélia Kahn, Marina Leslie, Carla Mazzio, Subha Mukherji, Erin Murphy, Vin Nardizzi, Noémie Ndiaye, Kaara Peterson, Nicholas Radel, Matthew Ritger, Katherine Vomero Santos, Alan Stewart, Misha Teramura, Catherine Tisdale, Lyn Tribble, Henry Turner, Wendy Wall, Sarah Wall-Randell, and Adam Zucker. I am particularly grateful to Jessica Beckman, Simone Chess, Stephanie Elsky, Colby Gordon, Derrick Higginbotham, Sawyer Kemp, Christine Varnado, Jordan Windholz, and Leah Whittington for making this profession as warm and inviting as it is intellectually stimulating. The same can be said of Jean Howard, Jeff Masten, and Paul Yachnin, each of whom played a vital role in the development of this project and continue to inspire my work and thinking.

I marvel at the good fortune that brought me to Babson College, where I am surrounded by friends, colleagues, and students of the highest calibre. These include the members of the Arts & Humanities and History & Society divisions, *omnes*, whose compassion, erudition, and dedication to our shared undertaking are daily sources of inspiration. I especially wish to thank my division chairs, Julie Levinson and Jenny Rademacher, for their unwavering support and encouragement throughout the tenure process; Stephen Deets, Marjorie Feld, Mary O'Donoghue, Fred Opie, Mary Pinard, Kerry Rourke, Elizabeth Swanson, and Beth Wynstra for their sage counsel and good cheer; and Pamela Dietrich, Cathy Schaus, and Nancy Wright for their tireless support and enduring kindness. Finally, it is my great pleasure to thank my students, both at Babson and beyond, for all that have taught me; for the courage, enthusiasm, and insights they have brought to our collective journeys; and for the better worlds that they at once represent and are in the process of creating.

My relationship with Oxford University Press begins with Elaine Treharne, who recognized the promise of this project at Stanford, encouraged me to submit a proposal to the Oxford Textual Perspectives series in which it now appears, and introduced me to the equally incomparable Greg Walker. I thank both Elaine and Greg for their warmth, generosity, patience, and editorial brilliance. So too, I thank Jo Spillane and Phoebe Aldridge-Turner for their exceptional work shepherding this book through the publication process at OUP; Melissa Flamson for securing permissions and reproductions for the images which appear in the pages that follow; and Amanda Speake for expertly assembling the index. An earlier version of Chapter 2 appeared in *The Oxford Handbook of Shakespeare and Embodiment: Gender, Sexuality, and Race*, ed. Valerie Traub (Oxford: Oxford University Press, 2016), 93–111; and a prior version of Chapter 5 was published in *Shakespeare Survey* 67 (2014), 310–326. I am grateful to the editors and presses for their permission to reprint that material in revised form.

I would be remiss were I not to acknowledge the many teachers and mentors who invested in me long before this project took shape, and whose influence upon my life remains palpable despite the years that have passed since our acquaintance. Any such list necessarily begins with Bethany Prunier, who introduced me to the joys of reading and who encouraged me, alongside other outstanding faculty members at Souhegan High School, to pursue essential questions rather than fixed answers. At Brown, Karl Jacoby was a vital mentor during an especially challenging period. At St. Paul's School, numerous colleagues took me under their wing and helped me recognize my calling, including the late David Newman, who rekindled my interest in Shakespeare. At the Bread Loaf School of English, Oliver Arnold and Susanne Wofford set that interest aflame, prompting a turn to full-time graduate study. At Dartmouth, Lynda Boose, Jonathan Crewe, Cecilia Gaposchkin, Carl Estabrook, and Don Pease channelled my attention to historical and theoretical questions that continue to animate my thinking and enliven my life. I especially wish to thank Lynda who, as these acknowledgements reveal, was one of many feminist critics who played a formative role in my intellectual development, and without whom—alongside Barbara Hodgdon and Valerie Traub—this study is simply unthinkable. It is my great pleasure to dedicate the book to them.

Countless friends and family members have accompanied me along this journey. Special thanks are due to Kristen Blanchette Roy, Hap Bradley, and Asynith Palmer for their enduring friendship; to Sue Spiess, Paul Spiess, and Jen Spiess Gupta for their boundless love (and patience); and to Lindsey Braverman, Ayla Spiess, and Annabel Spiess for enriching my life beyond measure. I wish for my daughters, and all of us, a better world to come.

CONTENTS

LIST OF ILLUSTRATIONS

Introduction

Epistemology of the Early Modern Whore

Midway through the sixth book of *ΓUNAIKEION: or, NINE BOOKES of Various History Concerninge Women* (1624), his encyclopaedic catalogue of women historical and mythological, Thomas Heywood concedes that the time has come for a proper definition. His is, after all, a work of didactic aims if not ontological ambitions: a 466-page treatise that endeavours to distinguish the chaste from illicit woman, and thereby instruct readers how to do the same.[1] Inscribed to Erato, the muse of sacred and profane love, and dedicated to the 'Treating of Chast[e] women, and of Woman Wantons' (sig. Aa2r/267), the sixth book appears well suited to delivering such social and sexual clarity. Yet as throughout the broader work, Heywood here privileges capacious portraits over concise definitions, offering protracted accounts of renowned virgins, such as the biblical Mary, and chaste wives, like Homer's Penelope, alongside detailed histories of Lais (the 'strumpet of Corinth'), Phrine (the Boeotian 'Courtizan'), and Harlotta (mother to William the Conqueror and namesake, Heywood alleges, to the

[1] Heywood's book participates in a much longer tradition that aims to differentiate between 'the Faire and Foule, Chaste and Wanton' (sig. A4r/n.p.). Relevant examples include Abraham Vele, *The Deceyte of Women* (1557); Barnabie Rich, *THE EXCELLENCY of Good Women* (1613); Nicholas Breton, *THE GOOD AND THE BADDE* (1616); Richard Brathwaite, *THE ENGLISH GENTLEWOMAN* (1631). Except for the prefatory materials (gather A), the 1624 edition of *ΓUNAIKEION* includes signature markers as well as page numbers. For ease of reference, I include both in what follows.

contemporary 'Harlot').[2] Amidst these thick descriptions, it is therefore a touch surprising when Heywood shifts from the expository to the definitional and concedes 'that I should define vnto you, what these prostitutes and common women are'. It is as if, after 286 pages of the seemingly endless anecdotes and *exempla*, epigrams and fables, tales and 'discourses' that constitute this paragon of Renaissance copiousness,[3] Heywood realizes that he must clarify the conceptual foundations upon which his project depends. Having thus primed readers for definitional deliverance, he suddenly swerves again and, adopting a decidedly offhand tone—as if sharing an insight so obvious as to barely merit acknowledgement—releases himself from any such obligation: 'But what need I trouble my selfe so farre, when in these corrupt daies almost euerie Boy of fifteene or sixteen yeres old, knowes what a strumpet is, better by his own practice than I can illustrate to him by all my reading' (sig. Bb6r/287).

In his dismissive certainty and definitional elusiveness, Heywood aptly if ironically figures early modern 'whoredom' less as a site of conceptual stability and ready knowability than as a nexus of power and knowledge relations that masquerades as an agreement in signification.[4]

[2] *ΓUNAIKEION*, sigs Cc1r/289, Cc3r/293, Cc6v/300. Heywood also refers to Lais's 'common prostitution' (sig. Cc1r/289), designates Phrine as a 'prostitute in Thespis' (sig. Cc2v/292), and, in his etymology of Harlot(ta), suggests that 'prostitutes and common wenches are to this day in our vulgar Tongue called Harlots' (sig. Cc6v/300).

[3] See Heywood's 'To the Reader', which opens by figuring the work as a 'Discourse of Women'. *ΓUNAIKEION*, sig. A4r/n.p. On Renaissance copiousness and the 'problems of reading and writing' that it animates (xvi), see especially Cave, *The Cornucopian Text*.

[4] A quick note on quotation marks: as is well known, it is common practice for scholars to place unstable terms in quotation marks, a move that both puts the selected term in question and acknowledges its necessarily provisional status. To the extent that this book foregrounds the instabilities and incoherences of early modern 'whoredom', all such usages of the term—and its manifold correlatives—should be understood as in quotation marks. That said, and to avoid readerly fatigue, I henceforth refrain from bracketing all such terms in quotation marks unless identifying a direct textual citation. I have adopted 'whoredom' as my governing term for two reasons: first, this usage acknowledges the prominence of 'whore[dom]' vis-à-vis its correlatives both in early modern discourse and present-day scholarship, even as my argument reveals that other 'terms of whoredom' appear with greater frequency in select early modern discourses: 'harlot' in the 'King James Bible', for instance, or 'bawd' and 'wench' in Shakespearean drama. Second, in its capacity to incorporate elements that are, I suspect, at once familiar ('whore') and strange ('whoredom') to modern readers, the term both underscores the complex historical character of 'whore[dom]' and activates the relations of recognition and befuddlement, knowledge and ignorance, that, I will argue, are essential to understanding both this category and its attendant epistemology.

In a text ostensibly oriented towards female readers,[5] he locates sexual knowledge in the minds and 'practice[s]' of teenage boys; privileging the experiential over the textual, he enacts an epistemological distinction that loosens the didactic purchase of his own project; presenting the illicit sexual woman as readily intelligible, he infers a conceptual stability that is belied not only by the multiplicity of persons, relations, and meanings that populate the *ΓUNAIKEION*'s nine books but those detailed in the very sentence which follows his brash declaration:

> And for Concubines wee need not trauell so farre as the Turkes Seraglio, since but few kings pallaces are without them. And for such as wee call Sweet-hearts, Friends, or Good wenches, should we but search noble mens Diaries, gentlemens Summer-lodges, or cittisens Garden-houses, and trauell no further, wee should no question find plentie sufficient. (sig. Bb6r/287)

As 'strumpets' collide with 'Concubines' and 'Sweet-hearts', English 'pallaces' merge with Turkish 'Seraglio[s]', and 'cittisens Garden-houses' seem indistinguishable from brothels, Heywood's definitional praxis proves less clarifying than confounding, animating rather than resolving the question(s) at hand: 'what [are] these prostitutes and common women?' How do such figures compare to, and diverge from, the 'strumpets', 'sweet-hearts', 'friends', and 'good wenches' with whom they are here aligned? What does 'almost euerie Boy of fifteene or sixteen yeres old' know about early modern English 'strumpets', how is such knowledge attained, and upon what terms, standards, interpretive logics, and material practices does it depend? How does this knowledge align with, and diverge from, that of the inquisitive (ignorant, confused, baffled, oblivious) reader who presumably seeks to know? In its efforts to render such questions insignificant, to bury them beneath the 'three thousand' lives catalogued therein (sig. A3r, n.p.), Heywood's *ΓUNAIKEION* evinces in strong form what I call the 'making of English whoredom': the ongoing and contestatory labour necessary to produce and sustain the fiction of the 'whore' as a fixed, coherent, and readily apprehensible object of knowledge in early modern England.

[5] *ΓUNAIKEION*, sig. A4r/n.p.: 'Wiues may reade here of chast Virgins, to patterne their Daughters by, and how to demeane themselues in all Coniugall loue towards their Husbands: Widowes may finde what may best become their solitude, and Matrons those accomplishments that most dignifie their grauitie: and so of the rest.'

Shakespeare and the Making of English Whoredom is a book about this cultural and discursive labour, both as it unfolds in early modern England and in present-day efforts to elucidate the contours of that historical culture. It is, in other words, a book about the making of a category of sexual knowledge, as well as the epistemological structures, assumptions, and impasses that such labour engenders and reveals. It is also, and therefore, a book about unmaking and unknowing whoredom, and what emerges when a seemingly familiar category of social and sexual life becomes—or is revealed to be—unfixed, unstable, or unintelligible. Attending to whoredom as a knowledge relation and a material process, I diverge from prior studies of prostitution and whoredom in early modern England, where historicist and feminist scholars have demonstrated that illicit sexual figures provided early moderns with a potent vocabulary to explore and police matters of religion, gender, social status, economic authority, theatricality, and sexual practice, among a range of other topics.[6] This scholarship, it must be stressed, has played a vital role in enhancing our understanding of the contours and complexities of early modern social life, including its gendered asymmetries and disciplinary apparatuses. It has also, as I detail below, illuminated a range of historiography and hermeneutic quandaries that

[6] A vital thread of early feminist literary scholarship, for instance, examined the relationship between male anxieties and women's economic and sexual agency. Essential studies include Gohlke, 'I wooed thee with my sword'; Woodbridge, *Women and the English Renaissance*; Parker, *Literary Fat Ladies*; Rose, 'Sexuality in the Reading of Shakespeare'; Jardine, 'Why Should He Call Her Whore?'; Cook, 'The Sign and Semblance of Her Honor'; Stallybrass, 'Patriarchal Territories'; Newman, *Fashioning Femininity and English Renaissance Drama*; Adelman, *Suffocating Mothers*; Traub, *Desire and Anxiety*; Howard, *The Stage and Social Struggle in Early Modern England*; and Boose, 'The Priest, the Slanderer, the Historian, and the Feminist'. More recent studies include Howard, *Theater of a City*; DiGangi, *Sexual Types*; Alfar, *Women and Shakespeare's Cuckoldry Plays*; and Fox, 'Cosmopolitan Desire and Profitable Performance in *The Dutch Courtesan*'. On relations of theatre, theatricality, and prostitution in the period, see Cook, 'Bargaines of Incontinencie' and *The Privileged Playgoers of Shakespeare's London*; Howard, 'Women as Spectators, Spectacles, and Paying Customers'; Lenz, 'Base Trade'; Mullaney, *The Place of the Stage*; Varholy, 'Rich Like a Lady'; and Gillen, *Chaste Value*. Among many indispensable studies of the complex interrelations of gender, sexuality, and religious difference in the period, see especially McEachern, 'A Whore at First Blush Seemeth Only a Woman'; Dolan, *Whores of Babylon*; Loomba, 'Delicious Traffick' and 'Break Her Will, and Bruise No Bone, Sir'; Nocentelli, *Empires of Love*; Vitkus, *Turning Turk*; Britton, *Becoming Christian*; Degenhardt, *Islamic Conversion and Christian Resistance on the Early Modern Stage*; and Sanchez, *Queer Faith*. Additional citations can be found throughout the remainder of this Introduction.

situate whoredom as an important site for methodological reflection and experimentation. In what follows, I argue that a necessary corollary to this scholarship is the study of whoredom as a conceptual category whose stability and social legibility emerges only through considerable discursive work. To illuminate some of the social, textual, and linguistic processes through which early modern whoredom and the figure of the whore are materialized, I therefore shift the analytic lens away from questions of representational verisimilitude, social discipline, and authorial perspective to those of signification and knowledge. This move allows me to examine an array of material practices that emerge to mediate problems of sexual knowing in specific historical contexts, including literary and dramatic representations by writers such as Shakespeare, Heywood, Gervase Markham, Thomas Dekker, and John Taylor, as well as dictionary entries, public proclamations, and conversion rituals. It also channels critical attention to the constitutive roles played by ambiguity, ignorance, opacity, and impasse to the meanings and makings of English whoredom as well as its attendant epistemology, revealing their structural centrality both to this cultural category and the discursive processes through which it has been, and continues to be, rendered intelligible as an object of sexual knowledge. Scrutinizing the contradictions and aporia that emerge by way of this discursive production, I demonstrate, allows us to discover both a category and an epistemology in-the-making, rather than a stable substrate of facts awaiting historical recovery.

As we shall see, an epistemological approach requires that we reexamine the conceptual foundations upon which categories such as early modern whoredom have been—and continue to be—constructed and understood, both in that era and our own. It necessitates that we tarry at sites where sexual knowledge breaks down and attend to the complexities and consequences of the material practices, cultural logics, and social affects that emerge to mediate these impasses. And, to the extent that this double helix of making and unmaking swirls both in early modern England and in present-day scholarship that aims to elucidate its contours, it demands a rethinking of some of our most ingrained ideas about what whoredom 'is', what it means, and how it operates within and across seemingly discrete historical cultures. With these axioms in mind, the remainder of this Introduction examines a series of problems—linguistic, historiographic, hermeneutic, methodological, political—that continue to animate the meanings and makings of early modern whoredom. First, I revisit the sign of early modern whoredom and unfold the importance of the categorical confusions that it incorporates and engenders. Central to this analysis is a methodological foray into what I call 'unknowing': an act of critical imagining that animates the experience of sexual-conceptual incoherence in and across historical time. Second, I examine the '(un)structures' of English whoredom: the political, legal, ideological, and geographic contours of illicit sex in early modern London, but also the ambiguities and opacities that attend and unsettle them. I argue that these and other evidentiary, hermeneutic, and historiographic impasses are essential to understanding how whoredom operates in that culture, including its dramatic representations. Third, I describe how my epistemological approach intervenes in the contemporary scholarship and offers a new analytic framework for accessing and interpreting issues that extend far beyond the 'whore' as a historical personage or literary trope. I conclude by detailing the questions, texts, and contexts that inform the book's six chapters, and which collectively constitute its broader argument.

The Sign of Early Modern Whoredom

Let us begin again with an act of unknowing. Imagine, for a moment, that you do not know what a 'whore' is, or what 'whoredom' means, or who among your compatriots is most likely to find themselves affixed to such terms.[7] In this imagined life, you find yourself in London during

[7] By 'unknowing', I designate a heuristic that both acknowledges the shaping force of a prominent conceptual category and, to the degree possible, attempts to 'unthink' it through an act of strategic forgetting whereby the critic, through an act of imagination, endeavours to process its meanings and contours, including by reference to related categories, ideologies, and experiences, as if they are being introduced to it for the first time. As will be clear, this heuristic aims to illuminate, and linger within, the various incoherences, contradictions, and aporia that attend 'whoredom' as it is defined in a specific cultural context. Centred on an influential early modern text, the analysis that follows is at once historicist, in that it seeks to restore an experience of early modern sexual knowledge making; deconstructive, in its unrelenting attention to questions, inflections, implications, and relations that unsettle the coherence of a category in the very process of its unfolding; and self-consciously imaginative, in a structuring conceit that is fundamentally allegorical rather than mimetic in its aims and effects. It aims, in other words, to animate a self-reflexive hermeneutic praxis whereby readers are encouraged to grapple

the first decade of the seventeenth century attending a church service, where you hope to acquire such knowledge so that you might better understand the world and society in which you reside. You are, as such, relieved to learn that today's sermon will incorporate the famous 'Homilie of Whoredome and uncleannesse', one of twelve discourses printed in the state-sponsored *Book of Homilies* (1547).[8] You pay close attention.

Whoredom, you quickly apprehend, is an imminent concern. While 'great swarms of vices' threaten the commonwealth, it is 'the outrageous seas of adultery (or breaking of wedlock), whoredom, fornication, and uncleanness' which, the pastor intones, constitute the most pressing threats to self and state, having 'overflowed almost the whole world unto the great dishonor of GOD, the exceeding infamy of the name of Christ, the notable decay of true Religion, and the utter destruction of the public wealth'. Elevating this vile quartet above all other sins, the pastor then parses another distinction in kind by figuring 'whoredom and fornication'—but not 'adultery' and 'uncleanness'—as especially 'odious, hateful, and abominable' to 'GOD and all good men'. Given the gravity of such terms, you yearn for still greater definitional precision, so that you might better know how to proceed: what, again, are 'whoredom and fornication?' At the very least, these acts or states or conditions appear interchangeable at present: bound together by the pastor's rhetoric, they assume a shared shape and form as 'this most detestable sin of whoredom and fornication' (5). A sin, then, but what constitutes or defines it—or them?

As if intuiting your confusion, the pastor draws an analogy. To 'perceive that fornication and whoredom... are most abominable sins', he suggests, you should 'call to remembrance this commandment of GOD, "thou shalt not commit adultery"'. You might note, amidst this flurry of terms and allusions and relations, that the pastor's pluralization ('sins')

with their own assumptions about the category in question, both in the early modern period and our own. Thus, to the extent that this imagined scenario may be taken to assume a present-day knowingness about whoredom and its meanings that readers must discard ('forget') to animate the heuristic at hand, my allegorical orientation in this section argues the opposite point: what must be forgotten is not a fixed and coherent understanding of what whoredom is and means in the present historical moment but rather the illusion thereof.

[8] *Certayne sermons or homilies* (1547). Reprinted in Davis, *Sexuality and Gender in the English Renaissance*, 5–15, which is cited in what follows.

suddenly renders discrete and singular what appeared, just moments earlier, synonymous and unitary ('this most detestable sin of whoredom and fornication'), but such subtleties can be difficult to intuit in real time, especially when the speaker is unfolding yet another conceptual relation: in this case, bringing whoredom (and/or fornication) into alignment with 'adultery'—a term that, you might recall, he has already defined as a 'breaking of wedlock'. Aligning whoredom-fornication-adultery, the pastor thus loosens the other conceptual distinction that he had introduced moments earlier, wherein whoredom and fornication appeared to supersede adultery (and uncleanness) as offenses unto God. He then further muddies these conceptual waters by noting that adultery, while 'properly understood' as extramarital intercourse, also encompasses 'the unlawful use of those parts which he ordained for generation'. Thus, and to the extent that you follow the pastor's unfolding logic and the rapid analogies upon which it depends, whoredom (-fornication-adultery) seems to connote (a) conjugal infidelity and/or (b) non-procreative genital activity—but the specific 'laws', 'uses', and 'parts' implicated in this activity are otherwise unstated (5–6). Given the proclaimed stakes, these are troubling opacities indeed.

If you could slow things down, you might assuage yourself with the knowledge that whoredom-fornication-adultery thus far appears to be a fundamentally transitive activity (i.e. something that you 'do', either to yourself or with another person) that is essentially genital ('those parts...ordained for generation') in nature. In other words, the pastor appears to have introduced parameters that support conceptual clarity by distinguishing between licit and illicit acts (conjugal versus non-conjugal), the body parts that they encompass (genital versus non-genital), and the aims towards which such acts proceed (procreative versus non-procreative). Yet just as this definition begins to cohere, the pastor unravels it by arguing that you and your fellow congregants must also recall Christ's admonition that 'whosoever seeth a Woman, to have his lust of her, hath committed adultery with her already in his heart' (6). Improper thoughts, adulterous yearnings, and impure hearts, therefore, are also signs and symptoms of whoredom-fornication-adultery.

As with all that has come before, the pastor's turn to 'spiritual whoredom' concomitantly expands and restricts the conceptual field that you are attempting to envision. First, expansion: in its shift from the material to the spiritual, from flesh to faith, the homily presses towards that transcendent vision of whoredom proffered in *The Demaundes of Holy Scripture* (1564), where Thomas Becon responds to his own question, 'What is an harlotte or whore?', by declaring 'it is the unfaithfull soule (whether it be man or woman) which seketh health other where than of Christ, apostasyng and ronnyng away from gods worde and fayth in Christ unto mans tradicions'.[9] For Becon, whoredom(-harlotry) is less a discrete act, relation, or use of the body than a movement of soul and spirit, a turning away from God and Christ, that occurs in men and women alike. It is, in essence, a spiritual transgression whose material enactments can encompass, but are not restricted to, specific genital acts and (extra-)conjugal relations. In your mental catalogue, therefore, 'evil thoughts' and 'carnal desires' now swim alongside 'fleshly consents' as intrinsic to, and evidence of, whoredom(-fornication-adultery-harlotry-apostasy). As whoredom's definitional parameters increase, so too do its potential referents. Insisting that 'whoredom, fornication, and all other uncleanness [is] forbidden to all kinds of people, all degrees, and all ages without exception', and that 'Christ our Master commanded us that we should all forsake uncleanness and filthiness, both in body and spirit' (6), the pastor leverages these rapid metonymies to advance a universalizing framework in which whoredom emerges as a state or condition applicable to all. Whether man or woman, 'king' or 'subject', 'common officer' or 'public person', we are all (potential) whores (7). Indeed, the pastor is at pains to suggest, one might be a whore and not even know it. Such an insight appears central to the pastor's allusion to Matthew 5.27–28, in which Christ, that 'perfect teacher of all truth', locates whoredom-fornication-adultery-harlotry-apostasy not in the female body but rather in the male 'heart'—a configuration that contravenes the commonly held belief that whoredom is an intrinsically if not exclusively female trait and sin.[10]

[9] *The Worckes of Thomas Becon whiche he hath hitherto made and published*, sig. LLLLlliir/1460. On Becon's career and influence, see Patterson, *Domesticating the Reformation*, 79–156.

[10] The sermon cites the passage in full: 'Ye have heard (sayth Christ) that it was said to them of old time, Thou shalt not commit adultery. But I say unto you, whosoever seeth a Woman, to have his lust of her, hath committed adultery with her already in his heart' (6).

Just as this emerging portrait appears all inclusive, the pastor's rhetoric also calls to mind the 'spirituall whoredome' or 'fornication spirituall' that writers like John Downame and John Bale have long associated with the 'great whore of Babylon', i.e. the Catholic Church and its practitioners.[11] Perhaps, that is, you recognize it as an anti-Catholic commonplace that connects whoredom(-fornication-adultery-harlotry-apostasy) to the various rituals, beliefs, and practices commonly associated with that 'filthy famelye of spiritual whoremongers': the 'Idolatryes, witchcraftes, sectes, superstitions, papacyes, priesthoodes, relygions, shauings, anointings, blessings, sensings, processio[n]s' through which, Bale implies, their whoredom not only manifests but can be recognized and known.[12] It animates, in other words, a restrictive or minoritizing framework that operates alongside the expansive, universalizing framework detailed above.[13] If you are Protestant, this minoritizing inflection may bring a sense of a relief, suggesting as it does that whoredom resides elsewhere and, again, that it might be recognized and known by way of such markers. Should you follow this line of thought, you might recall the extraordinary depiction of the Whore of Babylon in the 1560 Geneva bible, wherein this figure arrives 'araied in purple & skarlat, & guilded with golde, & precious stones, and pearles, and had a cup of golde in her hand, ful of abominations, and filthiness of her fornication'.[14] Again, perhaps you feel a touch of relief: such monstrous figures, you imagine, must be easy to identify.[15]

[11] Downame, *A Treatise Against Fornication and Adulterie* (1609), sig. S3r; Bale, *The Image of both Churches* (1570), sig. R8v. Elsewhere, Bale refers to the church as that 'abhominable harlot' (sig. Ddd2r) and the 'abhominable stru[m]pet Iesabel' (sig. E2v). The concept reaches it textual apogee in 1647 with the publication of Thomas Case's *Spiritual Whoredom Discovered*. On the tight conceptual linkages between Catholicism and disorderly femininity in early modern England, see Dolan, *Whores of Babylon*.

[12] Bale, *The Image of both Churches*, sigs Ddd2r, R7v.

[13] On the unrationalized coexistence of universalizing and minoritizing frameworks, see Sedgwick, *Epistemology of the Closet*. For a related application of Sedgwick's framework to the study of early modern sexual discourse, see Friedlander, *Rogue Sexuality in Early Modern English Literature*, esp. 11.

[14] Revelation 17:4, *The Bible and Holy Scriptvres Conteyned in the Olde and Newe Testament* (1560).

[15] For a related argument on the epistemological implications of apocalyptic imagery, particularly as it is routed through a prominent discursive figure (the 'Sodomite'), see Bray, *Homosexuality in Renaissance England*. As Bray famously argues, the extremity of the rhetoric that animates the discourse of early modern sodomy facilitates a 'cognitive dissonance' whereby subjects were less likely to locate friends and neighbours who

Yet even this most extraordinary of whores evades easy conceptual resolution. You might therefore find yourself navigating that strange dance of clarity and confoundedness that materializes in the marginal glosses which attend this famous passage in the *Newby Bible* of 1580:

> d The beast signifieth ye ancient Rome: ye woman that sitteth thereon, the newe Rome which is the Papistrie, whose crueltie and blood shedding is declared by skarlat.
> e Ful of idolatrie, superstition, and contempt of the true God.
> f This woman is the Antichrist, that is, the Pope, with ye whole bodie of his filthie creatures... whose beautie onely standeth in outwarde pompe & impudencie and craft like a strumpet.[16]

As allegorical keys, these glosses aim to bridge the gaps between discourse and reality, figuration and denotation, connecting the allegorical whore to its earthly embodiments and materializations. But let us imagine, for a moment, the pastor giving voice to these glosses, either amidst the homily at hand or during another service. Who or what is this whore? City and institution. Man and woman. Pope and Antichrist. Filthy and beautiful. Allegorical figure and human referent. A sign of the apocalypse in the guise of an everyday strumpet. In its (un)familiarity, the Whore of Babylon broadly evokes—we might even say allegorizes—the confounding capaciousness of the early modern whore as a discursive and conceptual category: its capacity to incorporate a range of seemingly disparate ideas, entities, and inflections but also, and in so doing, to blur the lines that set them apart.

These confusions only proliferate, we must imagine, as you depart the church and turn your mind to some of the many other texts, discourses, and institutions that contribute to the making and unmaking of whoredom in early modern England: the court sessions and medical tracts, marriage manuals and memory treatises, conversion narratives and historical chronicles, cant dictionaries and character books, pedagogical colloquies and everyday colloquialisms, stage dramas and antitheatrical tracts, lyric poems and bawdy ballads, royal proclamations

engaged in sodomitical acts or relations under the monstrous sign of 'Sodomy'. As he puts it, 'There was an immense disparity in this society between what people said—and apparently believed—about homosexuality and what in truth they did' (9).

[16] Passage and glosses reprinted in Stallybrass, 'Books and Scrolls', 60.

and prose satires. If Rome and Israel 'play the whore' in contemporary biblical and anti-Catholic discourses, it is Jerusalem—and, by analogy, London—which Thomas Nashe figures as a 'gorgious strumpet' in *CHRISTS TEARES OVER IERVSALEM* (1594), and Venice that emerges as 'the Turk's Courtesan' in contemporary jargon.[17] 'Fortune' may be a 'strumpet' to Hamlet,[18] an 'arrant whore' to Lear's fool,[19] and 'a bitch, a mere strumpet' to Gismund in *A Christian Turned Turk*,[20] but it is the 'strumpet wind' that, Gratiano alleges in *The Merchant of Venice*, prevents boats from returning home on time.[21] If 'Eloquence', for Philip Sidney, is 'appareled, or rather disguised, in a courtesan-like painted affectation',[22] and 'Vild double-fac't Oratory' appears, to Nashe, 'the whorish painter of imperfections',[23] it is 'that clever harlot, our natural reason', Martin Luther alleges, that turns men from marriage by forecasting the domestic duties that will await them at home.[24] Even 'knowledge' itself, Francis Bacon alleges, 'is but a courtesan' when it 'tendeth but to satisfaction... for pleasure and not for fruit or generation'.[25] And if such tropes, in their different inflections and incarnations, nevertheless broadly converge around the idea that whoredom is, at the very least, ignominious, it is much harder to intuit how one should interpret John Donne's suggestion that the true church is 'most true and pleasing to Thee' when, like a whore,

17 Nashe, *CHRISTS TEARES OVER IERVSALEM*, sig. A1r. On 'the Turk's Courtesan' as a common 'sobriquet' for Venice, see Dursteler, *Venetians in Constantinople*, 5–6. As with Whore of Babylon (Rome), such metaphors underscore that the meanings and making of English whoredom emerged in the context of a broader European discursive field.

18 Shakespeare, *The Tragedy of Hamlet*, 2.2.230–231.

19 Shakespeare, *King Lear*, 2.2.242.

20 Daborne, *A Christian Turned Turk*, 1.1.4.

21 *The Merchant of Venice*, 2.6.16. The complicated metaphor not only figures the boat as a prodigal child but genders both as feminine: 'How like a younger or a prodigal / The skarfed bark puts from her native bay— / Hugg'd and embraced by the strumpet wind! / How like the prodigal doth she return / With over-weather'd ribs and ragged sails— / Lean, rent, and beggar'd by the strumpet wind!' (2.6.14–18).

22 *An Apology for Poetry*, 119.

23 *CHRISTS TEARES OVER IERVSALEM*, sigs L4v–M1r.

24 'The Estate of Marriage, 1522', 31.

25 *Valerius Terminus of the Interpretation of Nature*, n.p. On this unpublished manuscript, likely penned around 1603, including Bacon's authorship and use of pseudonyms, see Serjeantson, 'Francis Bacon's *Valerius Terminus* and the Voyage to the "Great Instauration"'.

'she is embraced and open to most men', much less George Herbert's figuration of his beloved Temple as a 'house of pleasure', one of the period's most common cognates for a brothel.[26]

As readers will surely note, this cacophony of citations and connotations broadly trends toward a general shape and form, one that is predominantly female in character, arrant in nature, meretricious in conduct, and corrupt in essence. But it also, in revealing some of the paradoxes and aporia that emerge by way of this conceptual (un)making, intimates the cultural labour necessary to stabilize the often-axiomatic assumption that whoredom inevitably indexes the sexually illicit woman and/or the exchange of sex for money in early modern England. As a heuristic, therefore, our thought experiment demonstrates not only the analytical value of 'unknowing' a prominent conceptual category but of curating and scrutinizing the often-bewildering multiplicity of terms, ideas, relations, impasses, contradictions, and aporia that emerge when we suspend what we 'know' about whoredom and linger anew in its confounding polysemy. Whoredom in early modern England is not simply a legal offense, or a verbal weapon, or an act of sexual commerce, or a spiritual condition, or an allegorical figure, or a social 'character', or a labile trope, or a metaphysical construct, or a gendered discourse, or a confounding category: it is all these things at once.

The confusions that attend the sign of whoredom disclose several foundational insights that I revisit and develop throughout this book. First, the making of English whoredom unfolds across a range of discourses, assuming differing shapes and resonances depending upon the social and textual sites of its articulation. This is particularly the case in Chapter 1, where I examine an emergent English lexicographic project, and Chapter 3, where I scrutinize some of the governing paradigms through which early modern whoredom has been brought into clarity, both in that era and our own. Second, whoredom overlaps with a variety of prominent terms and conceptual categories in early modern England—including but not limited to adultery, apostasy, bastardy,

[26] Donne, '2 (XVIII) Show me, dear Christ', in *John Donne's Poetry*, 119; Herbert, 'Church-Music', in *The Complete English Poems*, 59. On the sexual inferences at play in each poem, see Rambuss, *Closet Devotions*, 59.

bestiality, bigamy, incest, fornication, lust, pride, roguery, sodomy, and witchcraft—in ways often difficult to parse, not only from our historical distance but in the period under analysis. Third, and as Nashe's strumpet-city, Sidney's courtesan-like eloquence, and Donne's whore-church reveal, the fecundity of whore tropes which circulate in early modern England foster not only a range of unexpected relations but the problems of interpretation that attend them. These include the various relationships that emerge between whoredom and the multiplicity of contemporary issues and topics—many of which are neither obviously nor self-evidently concerned with sex, gender, criminality, and morality per se—whose meanings, instabilities, and complexities, as scholars have long demonstrated, were shaped and mediated by a variety of whore tropes: beauty, charity, commercialism, conversion, cosmetics, cosmopolitanism, disease, domesticity, economic agency and exchange, eloquence, ethnicity, Englishness, evil, faith, foreignness, fortune, immigration, infanticide, language use, nationality, natural reason, politics, political participation, poverty, religion and religious identity, race, rhetoric and rhetorical properties, social (dis)order, social mobility, theatre and theatricality, treason, urban development, usury, and vagrancy, among other issues and concerns.[27] From these foundational

[27] Indeed, and as scholars have long recognized, one of the defining characteristics of early modern whore tropes is their capacity to forge metonymic linkages across a range of discourses, entities, and/or realms of social experience, facilitating a kind of conceptual blending wherein, for instance, ideologies of women's language use, domestic confinement, and sexual practice merge with anxieties about foreigners, infectious diseases, and the integrity of the English body politic. See Cady, 'Linguistic Dis-ease'. Given their deployment across a wide range of early modern texts and discourses, the literature on early modern whore tropes is equally diverse and voluminous. A survey of the relevant scholarship that aims to illuminate the breadth and diversity of this tropological field, therefore, might include Crane, 'Players in your Huswifery'; DiGangi, 'Sexual Slander and Working Women in *The Roaring Girl*'; Dolan, *Whores of Babylon*, 45–94; Friedlander, *Rogue Sexuality*, 69–125; Fox, 'Cosmopolitan Desire and Profitable Performance in *The Dutch Courtesan*'; Healy, *Fictions of Disease in Early Modern England*, 123–87; Helms, 'The Saint in the Brothel'; Hentschell, 'Luxury and Lechery'; Horbury, *Prodigality in Early Modern Drama*, 211–256; Howard, *Theater of a City*, 114–161; Karim-Cooper, *Cosmetics in Shakespearean and Renaissance Drama*, 1–66; Lenz, 'Base Trade'; Mallin, 'Charity and Whoredom in *Timon of Athens*'; McEachern, 'A whore at the first blush'; Mullaney, *The Place of the Stage*, 135–52; Newman, *Fashioning Femininity and English Renaissance Drama*, 129–144; Orlin, 'Women on the Threshold'; Panek, 'This Base Stallion Trade'; Rubright, 'Going Dutch in London City Comedy'; Twyning, *London Dispossessed*, 20–91; Varholy, 'Rich Like a Lady'; Vitkus, *Turning Turk*, 77–162. As

insights, this book elaborates the following principles that inform the meanings and making of early modern English whoredom:

1. Whoredom is a nexus of power and knowledge relations that masquerades as an agreement in signification.
2. Whoredom is not universal, transparent, autonomous, or neutral. Lacking a singular or fixed meaning in early modern England, it accrues value by comparison to a range of other figures, practices, institutions, and conceptual categories. These relations are dynamic rather than static and configured across axes both synchronic and diachronic.
3. It is often in the interests of patriarchal hegemony that whoredom be figured as a discrete ontological category and discernible object of knowledge. A significant amount of cultural labour is necessary to produce and sustain this illusion.
4. This labour takes place across a range of institutions and cultural discourses, including those neither obviously nor self-evidently concerned with sex, gender, and morality. It persists into the present era, where studies of early modern literature and culture continue to insist upon the whore's conceptual stability and social legibility.
5. An enabling fiction, the fixity of early modern whoredom serves as an efficient means of bypassing problems of knowledge and (un)knowability, including but not limited to those of sexual status, desire, and meaning. Concurrently, whoredom offers a point of departure for accessing those problems, for sounding out their implications and effects, and for querying the various cultural processes and logics through which they are mediated, managed, and 'resolved'.

Kim F. Hall, Lara Bovilsky, and Katherine Gillen remind us, the meanings and functions of early modern whoredom are concurrently structured by contemporary discourses of chastity and its race-making cognates: beauty, fairness, innocence, purity, and whiteness along with foulness, sexual impropriety, impurity, darkness, and racialized blackness. See Hall, *Things of Darkness*, 62–122; Bovilsky, *Barbarous Play*, 37–66; Gillen, *Chaste Value*, 33–86.

6. Whoredom's fixity emerges in tension with its status as a privileged emblem for artifice, changeability, counterfeit, dissimulation, falsehood, impurity, and inauthenticity in early modern England. This dynamic tension—what we might call whoredom's 'counterfeit ontology'—not only animates its manifold representations but implicates them in broader questions of sexual epistemology.
7. A sign of (improper) signification, whoredom overlaps with, and functions as a metonym for, both linguistic excess and theatricality in the period. The constitutive interrelations of this 'mimetic triad' not only enhance whoredom's disruptive potential but render it a productive site for epistemological inquiry: a representation of (anxieties about) representation, whoredom offers an alternative site for thinking relations of signification and knowledge, fiction and reality, discourse and materiality in the age of Shakespeare.
8. To acknowledge these linguistic, discursive, and epistemological dimensions, including the various contradictions and opacities that attend them, neither diminishes nor denies the material realities of whoredom as a disciplinary regime. Rather, it is to insist that whoredom possesses no essential substance prior to its materialization in historically specific terms, texts, bodies, and relations. It is also, and concurrently, to understand that this materialization was lived, felt, and experienced by historical subjects.
9. Whoredom is, in this sense, performative: a citational, reiterative, and sedimentary process that constitutes social entities, as well as the fields of intelligibility through which they can be thought, named, known, and regulated.[28]
10. What is known, unknown, and (un)knowable about early modern whoredom—and its correlatives—is therefore

[28] As should be clear, both this and the preceding axiom are indebted to the groundbreaking work of Judith Butler, especially *Bodies That Matter*. For a useful discussion of Butler's relevance to the culture under analysis here, see DiGangi, 'Early Modern Bodies That Matter'.

ineluctably linked to the material processes by which it is made to signify.[29]

11. These processes are historically contingent, culturally diverse, variable in efficacy, and unpredictable in effect. By parts contradictory and mutually constitutive, they are also inexhaustibly productive—fuelling a proliferation of terms, bodies, narratives, and paradigms through which individuals might identify, 'know', and assign meaning to early moderns as sexual, gendered, religious, domestic, racialized, criminal, human, and historical subjects.
12. In their multiplicity and fecundity, their iterability as well as contingency, these processes likewise open onto the complex relations of signification, intelligibility, and knowability in the age of Shakespeare—as well as onto the various assumptions, practices, and paradoxes through which those relations are forged and contested, both in early modern England and present-day scholarship that aims to elucidate the contours of that historical culture.
13. The making of English whoredom, therefore, is not simply the aggregate social, linguistic, and textual processes that help to materialize the 'whore' as a discernible object of social and sexual knowledge but also and concurrently the social, linguistic, and textual processes that introduce and sustain the epistemology through which this discursive figure can be defined, recognized, and known as such in a given historical context.
14. Where early modern whoredom is made, it is also and continually re-made. Always in process, its meanings and relations are therefore precarious, subject to contestation, and open to disarticulation.
15. Undoing whoredom is a necessary and vital task. To participate in this project, one must reject both a metaphysics of whoredom and the moral frameworks which subtend it. This is, I believe, a far more challenging practice than we have heretofore appreciated.

[29] My thinking here is especially indebted to Traub, *The Renaissance of Lesbianism in Early Modern England* and *Thinking Sex with the Early Moderns.*

The (Un)Structures of English Whoredom

Perhaps there was a time when the structure of prostitution in early modern England was readily intelligible to all who sought to know and map its contours. Scholars once spoke, for instance, of an Elizabethan 'underworld': an alternative universe of disorder, decadence, and play that was located in—and restricted to—London's suburban 'liberties', governed by its own (mis)rules and languages, and populated by the 'base string' of humanity.[30] A social, moral, and topographical counterpart to the city and court, this Falstaffian anti-world of brothels and theatres, actors and sex workers was thought to define the princely and the proper by way of binary opposition. If such a perspective appears quaint today, the residue of older structural and historicist approaches to early modern literature and culture, it nevertheless evokes the ideological benefits of a clearly demarcated sexual sphere, one whose unique geographic, demographic, and even linguistic contours were thought to operate as evidence that worked to resolve some of the conceptual ambiguities detailed in the preceding section.

In what follows, I revisit the histories of commercial sex in medieval and early modern London, including its suppression by royal proclamation in 1546 and subsequent persistence in altered forms. Highlighting some of the absences and aporias that attend the proclamation and its afterlives, I detail how this shift in official policy animates other ambiguities and opacities—legal, topographical, semiological, spatial, conceptual, hermeneutical—that unsettle the fixity and presumed intelligibility of early modern whoredom. Where this history broadly corroborates the semantic argument outlined in the preceding section, it also discloses a critical tendency to counter this ambiguity by narrowing or restricting the sign of early modern whoredom to whoredom-as-sexual commerce. This inclination not only underwrites historical and literary critical studies that acknowledge the whore's semantic lability but also feminist approaches which have, however unwittingly, relied upon and reproduced a binary—and implicitly moralized—distinction between 'real'

[30] Salgado, *The Elizabethan Underworld*; Berlin, *The Base String*. For an influential account of the ideological benefits of London's 'liberties', including Southwark, see Mullaney, *The Place of the Stage*. Critiques of Mullaney's thesis can be found in Kozusko, 'Taking Liberties'; Salkeld, 'Shakespeare, Theatre and Transgression'; and Somerset, 'Cultural Poetics, or Historical Prose?'.

and 'discursive' whores. The histories of commercial sex in early modern London thus open onto a range of absences, impasses, and double binds—evidentiary, archival, discursive, political—that continue to define the broader scholarship of English whoredom.

Focusing on these quandaries, I argue that the manifold incoherences and opacities of English whoredom are not historiographic and hermeneutic problems that will be resolved through the discovery of additional records, or the adoption of more precise definitions, or the development of better methodologies. Rather, they are part and parcel of an epistemology-in-the-making that churns in early modern England but also, and perhaps more provocatively, in our own historical moment. Whoredom, in other words, is as much a problem of knowledge and knowability in the age of Shakespeare as it is for present-day scholars aiming to delineate the contours of that historical culture, even if the forms of its attendant epistemologies are shaped and unsettled by institutions, discourses, practices, ideologies, bodies, terms, texts, concepts, memories, and affects unique to each cultural milieu.

This insight sheds new light on another defining characteristic of early modern English whoredom: its extraordinary ubiquity beyond the juridical archive. Simply put, whores are everywhere in the broader textual tradition. Surfacing in Protestant sermons and royal proclamations, bawdy poems and English bibles, broadside ballads and allegorical emblems, prose romances and utopian fictions, devotional poems and anti-theatrical treatises, character sketches and miscellany drawings, stage plays and coterie poems, multi-lingual dictionaries and medical treatises, and so on and so forth, the terms, tropes, images, and signs of early modern English whoredom are as pervasive as they are polymorphous, assuming a multiplicity of shapes and meanings across a range of texts and contexts. This discursive surplus encourages us to recast the relations between whoredom's manifold presences and absences, its interpretive aporias and its material effects, its social opacities and its textual ubiquity, less as problems to be resolved than evidence of a broader and constitutive relationship between cultural production and sexual epistemology, i.e. how cultures 'make' sexual knowledge. It also underscores the pivotal role played by the representative arts in delivering and deconstructing the very epistemologies through which this sexual knowledge is constituted, recognized, and reaffirmed as such. To bring these relations into better visibility, we must revisit the histories of sexual commerce in early modern London.

On 14 April 1546, an unknown representative of the English crown walked the streets of London broadcasting the terms of Tudor Royal Proclamation 265, 'Ordering London Brothels Closed'. The proclamation signalled a decisive shift in English social and sexual policy, yet the conditions surrounding its publication remain a mystery: this non-event appears inconsequential in historical studies of Henry VIII's final years. We are left to imagine why the act came about, how Londoners received the proclamation, and how its meanings materialized in the practices of everyday life. Such lacunae prove especially significant given what scholars do know about English prostitution: first, that illicit sexual commerce persisted despite the royal prohibition;[31] and second, that 'prostitutes' and 'whores' would come to saturate the stages and pages of Elizabethan and Jacobean England.

Let us linger, for a moment, with that anonymous representative of the English crown, walking London's streets in the middle of the sixteenth century. As noted, there is no record of these perambulations, of the timbre of his voice, of what responses this proclamation garnered from the varying Tudor subjects going about their daily lives on that April day in 1546. We might imagine, therefore, a figure like Shakespeare's Mistress Overdone, *Measure for Measure*'s bawd, who proclaims, in response to a Viennese proclamation intent on suppressing urban prostitution, 'Why here's a change indeed in the Commonwealth!'[32] Official repression, in other words, may have catalysed a stark and recognizable change in the city's sexual policies and politics. Yet this literary and historical trace appears over fifty years later, by which time Henry VIII had long since passed, and his second daughter was herself navigating the final stages of life. And, of course, Overdone's line appears in a playtext written for performance, likely uttered by a boy actor onstage, and first published in the 1623 First Folio. Indeed, we do not know if there was a proclamation in its verbal sense, for the term's early modern connotations included public speech and utterance as well as acts of printing, publishing, and declaring

[31] Archer, *The Pursuit of Stability*; Griffiths, 'The Structure of Prostitution in Elizabethan London'; Dabhoiwala, 'The Pattern of Sexual Immorality in Seventeenth and Eighteenth Century London'; Ungerer, 'Prostitution in Late Elizabethan London'.

[32] Shakespeare, *Measure for Measure*, ed. Bawcutt, 1.2.113–114.

law (OED, *n*.1–4).[33] In *A Survay of London* (1598), John Stow offers an alternative vision of the event, arguing that the 'kings commandment...was proclaymed by sounde of Trumpet',[34] almost as if this sonic pall were language enough, its divine reverberations instantly perceived and its effects immediately felt across London's sexual landscape.

Amidst these varying performances, speech act and music and play, we have a document, Tudor Royal Proclamation (TRP) 265, according to which the:

> King's most excellent majesty, considering how by toleration of such dissolute and miserable persons...have been suffered to dwell beside London and elsewhere in common, open places called the stews, and there without punishment or correction exercise their abominable and detestable sin, there hath of late increased and grown such enormities as not only provoke instantly the anger and wrath of Almighty God, but also engender such corruption among the people...[the King thus] hath by advice of his council thought requisite utterly to extinct such abominable license and clearly take away all occasion of the same.[35]

Historians have debated what perceived 'enormities' stimulated suppression, whether increased outbreaks of syphilis,[36] rising concerns about male lust,[37] fears of vagrancy and criminality,[38] or, as the document's biblical rhetoric suggests, 'shifts in morality' linked to the era's contentious religious climate.[39]

[33] According to historian Chris R. Kyle, proclamations were usually disseminated both orally and in print to 'ensure that as many people as possible were informed'. This two-pronged approach, Kyle argues, aimed not only to reach the widest possible audience but also, and more significantly for our purposes, to counter the most common of excuse advanced by proclamation offenders, i.e. 'that of ignorance'. I address the latter at greater length below. See 'Monarch and Marketplace', 784–785.

[34] *A Survey of London*, 332.

[35] *Tudor Royal Proclamations*, I.365.

[36] Porter, *London*, 56.

[37] Archer, *The Pursuit of Stability*, 211.

[38] Johnson, *Southwark and the City*, esp. 65–68; Carlin, *Medieval Southwark*, 225–226.

[39] Although little work has been done examining the impact of Reformation thinking upon English prostitution, Lyndal Roper and Tessa Storey have examined these relations in early modern Germany and Italy, respectively. Roper, 'Discipline and Respectability', and Storey, *Carnal Commerce in Counter-Reformation Rome*. In *Whores of Babylon*, Frances Dolan examines how representations of English Catholic and anti-Catholic sentiment informed and reflected issues of gender in the period but does not specifically address

What is clear, however, is that the document proclaims a definitive break from the 'abominable license' of past sexual commerce: the 'toleration' of public brothels, those 'open places called the stews', in and around the city for at least three centuries. While scholars agree that the sex trade was largely tolerated in segregated sections of the city,[40] barring the occasional raid or abolition campaign, prior to the 1546 suppression, it is unclear exactly what happened after the proclamation was issued. Such uncertainty partly reflects the dubious legal status of royal proclamations as official acts of lawmaking: their jurisdictional authority and legality were both subject to considerable debate in sixteenth-century English legal circles.[41] Scholars thus disagree whether the proclamation remained in force throughout the century or was nullified upon the death of its issuing monarch, Henry VIII. Roy Porter, for example, suggests that the stews reopened upon Edward VI's accession were suppressed once more by Mary Tudor, then returned and 'prospered' under Elizabethan rule.[42] Gamini Salgado offers a similar account, differing only in the assertion that brothels persisted 'more or less unmolested' under the Marian regime, as well as those of her half-siblings.[43] Yet such present-day attempts to delineate the precise legal status of London prostitution mask what was conspicuously—and productively—opaque in the period: as historians have long acknowledged, the 'rule of the law' regarding royal proclamations 'was ill-defined' and not always rigorously upheld throughout the sixteenth century.[44] Proclamations, in other words, instantiated not only relations of power but of knowledge, whereby the precise nature of the former

English prostitution. I address Thomas Fuller's seventeenth-century interpretation of the 1546 suppression in Chapter 3.

[40] As Howard underscores, this is not to suggest that sex work was fully and effectively restricted to such areas prior to the 1546 suppression. See 'Sex and the Early Modern City', 119.

[41] Holdsworth, *A History of English Law*, esp. 53–104, 294–307; *Tudor Royal Proclamations*, I.xxi–xliii. This history includes the short-lived Act of Proclamations, enacted in 1539 but repealed in 1547, which aimed to deliver both a statutory framework and an enforcement mechanism for Tudor royal proclamations—thus reflecting concerns regarding their validity and enforceability—only to have had little practical effect. See Elton, 'Henry VIII's Act of Proclamations'; Bush, 'The Act of Proclamations'.

[42] Porter, *London*, 56.

[43] Salgado, *The Elizabethan Underworld*, 52.

[44] Holdsworth, *A History of English Law*, 101–102. See also Elton, 'Henry VIII's Act of Proclamations'; Bush, 'The Act of Proclamations'; Kyle, 'Monarch and Marketplace'.

was (often explicitly) negotiated by way of the latter: as historian Chris R. Kyle notes, the most common of excuse advanced by proclamation offenders was 'that of ignorance... not knowing about the proclamation, or not hearing it'.[45] Indeed, if TRP 265 documents an official (monarchical) position vis-à-vis prostitution by the middle of the sixteenth century, it seems neither to have abolished sexual commerce nor made its perpetrators more vulnerable to prosecution than in prior eras.

While references to prostitution disappear from Tudor and Stuart records after 1546,[46] sexual commerce clearly persisted well into the seventeenth century.[47] But it did so in altered forms: formally condemned by the monarchy, it was largely tolerated in practice and subject to only sporadic regulation by other social and legal authorities, predominantly the ecclesiastical and Bridewell courts.[48] The semiotics of London sexual commerce further inflected these legal, social, semantic, and sexual opacities. As the 1546 proclamation itself suggests, the conspicuous visibility of the bankside stews, specifically those 'houses white and painted with signs on the front for a token of the said houses',[49] enabled a sense of social and geographic containment, however illusory, prior to suppression: illicit sexual practices could be restricted, conceptually at least, to the 'moral geographies' of the London bankside.[50] As Stow notes, Henry's suppression thus altered the material and

[45] Kyle, 'Monarch and Marketplace', 784–785.

[46] *Tudor Royal Proclamations*; *Stuart Royal Proclamations*. For references to commercial sexuality before 1546, see TRP 13 (6 June 1487), 'protecting women of all kinds from ravishment', including 'common women not allowed to follow king's garrison'; TRP 73 (15 May 1513), which includes a section on keeping brothels, and TRP 250 (26 May 1545), which associates vagabonds with sexual licentiousness on the London bankside and 'such like naughty places where they much haunt and in manner lie nightly for the accomplishment and satisfying of their vile, wretched, and filthy purposes'.

[47] Archer, *The Pursuit of Stability*; Griffiths, 'The Structure of Prostitution'; Dabhoiwala, "The Pattern of Sexual Immorality'; Gowing, 'The Freedom of the Streets'; Ungerer, 'Prostitution in Late Elizabethan London'.

[48] As I argue in Chapter 5, TRP 265 memorializes not an end but an evolution, not an erasure but an inauguration of official forgetting: a transition in the histories of London prostitution, informed especially by an emergent memory practice that enabled a practical toleration of sexual commerce. On the ecclesiastical and Bridewell courts in early modern London, see Gowing, *Domestic Dangers*; Griffiths, *Lost Londons* and 'The Structure of Prostitution'; Ingram, *Church Courts, Sex, and Marriage in England, 1570–1640* and *Carnal Knowledge*; Hair, *Before the Bawdy Court*; Hubbard, *City Women*; Mowry, 'London's Bridewell'.

[49] *Tudor Royal Proclamations*, I.365–366.

[50] I draw the phrase 'moral geographies' from Griffiths, 'Overlapping Circles', 135.

literal 'signes' by which London prostitution had been and could be known: beforehand, 'allowed stewhouses had signes on their frontes, towardes the Thames, not hanged out, but painted on the walles, as a Beares heade, the Cross Keyes, the Gunne, the Castle, the Crane, the Cardinals Hat, the Bell, the Swanne, &c.' What happened when these 'signes' were painted over and 'this row of stewes in Southwarke was put downe by the kings commandment'?[51]

According to contemporary accounts, this erasure had the paradoxical effect of making sexual commerce appear all the more visible to discerning eyes. In a sermon delivered in the presence of Edward VI, Hugh Latimer decried not simply the persistence but the metamorphosis of London 'whoredom', just three years after its supposed suppression:

> You have put down the stews: but I pray you what is the matter amended? What availeth that? Ye have but changed the place, and not taken the whoredom away.... There is more open whoredom, more stewed whoredom, than ever was before. For God's sake let it be looked upon; it is your office to see unto it.[52]

Latimer's emphases on perception are especially significant: Edward, the Bishop implies, is blind to the 'open' proliferation of 'stewed whoredom'. The king must therefore shift his gaze and see clearly what is obvious and easily perceptible to others. Yet as Latimer's allusion to multiple whoredoms ('open whoredom', 'stewed whoredom') suggests, perception depends not only on 'place' but on one's definitions and accepted significations. What does the Bishop see? What does the King not see—or choose not to see? As Laura Gowing argues, Henry's proclamation, however unwittingly or paradoxically, amplified the conceptual parameters of London prostitution:

> While before 1546 the regulation of London prostitution focused on restricting it to Southwark, by the late sixteenth century no single place could be identified with prostitution... in the intensely (though frequently unsuccessfully) regulated city streets of the 1580s–1640s, the shadow of illicit sex and prostitution could be seen or imagined everywhere.[53]

51 Stow, *A Svrvay of London*, 332.
52 Latimer, 'The Third Sermon of M. Hugh Latimer'.
53 'The Freedom of the Streets', 145.

No longer the province of bankside brothels, illicit sex pervaded the urban landscape: it could be 'seen or imagined' anywhere: in streets, shops, taverns, alehouses, inns, barbershops, churches, theatres, fields, alleys, and even ditches.[54] Without the clear signs and white walls of Southwark, all buildings were potential sites of sexual commerce, including Westminster Abbey, Saint Paul's Cathedral, and Whitehall.[55] As elsewhere, I do not mean to imply that illicit sex and its practitioners were readily intelligible prior to the 1546 suppression, nor that TRP 265 catalyses a break in the epistemology of the whore. Rather, I suggest that the suppression enabled the emergence of an ideological and affective structure whereby legal prostitution was retrospectively imagined to have once facilitated a clear distinction between licit and illicit sexual exchanges.

The question of course, was not only where illicit sex was located but who was doing it. In *A Common Whore* (1622), the poet John Taylor suggests how London's shifting sexual semiotics extended to the interpretation of individual identities:

> The Stews in *England* bore a beastly sway,
> Till the eight *Henry* banish'd them away:
> And since those common *whores* were quite put downe,
> A damned crue of Priuate *whores* are growne. (sig. B3r)

Taylor's distinction between 'common' and 'Priuate' encodes differences of perceived accessibility, official legitimacy, and visibility. While English sumptuary restrictions concerning prostitution were not as strict as on the continent, the 1546 proclamation nonetheless would have made officially prescribed sartorial signifiers uncommon, if not altogether obsolete.[56] The question, therefore, is what signifying practices emerged or evolved in absentia. Whereas shorn hair or striped hoods may have identified medieval prostitutes, such conspicuous markers were less

[54] In addition to studies already cited, see Bly, 'Carnal Geographies'; Johnston, '"To What Bawdy House Doth Your Maister Belong?"'; Manzione, 'Sex in Tudor London'.

[55] Bly, 'Carnal Geographies'; Shugg, 'Prostitution in Shakespeare's London'.

[56] As Roper ('Discipline and Respectability') notes, sumptuary regulations made legible not only the prostitute but also, by way of difference, their 'honest' counterparts. On clothing as a means of constituting the early modern subject, see Jones and Stallybrass, *Renaissance Clothing and the Materials of Memory*.

likely following the Henrician suppression.[57] Other forms and means of signification persisted into the seventeenth century, including social and symbolic exclusions such as those pertaining to church attendance and seating, access to communion, and even distinction in burial; Stow recalls, for example, a distinct 'plot of ground, (called the single womans Churchyard) appointed for [prostitutes], farre from the parish Church',[58] while suspected whores and whoremongers could be subject to public fines, stocks, whipping, carting, or other spectacles of public shaming.[59] Yet even as such practices offered one means of identifying and marking the sexual transgressor, it is far less clear what kinds of knowledge were produced in and through these disciplinary inscriptions. As Foucault reminds us, even the most violent expressions of power can work in unpredictable ways, producing meanings and relations that contravene the official 'truths' they are intended to deliver.[60]

Gender was a central signifying category in the making of English whoredom and thus a primary means through which early modern whores were recognized, adjudicated, and known. Unquestionably, women were both the primary subjects of early modern whore discourse and the primary objects of its disciplinary inflections and materializations. Without losing sight of this vital insight, scholars have begun to revisit the gender dynamics of early modern whoredom in a variety of productive ways, channelling attention to the various and complex ways in which men surface in contemporary whore discourse as well as to the interpretive and historiographic quandaries that attend their textual presences and absences. In a striking analysis of 'he-whores', for instance, Jennifer Panek identifies a variety of allusions to men who provide sex to women in exchange for compensation in the literature of the period. While acknowledging the paucity of evidence of male sex

[57] Karras, 'The Regulation of Brothels in Later Medieval England'; Carlin, *Medieval Southwark*.

[58] Stow, *A SVRVAY OF LONDON*, 332.

[59] The literature on shaming spectacles in early modern England is vast. For historical studies of punishments related to illicit sexual behaviour, see Gowing, *Domestic Dangers*; 'The Freedom of the Streets'; Walker, *Crime, Gender, and Social Order in Early Modern England*; Ingram, *Church Courts, Sex, and Marriage*; 'The Reformation of Manners in Early Modern England'; and *Carnal Knowledge*; Ungerer, 'Prostitution in Late Elizabethan London'. On physical and symbolic violence directed towards transgressive women on Shakespeare's stage and its relations to these material histories, see Boose, 'Scolding Brides and Bridling Scolds'.

[60] See, for instance, *Discipline and Punish*, 3–69. See also the responses to Jeanne la Pucelle's public execution, which I discuss on page 118.

work in the Bridewell court books and related ecclesiastical records,[61] Panek advances a compelling argument that 'stallions' and 'he-whores' were available to early modern subjects, at the very least, as figures of imagination and sexual fantasy.[62] In a pair of studies that draw heavily on the very archives that prove (largely) silent on the topic of male prostitution, historians Laura Gowing and Bernard Capp have demonstrated, through close attention to contemporary slander litigation, that women were among the most vociferous enforcers of the sexual double standard.[63] Channelling attention to relations, desires, spaces, and practices that contravene the conventional binary distinctions between male-clients/female-sex workers, male-oppressors/female-victims, these studies enable more nuanced understandings of early modern whore discourse and patriarchal hegemony more broadly.[64] As Valerie Traub has argued in another context, moreover, absences in the early modern juridical archives may tell us as much about contemporary expectations and ideologies as they do about actual practices: gendered assumptions regarding male clients and female sex workers, for instance, may have enabled a variety of non-normative sexual relations, practices, and eroticisms in early modern England precisely because they did not signify as such.[65]

Additional absences and opacities structure the privilege historical archive of early modern English prostitution. Where Ruth Mazo Karras illuminates the structures of medieval English prostitution by reference to the array of tax, ordinance, and legal documents

[61] Near the end of her article, Panek identifies two accounts of women paying men for sex, in 1622 and 1627, respectively (390). See also Bray, *Homosexuality in Renaissance England*; Griffiths, 'The Structure of Prostitution'; Salkeld, *Shakespeare Among the Courtesans.*

[62] Panek, '"This Base Stallion Trade"'. See also Bly, *Queer Virgins and Virgin Queans on the Early Modern Stage.*

[63] Gowing, *Domestic Dangers*; Capp, *When Gossips Meet.* See also Orlin, 'Women on the Threshold'.

[64] As Capp reveals, early modern women could also weaponize men's anxieties about their 'good names' to various ends. See 'The Double Standard Revisited', 72 and passim; *When Gossips Meet*, 252–263.

[65] Traub, *The Renaissance of Lesbianism*, 158–187 and passim. See also the vital work emerging in early modern trans studies, which has undermined the viewpoint that gender is best understood as operating according to a fixed binary in early modern England. Essential studies include Chess, *Male-to-Female Crossdressing in Early Modern English Literature*; Gordon, *Glorious Bodies*; and the essays collected in Chess, Gordon, and Fisher, 'Early Modern Trans Studies'.

produced to regulate what was, at the time, a legal trade,[66] and Judith Walkowitz draws on the range of medical, military, and judicial records produced by the Contagious Diseases Acts (1864, 1866, 1869) in two studies of prostitution in Victorian England,[67] scholars working *in medias res* have stressed the dearth of similarly 'official' records and the invisibility of 'real' sex workers in the juridical archives. Among these absences, none are more important than those which structure the records of London's Bridewell court, the preeminent institution for the adjudicating social and moral offenses in the era and thus the privileged historical archive.[68] As scholars have long acknowledged, these records are riddled with gaps: not the occasional occlusion or illegible entry, but rather entire years—indeed decades—missing from the register. These include all accounts for the years spanning 1562–1574, 1579–1597, and 1611–1618: in total, thirty-six years of absence built into the archival structure of London prostitution and whoredom.[69] It is historically accurate, therefore, to say that absence is a defining characteristic of the privileged archive that historically has structured the study of illicit sexual behaviours and identities in early modern London. This elemental absence can result in disproportionate weight being accorded to the Bridewell records that do come to us from that era, as scholars extrapolate across large swaths of time in their efforts to piece together a broader understanding of official efforts to regulate commercial sex in Elizabethan London. Certainly, other records can supplement our understanding of social and sexual regulation in the era—quarter session books, rolls, and registers from local counties; parish account books; privy council registers; Star Chamber records; royal proclamations and other state papers; and, most notably, the records of other ecclesiastical or 'bawdy' courts—but these documents bear their own opacities and

[66] Among many works, see especially *Common Women*.

[67] *Prostitution and Victorian Society*; *City of Dreadful Delight*.

[68] Historical studies that draw heavily on the Bridewell archives include Archer, *The Pursuit of Stability*; Griffiths, 'The Structure of Prostitution'; *Lost Londons*; and 'Meanings of Nightwalking in Early Modern London'; Ingram, *Carnal Knowledge*; Manzione, 'Sex in Tudor London'; Ungerer, 'Prostitution in Late Elizabethan London'. Works by literary critics that annex these archives in conversation with contemporary literary representations include Twyning, *London Dispossessed*; Salkeld, *Shakespeare among the Courtesans*; Mowry, 'London's Bridewell'; and Varholy, '"But She Would Not Consent"'.

[69] Griffiths, *Lost Londons*, 19–21.

interpretive challenges.[70] Consider, for instance, the following entry, which comes to us from parish records of West Rudham, Norfolk, in 1597:

> Edmund Hopper. He harboreth a lewd woman in his house. *He replies* that he harboured noe suche woman.[71]

Principium et finem. What is recorded here? In addition to the name of the accused, the account specifies a behaviour (harbouring) and kind of a person (lewd woman) deemed unacceptable in a particular parish at a particular point in time. Documenting the arraignment of a man for inappropriately sheltering—or billeting or concealing or entertaining or hunting[72]—a disreputable woman in his domicile, the entry suggests local interest in the policing of male behaviors and practices vis-à-vis the kinds of women with whom they interact; significantly, it is Hopper who is arraigned here, not the woman. That this 'lewd woman' goes unnamed intimates her status as an outsider or non-resident of West Rudham, in contrast to Hopper who is at least nominally recognized by the court, but her identity—indeed, her very existence—otherwise remains uncertain. And while the terms 'lewd' and 'harboreth/harboured' intimate an illicit sexual relationship of some sort between the two, it is equally possible that they simply connote the presence of

[70] See, for instance, Ingram, *Carnal Knowledge*, in which the historian, on the one hand, repeatedly acknowledges the historiographic problems that attend his analysis of sexual regulation in late medieval and early modern England—absent and fragmentary records, jurisdictional conflicts, variable recording practices, semantic ambiguities and opacities, terminological and categorical inconsistencies, the intensely local character of each regulatory system, and so on and so forth—yet repeatedly insists, on the other hand, that his (often quite localized) archival findings reveal an 'unusually intense regime' of sexual regulation in both pre-Reformation and Elizabethan England (78). For Ingram, in other words, absence and opacity are never seriously considered as signs of communal flexibility, tolerance, understanding, pragmatism, or indifference regarding the sexual practice of others—even as his study delivers a multiplicity of examples that support this perspective, and which thereby undermine the scale and scope of his thesis. For an alternative account of English sexual regulation, see Eleanor Hubbard's excellent *City Women*, in which she reveals that London magistrates and communities, when forced to decide between punishing sexual offenders and preserving domestic and economic stability, tended to privilege the latter over the former, prioritizing reconciliation and resolution over discipline. Significantly for our purposes, this inclination extended to cases of women's adultery, where betrayed husbands, Hubbard finds, often faced considerable pressure to forgive their wives so that 'the household might be patched together' (171).

[71] Hair, *Before the Bawdy Court*, 46, emphasis in the original.

[72] 'Harbour | Harbor, V.', *Oxford English Dictionary Online*.

wrong person in the wrong house at the wrong time. It is also equally possible, we must note, that Hopper—as he claims—'harboured noe suche woman'; that the 'woman' in question was not 'lewd'; or that event in question never occurred. Indeed, the most significant aspect of this legal entry—and it is in this sense, especially, that this entry is emblematic of the legal records that survive from the era—is the absence of a verdict or any other information regarding how the case played out. Simply put, we do not know what happened to Edmund Hopper, nor to the (supposedly) 'lewd' woman whom he (supposedly) harboured. Such gaps are, as scholars have long acknowledged, central to the historiography of English whoredom. Where it is 'frequently impossible to trace the whole course of a single case' in the surviving legal and ecclesiastical archives and, as such, we rarely 'know whether a person presented was found guilty or not',[73] scholars face a series of interpretive impasses that at once solicit analysis and deny evidence essential not only to the contours of the cases in question but to their very facticity. Similar impasses extend even to those cases in which a verdict is recorded: the fact that an individual is deemed a 'whore' by a jury of their peers may provide valuable insights about social or sexual reputations in early modern England, or the sexual scripts, metaphors, and narratives that contemporary juries found most compelling, or the kinds the evidence that they accepted as proof of iniquity, but they rarely, if ever, deliver specific details regarding the sexual practice(s) in question.[74] Even public confessions of whoredom, as I argue at the outset of Chapter 3, may tell us less about specific sexual acts, practices, desires, and identities than the narrative and rhetorical structures through which whoredom was rendered intelligible as a common sexual plot in the period.

While historians and literary scholars have long grappled with whoredom's archival gaps, what is most striking about this critical history is not the emergence of a methodological consensus but rather the recurrence of seemingly intractable political and hermeneutical impasses. Focusing on these quandaries in what follows, I argue that rather than framing these as critical antitheses—between, for instance, history and literature, agency and victimization, reality and representa-

[73] Hair, *Before the Bawdy Court*, 19.
[74] Gowing, *Domestic Dangers*, passim; Traub, *Thinking Sex with the Early Moderns*, 191–193.

tion, structure and play, etc.—we ought instead to conceptualize them as structuring antinomies whose interplay is itself part and parcel of the epistemology of the early modern whore. In other words, I argue that the persistence of these critical impasses can profitably be leveraged to illuminate our understandings of early modern whoredom and the various incoherences and contradictions that it incorporates. In an influential historical study of Elizabethan prostitution, for instance, Paul Griffiths argues that absences in the 'archive'—by which he means legal, royal, and medical documents—necessitates that historians 'must conceptualize and contextualize, and read literary sources in the light of the archival record'.[75] While the assertion usefully highlights differences among varying textual forms, his subsequent declaration that 'the pamphlet, ballad or play must adopt a supporting role to the court-book', implies an evidentiary privilege that elides certain forms of knowledge in the very process of making other meanings or relations visible.[76] As Karen Newman notes, while court records can suggest where sexual exchanges took place in early modern England, how much they cost, and what kind of persons where involved, they 'rarely…consider questions of language, affect, dress, motivation, desire, or performance'.[77] Moreover, Griffiths's claims that 'we are perhaps closer to the authentic voice of the bawd or prostitute' in Bridewell records overlooks the ways in which archival voices are themselves mediated by the questions asked, by the narrative conventions of the court confession, and even by a scribe's recording practices.[78]

Literary scholars are by no means exempt from this critique. Early studies of prostitution in Shakespeare's plays, for example, adhered to a

[75] While the Bridewell court records serve as Griffiths's archive, his assertions of 'absence' even here have been challenged by Gustav Ungerer, who notes that both Griffiths and Ian Archer limit their searches to the 1570s. By expanding his chronological parameters into the seventeenth century, Ungerer locates further materials for scholarly analysis. See 'Prostitution in Late Elizabethan London'.

[76] Griffiths, 'The Structure of Prostitution', 53–54.

[77] Newman, 'Sex in the City', 136.

[78] Griffiths, 'The Structure of Prostitution', 51. On 'voice' and mediation in early modern court records relevant to this study, see Gowing, *Domestic Dangers*; Storey, *Carnal Commerce*. More recently, Valerie Traub has argued that critics need to pay more attention to the use of stock phrases in legal depositions, which not only adhere to formulaic conventions but manifest a 'particular form of indeterminacy' about the sex acts that scholars have conventionally taken them to signify. See *Thinking Sex with the Early Moderns*, 190–193.

form of old historicism that often rendered literary and dramatic representations as mere reflections of social reality. Such approaches effaced the ways in which cultural performances produce or mediate a subject's experience of that very reality, while at the same time conflating the theatrical with the quotidian.[79] Thus Normand Berlin, Gamini Salgado, and Wallace Shugg, reading Shakespeare's plays as evidence of daily life, located prostitutes as part of a distinct criminal subculture restricted to London's Southwark liberty.[80] While such studies usefully highlighted the geographical proximity of the Globe Theater to suspected bawdy houses, they frequently reproduced the ideological work performed by the texts under analysis, lending a sense of organization, as well as social and geographic containment, since exposed as illusory.[81] Similar limitations encumber Anne Haselkorn's *Prostitution in Elizabethan and Jacobean Comedy* (1983), a tropological analysis that located an 'extensive concern or interest or absorption with the plight of the prostitute' on the London stage, identified a 'range of attitudes poised somewhere between severity and liberality' in these texts, and argued that the prostitute, as a dramatic role, offered early modern writers a fecund figure for examining the shifting status of women in an increasingly capitalist society. While detailing how a specific dramatic genre, London city comedy, emerged as a vital site for exploring 'sensitive sexual issues' in a particular historical moment (147), Haselkorn—like other early contextualist studies of prostitution on the early modern English stage—relied heavily and uncritically on the pseudo-historical scholarship of E. J. Burford, whose 'fantastical' studies have been either ignored or denounced by professional historians.[82]

The theoretical turn in early modern studies brought increased attention and methodological rigour to these relations between the theatrical and social in early modern England. Whereas Haselkorn noted potential links between misogynist representations and female economic mobility, as well as what might be termed dissident voices or narrative faultlines in the plays under analysis, for instance, Jonathan Dollimore and Jyotsna Singh turned attention to the political and methodological

[79] Howard, 'The New Historicism in Renaissance Studies'.

[80] Berlin, *The Base String*; Salgado, *The Elizabethan Underworld*; Shugg, 'Prostitution in Shakespeare's London'.

[81] See especially Salkeld, *Shakespeare among the Courtesans*, 1–26.

[82] See, for instance, Kelly, 'Bishop, Prioress, and Bawd', 349.

quandaries generated by, as the latter put it, the slippery 'relationship between women's experience and the construction of women in cultural representation'.[83] Where Dollimore focused on problems of archival absence, critiquing a scholarly tendency to anachronistically 'back-project' postmodern desires and identities onto early modern figures,[84] Singh channelled attention to representational absences: what was missing, unstated, or actively elided in early modern narratives of whoredom. Noting that 'prostitution was a way of making a living for many women facing material needs' in the period, Singh detailed how the tendency to elide these material realities facilitated a scapegoating strategy that positioned such figures as fully responsible for their own abjection.[85]

Published in 1994, the Dollimore and Singh essays remain relevant as harbingers of the methodological orientation (feminist materialism) that has broadly governed literary-critical approaches to early modern English whoredom for the past three decades. The most influential figure in this critical genealogy is unquestionably Jean Howard, whose own brand of feminist materialism delivers both a sophisticated theoretical framework and an applied methodology for apprehending the cultural politics of representing early modern whoredom.[86] Equally attentive to the materials conditions of performance, the shaping powers of drama, and the ideological contradictions that such works generate and disclose, Howard has repeatedly channeled critical attention to the various brothels, bawds, and whores of the London stage, foregrounding their centrality to a range of contemporary debates while revealing the analytical benefits of examining their dissident and disciplinary inflections. Thus, even as Howard demonstrates that whore tropes provided dramatists with a potent symbolic repertoire for navigating contemporary anxieties about women's identities, social mobility, and sexual agency—as well as broader concerns regarding cosmopolitanism and 'Englishness'—in a developing market economy, she insists upon the historical and political

[83] Singh, 'The Interventions of History', 9.

[84] Dollimore, 'Shakespeare Understudies', 135.

[85] Singh, 'The Interventions of History', 9.

[86] *Theater of a City*, esp. 114–161. See also 'Mastering Difference in *The Dutch Courtesan*'; 'Civic Institutions and Precarious Masculinity in Dekker's *The Honest Whore*'; 'Prostitutes, Shopkeepers, and the Staging of Urban Subjects in *The Honest Whore*'; and 'Sex in the Early Modern City'.

necessity of examining how the 'bawdy houses and whores of London comedy...exceed their predictable function as the site and emblems of urban vice and abjection'.[87] By attending to how such figures and spaces concomitantly annex and unsettle hegemonic ideologies, her critical methodology curates those alternative possibilities for social relationality that inhabit even the most reductive of cultural representations and facilitates a nuanced vision of how cultures 'work' by and through representations of illicit sexual persons, places, and practices.[88] For Howard, the prostitutes and whores on the early modern stage are best understood not as reflections of social struggle but as one of the primary sites through which that struggle was enacted and bodied forth.

Feminist materialism operated as the dominant if not consensus methodology for literary critical approaches to early modern English prostitution and whoredom as the first decade of the twenty-first century drew to a close.[89] While there are many reasons why specific methodologies come to govern the study of a particular topic at a given time, including broader critical trends, one of the enduring strengths of feminist materialism—and thus its utility to scholars attuned to the histories and politics of gender—undoubtedly lies in its capacity to illuminate

[87] *Theater of a City*, 161. As Howard details, such excesses are the byproduct of the sustained analytical pressure that 'prostitute drama[s]' bring to bear upon the supposedly discrete categories of maid, wife, widow, and whore (135). In this, her work is emblematic of a broader scholarly tradition which has long identified London 'city comedy' as a site in which these and other seemingly discrete categories were examined, mediated, and/or brought into conceptual crisis. See especially Kahn, 'Whores and Wives in Jacobean Drama'; Twyning, *London Dispossessed*; Leggatt, *Citizen Comedy in the Age of Shakespeare*; Leinwand, *The City Staged*; DiGangi, *Sexual Types*. Similarly, her work reflects a vital strain of feminist scholarship that has channelled attention to the relationship between these onstage representations and early modern women's lives. See, for instance, Dowd, *Women's Work in Early Modern English Literature and Culture*. I address women's life cycles at greater length in Chapter 3. For a recent study of cosmopolitanism and the London sex trade, see Fox, 'Cosmopolitan Desire and Profitable Performance in *The Dutch Courtesan*'.

[88] Howard addresses her methodological commitments more broadly in 'The New Historicism in Renaissance Studies', *The Stage and Social Struggle in Early Modern England*, and the introduction to *Theater of a City*, 1–28.

[89] Relevant scholarship from the period that broadly aligns with feminist materialist principles, albeit to various ends, includes Panek, '"This Base Stallion Trade"'; DiGangi, 'Sexual Slander and Working Women in *The Roaring Girl*'; Twyning, *London Dispossessed*; and Varholy, 'Rich Like a Lady'. More recent works include DiGangi, *Sexual Types*, 192–220; Fox, 'Cosmopolitan Desire and Profitable Performance in *The Dutch Courtesan*'; and Tisdale, 'Stranger Compass of the Stage'.

the material realities of women's oppression without foreclosing possibilities for agency and anti-patriarchal resistance. Put differently, in its bipartite insistence upon the shaping powers of history and literature, feminist materialism allows consideration of the often-dynamic power relations that subtend early modern whoredom and its representations. In so doing, it offers a methodological means of navigating a series of prominent antinomies—between reality and representation, subversion and containment, (whore as) victim and agent, patriarchal and feminist Shakespeare—that, at one time, threatened to paralyze feminist approaches to Shakespeare and early modern culture by pressing scholars into restrictive binaries.[90]

Just when one might have argued for a 'feminist materialist settlement' in the relevant scholarship, however, new monographs by Duncan Salkeld and Kay Stanton suggested a growing dissatisfaction with this critical praxis on the grounds of its perceived historical veracity (Salkeld) and feminist political utility (Stanton).[91] Returning to the practices and poetics of early modern English prostitution yet diametrically opposed in their interpretive praxes and readings of female agency, they concurrently signalled a resurgence of the political and hermeneutical impasses noted above to the scholarship of early modern whoredom. In so doing, they granted scholars a unique opportunity to reassess the status—and stakes—of feminist literary history. In *Shakespeare among the Courtesans* (2012), Salkeld positions Howard as emblematic of a broader critical tendency to privilege representational ambiguity over historical facticity which has culminated, he charges, in an idealized vision of the Renaissance courtesan that effaces the 'starker realities and difficulties of women's lives at this time' (4). Practicing a 'forensic' historicism which restores interpretative primacy to the juridical archive, Salkeld argues that the 'prevailing literary myth of the [empowered, agentic] dramatic courtesan' is belied by 'historical reality' (157–158). From a contextual perspective, this approach yields valuable results, illuminating suggestive evidence of brothel attendance by foreigners and black servants; child prostitution; bawdy houses run by married couples; methods of restitution that included gift-giving, payment of rents, and

[90] For an important early account of these tensions in feminist approaches to Shakespeare, see Boose, 'The Family in Shakespeare Studies'.

[91] Salkeld, *Shakespeare among the Courtesans*; Stanton, *Shakespeare's 'Whores'*.

compensation in fabric; and a sexual economy that far transcended its purported restriction to the city's marginal geographies. But as a method for literary analysis, Salkeld's 'forensic' historicism is characterized by a perfunctory engagement with literary texts and an implicitly mimetic theory of representation that ultimately renders literature impotent: able only to validate, falsify, or 'acknowledge' the autonomous social sphere from which it springs.[92]

In *Shakespeare's 'Whores'* (2014), Stanton employs a presentist hermeneutics that resituates the Stratford playwright as a proto-feminist whose 'gynogenic perspective on female divinity' offers an as yet untapped paradigm for women's political resistance and erotic liberation (137). Where Salkeld urges scholars not to 'lionize' Renaissance courtesans 'as figureheads of social freedom or female agency',[93] Stanton instead channels attention to select Shakespeare women who, she argues, offer models of political resistance to present day women given their propensity, 'when pondering a problem, to look and then empathize or identify with various figures in similar situations from myth and/or earlier literature' (8).[94] These identification politics lead Stanton to pursue a far longer history—an 'idea of female divinity' predating Graeco-Roman and Judaeo-Christian phallocentrism (148)—whose traces, she claims, subtend Shakespeare's sexual and gendered poetics. Bypassing both Shakespeare's own historical moment and a variety of more problematic representations (Gertrude, Lady Macbeth, Tamora, Volumnia, etc.), Stanton contends that the political needs of the present moment are best served through strategic reading praxes that curate models and histories of resistance and eschew those which fail to align with the critic's preferred socio-political order.[95]

While Salkeld and Stanton signal a return to foundational debates about agency and victimization, literary representation and historical reality, a different set of antinomies—between what we might call discursive and aesthetic structures of meaning—can be detected through a

[92] Salkeld, *Shakespeare among the Courtesans*, 67.

[93] Ibid., 24.

[94] Stanton focuses primarily on Cleopatra, Rosalind, and Venus as such models.

[95] Thus, while I share Stanton's desire to undo 'phallocentric misogynist hegemony' (148), I would challenge the implicit homophobia which subtends the vision of feminism that she advances in *Shakespeare's 'Whores'*, one that is characterized by a steadfast refusal to identify, much less engaged with, queer scholarship relevant to the plays.

comparative analysis of two recent studies by Will Stockton and Cristina León Alfar. Reviewing the case of Desdemona's contested chastity, Stockton argues that *The Tragedy of Othello* doesn't so much confirm her virtue as it 'mercilessly deconstructs...chastity as an object of certain, critical knowledge'.[96] Noting that feminist critics have increasingly defended Desdemona's chastity, insisting upon her 'fidelity, honesty, constancy, and innocence' (199), Stockton demonstrates the relative ease with which one can prove the opposite, noting how any number of her actions or affects—sneaking out of her father's house, eloping without patriarchal consent, speaking openly and passionately of her desires, bantering with her husband's subordinates, even laughing at Iago's sexually inflected jokes—could render her unchaste according to early modern discourses of female virtue.[97] Stockton's point is not to defame Desdemona—to argue that she is, truly, a 'whore'—but rather to shift from a feminist praxis that, however unwittingly, implicitly links Desdemona's chastity to her right to life toward a queer ethical praxis which defends her right to life even if unchaste.

If Stockton underscores how broader discursive structures of sex can play a vital role in shaping both what and how audiences 'know' the sexual status of onstage characters, Alfar contends that any such sexual knowledge (at least as it pertains to Shakespeare's slandered wives) is primarily determined by—and can be verified by scholarly attention to—the shaping forces of dramatic structure, aesthetic coherence, and (implicitly) authorial design.[98] By shifting from extrinsic to intrinsic

[96] Stockton, 'Chasing Chastity', 201.

[97] Ibid., esp. 202–206.

[98] Given both the sophistication of Alfar's vital study and a range of significant homologies between her work and my own, it is important to address her argument at greater length. In *Women and Shakespeare's Cuckoldry Plays*, Alfar carefully details how characters like Desdemona, Cressida, Hero, Imogen, and Paulina wrest control of their slander narratives by annexing what we today call the performative and citational dimensions of language: coopting the rhetorical and narrative frameworks deployed by their oppressors, they secure a form of limited agency within the scenes of their constraint. Central to this argument, as I suggest above, are the determining forces of dramatic structure, aesthetic coherence, and (implicitly) authorial design: by 'stage[ing] a structure of accusation and defense that unravels the authority of husbands to make and unmake wives', Shakespeare's plays—'in contrast to [those] written by many of his contemporaries'—disclose a critically constitutive 'relationship between repression and collective counter-action' whereby women's capacity for resistance is inextricably 'tied to the formations of power that officially demand their subjection' (1–3). In other words, and as she puts elsewhere, 'the discursive making and unmaking

structures of theatrical meaning, from discourse to form, Alfar secures a seemingly stable sexual epistemology in Shakespeare's 'cuckoldry plays' that ultimately necessitates, she argues, the (physical) virtue of defamed women. As she puts it in a critical passage, 'Shakespeare's cuckoldry plays repeatedly stage the lack of foundation on which men make their stories. *In order to make that point, wives must be virtuous*' (3, emphasis added). Both this axiom and the apodictic certainty that it conveys helps to illuminate a defining difference between our otherwise closely related studies. For Alfar, the 'women accused of sexual betrayal [in these plays] are innocent' (1); they are bereft of 'sexual duplicity and bodily pollution' (1); they 'maintain a bodily continence' (4); and 'none of the accusations' levelled against them 'have any basis in fact' (6). In other words, what Shakespeare's slandered wives are *not*—what they *cannot* be—are 'whores'. These latter figures, by way of binary opposition, are therefore defined by their sexual duplicity, bodily pollution, and bodily incontinence. Alfar goes on to note:

> I do not mean to suggest that no women were whores in the sixteenth and seventeenth centuries or that no women cheated on their husbands. Rather, I suggest that the cuckoldry plays proceed from a rhetorical position that interrogates the methods and tropes needed to construct such stories, and, therefore, they discredit the story's underpinnings. (7)

This composite definition does a few things. It advances a transitive understanding of whoredom, one that is extramarital in practice and corporeal in nature. It eschews, as such, the more capacious definitions of whoredom circulating in the period, such as those advanced by Bale, Becon, and Downame, as well as the spiritual, spatial, habitual, and affective dimensions that attend and inform them. It reproduces an implicit but essential distinction between 'real' and 'discursive' whores, and its concomitant binaries of guilt and innocence, pollution and

of women into whores is licensed by a discourse of masculinist power that the plays connect to a tyrannical structure of relations' (11). *Shakespeare and the Making of the English Whoredom* thus holds much in common with Alfar's study, from our shared emphases on whoredom's narrative and performative dimensions to our joint understanding of the early modern stage—and Shakespeare's corpus in particular—as a vital site for scrutinizing the double helix of its discursive making and unmaking. As I reveal above, such a close kinship helps to illuminate the subtle yet defining difference between our respective studies and the methods that subtend them.

purity, duplicity and honesty. It associates aesthetic coherence with conceptual coherence, suggesting that the former requires the latter. In other words, and here it is useful to recall Stockton's essay, Alfar ties the emotional and aesthetic force of plays like *Othello* to their capacity to determine—rather than 'deconstruct'—the questions of sexual knowledge upon which they pivot.

The productive irony, of course, is that Stockton and Alfar are both correct. By this, I do not mean that (a) *The Tragedy of Othello* resolves Desdemona's sexual status, nor (b) that this status can be conclusively determined by examining broader discursive structures of sex. Rather, it is to insist that her chastity/whoredom is a critical antinomy that can be resolved only through the privileging of certain kinds of evidence over other forms of evidence. We might therefore better understand sexual status in *The Tragedy of Othello* less as a fact to be discerned than as a Rorschach test that reveals the affordances and limitations of our own interpretive methods and the criteria that subtend them. In its capacity to enlist audiences into this interpretive work, to implicate us in early modern whoredom as a knowledge relation, the play suggests that the force, persistence, and effectiveness of this disciplinary regime is intimately linked, and sustained by, our own desires—however well-intentioned—to adjudicate and resolve its 'proper' meanings.

Collectively, Salkeld, Stanton, Stockton, and Alfar reveal that early modern whoredom remains not only an important topic for contemporary critical inquiry but a vital site for methodological exploration and contestation. In their capacity to raise difficult questions concerning the methods (materialist, presentist, poststructuralist, formalist, feminist, queer) that we employ to make sense of the past and the consequences (historical, political, ethical, hermeneutical) that attend their adoption, they channel attention to the dynamic relations between critical methodology and historical epistemology: how, that is, the methods that we deploy to make sense of the past, and the theoretical frameworks which subtend them, inform both what we know about the past and how we know it. Central to these relations, I have suggested, are not only hierarchies of evidence (what counts as evidence, which kinds of evidence are accorded the most weight, how to interpret absence and ambiguity, etc.) and scholarly responsibility (to history, politics, ethics, etc.), but of representation and reality, discourse and aesthetics, agency and victimization, and which therefore return us to some of the defining antinomies of feminist literary history. In so doing, this critical tradition reveals that whoredom in early modern England is, to recast one of my earlier formulations, not only a definitional problem, or an evidentiary problem, or a hermeneutic problem, or a political problem, or an epistemological problem, but all these things at once. In short, the problem of whoredom is not defined by the accretion of various conceptual impasses but is itself an anvil upon which early modern England's social, sexual, and linguistic concepts were being forged.

Queer Epistemology and the Making of Sexual Knowledge

Ever since Michel Foucault distinguished the premodern 'sodomite' from the modern 'homosexual', arguing that the latter did not exist—as a word, conceptual structure, and subjectivity—until the late nineteenth century, the history of sexuality has been in part a history of the terms and concepts through which 'sex' and its meanings have been identified, adjudicated, and known in various historical cultures.[99] Channelling critical attention to the relationship between historically contingent terms and categories and the kinds of sexual knowledge that these enable and foreclose, this scholarship has disclosed a vital link between signification and epistemology: i.e. between how words signify, fail to signify, and/or are made to signify in specific historical contexts, and what scholars therefore can(not) know about sex and its meanings in cultures past.[100] In early modern studies, for instance, feminist and queer critics have scrutinized the historicity, semantic lability, and analytical utility of a range of (potential) 'sexual' signifiers, from 'bawdy',[101] 'boy',[102]

[99] Foucault, *The History of Sexuality*, Vol. I.

[100] See especially Traub, *The Renaissance of Lesbianism* and *Thinking Sex with the Early Moderns*; Masten, *Queer Philologies*.

[101] DiGangi, 'Shakespeare's Bawdy'.

[102] Arvas, *Boys Abducted*; Chess, 'Queer Residue'; Fisher, *Materializing Gender in Early Modern English Literature and Culture*; Masten, *Queer Philologies*, esp. 109–174; Orgel, *Impersonations*; Rackin, 'Androgyny, Mimesis, and the Marriage of the Boy Heroine on the English Renaissance Stage'; *Shakespeare and Women*, 72–94; B. Smith, *Homosexual Desire in Shakespeare's England*; Stewart, *Close Readers*.

'favourite',[103] 'friend',[104] 'Ganymede',[105] and 'girl'[106] to 'ingle',[107] 'lesbian',[108] 'minion',[109] 'rogue',[110] 'secretary',[111] 'sex',[112] 'sodomite',[113] 'straight',[114] 'tribade',[115] 'virgin',[116] and beyond.[117] Parsing similarities and differences between pre- and postmodern usages, as well as the conceptual incoherences, discursive intersections, and/or historical anachronisms that attend their deployment, this scholarship has underscored the vital

[103] DiGangi, *The Homoerotics of Early Modern Drama*, esp. 100–133; and *Sexual Types*, esp. 192–220.

[104] Andreadis, *Sappho in Early Modern England*, esp. 101–149; Bray, *The Friend*; DiGangi, *The Homoerotics of Early Modern Drama*; Masten, *Queer Philologies*, esp. 69–105; Shannon, *Sovereign Amity*; Stewart, *Close Readers*; Traub, *The Renaissance of Lesbianism in Early Modern England.*

[105] Arvas, *Boys Abducted*; Barkan, *Transuming Passion*; DiGangi, *The Homoerotics of Early Modern Drama*; Masten, *Queer Philologies*, esp. 109–174; Orgel, *Impersonations*, esp. 31–82; 'The Further Adventures of Ganymede'; Parker, *Shakespearean Intersections*, esp. 273–297; Rambuss, *Closet Devotions*, esp. 11–72.

[106] J. Higginbotham, 'Fair Maids and Golden Girls'; 'Girls and Sexuality in Seventeenth-Century Love Lyrics'.

[107] Bly, *Queer Virgins and Virgin Queans on the Early Modern Stage.*

[108] Andreadis, *Sappho in Early Modern England*; Blank, 'The Proverbial "Lesbian"'; Giffney, Sauer, and Watt, *The Lesbian Premodern*; Traub, *The Renaissance of Lesbianism in Early Modern England* and *Thinking Sex with the Early Moderns*, esp. 82–100, 265–293.

[109] Bartels, *Spectacles of Strangeness*, 143–172; DiGangi, *The Homoerotics of Early Modern Drama*, esp. 100–133; Goldberg, *Sodometries*, 105–144; B. Smith, *Homosexual Desire in Shakespeare's England*, 189–224.

[110] Friedlander, *Rogue Sexuality in Early Modern England.*

[111] J. Crawford, 'Women's Secretaries'; Stewart, *Close Readers.*

[112] Bromley and Stockton, *Sex before Sex*, 1–23; Traub, *Thinking Sex with the Early Moderns*, 1–34 and passim.

[113] Bredbeck, *Sodomy and Interpretation*; DiGangi, *The Homoerotics of Early Modern Drama*, 21–59; Fisher, 'Queer Money'; Goldberg, 'Sodomy and Society'; *Sodometries*, esp. 1–27, 105–144; Greene, 'You Must Eat Men'; I. Smith, 'The Queer Moor'; Stewart, *Close Readers.*

[114] Gamble, *Sex Lives*, 57–74.

[115] Park, 'The Rediscovery of the Clitoris'; Traub, *The Renaissance of Lesbianism.*

[116] Bly, *Queer Virgins and Virgin Queans on the Early Modern Stage*; Carroll, 'The Virgin Not'; Jankowski, *Pure Resistance*; Kelly and Leslie, *Menacing Virgins*; Loughlin, *Hymeneutics*; Peterson, 'Elizabeth I's Virginity and the Body of Evidence'; 'The Ring's the Thing'; Schwarz, 'The Wrong Question'.

[117] As should be clear, the terms presented here align closely with identities or categories of persons. Such a list expands greatly when one adds scholarship on terms associated with sexual or erotic acts, affects, body parts, scenarios, etc.: 'angling', 'bawdy', 'case', 'chastity', 'conversation', and more. On these lexicons and the interpretive problems that attend them, see especially Traub, *Thinking Sex with the Early Moderns*, 171–226. For a recent account of the limitations of 'homoeroticism', one of the field's governing categories of analysis, see Gamble, *Sex Lives*, 95–104.

insight that the histories of signification are ineluctably epistemological in nature—even if they have not been always been framed in these terms. In their attention to the various strategies through which critics and editors have sought to manage—activate, suppress, veil, disavow—the meanings (and knowledges) that circulate through these often-unruly terms, moreover, queer critics have underscored the materiality of these histories and knowledges, not only in the sense that they are forged and contested through a range of historically situated social, textual, and linguistic processes, but that this discursive work is inextricably linked to, and often participates in the reproduction of, contemporary ideologies of sex, gender, and morality.[118] By pushing these insights to the analytical foreground in what follows, I advance a critical methodology that is broadly epistemological in orientation, genealogical in practice, materialist in application, and informed by a range of feminist, queer, and deconstructive insights. I call this 'queer epistemology'. Thus, while this book extends a longstanding scholarly tradition in its sustained attention to a prominent 'sexual' category, the terms that circulate in and around it, and the battles that attend its meanings and usage in a specific historical context, its primary contributions unfold at the levels of critical methodology and sexual epistemology: how we read, write, and claim to know the histories of early modern sex, particularly the terms, categories, textual practices, interpretive impasses, and analytical procedures upon which such knowledge depends.

This book builds on the essential scholarship of Eve Kosofsky Sedgwick and Valerie Traub, each of whom has insisted upon the epistemological significance of ignorance and opacity, arguing that these are neither extrinsic nor antithetical to 'knowledge' as it is shaped and contested in specific historical contexts, but rather intrinsic—indeed, structurally central—to 'major nodes of thought and knowledge' in the cultures that they analyse.[119] As Traub puts it in *Thinking Sex with the Early Moderns* (2016), 'an epistemological approach—by asking *what*

[118] See especially Traub, *Thinking Sex with the Early Moderns*, 171–226; Masten, *Queer Philologies*, 213–230; Gamble, 'Please Ask, Please Tell'; Spiess, 'The Confounding Gloss'.

[119] Put differently, Sedgwick and Traub advance a deconstructive understanding of ignorance and opacity as structurally central to knowledge and clarity, and therefore sites of meaning and analysis in their own right, rather than obstacles or impediments that scholars must overcome in order to apprehend 'knowledge' as it is constituted and operates within a given historical culture. Sedgwick, *Epistemology of the Closet*, 1; Traub, *Thinking Sex with the Early Moderns*.

can be known as well as *how* it is known—recasts the dynamics among sex, representation, signification, and historiography as a problem of knowledge relations: constituted not only by social interchange but by implicit understandings of what counts as knowledge and what eludes or baffles as ignorance'.[120] The significance of this insight cannot be overstated. First, and by repositioning that which appears to impede or block access to knowledge as constitutive of knowledge, an epistemological approach reconfigures ambiguity, contradiction, impasse, incoherence, opacity and other 'problems' of knowledge production as evidence that in themselves can encode vital insights about our objects of inquiry, as well as the broader cultures in which they circulate. Whereas Sedgwick demonstrates how the contradictions and incoherences that inhere within twentieth-century understandings of the homo/hetero-sexual binary can be leveraged to illuminate the workings of discursive power,[121] Traub recasts opacities and impasses in the history of sexuality as evidence of the 'difficulty of knowing sex' in and across historical time that can be scrutinized to reveal the benefits and limitations of the critical praxes that we develop to understand sex and its meanings; the axioms and assumptions that inform varying disciplinary approaches to, and perspectives on, sex as an object of historical knowledge; and the political, ethical, and/or pedagogical aims that we hope to realize through such scholarship.[122] Second, by foregrounding the material effects of what Traub calls 'presumptive knowledge about what sex is and what it means' (147), and what Sedgwick characterizes as the 'dismissive knowingness' through which scholars historically have disregarded

[120] Traub, *Thinking Sex with the Early Moderns*, 5; emphasis in the original.

[121] In a critical passage, Sedgwick defines these 'contests for discursive power' as 'competitions for the material or rhetorical leverage required to the set the terms of, and to profit in some way from, the operations of such an incoherence of definition'. In that same paragraph, she contends that the incoherences and knowledge relations embedded within the homo/hetero binary constitute a range of other culturally productive binaries—an 'entire cultural network of normative definitions'—in twentieth-century Western culture. See *Epistemology of the Closet*, 11.

[122] *Thinking Sex with the Early Moderns*, 11. See also her claim that 'the obstacles we face in *making* sexual history can illuminate the difficulty of *knowing* sexuality, and both impediments can be productively adopted as a guiding principle in historiography, pedagogy, and ethics' (4, emphasis in the original). On the acquisition of 'sexual-logistical knowledge' in early modern England, i.e. how early moderns learned 'to have sex', and the constitutive role of ignorance in these knowledge relations and processes, see Gamble, *Sex Lives*.

insights and questions which disturb the normative sexual order (53), this approach situates scholars within the very knowledge relations that they seek to analyse. In other words, we do not stand outside of sex as a category of knowledge, even when attempting to delineate its contours in cultures and time periods different from our own.

The material effects of scholarly 'knowingness', as Melissa Sanchez points out, are readily evident in a critical tradition in which the 'claim that a text represents queer sex' is subjected to 'a heavier burden of proof than the assumption that it depicts straight sex'.[123] The force of this injunction and the weight of the tradition that lies behind it undoubtedly have shaped the histories of early modern sex, establishing parameters on the hermeneutic procedures that scholars historically have been allowed to deploy, the evidence they have been permitted to introduce and analyse, and the knowledge claims they have been able to advance within specific historical contexts.[124] To the extent that this unequal 'burden of proof' has encouraged greater methodological, hermeneutic, and epistemological self-reflexivity in queer critical approaches to early modern sex, it has facilitated a wealth of new scholarship that challenges *a priori* assumptions about what constitutes sex, what counts as erotic, and what passes as 'heteroerotic unless proven otherwise' in early modern literature and culture (95). By pursuing these and related questions, Sanchez notes, queer critics have excavated a range of 'non-normative and non-reproductive' erotic practices available to early modern subjects; explored 'acts and fantasies that may not register as sexual now but that were saturated with erotic significance in early modern culture'; and forcefully confronted the implicit heterosexism that underlies conventional approaches to interpretive ambiguity and impasse.[125] Foregrounding the critical significance of previously

[123] Sanchez, *Shakespeare and Queer Theory*, 94.

[124] It is in this sense, especially, that one detects Foucault's influence in Traub's configuration of 'sex as a knowledge relation'—a phrase that palpably evokes, and undoubtedly draws upon, the philosopher's central insight regarding on the constitutive link between knowledge and power. Knowledge relations, in other words, are always already power-knowledge relations.

[125] Sanchez, *Shakespeare and Queer Theory*, 94–97. In 'Thinking Kink', Will Fisher presents a rich bibliography of scholarship attending to 'kinky sex practices' in early modern literature and culture, including accounts of: agalmatophilia, anilingus, autoerotic asphyxiation/breath play, bondage, chin-chucking, cross-species eroticism/bestiality, dendrophilia, dildo use, enemas, erotic humiliation/impotence, erotic instrumentality, felching, fetishisms, fisting, flogging/spanking, forced feminization, forniphilia, golden

overlooked or elided evidence, as well as of the assumptions and interpretive practices that facilitated their prior omission, such scholarship has reshaped the field of early modern sex studies: altering not only what is known but the various analytical procedures through which such knowledge might be identified and analysed.[126]

In crafting this critical genealogy, I have argued for an epistemological substrate that has long animated queer literary criticism and theory and therefore preceded and laid some of the conceptual groundwork for the so-called epistemological turn in early modern sex studies. At the same time, I have argued that what uniquely defines an epistemological approach to early modern sex, especially as conceptualized by Traub, is the attention that it places on the hermeneutic value of that which impedes, eludes, or frustrates sexual knowledge in and across time. While such obstacles include critical practices that suppress or deny evidence, practices, and/or significations that run counter to governing sexual and moral ideologies, queer epistemology also focuses attention on the various textual, linguistic, historiographic, hermeneutic, and political impasses that attend the study of early modern sex: polysemous texts, unstable definitions, euphemistic language, stock phrases, archival absences, and political double binds. In *Shakespeare and the Making of English Whoredom*, I argue, apropos of Sedgwick, that the definitional incoherences of early modern whoredom are at once culturally productive, i.e. catalysing a range of social and material processes that aim to resolve them, and epistemologically deconstructive, i.e. opening onto a dynamic interplay between knowledge and its undoing that, I reveal, can be leveraged to illuminate some of the terms, assumptions, criteria, evidence, and meanings upon which the epistemology of the early modern whore depends. Drawing upon Traub, I insist upon the analytical benefits of dilating the absences, opacities, impasses, and aporias that attend early modern 'whoredom' and its materializations,

showers/water sports, incest, intercrural sex, kataklysis, macrophilia, masochism, masturbation, necrophilia, pony play, puppy play, role-playing, scat play, urophagia, voyeurism, and voluntary cuckoldry. Other essential studies include Bromley and Stockton, *Sex before Sex*, and Gamble and Knoll, *The Kinky Renaissance*. On the implicit heterosexism that informs scholarly readings of sexual allusion or innuendo on the early modern stage, see Varnado, 'Invisible Sex!'

[126] To these, we must also add the burgeoning field of early modern asexuality studies, a bibliography for which has been assembled by Blake et al. at https://tinyurl.com/earlymodacebib.

and which thereby help to render visible the cultural and discursive labour necessary to craft and sustain the fiction of the 'whore' as a fixed, coherent, and readily apprehensible object of knowledge. Building on the legacy of both, I bring queer and deconstructive methodologies to a topic that bears significant historical and feminist dimensions. In so doing, I do not argue the primacy of my approach or methodology but rather its capacity to supplement prior understandings and enable yet new questions and critical praxes.

Shakespeare and the Making of English Whoredom is, therefore, an avowedly feminist project that is animated by a queer epistemological method. While one of the aims of this book is to persuade readers that whoredom possesses no essential substance prior to its materialization in historically specific terms, texts, bodies, and knowledge relations, it concurrently recognizes that whoredom's material effects are overwhelming disciplinary in nature and disproportionately experienced by women, both in that historical culture and our own. A second aim of this study, therefore, is to show how the methods and insights of queer epistemology can profitably be applied to topics of vital feminist concern, such as whoredom, while resisting the identitarian or ontological logics that such categories seek to install in the first place. This is not to abandon the necessary work of social and political resistance. It is, rather, to suggest how queer epistemology—in its close attention to the social, textual, and linguistic sites and processes through which prominent socio-sexual categories are made and unmade, as well as to the knowledge relations that attend this cultural work—not only can help us better understand how cultures work but, in so doing, can illuminate previously unrecognized sites for resistance and contestation. As we shall see, these include: acts of terminological redefinition and undefinition (Chapter 1); discursive tactics that expose and parody illogics of gendered oppression (Chapter 2); the mapping of conceptual, narrative, and temporal incoherences that belie seemingly fixed cultural logics (Chapter 3); dramatic structures that implicate audiences in the sexual-conceptual work being depicted onstage (Chapter 4); dramatic structures that enlist audiences into the sexual memory work being depicted onstage (Chapter 5); and the deployment of rhetorical figures that prompt readers to contemplate how instabilities of sex, language, gender, and the book (de)construct the very knowledge that each helps to shape and materialize in the world (Epilogue).

As these examples suggest, the mode of queer epistemology pursued in *Shakespeare and the Making of English Whoredom* places special emphasis on literary texts, and stage drama in particular, as vital sites for scrutinizing the broader cultural processes and knowledge relations that attend early modern category construction. As is well known, the literary and dramatic texts that come to us from the period frequently channel attention to the instabilities of language, textuality, and embodiment that underwrite their representational practices. In the texts of English whoredom, as we shall see, these meta-reflexive capacities are often leveraged in ways that force audiences not only to contemplate the unfixity of a particularly socio-sexual category, but to experience what happens when such a seemingly familiar category becomes—or is revealed to be—unfixed, unstable, or unintelligible. By immersing readers and playgoers in the problems of signification and knowledge that animate the making of English whoredom, in other words, the literary and dramatic texts explored in what follows invite audiences into the very knowledge relations and material processes that they depict on stage and page.

Outline of the Present Work

Shakespeare and the Making of English Whoredom advances from the whore as a problem of sexual knowledge that emerges and is mediated at the levels of semantics, evidence, and archive (introduction); language and textuality (Chapter 1); discourse and embodiment (Chapter 2); sexual time and narrative knowing (Chapters 3–4); history and memory (Chapter 5). But the book can also be experienced as a collection of individual essays that each approach early modern whoredom and its epistemological quandaries from a distinct analytical perspective: language, embodiment, time, narrative, memory. Thus, while several chapters develop their argument through the reading of a specific literary or cultural text—and insist upon the necessity of such intimate engagement—the primary organizational framework here is epistemological rather than textual or authorial. As such, texts have been chosen for their capacity to illuminate the complex materiality and epistemology of the early modern whore, as well as broader questions of sexual knowledge production germane to that historical culture and our own.

Along the way, I introduce a range of analytical tools or heuristics—'unknowing', 'terms', 'puzzling', 'proclamation', 'chronologics', and 'chastisement'—whose utility extends beyond the study at hand. So too the epistemology of the whore partakes of far more texts than covered in this account. This book therefore aims to provide an impetus for additional studies that build upon and productively challenge the arguments advanced here.

Before turning to the chapters, it is important to note what this book is not doing. In the pages that follow, I do not suggest that 'whoredom' emerges as a novel category of socio-sexual thought in early modern England, and that this emergence can be therefore leveraged to differentiate between presumably discrete historical periods and cultural formations. I do not, for that matter, chart the development of a collective consciousness,[127] nor do I contend that the 'making' under analysis here advances towards a coherent final product that retrospectively can be leveraged to illuminate the 'true' or 'real' meanings of early modern whoredom. Indeed, this book is decidedly not about what whoredom is or means but rather how it is made-to-mean—and the consequences of this cultural and discursive work. Nor, finally, do I claim to deliver a comprehensive history of English whoredom. Instead, I contend that both whoredom and its attendant epistemology are 'in-the-making' during the period under analysis in this study; that this work unfolds across a range of discourses and material practices; that it incorporates a multiplicity of terms, bodies, acts, relations, affects, and meanings; and that, as such, it generates excesses and aporias that work against—and unmake—the very solidity and conceptual fixity that writers like Heywood aim to deliver.

Chapter 1, 'The Terms of Whoredom', locates the whore in the history of material texts. I begin by revisiting the basic problem of definition with which we opened this study: who—or what—was connoted by the term 'prostitute' in early modern England? How did such definitions compare to, or contrast with, those for 'whore', 'strumpet', 'trull', and other related words? While scholars have long positioned 'whore' as the governing term for illicit female behaviour in the period, I reveal that early moderns struggled mightily to achieve any such categorical clarity. Central to this argument is my reading of an emergent lexicographic

[127] Cf. Thompson, *The Making of the English Working Class.*

project, one whose pointedly experimental ethos fostered a range of textual practices—varying systems of lexical arrangement and visual presentation, differences of typeset and pagination, the use of ideograms, etc.—that concomitantly informed and unsettled the terms of everyday life. Analysing a range of linguistic, scholastic, and academic texts including John Rider's *Bibliotheca Scholastica* (1589), I detail how efforts to stabilize the whore's meanings on the dictionary *mise-en-page* amplified rather than restricted contemporary sexual connotations, producing a far broader field of meanings and relations than previously acknowledged. This chapter thus catalogues almost seven hundred 'terms of whoredom', a proliferation that not only exposes the tight conceptual links between signification and knowledge that such texts claim to forge in their introductory epistles but reveals semantic linkages between this lexicon and early modern discourses of race, nationality, domesticity, husbandry, and animality yet underexamined in contemporary scholarship. What, I ask, can the richness and complexity of this lexicon—which incorporates terms as disparate as 'milk white doe', 'Choir of Nuns', 'easie-paced Gennets', and 'cunny-fur'—tell us about sexual knowledge making in and across time? While routed through the unique definitional problematics of early modern whoredom, Chapter 1 thus opens onto broader semantic relations and quandaries relevant to the production of sexual knowledge from early modernity to the present day.

Linking questions of signification and textuality to those of embodiment and agency, Chapter 2, 'Puzzling Embodiment: Proclamation, *La Pucelle*, and *The first Part of Henry the Sixth*', examines how words materialize (and fail to materialize) medieval and early modern bodies. Reading three representations of 'Joan of Arc'—at her trial and execution in medieval Rouen, in Shakespeare's play, and in scholarly accounts of that play—I reveal how 'heretic', 'witch', and 'whore' emerge, in historical succession, as operative terms for stabilizing her excess significance in medieval, early modern, and postmodern contexts. Reading the various forms of proclamation through which Joan's interlocutors have sought to render her legible, I focus upon who is served by these acts of proclamation, what is and is not known through such signifying practices, and how slanderous meanings have been materialized and contested. Throughout, I demonstrate how thinking embodiment-as-process, as a transitive and transformative action that brings the seemingly immaterial into the corporeal, enables new insights regarding the relations of bodies to discursive practices in medieval and early modern England.

Having examined how whoredom is made and unmade at the levels of language, textuality, and embodiment, the book's middle chapters turn to the relations between sexual time and narrative knowing. Chapter 3, 'The Times of Whoredom', opens with an act of narrative undoing: in 1589, Ursula Shepherd appears on the steps of her local church, confesses to having 'played the whore', and pledges to 'hereafter lead a chaste life'. Turning from whoredom to chastity, Shepherd not only inverts contemporary logics of sexual sequence but challenges a theory of sexual time whereby whoredom leads inexorably to death and damnation. Alongside other repentant whore narratives, her tale discloses the necessity of scrutinizing how theories of sexual time inform and unsettle narrative knowing. To bring this relation into visibility, I pursue a two-part analysis that unfolds across this chapter and the next. I begin by excavating the multiple and often conflicting temporal logics that underwrite the governing paradigms ('the necessary evil', 'life cycles', 'characters, persons, and types', 'the fallen woman', and, by way of binary opposition, 'virginity' and 'chastity') through which early modern whoredom has been brought into clarity, both in that era and our own. These explanatory frameworks and the mixed temporalities that underlie them reveal both the extraordinary discursive labour necessary to demarcate the early modern whore and the various fissures and contradictions upon which any such knowledge depends. But they also channel attention to the often-explicit temporal considerations that inform early modern thinking about whoredom, revealing a critical tension between sexual narrativity and sexual time: just as the former depends upon a theory (or theories) of sexual temporalities, the latter's labile and shifting nature threatens to undo the very conceptual stability that narrative traditionally aims to secure. In the chapter's conclusion, I argue that the tension between sexual narrativity and sexual time enables the development of new methods for reading early modern whore plots.

In Chapter 4, 'Making and Unmaking Whoredom: Turning Chaste in *The Honest Whore*', I demonstrate what this looks like by analysing Thomas Dekker and Thomas Middleton's *The Honest Whore, With, the Humours of the Patient Man, and the Longing Wife* (1604). Extraordinarily popular in its time, the play examines a range of figures who defy or unfix the social, sexual, and gendered narratives within which they might otherwise be conscripted, as well as the often-powerful affects that emerge in response to the categorical trouble that they elicit and body forth. These include Bellafront, the titular 'honest whore', whose efforts to 'turn chaste' evoke not only anger, confusion, and disbelief in other characters but recourse to the temporal logics detailed in the preceding chapter. By scrutinizing how, when, and by whom these logics are introduced, as well as how they inform and unsettle the work of knowing Bellafront's sexual status as a product of narrative time, I argue for a new understanding of the play as an active dramatization of the problems of knowing (honest) whoredom. Of particular importance is what I call the 'chastising process': a mode of sexual and gendered becoming whose performative requirements, I reveal, can be profitably leveraged to illuminate contemporary ideological structures of sex, gender, race, religion, and their complex intersections.

While attuned to relations of language, body, time, and narrative, my final chapter, 'The Measure of Sexual Memory', explores the broader cultural legacies of English prostitution on the Jacobean stage. Focusing on Shakespeare's *Measure for Measure* (1604), I examine how that play makes dramatic use of the complex materiality and the epistemology of early modern whoredom, enabling an interrogation of the social and conceptual costs of the shifting historical relation between law and prostitution in early modern England. I begin by examining the relationship between memory practices and authoritarian power in Shakespeare's play. While scholars have long attended to the play's depiction of criminality, transgression, and authority, their relations to sexual memory have gone unnoticed. The drama, however, both begins and concludes at sites of remembrance, figuring Duke Vincentio's control of memory as the manifestation of his social authority. Troubled by his own longstanding 'license' of public prostitution, the Duke labours to dissociate his bodies natural and politic from the very 'thought' of sex, only to find his memory practices challenged by Lucio, a sexual dissident who recalls precisely those erotic desires, relations, and histories that the state yearns to forget. Construing sexual memory as an ongoing, collaborative, and contestatory process, *Measure for Measure* not only recalls the histories of English prostitution—including its suppression in 1546 and subsequent persistence throughout the remainder of the century—but in so doing, participates in the very memory work that the play puts to the question.

Shakespeare and the Making of English Whoredom concludes with a brief Epilogue in which I argue that the full potential of 'Undoing Whoredom' lies not simply in harnessing that category's capacity to undo itself—i.e. to disclose its own instabilities and incoherences, and thereby to allow scrutiny of the knowledge relations and material processes that contribute to its making and unmaking in specific historical contexts—but to reveal and animate the undoing of other conceptual categories and systems of meaning-making in early modern England. To do so, I turn to John Taylor's *A Common Whore* (1622), a cornucopian verse pamphlet that conspicuously leverages the instabilities of whoredom to think with and through instabilities of language, of gender, of the book, and ultimately of the knowledge that each helps to shape and materialize in that world. In so doing, Taylor's pamphlet opens onto a deeper insight that underpins the broader argument advanced in my book: that what it is ultimately at stake in the making of English whoredom is not simply a reckoning with the instabilities that attend and animate a particular socio-sexual category, or an emergent lexicographic project, or strategies of gendered embodiment, or acts of conversion, or interpretive logics of sex, or theories of sexual time, or depictions of English sexual history and memory on the London stage, but with the making of what passes for knowledge itself, and with the unique capacities of literary and dramatic texts to disclose this epistemological work, the knowledge relations that it incorporates, and the material processes through which it is puzzled out.

Shakespeare and the Making of English Whoredom. Stephen Spiess, Oxford University Press.
 DOI: 10.1093/9780191851223.003.0001

1

The Terms of Whoredom

Whoever is ignorant of words shall never judge well of things.

Thomas Blount, *Glossographia* (1656)

Term, n.

I. A point in time; a span of time.
II. A condition or stipulation; a state or situation.
III. A physical or conceptual limit or end point; a space or span bounded by such limits.
IV. A word or expression, and related senses.

Oxford English Dictionary

In the final pages of *The Rich Cabinet* (1616), a collection of 'Excellent discriptions, exquisite Charracters, witty discourses, and delightfull Histories, Deuine and Morrall', Thomas Gainsford inaugurates an entry on 'A Whore' by distinguishing between that figure's nominal multiplicity and what he presents as its semantic essence: 'A Whore hath many significant names, as filth, curtisan, queane, strumpet, puncke, light-hus-wife, concubine, leman, Iove, mistresse, and infinite other fictions, according to mens fantasies; but all concluding, breach of chastity, and contempt of loyaltie, either to virginitie or marriage' (sig. Y4v). Situating his privileged term within a capacious lexical field, Gainsford immediately moves to foreclose the significance of this linguistic relationality. At the precise moment that readers might contemplate the differences between a concubine, courtesan, light huswife, and mistress—or the transgressive homonymy of queane and queen; or the presence of Love/Jove in this illicit lexicon; or the gendered 'fantasies' that feed this linguistic proliferation; or *why* a 'Whore hath [so] many significant names'—Gainsford urges them not to get bogged down by such concerns. The terms of whoredom may be 'infinite', he allows, but in the end they all boil down to the same thing: a state or condition antithetical to loyalty, virginity, and/or chaste conjugality. The whore's 'many significant names', in other words, must be rendered insignificant—products of fancy ('fictions', 'fantasies'), rather than semantic variability—lest they imperil understandings of what such a figure is or really means in early modern England.

In this double movement, Gainsford anticipates modern accounts of that historical culture, where scholars have broadly acknowledged the fluidity and instability of whoredom as a conceptual category yet either dismissed its lexical variability or attempted to pin down its essential meanings. Take, for instance, historian Laura Gowing's groundbreaking study of early modern defamation, *Domestic Dangers*, which finds an extraordinary 'language of insult' in London's ecclesiastical court records, where 'bawds', 'jades', 'queanes', 'strumpets', and 'whores' jostle alongside 'mangy carrion', 'tinkers truell[s]', 'pockey lousey hedge whore[s]', 'welshe jade[s]', 'scurve fatt arst queane[s]', and other 'inventive elaboration[s]' on these and related terms.[1] Noting the creativity and cross-discursive thinking evinced by such a lexicon, Gowing nevertheless eschews the differences that set such terms apart by figuring them as variations on the same: in London's bawdy courts, at the very least, the manifold monikers of female misconduct almost inexorably point to 'whore', the period's slanderous signified. Gowing thus figures the early modern 'whore' as a 'generic term of abuse' that absorbs and refracts a range of female transgressions, including those unrelated to sexual misconduct.[2] It operates, in other words, as a kind of lexical-conceptual hostel: a capacious gathering space that accommodates not only perceived synonyms—'queane', 'jade', 'strumpet', and the like—but a range of connotations that, Gowing suggests, belie that term's actual linguistic content. This latter distinction, between social connotation and sexual denotation, surfaces obliquely throughout the study, as

[1] *Domestic Dangers*, 66 and passim.

[2] Ibid., 66, 118. See also Capp, *When Gossips Meet*, esp. 189–197. In *City Women*, Eleanor Hubbard offers several examples that underscore Gowing's essential insight, including a woman termed a 'whore, common whore, pocky whore' for beating her servant (38); another identified as a 'barbarous whore' after her husband beat a servant (38); and a maidservant called a 'whore'—and beaten with a wooden candlestick—by her master for attempting to defend her battered mistress (141).

when Gowing contends that '[t]he 'whores' of the language of insult are not, generally, *real whores*', and alludes to the 'stringent regulation of *real whores*' by city authorities in 1570s (emphasis added).[3] By this alternative phrase, Gowing appears to have in mind 'real prostitute[s]', an idiom that she elsewhere links to 'financial implications'.[4] If the relationship between 'whores' and 'prostitutes' thus remains opaque in her study, what is clear is how such constructions instantiate, however implicitly, a referential 'real[ity]'—what we would today call 'sex work'—against which the semantic lability of the early modern 'whore' is to be understand and adjudicated. Gowing's rhetoric of 'real[ness]' thus participates, however unwittingly, in a definitional project not all that dissimilar from that of Gainsford: one that encourages readers to distinguish, whether implicitly or explicitly, between 'real whores' and their 'fiction[al]' counterparts in early modern England.

Gowing is far from alone in wrestling with the linguistic relations that inform the terms of whoredom in early modern England. Over the past two decades, scholars have variously defined and undefined the early modern 'whore' and 'whoredom' as connoting 'a professional sex worker';[5] 'a prostitute';[6] 'not prostitution, but sexual promiscuity';[7] a woman's 'indiscriminacy in her choice of sexual partners';[8] 'any woman who had sexual relations outside marriage, irrespective of her promiscuity, social position or remuneration';[9] 'a woman who has or is suspected of having sex outside of the (typically male) speaker's range of acceptable contexts'.[10] As these definitions suggest, even as scholars increasingly have underscored the semantic lability of these and related terms in early

[3] Gowing, *Domestic Dangers*, 115, 272.

[4] It is a distinction that Gowing at once introduces and unsettles, noting, for instance, that 'the word "whore" rarely meant a real prostitute' (59), and that '"Whore" does not necessarily have the financial implications of prostitution, although defamers sometimes specify them' (66). As with the phrase 'real whores', Gowing twice refers to 'real prostitutes'. In addition to the passage cited above, see 'Real prostitutes were circumscribed in the same way, through the branding introduced under Henry VIII, their control through marked brothels, and the confinement to particular areas that was enforced in other European cities' (100). As noted in the Introduction, there is no evidence that whores were actually branded in Tudor England.

[5] Stanton, *Shakespeare's Whores*, 1.

[6] Howard, *Theater of a City*, 114.

[7] DiGangi, 'How Queer Was the Renaissance?', 129.

[8] Varholy, 'But She Woulde Not Consent', 51.

[9] Dabhoiwala, 'The Pattern of Sexual Immorality', 87.

[10] Mallin, 'Charity and Whoredom in *Timon of Athens*', 82.

modern England—noting, for instance, that 'whore' possesses a 'most slippery definition';[11] that 'precise delineations' cannot be drawn between 'a courtesan...and a whore';[12] that 'even in the most extreme case, of women prosecuted for whoring, it is often impossible to distinguish categorically between those who were 'professional' and those who engaged in sexual trade only on an 'amateur' or 'part-time' basis; or between 'prostitutes', 'mistresses', and other sexual offenders'[13]—they nevertheless insist that 'whore[dom]' is an intrinsically sexual category and offense. In so doing, they posit a relatively concise semantic field that contravenes the broader recognitions detailed in this book's introduction: (1) that the sign of whoredom overlaps with a variety of germane terms and categories in early modern England, including adultery, apostasy, bastardy, bestiality, bigamy, incest, fornication, lust, pride, roguery, sodomy, and witchcraft; (2) that, as one of the era's preeminent tropes, it provided a trenchant language through which early moderns shaped and contested contemporary understandings of everything from beauty, criminality, ethnicity, evil, fairness, and fortune to natural reason, politics, religious conversion, race, rhetorical processes, spiritual incontinence, theatricality, treason, urbanity, and usury, among others; and (3), as Gowing and others remind us, that the terms of early modern whoredom index a range of transgressions that may intersect with, but are irreducible to, sexual misconduct per se: dressing inappropriately, speaking too much, appearing in the wrong place at the wrong time, lying, thieving, blushing, laughing, walking alone, consorting with disreputable persons, gambling, acting, attending a play, failing to attend church, espousing false doctrine, challenging patriarchal authority, and so on.[14]

Such efforts to dismiss the whore's nominal and semantic ambiguities reveal its vital significance as a definitional problem, both in early modern England and in present-day scholarship that aims to elucidate the contours of that historical culture. Whoredom thus offers a unique site for exploring relations-in-language, including among terms associated with sexual acts, behaviours, and identities. In their efforts to resolve the whore's meanings, what Gainsford, Gowing, and their contemporaries

[11] Stanton, *Shakespeare's Whores*, 17.

[12] Salkeld, *Shakespeare among the Courtesans*, 7.

[13] Dabhoiwala, 'The Pattern of Sexual Immorality', 90.

[14] Gowing, *Domestic Dangers*; Hubbard, *City Women*; Ingram, *Carnal Knowledge*; Stockton, 'Chasing Chastity'.

ironically suppress is the extraordinary linguistic energy and creativity that attends the making of English whoredom, including, as we shall see in this chapter, efforts to delineate these and related terms as part of an emergent lexicographic project. Analysing the terms of whoredom, as I will demonstrate, reveals sexual language-making to be an intrinsically imaginative process, one that operates through a dialectic of enablement and constraint animated by the fecundity of the English language, the instabilities of early modern sex, and the various textual practices through which early modern lexicographers attempted to codify the terms of everyday life. While scholars have long turned to such dictionaries to illuminate the sexual lexicons of early modern England, I argue that such texts must be understood less as repositories of historical meanings than as active sites of cultural, sexual, and linguistic meaning-making.

To illuminate the investments, assumptions, and knowledge-relations that subtend this ongoing work, I leverage the multiple senses of the 'terme[s]/tearme[s]/term[s]' noted in my second epigraph. In their semantic reach, 'terms' differ from 'words' in their capacity to signal at once a moment in time and a relation across time; a contract, condition, or law; a threshold, boundary, or terminus; and, always again, a word, utterance, or signifier.[15] Embedded within these senses, one finds terms that index periods of educational instruction (I.4.c.), menstruation (I.5.a.), and 'normal pregnancy' (I.5.b.), that characterize a relationship or agreement between individuals (II.7–8, P4.a), and that betoken a specialized idiom or 'piece of jargon' (IV.11.a). Attending to the terms of a given word, text, discourse, or practice, therefore, is to illuminate—and hold in productive tension—relations of synchrony and diachrony, force and play, possibility and delimitation. It is also to scrutinize norms of language, gender, class, and sexuality; to query scenes and temporalities of instruction; and, perhaps most provocatively, to examine the perceived endpoints or boundaries—the term-limits, so to speak—of privileged and/or hegemonic terms, including how and where they have been erected, by whom, and to what ends.

[15] Cf. 'word, n. and int.', *OED Online*. To avoid readerly fatigue, I henceforth refrain from bracketing 'terms' in quotation marks, with the obvious caveat that each usage should be seen to evoke—and, critically, put to the question—the manifold inflections traced out in this paragraph. On my use of quotation marks here and throughout the book, see n. 4 in the Introduction.

So conceived, terms possess a meta-critical orientation that can be leveraged to illuminate faultlines and impasses—how and where one's terms fail, flounder, or fall short—but also the relations of power and knowledge that circulate within the chosen terms that govern our own scholarly discourses. A rhetoric of terms, I therefore suggest, is particularly well suited to the study of early modern definition writing, if not also to the lexicons of early modern life more broadly.[16]

My argument proceeds in four parts. First, I introduce the English lexicographic project and describe how its experimental ethos fostered a range of textual practices that concomitantly informed and unsettled the terms of early modern life. These include, as I demonstrate through an extended reading of the entry 'To Commit Whoredome' in John Rider's *Bibliotheca Scholastica* (1589), systems of lexical arrangement and visual presentation that play a critical—and critically unexamined—role in these definitional processes and the ideologies of semantic stability that subtend them. Second, by comparing Rider's methods to those adopted by his contemporaries, I detail how the visual, textual, and semantic trials of early modern English lexicography amplified rather than restricted contemporary sexual connotations, producing a far broader field of meanings and relations than previously acknowledged. Third, I illuminate the breadth and complexity of this sexual-lexical matrix by cataloguing over seven hundred early modern 'terms of whoredom'. Fourth, I explore the methodological, historical, discursive, and epistemological questions embedded within this archive; detail some of the insights and aporias that it renders visible; and describe how it can be leveraged to illuminate broader questions of sexual knowledge production from early modernity to the present day. In so doing, I demonstrate how the making of early modern whoredom is inextricably linked to the history of the material text.

Throughout, I argue for the importance of lingering at sites of sexual definition-making; of curating the manifold terms and relations that emerge when early modern writers imagine and define the terms of

[16] For the reasons detailed here, 'terms' is an analytical tool well suited to the 'new philologies' in Renaissance studies, which have brought renewed attention to the problems of language and textuality long central to traditional philology while concurrently insisting that such problems be examined in the broader historical, political, ideological, and cultural contexts in which they emerge and are mediated. See, for instance, Masten, *Queer Philologies*; Rubright and Spiess, *Logomotives*.

whoredom; of querying the contradictions and aporia that arise by way of this sexual-lexical work; of detailing the various textual practices through which writers attempt to enable or constrain this linguistic proliferation; and of scrutinizing the often-implicit theories of language and (sexual) signification that subtend this definitional work. It is only in such careful linguistic labour that we can fully account for the centrifugal force that whoredom's dialectical linguistic movements enact upon both early modern England's culture and our own.

'To Signify & Shew': Envisioning Meaning in the Dictionary *Mise-en-Page*

In an introductory epistle to 1589's BIBLIOTHECA SCHOLASTICA [*The Scholar's Library*], the first dictionary that 'hath the English before the Latine', John Rider offers a traditional if relatively concise *apologia*, locating his text within an extended lexicographic genealogy while defending its status as a unique contribution to this 'learned' project.[17] Confessing 'I may seeme to some over bold in setting forth a newe treasure of wordes vnto the world, when the works of so honorable and learned men, who have labored in this kinde, are so learnedly penned, and highly esteemed', he nonetheless positions his edition as a new type of 'Dictionarie', one that serves as both an aggregation and condensation of previous works. Whereas contemporary volumes had proven increasingly expansive and expensive, he 'thought it good...to epitomize and contract the learned works of all the learnedst and best Dictionaries in England, with us now extant, into a portable Enchiridion [handbook]'. Pitched as leaner, cheaper, and more accessible than its peers, the BIBLIOTHECA SCHOLASTICA, Rider alleges, offers a storehouse of 'treasures' to 'students' too 'poore' to 'furnish themselues with [other] such Dictionaries'. As individual units of knowledge, conjoining words and meanings, the terms of early modern England represent, in such a construction, emergent forms of social, intellectual, and material currency in an evolving print culture.

[17] Rider, 'To the Reader', BIBLIOTHECA SCHOLASTICA, n.p. All citations in this paragraph are from this (unnumbered) page.

Such materiality derives, in part, from the *BIBLIOTHECA SCHOLASTICA*'s status as one of many manuscript and print texts produced in late medieval and early modern England that work to codify, define, aggregate, stabilize, and/or animate the terms of everyday life. This textual history precedes the advent of the printing press in England, originating in the codification of marginalia in medieval monasteries. When negotiating difficult words or passages in antique texts, monastics inscribed personal definitions between lines or along the margins of the manuscripts they were working on. To locate meanings in such texts, subsequent readers had to navigate an interactive *mise-en-page*, conjoining the imprinted and the inscribed, the entry proper and the marginal notation. As such methods became increasingly common, scribes began to collate these glosses in separate manuscripts, creating reference texts to be studied in their own right. The emergence of print further catalysed such practices, but the project remained, by the late sixteenth century, less a codified field of study possessing specific rules or guidelines than a site—and sight[18]—for textual and lexical experimentation.[19] I refer to the production of these texts as lexicography, using the term to indicate the writing of 'meaning or meanings'.[20] Such

[18] Throughout this chapter, I use 'site' to indicate both those textual spaces wherein writers explored and experimented with meanings (i.e. 'site' as location) and the material product visible to the human eye (i.e. 'sight'). On the dictionary as a textual site/sight wherein historical contingent structures of knowledge become visible see Foucault, *The Order of Things*; Williams, *Keywords*; Kuhn, *The Structure of Scientific Revolutions*.

[19] As Gabriele Stein and John Considine have argued, these textual practices precede—and later coincide with—the development of English philology, etymology, and orthography, among other fields. As such, these texts defy boundaries separating seemingly distinct modern textual genres, including dictionaries, encyclopaedias, lexicons, thesauruses, and glossaries. A single lexicographic text from the period may include any number of the following characteristics: word lists, etymological clusters, field-specific vocabularies, singular or multiple definitions, extensive glosses, encyclopaedia-length definitions, famous quotations, biblical parables, English and polyglot synonyms, antonyms, rhymes, mnemonic verses, rhetorical forms, pictures, drawings, proper names, social types, and/or parts of the human anatomy. Although writers often copied definitions verbatim from other texts, adopted nearly identical typographies, and/or reproduced previous organizational axioms, their products also diverged widely along these very same axes. See Stein, *The English Dictionary before Cawdrey*; Considine, *Dictionaries in Early Modern Europe*. See also Schafer, *Early Modern English Lexicography*. Scholars generally date the birth of the 'modern dictionary', predicated upon the establishment of consistent 'lexical laws', with Samuel Johnson's *Dictionary of the English Language* (1755). See de Grazia, 'Homonyms before and after Lexical Standardization', 150.

[20] I adopt this definition from the *Oxford English Dictionary* ('Dictionary' 1a), as opposed to the more limited sense of lexicography as 'the writing or compilation of a

a definition captures the inchoate state and 'experimental spirit' of the lexicographic project,[21] but also its fundamentally creative character: organizing words and definitions in print, writers inscribed as they transcribed, added where they assembled, constructed when they codified. English lexicography thus provided a 'powerful instrument' through which contemporary writers could explore—and produce—English heritage, cultural history, and ethnic identity,[22] as well as ideologies of race and gender,[23] but also theories of signification and the production of meanings in an evolving print culture. Engaging terms possessing multiple connotations, lexicographers moulded meanings through a variety of complimentary—and competing—factors, forces, and systems of organization. Such a dynamic encourages attention to the interactions among and between the signifying components of the lexicographic text, especially its visual, textual, and linguistic characteristics.

But let us return, for a moment, to Rider's opening conceit. Positioning his text as a linguistic repository, a 'treasure of wordes', Rider intimates not only the value of the words deposited therein but their inherent stability: akin to coins that can be possessed or traded, the contents of his collection are configured as autonomous material assets—concrete, tangible, immutable—awaiting procurement by

lexicon or dictionaries ('Lexicography' 1a). See the preceding footnote for this rationale. I acknowledge the potentially anachronistic status of this latter term; according to the *OED*, the first known use of 'lexicography' to indicate a distinct practice or profession does not appear until 1680, when George Dalgarno notes, in *Didascalocophus*, that he 'shall therefore only make some few reflexions upon Etymology and Syntax, supposing Orthography to belong to Lexicography'. Nonetheless, Dalgarno's entry indicates the intimate relations between these varying fields. Such terminological imprecision poses a taxonomic quandary for modern scholars. Robert Cawdrey's *A Table Alphabeticall* (1604), for example, has been cited as the 'first English Dictionary' yet this assertion derives from its status as a monolingual text, thus differentiating Cawdrey's effort from earlier bilingual (e.g. Rider's *Bibliotheca Scholastica*) and polyglot (e.g. John Barret, *An Alvearie or triple dictionarie in Englishe, Latin, and French*, 1574) compendiums, as well as word-lists and grammar books. Significantly, Cawdrey himself never uses the term 'dictionary', referring to his text solely as a 'true Orthography' (sig. A2r).

[21] Stein, *The English Dictionary before Cawdrey*, 59.

[22] Blank, 'The Babel of Renaissance English'; *Broken English*; Considine, *Dictionaries in Early Modern Europe*; H. Crawford, *Etymology and the Invention of English in Early Modern Literature*; Rubright, *Doppelgänger Dilemmas*; 'Incorporating Kate'.

[23] Fleming, 'Dictionary English and the Female Tongue'; Masten, *Queer Philologies* Phillips, 'Schoolmasters, Seduction, and Slavery'; Rubright, 'Becoming Scattered'. See also the various dictionary entries included in Burton and Loomba, *Race in Early Modern England*.

'Covrteovs Reader[s]'.[24] Noting the addition of 'some smal mites [i.e. coins] of mine owne, which amount to 4000 wordes more then [sic] any one Dictionarie nowe extant affords', Rider extends the materiality of the metaphor, reinforcing its economic and linguistic inflections. In the contexts of an early modern print economy, it is a savvy if familiar marketing ploy.[25] In the contexts on an emergent lexicographic project, it is something far more audacious: an implicit promise that the instabilities and vagaries of language might be hammered out; that the relationship between signifiers and signifieds can be concretized and shorn of excesses; that readers can therefore locate the true meaning—the true value—of the words they seek to know and subsequently can deposit them in their mental banks.[26] In so doing, he implicitly associates terminological acquisition with personal development: procurement as a means of enhancing intellectual wealth.[27]

If this path to erudition appears tangible, the lexicographic promise implicitly depends upon the writer's ability to 'Signifie & shew'.[28] Does the lexicographer, like Rider, provide a comprehensive list of possible

[24] Rider, 'To the Reader', *Bibliotheca Scholastica*, n.p. William Mulcaster draws a similar analogy in *The First Part of the Elementarie* (1582), a rhetorical handbook which includes a table of eight thousand 'hard words', where he suggests that words provide the elemental 'f[o]undation' necessary to advance 'students to the attainme[n]t of learning' and help 'the learned to aduaunement of liuing', dedicatory epistle, n.p.

[25] See, for instance, Hyspanus, *The Treasury of Health of Health conteynyng many profitable medycines, gathered out of Hypocrates, Galen and Auycen* (1550); Partridge, *The Treasurie of commodious Conceits, & hidden Secrets* (1573); Huberinus, *A riche Storehouse, or Treasurie, for the Sicke, full of Christan counsels, holesome doctrines, comfortable persuasions, and godly meditations* (1578); Hollyband, *The Treasurie of the French Tong* (1580); Meres, *Palladis Tamia. Wits Treasvrie Being the Second part of Wits Commonwealth* (1598); and Cawdrey, *A Treasvrie or Store-Hovse of Similes* (1600).

[26] Construed thus, Rider's metaphor challenges Margreta de Grazia's contention that the 'linguistic ideal of one linguistic sign per epistemological signified' postdates the era, suggesting instead that, while the contours of such an 'ideal' may have been inchoate, the dream of what Thomas Wilson and Robert Cawdrey refer to as 'apt words' had already been dreamt. See de Grazia, 'Homonyms', 155. On Wilson and Cawdrey, see n. 29 in this chapter.

[27] This belief, which permeates lexicographic texts in the period, also assumes nationalist connotations. See, for instance, Mulcaster, *The First Part of the Elementarie*.

[28] The phrase comes from Rider's entry for signification, which critically conjoins these two verbs (sig. Ee7v, 1333.59–1334.28). As with 'To commit Whoredome', the entry 'To Signifie & Shew' expands rather than restricts the meaning of signification, with various sub-entries that differentiate between '*To signifie, betoken, or foresee*', '*signified*', '*A signification, or meaning of a thing*', '*An expresse signification of that which is entended*', '*Signifying*', '*Signifying but one thing*', '*Signifying many things*', '*That signifieth a thing to be at hand*', '*With some significations*', and '*With many significations*'.

significations? Does he, like Robert Cawdrey, seek definitional precision—'apt words, that properly agree vnto that thing, which they signifie, and plainly expresse the nature of the same?'[29] In most cases, lexicographers pursued a combination of the two. Tensions between precision and breadth drove the lexicographic market, encouraging experimentation and imitation, production and reproduction.[30] Fuelled by these frictions, lexicography provided a textual site to explore the making of meanings in print. As we shall see, the organizational structure that underpins Rider's *BIBLIOTHECA SCHOLASTICA* neither reflects nor emblematizes English lexicography; instead, the text proves lexicographic in its unique and experimental, rather than orthodox or programmatic, qualities.

Given the intimate associations of signifying and 'shew(ing)' in these texts, let us look at where, and how, Rider's entry 'To commit Whoredome' is located in the *BIBLIOTHECA SCHOLASTICA* (Fig. 1.1). As this page reveals, to locate entries and meanings in the *BIBLIOTHECA SCHOLASTICA*, readers must first negotiate the visual order imposed by Rider's *mise-en-page*.[31] The tripartite pagination departs from the most

[29] *A Table Alphabeticall*, sig. A4v. Cawdrey here echoes Thomas Wilson, *The Arte of Rhetorique* (1553): 'Suche are thought apt words, that properly agre[e] unto that thing, whiche thei signifie, and plainly expresse the nature of the same' (sig. Y4r). On the moral connotations of 'proper' and 'improper' signification in the early modern rhetorical tradition, see Crewe, *Unredeemed Rhetoric*; Menon, *Wanton Words*; and Felperin, '"Tongue-Tied Our Queen?"'

[30] By altering content and organizational axioms, lexicographers marketed their products simultaneously as new editions—reproducing popular and/or essential components from preceding texts—and innovative productions in their own right. To attract readers (and buyers), for example, Rider stresses both the *BIBLIOTHECA SCHOLASTICA*'s proximity to its forebears and its unique and experimental attributes. These latter characteristics include not only differences of size, price, and accessibility, but also the imposition of an innovative organizational structure and indexical system. Such diversity promulgated calls for standardization and even, by the mid-seventeenth century, attempts to establish a new, 'perfect' language, such as Francis Lodowyk's *THE GROUND-WORK, OR FOUNDATION LAID (or so intended) For the Framing of a New Perfect LANGUAGE* (1652). Focusing on English grammar school education, Mulcaster argues that lexicographers must codify a terminological 'fundation' for the English tongue. The 'grammar maister', he laments, 'hath no Elementarie principle'—neither a codified set of rules nor definitional consenses—from which to draw. Lexicography, Mulcaster argues, needs to identify stable 'elem[n]ets or principles, which children ar[e] to deal with', without which national-linguistic 'vnity' will prove impossible. See *THE FIRST PART OF THE ELEMENTARIE*, sig. Ff4r.

[31] On the *mise-en-page*'s constitutive role in the production of lexicographic meanings, see Rubright, *Doppelgänger Dilemmas*, esp. 110–161.

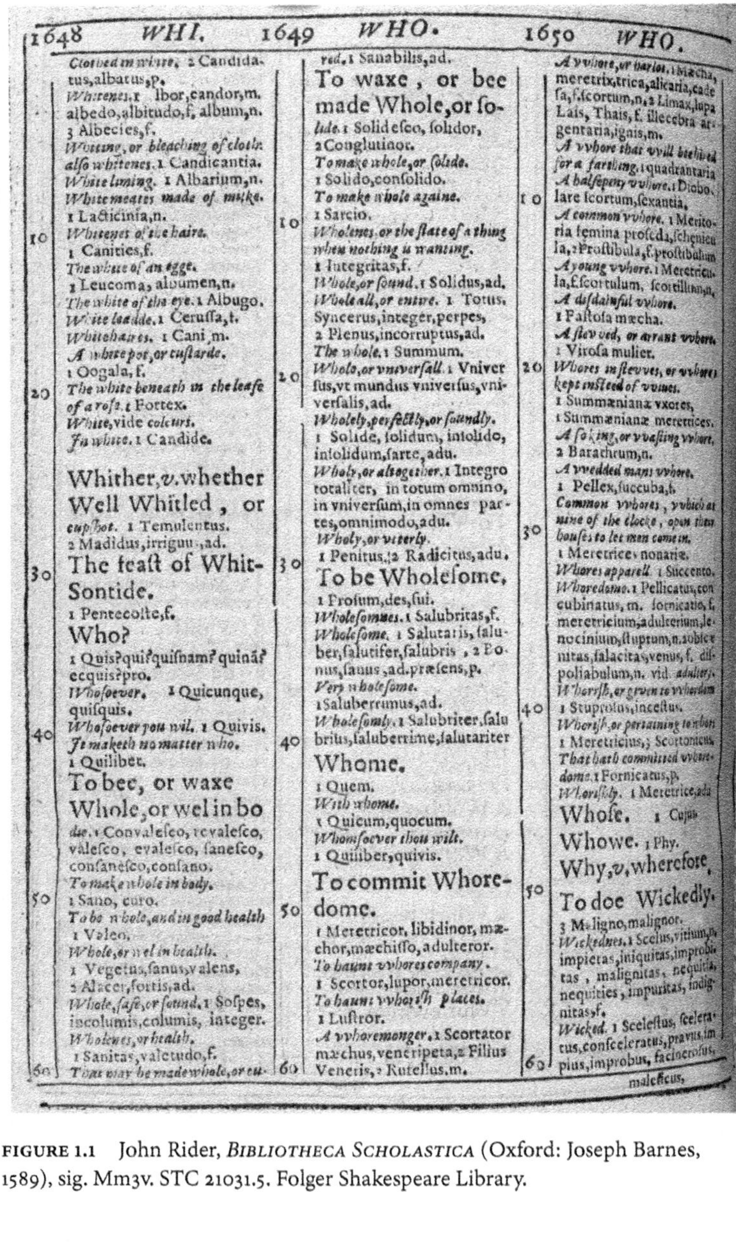

1648 *WHI.* 1649 *WHO.* 1650 *WHO.*

Clothed in white, 2 Candidatus, albatus, p.
Whitenes. 1 Ibor, candor, m. albedo, albitudo, f. album, n. 3 Albecies, f.
Whiting, or bleaching of cloth: also whitenes. 1 Candicantia.
White liming. 1 Albarium, n.
White meates made of milke. 1 Lacticinia, n.
Whitenes of the haire. 1 Canities, f.
The white of an egge. 1 Leucoma, albumen, n.
The white of the eye. 1 Albugo.
White leadde. 1 Cerussa, f.
White haires. 1 Cani, m.
A white pot, or custarde. 1 Oogala, f.
The white beneath in the leafe of a rose. 1 Fortex.
White, vide *colours.*
In white. 1 Candide.

Whither, *v.* whether

Well Whitled, or *cupshot.* 1 Temulentus. 2 Madidus, irriguus, ad.

The feaſt of Whit-Sontide. 1 Pentecoſte, f.

Who? 1 Quis? qui? quiſnam? quinā? ecquis? pro.
Whosoever. 1 Quicunque, quiſquis.
Whosoever you wil. 1 Quivis.
It maketh no matter who. 1 Quilibet.

To bee, or waxe Whole, or wel in bo*die.* 1 Convaleſco, revaleſco, valeſco, evaleſco, ſaneſco, conſaneſco, conſano.
To make whole in body. 1 Sano, curo.
To be whole, and in good health 1 Valeo.
Whole, or wel in health. 1 Vegetus, ſanus, valens, 2 Alacer, fortis, ad.
Whole, safe, or sound. 1 Soſpes, incolumis, columis, integer.
Wholenes, or health. 1 Sanitas, valetudo, f.
That may be made whole, or cu-red. 1 Sanabilis, ad.

To waxe, or bee made Whole, or ſo*lide.* 1 Solideſco, ſolidor, 2 Conglutinor.
To make whole, or solide. 1 Solido, conſolido.
To make whole againe. 1 Sarcio.
Wholenes, or the state of a thing when nothing is wanting. 1 Integritas, f.
Whole, or sound. 1 Solidus, ad.
Whole all, or entire. 1 Totus, Syncerus, integer, perpes, 2 Plenus, incorruptus, ad.
The whole. 1 Summum.
Whole, or universall. 1 Vniverſus, vt mundus vniverſus, vniverſalis, ad.
Wholely, perfectly, or soundly. 1 Solide, ſolidum, inſolido, inſolidum, ſarte, adu.
Wholy, or altogether. 1 Integro totaliter, in totum omnino, in vniverſum, in omnes partes, omnimodo, adu.
Wholy, or utterly. 1 Penitus, 2 Radicitus, adu.

To be Wholeſome, 1 Proſum, des, ſui.
Wholesomnes. 1 Salubritas, f.
Wholesome. 1 Salutaris, ſaluber, ſalutifer, ſalubris, 2 Bonus, ſanus, ad. præſens, p.
Very wholesome. 1 Saluberrimus, ad.
Wholesomly. 1 Salubriter, ſalubrius, ſaluberrime, ſalutariter

Whome. 1 Quem.
With whome. 1 Quicum, quocum.
Whomsoever thou wilt. 1 Quilibet, quivis.

To commit Whoredome. 1 Meretricor, libidinor, mæchor, mæchiſſo, adulteror.
To haunt whores company. 1 Scortor, lupor, meretricor.
To haunt whorish places. 1 Luſtror.
A whoremonger. 1 Scortator mæchus, veneripeta, 2 Filius Veneris, 2 Rufellus, m.
A whore, or harlot. 1 Mæcha, meretrix, trica, alicaria, cadeſa, f. ſcortum, n. 2 Limax, lupa Lais, Thais, f. illecebra argentaria, ignis, m.
A whore that will be hired for a farthing. 1 quadrantaria
A halfepeny whore. 1 Diobolare ſcortum, ſexantia.
A common whore. 1 Meritoria femina proſeda, ſchęnicula, 2 Proſtibula, f. proſtibulum
A young whore. 1 Meretricula, f. ſcortulum, ſcortillum, n.
A disdainful whore. 1 Faſtoſa mæcha.
A stewed, or arrant whore. 1 Viroſa mulier.
Whores in stewes, or whores kept instead of wives. 1 Summænianæ vxores, 1 Summænianæ meretrices.
A soking, or wasting whore. 2 Barathrum, n.
A wedded mans whore. 1 Pellex, ſuccuba, f.
Common whores, which at nine of the clocke, open their houses to let men come in. 1 Meretrices nonariæ.
Whores apparell. 1 Succento.
Whoredome. 1 Pellicatus, concubinatus, m. fornicatio, f. meretricium, adulterium, lenocinium, ſtuprum, n. 2 obſcœnitas, ſalacitas, venus, f. diſpoliabulum, n. vid. *adultery.*
Whorish, or given to whoredom 1 Stuproſus, inceſtus.
Whorish, or pertaining to whores 1 Meretricius, 3 Scortonicus.
That hath committed whoredome. 1 Fornicatus, p.
Whorishly. 1 Meretrice, adu

Whoſe. 1 Cujus.

Whowe. 1 Phy.

Why, *v.* wherefore.

To doe Wickedly. 3 Maligno, malignor.
Wickednes. 1 Scelus, vitium, n. impietas, iniquitas, improbitas, malignitas, nequitia, nequities, impuritas, indignitas, f.
Wicked. 1 Sceleſtus, ſceleratus, conſceleratus, pravus, impius, improbus, facineroſus, maleficus,

FIGURE 1.1 John Rider, *Bibliotheca Scholastica* (Oxford: Joseph Barnes, 1589), sig. Mm3v. STC 21031.5. Folger Shakespeare Library.

common approach—usually bipartite or without columns—structuring contemporary texts, a divergence that enhances claims to textual distinction,[32] but also confers a sense of geometric order upon the *Bibliotheca Scholastica*. Integers progress horizontally across the top of each page, rendering each column uniquely identifiable in the work as a whole: where page 1 (sig. A1r), for instance, features columns 1–3, this page (sig. Mm3v) incorporates columns 1648–1650.[33] A second numeric scale then descends the vertical axes of each margin, marking line numbers by an order of ten (up to 60). This textual geometry produces a kind of terminological cartography: a coordinate system wherein latitude (columns) and longitude (lines) appear to secure precise locations for each individual entry. Suggesting order and extreme precision—attributes readers may extend to the terms and definitions listed within—Rider's *mise-en-page* implies that meanings are located with pinpoint accuracy in the *Bibliotheca Scholastica*. From a purely visual perspective, English 'Whoredome' resides at the intersections of column 1649, lines 49–50. Or so it seems.

Upon closer examination, Rider's coordinate system corresponds solely to Latin terms, the *Bibliotheca Scholastica*'s 'second' language. Indeed, Latin cartographic precision ultimately contrasts with English terminological breadth: whereas Latin entries seem fixed,

[32] A valuable reminder that such texts, regardless of their social 'utilitie', were produced as commodities for distribution within a developing English print economy. Assertions of textual kinship and distinction depend, perhaps unsurprisingly, on a reader's definitional parameters. Identifying the *Bibliotheca Scholastica* as a 'Double Dictionarie', Rider invites comparison to earlier compendiums such as *The Dictionary of Syr Thomas Elyot knyght* (1538) and William Salesbury's *A Dictionary of Englyshe and Welshe* (1547), both dedicated to Henry VIII, as well as contemporary works like Thomas Thomas's *Dictionarivm Lingvae Latinae et Anglicanae* (1587), printed just two years prior. In contrast to contemporaries like John Baret (*An Alvearie or Triple Dictionary in Englyshe, Latin, and French*, 1574) and John Florio (*A Worlde of Wordes*, 1598), however, Rider declines to identify specific influences, referring simply to the 'learned men' and 'works' that have preceded his text. Such imprecision enables subsequent claims to economic value and textual concision: it is difficult to the judge veracity when one does not know the field of comparison.

[33] One can therefore argue the *Bibliotheca Scholastica* is organized by column as opposed to page. While image 1, for instance, reprints columns 1648–1650, it appears on the 550th printed page of the text. The main body of the text includes approximately 1800 columns, or six hundred printed pages. This latter number, however, incorporates neither the text's prefatory materials nor the extensive Latin index (which nearly doubles the length of the manuscript).

exact, and condensed, English terms appear expansive and meaning-full.[34] Before turning to these English entries, however, it is important to note that such divergences emerge from differing systems of organization. The text adopts a different set of axioms for each language.

The terminological, geometric, and cartographic qualities ascribed to Latin are rendered visible in the *Bibliotheca Scholastica*'s indexical *mise-en-page* (Fig. 1.2). In this textual order, such coordinates imply not only indexical meticulousness but lexical stability: if located elsewhere, all meanings, readers are led to believe, have been accounted for and can be located. Compared to the main text (Fig. 1.1), where a range of subcategories divide English headwords, indexical entries are situated in close proximity to one another and occupy less space on the page: visual characteristics that suggest concision and approximation. In brief, meanings seem more exact, definitions more definite in the

Luſtror,aris,depo.Plaut.711,43
1649,56.
Luſtrum, ſtri, neut. Cic. 230,7.
351,40.418, 20.1169, 31. 1165,
51.1410,24.
Lūſus,a,um,p.a ludor,Cic. 403,
15.952,28.& 30.1100,37.
Luſus,us,m.a ludo,Cic.1066, 3.
1101,12.1199,4.1390,15.

FIGURE 1.2 Latin Index ('Lustror-Lusus'), in John Rider, *Bibliotheca Scholastica* (Oxford: Joseph Barnes, 1589), sig. Iiiir. STC 21031.5. Folger Shakespeare Library.

[34] Peter Stallybrass notes just such a distinction between Latin and English in the period, arguing that the 'Latinate fantasy of fixed meaning is forced to submit to the orthographic play of the [English] vernacular'. See 'Shakespeare, the Individual, and the Text', 601.

system of arrangement that govern the *Bibliotheca Scholastica*'s Latin index. By substituting coordinates for meanings, this *mise-en-page* also suppresses, if not outright elides, shades of distinction between potential significations. Readers do not see, for example, that while 'Lustror' signifies *specific* geographic sites at the coordinates 711,43 ('*to haunt stews*', or brothels),[35] the term indicates a *general* locale at 1649,56 ('*to haunt whorish places*').

In contrast to Latinate reduction, the *Bibliotheca Scholastica*'s English entries prove capacious and polymorphous. The entry 'To Commit Whoredome' illustrates this abundance, as well as the experimental 'principles of arrangement' that undergird this portion of the text.[36] It also reveals the breadth of meanings associated with early modern whoredom: as opposed to cartographic approximation, whoredom here emerges amidst a vast definitional field of associated terms, meanings, values, and interrelations. Rider's entry thus helps to illuminate the generative homology that links language to sex in the period, wherein the instabilities of each discursive field result in an animating paradox in which the very effort to pin down terms and meanings only proliferates yet more terms and meanings. In so doing, it gestures towards the broader insight that an epistemology of the early modern whore—or any conceptual category, for that matter—is also and concurrently an epistemology of the language(s) and textualities through which it is constructed and materialized.

Whereas the Latinate index proceeds in alphabetical order, Rider uses a different organizational structure in the English section of the *Bibliotheca Scholastica*. As he notes in the letter 'To the Reader' which precedes the dictionary proper: 'First I put the verbe (if it haue any) then the participle, after the Nownes substantives, and adjectiues, and lastly the Adverbs'. By adopting this system of organization for his primary entries, the first of its kind in English lexicography,[37] Rider alters relations of headwords and meanings. When listed alphabetically, as in the index, words assume no distinct value in their own right: textual positions are not ordered according to grammatical function, part

[35] Originally a pond or tank in which fish were kept, 'stews' operated as a common term for brothels in the period. See, for instance, Minsheu, *Ductor in Linguas, The Gvide Into Tongves* (1617), 468.

[36] Stein, *The English Dictionary Before Cawdrey*, 342.

[37] Ibid., 332–352.

of speech, or precision in signification, but rather by the sequence of letters that constitute the term(s) in question. To return to Fig. 1.2, for example, terms signifying the haunting of 'whorish places' (Lustror 1649,56), a 'cave for wild beasts in the wood' (Lustrum 230,7), and the act of being 'deceived' (Lusus 403,15) appear as equivalent terms: the text confers no distinctions between an activity bearing sexual connotations, a locale, and a passive action.[38]

Terminological and definitional reductions such as these appear particularly conspicuous in contemporary lexicographic texts. A quick glance at Cawdrey's *A Table Alphabeticall* (1604, Fig. 1.3), for example, equally implies terminological equity, not only between entries and definitions but among headwords ('baptist' and 'baud') and glosses

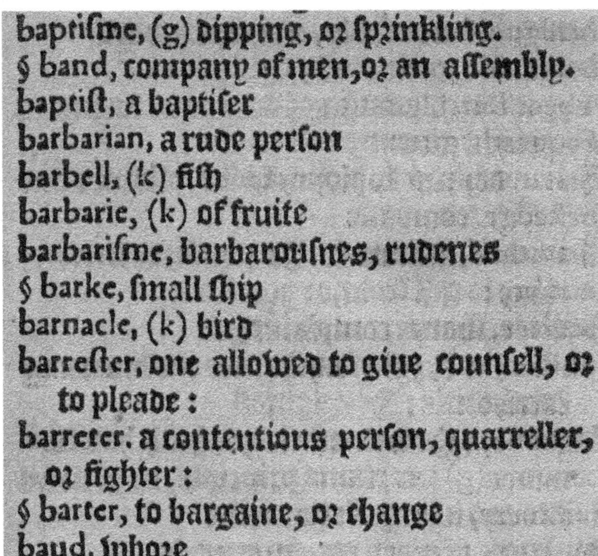

baptiſme, (g) dipping, or ſprinkling.
§ band, company of men, or an aſſembly.
baptiſt, a baptiſer
barbarian, a rude perſon
barbell, (k) fiſh
barbarie, (k) of fruite
barbariſme, barbarouſnes, rudenes
§ barke, ſmall ſhip
barnacle, (k) bird
barreſter, one allowed to giue counſell, or to pleade:
barreter. a contentious perſon, quarreller, or fighter:
§ barter, to bargaine, or change
baud, whore

FIGURE 1.3 From 'baptisme' to 'baud', in Robert Cawdrey, *A Table Alphabeticall* (London: I. Roberts for Edmund Weauer, 1604), sig. B8r. The Bodleian Libraries, University of Oxford, Weston Library, Arch. A, f. 141 (2).

[38] While indexical entries do identify a term's word-class (e.g. parts of speech), these categories do not impact the organizational structure of this section (as is the case in the English portion of Rider's text).

('a baptiser' and 'whore').[39] Cawdrey's use of type reveals another significant difference between his text and Rider's *Bibliotheca Scholastica*: by presenting glosses in a more striking (i.e., serif) font, Cawdrey accords greater prestige to glosses than headwords. Cawdrey's 'whore' is, quite literally, more prominent than 'baud': it not only operates as that latter term's sole definition but is presented in an enlarged and visually arresting font. Given Cawdrey's interest in defining 'hard words'—terms considered difficult to grasp at that time[40]—this *mise-en-page* furthermore situates the 'whore' as the familiar term, common enough to stabilize the assumedly more evasive 'baud'.

'Whoredome' and 'whore' assume quite different meanings in the *Bibliotheca Scholastica*. To return to Rider's unique organizational principles, this text suggests a range of values and relations according to terminological function (e.g. part of speech), derivational relationship, and subject-field orientation.[41] In this grammatical order, the act of committing 'whoredome' precedes the 'whore': visually and grammatically subordinate, the nouns of 'whoredome' derive from an action, implying that one becomes a whore—or whoremonger—through one's deeds. This derivational relationship proves especially significant given that other English nouns lack associative verbs, thus functioning as headwords in their own right. Entries such as '*an* Abbot' (Fig. 1.4), for instance, suggest an identity that precedes, or is irreducible to, the various actions or practices with which such figures might be associated. Solidified by differences of font and typography, the social and hierarchical implications of this particular entry are revealed in the subordination of

[39] Often positioned as the first monolingual dictionary in English, Cawdrey's *A Table Alphabeticall* offers another useful reminder of the lability of this category in the early modern period. Setting his task as the interpreting of 'hard vsuall English words, borrowed from the Hebrew, Greek, Latine, or French. &c.', Cawdrey's aim is not to codify and define the manifold terms that comprise the English language but rather to identify and gloss foreign words that have become 'Englished'. In a sense, therefore, one might best describe his entries as interlinguistic glosses, as opposed to dictionary entries that conjoin English headwords to English glosses. And yet, as Cawdrey himself notes, the terms that comprise his *Table* have been selected precisely because they have been operating as 'vsuall English wordes' and thus, even as he is at pains to mark their foreign origins, his entries might equally be described as intra-linguistic glosses; or, headwords and glosses; or, terms and synonyms.

[40] Schafer, *Early Modern English Lexicography*, 4.

[41] I adopt these categories from Stein, *The English Dictionary before Cawdrey*, 332–352. Subject-field orientation refers to sections organized by category, such as names of birds, herbs, numbers, etc.

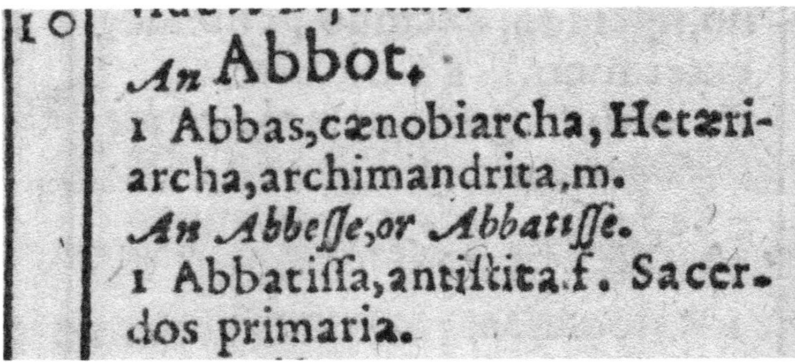
10

An Abbot.

1 Abbas,cænobiarcha, Hetæriarcha,archimandrita,m.

An Abbeſſe,or Abbatiſſe.

1 Abbatiſſa,antiſtita.f. Sacerdos primaria.

FIGURE 1.4 'An Abbot', in John Rider, *Bibliotheca Scholastica* (Oxford: Joseph Barnes, 1589), sig. A1r. STC 21031.5. Folger Shakespeare Library.

'*An Abbesse, or Abbatesse*': the masculine Abbot, quite literally, precedes—we might even say governs or gives birth to—the feminine Abbess. I will return to these gendered inferences momentarily, but first want to emphasize the manner in which terminological relations, in Rider's text, always begin with, and correspond to, privileged headwords: whereas the Abbot appears outside the province of an organizing verb, acts of 'committing whoredom' conspicuously govern (the meanings of) whores and whoremongers alike. 'Abbot', in other words, is presented as an identity unconnected to specific acts or actions, while 'whore' is presented as an identity that derives from an act of 'whoredome'.[42] Such relations prove especially intricate as readers navigate the various subdivisions that appear under headwords in the English portion of the *Bibliotheca Scholastica*. Take, for instance, the first lines of the entry 'To commit Whore-dome' (Fig. 1.5).

As this excerpt reveals, underneath English headwords and their subordinate entries (which are also rendered in the English), readers encounter Latin terms that are, as in the index, associated with specific

[42] Certainly, such a construction recalls Foucault's much-debated distinction, in *The History of Sexuality*, Vol. I, between premodern sodomy and modern homosexuality, wherein the former indicates an act, i.e. something that someone does, while the latter connotes an identity, i.e. what someone is. For a spirited debate on the applicability of Foucault's argument to the medieval prostitute, see Karras, 'Prostitution and the Question of Sexual Identity in Medieval Europe'; van der Meer, 'Medieval Prostitution and the Case of a (Mistaken?) Sexual Identity'; and Freccero, 'Acts, Identities, and Sexuality's (Pre)Modern Regimes'.

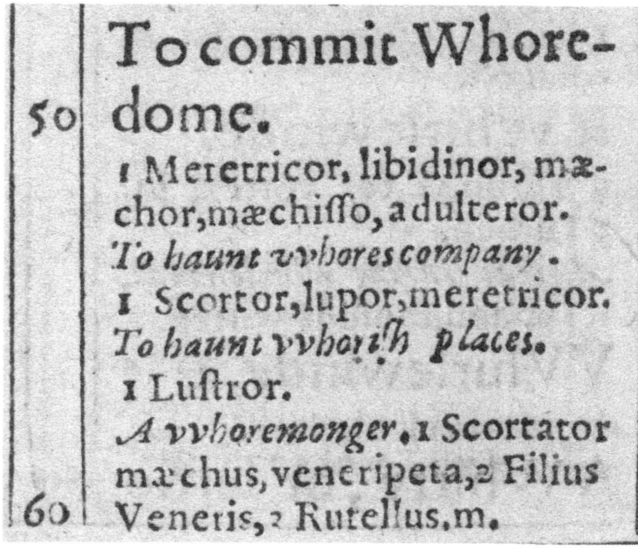
To commit Whore-
dome.
1 Meretricor, libidinor, mæ-
chor, mæchiſſo, adulteror.
To haunt vvhores company.
1 Scortor, lupor, meretricor.
To haunt vvhoriſh places.
1 Luſtror.
A vvhoremonger. 1 Scortator
mæchus, veneripeta, 2 Filius
Veneris, 3 Rutellus, m.

FIGURE 1.5 First lines of the entry 'To Commit Whore-dome', in John Rider, *Bibliotheca Scholastica* (Oxford: Joseph Barnes, 1589), sig. Mm3v. STC 21031.5. Folger Shakespeare Library.

numerals. In this case, however, these integers do not function as textual coordinates but rather designate literal, figurative, and archaic meanings. The first English dictionary to use subsections ordering figures of speech,[43] the *Bibliotheca Scholastica* thus confers, in these subentries, values according to precision in signification. The number 1, for example, denotes 'literal' translations—what Rider refers to as 'proper Latine word[s]'—for the English headwords. The number 2 then identifies 'figurati[v]e' meanings, subordinating figuration to supposedly direct signification. Some entries include a third numeral, listing definitions 'that be old and out of use'.[44] Within each subclass, Latin terms deviate from an alphabetical order. In each instance, therefore, sequence suggests proximity of translation, even among supposedly

[43] Stein, *The English Dictionary before Cawdrey*, 332–352.

[44] All three numerals can be glimpsed in the entry for '*A Whoremonger*' (Fig. 1.5): '1 Scortator mæchus, veneripeta, 2 Filius Veneris, 3 Rutellus, m'.

'literal' renderings: '*Meretricor*', generally signifying the sale of sex, for instance, appears closer to 'whoredome' than 'adulteror'. If intimately related, definitions possess varying degrees of kinship, both to their terminological peers and to the organizing headword.

Two verbal subcategories ('*to haunt whores company*' and '*to haunt whorish places*') follow this headword, preceding the 'No[u]nes substantives' of 'Whoredome'. Critically, both indicate relational activities: unspecified subjects commit whoredom by coming into contact with, or proximity to, persons or spaces seen as '*whorish*'. In the *Bibliotheca Scholastica*, the terms of whoredom thus transcend sexual activity: one can be whored by means of interpersonal associations or even their geographic location. Moreover, these actions both bear relational connotations and lack gendered subjects, appearing applicable to all persons and positions: imprecision suggesting a range of erotic pairings and practices. Rider's *Bibliotheca Scholastica* thus channels attention to the multiplicity of whoresons, whoremongers, whoremasters, and whore-gallants—as well as the 'masculine whore[s]', 'he-whores', and 'stallions' analysed by Jennifer Panek[45]—who surface in a range of early modern texts.

Gendered and sexual configurations prove especially intricate in the multiple substantives, as well as adjectival and adverbial constructions, that follow these two verbal entries. The first substantive entry, '*A whoremonger*', again identifies individuals associated with, or related to, the figure of the whore. It also possesses a tighter visual, textual, and conceptual bond to the act of 'whoredome' than to the various (substantive) 'whores' that follow in its wake: common, young, disdainful, stewed or arrant, soaking or wasting, etc. Whoredom thus appears, first and foremost, to be an activity committed by individuals adjacent to 'whores', rather than by whores themselves. The whore-as-subject first appears in a fourth subcategory of 'To commit Whoredome'. However, as opposed to a standalone substantive that configures the 'whore' as a singular or coherent entity—as is suggested in Cawdrey's *A Table Alphabeticall* (Fig. 1.4)—Rider identifies ten types of whoredom, indicating a range of associated terms and meanings (Fig. 1.6). These include distinctions of cost, age, attitude, clothing and behaviour. Although the '*Whore, or harlot*' appear[s] akin to the '*common*', '*young*',

[45] Panek, '"This Base Stallion Trade"'.

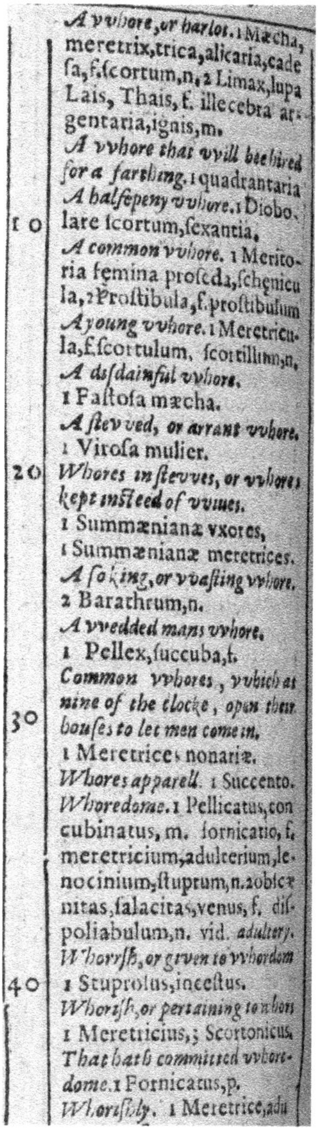

A vvhore, or harlot. 1 Mæcha, meretrix, trica, alicaria, cadesa, f. scortum, n. 2 Limax, lupa Lais, Thais, f. illecebra argentaria, ignis, m.
A vvhore that vvill bee hired for a farthing. 1 quadrantaria
A halfepeny vvhore. 1 Diobolare scortum, sexantia.
A common vvhore. 1 Meritoria femina proseda, schœnicula, 2 Prostibula, f. prostibulum
A young vvhore. 1 Meretricula, f. scortulum, scortillum, n.
A disdainful vvhore.
1 Fastosa mæcha.
A stevved, or arrant vvhore.
1 Virosa mulier.
Whores in stevves, or vvhores kept insteed of vviues.
1 Summænianæ vxores,
1 Summænianæ meretrices.
A soking, or vvasting vvhore.
2 Barathrum, n.
A vvedded mans vvhore.
1 Pellex, succuba, f.
Common vvhores, vvhich at nine of the clocke, open their houses to let men come in.
1 Meretrices nonariæ.
Whores apparell. 1 Succento.
Whoredome. 1 Pellicatus, concubinatus, m. fornicatio, f. meretricium, adulterium, lenocinium, stuprum, n. 2 obscænitas, salacitas, venus, f. dispoliabulum, n. vid. *adultery.*
Whorish, or given to vvhordom
1 Stuprosus, incestus.
Whorish, or pertaining to vvhors
1 Meretricius; Scortonicus.
That hath committed vvhoredome. 1 Fornicatus, p.
Whorishly. 1 Meretrice, adu

FIGURE 1.6 'To commit Whore-dome' (cont.), in John Rider, *Bibliotheca Scholastica* (Oxford: Joseph Barnes, 1589), sig. Mm3v. STC 21031.5. Folger Shakespeare Library.

or '*wedded mans*' whore, they are not equivalents. Degrees of relation surface even within subcategories, including this initial '*a Whore, or harlot*', where it is unclear whether the conjoined terms constitute a singular or dual entry. '*Whore*' precedes the '*harlot*' in this internal hierarchy, yet this shared conjunction—this critical 'or'—establishes an intimate kinship between the two terms, a bond closer than that shared with other phonetically related entries, such as the '*halfepeny whore*'.[46]

These polymorphous and polysemous whores reflect a different sense of definitional precision than that implied by Rider's Latin cartography. As opposed to numeric localization, these English terms conjoin definitional breadth to minute distinction. Minor discrepancies of cost (*farthing* versus *halfepeny*) and availability (the *common whore* versus *common whores* who 'open their houses to men' at 'nine of the clock'), for instance, suggest fields of relation and distinction configured by a range of variables. Paradoxically, therefore, attempts to codify meaning amplify the whore's meanings: precision becomes a means of production. Readers are left to wonder: what, then—or who—is a whore?

Just as Rider expands the referential possibilities of whore and whoredome, he suppresses distinctions between these and other English terms of whoredom, i.e., those composed of entirely different phonemes. In contrast to other lexicographers, that is, Rider eschews aggregating English metonyms in his glosses for foreign terms: readers find many whores, but only one trulls—in this entry. This type of terminological reduction transcends the number of English metonyms: whereas other lexicographers deploy a range of 'verbal discriminators' to indicate degrees of relation between terms—including 'properly', 'also', 'moreover', and 'sometimes'[47]—Rider relies primarily on 'or', a conjunction that implies substitution rather than distinction. 'Harlot', in other words, appears more synonymic than metonymic, more an apparent equivalent than a contiguous term. Similar conjunctive pairings permeate this entry and *mise-en-page*, including couplings of whores 'stewed' *or* 'arrans', 'in stewes' *or* 'kept instead of wiues', and 'soaking' *or* 'wasting'.

In lieu of verbal discriminators, the *Bibliotheca Scholastica* uses other visual and textual elements to indicate shades of distinction between terms and entries. In addition to a sequential privilege that, in this

[46] On the conjunctive properties of 'or' in dictionaries of the period, see Rubright, 'Shakespeare's Albion: The Racecraft of White Happiness'.

[47] Stein, *The English Dictionary before Cawdrey*, 322.

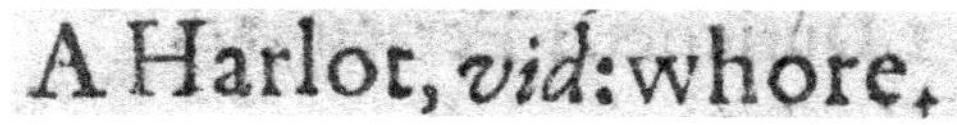
A Harlot, *vid:* whore.

FIGURE 1.7 'A Harlot, *vid*: whore', in John Rider, *Bibliotheca Scholastica* (Oxford: Joseph Barnes, 1589), sig. P6v. STC 21031.5. Folger Shakespeare Library.

entry, places the whore before the harlot (i.e. 'Whore, or harlot'), the 'whore' elsewhere is figured as the site—the place to look—to secure the harlot's meanings. That is, should readers turn to the entry for 'harlot' in the *Bibliotheca Scholastica*, they will find themselves referred to 'whore' (Fig. 1.7). Indeed, the abbreviation linking these two terms—'*vid*' (for the Latin *vide*)—underscores a critically visual dimension of lexical meaning-making in the *Bibliotheca Scholastica*. To define the harlot, readers must 'look to' or 'see' the whore. This verbal/visual coordinate not only underscores the ocular dimensions of lexicographic meaning-making but, by locating meaning elsewhere, instantiates a hierarchical relationship between the two terms. Lacking its own terms and subcategories, the 'harlot' appears insignificant in contrast to the plentiful 'whore'.[48] As this example suggests, meaning in the *Bibliotheca Scholastica* incorporates multiple relations and systems of relation: linguistic, visual, numerical, and sequential. It also produces aporias. In the referential circle that here encompasses 'harlot' and 'whore', something drops out: readers are encouraged, always, to look elsewhere for the meanings of whoredom.

Worlds of Words

Should readers compare Rider's work to contemporary lexicographic texts, the terms of whoredom increase dramatically. To reiterate an essential point, the *Bibliotheca Scholastica* proves lexicographic as an experimental rather than conventional work. The terms of English whoredom in early modern lexicography emerge both within a given text, such as the *Bibliotheca Scholastica*, and in conjunction with other texts, including those which seek single or 'proper' definitions.

[48] See also the entry for 'A Strumpet', which likewise simply reads '*vide* whore' (sig. Gg7v, 1432.7–8).

Whereas Rider, for instance, links 'whore' with 'harlot' in his dictionary, Cawdrey associates it with 'baud' in *A Table Alphabeticall* (1604), while Thomas Thomas conjoins 'common whore, harlot, or strumpet' when defining '*Prostibula*' in his *Dictionarivm Lingvae Latinae et Anglicanae* (1587).[49] When John Bullokar publishes *An English Expositor* in 1616, however, 'strumpet' disappears entirely, 'harlot' defines 'Curtezane', and the morpheme 'who[o]re' surfaces only within the terms 'Whoore-monger' and 'Whoore-dome', which are offered as definitions for 'palliard' and 'palliardise', respectively.[50]

Such relations are concise when compared to Timothy Bright's *Characterie* (1588), a rather paradoxical situation given this lexicographer's desire to locate, whenever possible, a one-to-one relationship between term and meaning. While successful in reducing most definitions to a single signifier, Bright nonetheless reuses these privileged meanings throughout the text. The 'whore', for example, proves particularly capacious, operating as a definition for 'Adulterer', 'Baude', 'Brothel', 'Buggerie', 'Chaste', 'Concubine', 'Defloure', 'Gille', 'Harlot', 'Lemman', 'Rauish', 'Ribaude', 'Stewes', 'Strumpet', and 'Vnchaste'.[51] Within such a configuration, the term signifies, among other things: spouses (ungendered) who violate the sacrament of marriage; buildings associated with sexual commerce; acts of sodomy; acts of defloration; and, paradoxically, both states of unchastity and chastity (Fig. 1.8).[52] As in the

chaſte | *whore*

FIGURE 1.8 'Chaste | *whore*', in Timothy Bright, *Characterie* (London: I. Windet, 1588), n.p. BAC 601812. The Huntington Library, San Marino, California.

[49] Cawrey, *A Table Alphabeticall*, sig. B8r; Thomas, *Dictionarivm Lingvae Latinae et Anglicanae*, sig. Bbbb4r. Similar to Rider, Thomas indicates an array of subtle distinctions among his entries, including differences of age (*Scortillum*: 'a little whore, a young whore', sig. Ggg5v) and location/behaviour (*Virosa mulier*: 'a stewed or arrant whore', sig. Qqq6r).

[50] Bullokar, *An English Expositor*, sigs E5r, M6v, L6v.

[51] Bright, *Characterie*, sigs A2r, A7r, A12r, A12r, B2v, B6r, B11v, D3r, D6r, E2r, F6r, G5r, G6r, G12v.

[52] Bright's incorporation of (apparent) antonyms is a product of his unique characterological system, which shifts from an alphabet-based language to an ideogrammatic language. In this latter system, several discrete signifiers—such the ideogram associated with

FIGURE 1.9 'Baud, whore', in Robert Cawdrey, *A Table Alphabeticall* (London: I. Roberts for Edmund Weauer, 1604), sig. B8r. The Bodleian Libraries, University of Oxford, Weston Library, Arch. A, f. 141 (2).

BIBLIOTHECA SCHOLASTICA, Bright's *mise-en-page* (re)configures meanings and relations, in this case by conjoining terms along a horizontal, as opposed to vertical, register.[53] And in contrast to other texts, such as Cawdrey's *A Table Alphabeticall* (Fig. 1.9) and Edmund Coote's *THE ENGLISH SCHOOLE-MASTER* (Fig. 1.10), which separate headwords and meanings by way of a single comma, Bright use a vertical bar to conjoin (and separate) the two. Yet just as all three of these texts use serif and/or italic fonts to distinguish between definitions (positioned on

'whore'—incorporate both synonyms and antonyms, with their 'final' signification ultimately determined by what we might today describe as a diacritical mark: i.e. if the writer wants to animate the 'consenting signification', the ideogram 'requireth the marke on the left side', whereas when they intend to activate the 'dissenting signification', this 'addition is to be placed on the right side' (sigs Bvr–v). The confounding nature of this proposed system is arguably best exemplified by the entry for 'Vnchaste', which is defined as 'Honest, or whore' (sig. G12v). While the former, presumably, reflects the 'dissenting signification', and the latter thus signals its 'consenting signification', readers nevertheless are encouraged, by the very nature of the entry itself, to perceive the signifier being defined ('Vnchaste') as incorporating *both* synonym and antonym—a fact which renders the addition of a consenting or dissenting diacritical mark fundamentally aporetic. Unsurprisingly, Bright does not offer an ideogrammatic cognate for the English 'Vnchaste'.

[53] In this sense, Bright's visual schema offers a fascinating counterpart to the Saussurean and Lacanian signs, each of which famously figure the relations of signifier to signified by way of a vertical—as opposed to horizontal—axis: whereas Saussure places the signified over the signifier, arguing the former's pre-eminence, Lacan inverts this relationship (i.e. places the signifier over the signified), then channels attention to the (horizontal) relations between metonyms which comprise the signifying chain. What is especially striking about Bright's arrangement, therefore, is how its visual rhetoric encourages readers to perceive the relationships of words (signifiers) and the ideas or concepts that they presumably index (signifieds) as one of (relative) equivalence rather than of hierarchy. As noted above, the precise nature of this dynamic could then be marked—arguably, theorized—through the use of varying fonts, etc., on the printed page. My point is not that Bright anticipates modern linguistic theory but rather that his visual schema delivers yet another pointed reminder of the visual, textual, and material bases upon which historically contingent theories of signification have been formulated and contested. For comparison, see how Saussure encourages readers to envision the linguistic sign in *Course in General Linguistics*, 67; and Lacan, in *Ecrits*, 416, 428–429.

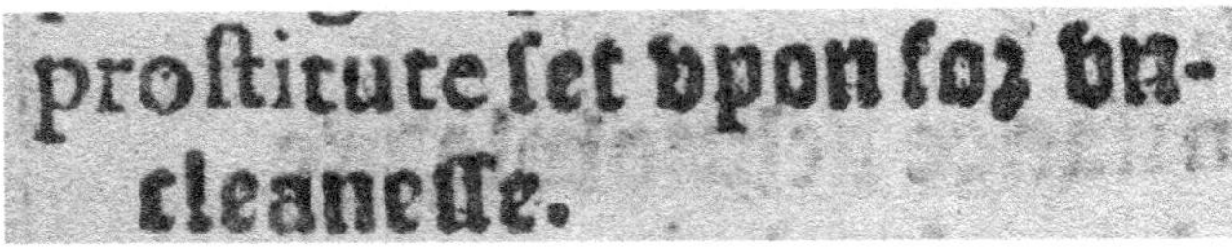
prostitute set vpon for vn-
cleanesse.

FIGURE 1.10 'Prostitute set upon for un-cleanesse', in Edmund Coote, *The English Schoole-Master* (London: Stationers, 1630), sig. M1r/p. 81. STC 5714. Folger Shakespeare Library.

the right) from the terms being defined (positioned on the left), they diverge in other ways: Coote's *The English Schoole-Master* (1630), for example, does not include entries for 'whore' or 'harlot'. Indeed, the entry for 'prostitute', which is again verbal rather than nominal, fails to mention 'whoredom' altogether, focusing instead on notions of filth and cleanliness, a description that suggests conceptual distinctions between prostitution and whoredom in the period.[54] John Florio, by contrast, appears to bridge the verbal and nominal in *Queen Anna's New World of Words* (1611), linking 'to prostitute or abandon to euery mans abusing for money' with 'to play the whore or bawde.... Also to practise whoredome or bawderie' (sig. Ll5v), yet this association disappears entirely in later texts by John Bullokar (1616) and Henry Cockeram (1623), where prostitution—without explicit reference to whoredom—relates to the sale of one's body.[55] In their efforts to distinguish between 'real' whores, i.e. sex workers, and their fictional counterparts, i.e. everyone else, modern critics elide the fact that such a distinction was itself being constructed and contested in the era.

The terms of whoredom prove especially opaque in multilingual dictionaries. Florio's *A Worlde of Wordes* (1598) and *Queen Anna's New World of Words* (1611), as well as Randle Cotgrave's *A Dictionarie of the French and English Tongves* (1611), include multiple English

[54] Coote's *The English Schoole-Master* represents one of the first, if not *the* first, English lexicographic text listing 'prostitute' as either a headword or definition; the term does not appear, for example, in Rider or Bright.

[55] Bullokar, *An English Expositor*: 'Prostitute: To set to open sale: to offer to euery man for money' (sig. M6v). While Cockeram replicates Bullokar's entry word for word in 1623's *English Dictionary* (Book 1, sig. I4v), he also uses 'prostitute' as a definition for 'to Set out ones body for money' (Book 2, sig. F1r) as well as for '*Baldraca*: a poore Maid that could not be brought to prostitute her body to the Emperor Otho, albe he proffered her great rewards' (Book 3, sig. H6v). See also the entries for 'Prostitute (*Prostituta*)' in Thomas Blount's *Glossographia* (1656): 'she that for money suffers herself to be abused by all that come, a common harlot' (sig. Ii7r).

definitions for each headword, materializing an array of intra-English relations alongside the inter-lingual bonds that emerge between Italian (Florio) and French (Cotgrave) headwords and the English definitions offered in these texts. Cotgrave's *A Dictionarie of the French and English Tongves*, for instance, provides several English cognates for each French term, creating a sequential list that intimates a semantic hierarchy organized by proximity to the French headword:

> *Gaultiere*: f. A whore, punke, drab, queane, gill, flirt, strumpet, cockatrice, mad wench, common hackney, good one.
> *Paillarde*: f. A whore, punke, drab, strumpet, harlot, queane, courtesan, callet.
> *Pimbesche*: f. a wilie queane, subtile wench, cunning drab; one that can finely execute her Mistresses knauish deuises.
> *Putain*: f. a whore, queane, punke, drab, flurt, strumpet, harlot, cockatrice, naughtie pack, light huswife, common hackney.
> *Rebut* ('*Madame de rebut*'): A loathsome queane, rascallie drab, ouerworne punke, pockie whore.[56]

Within this order, the 'whore', 'queane', 'punk', and 'drab' accrue privilege according to proximity as well as frequency of citation, with the three appearing in almost every entry. By contrast, 'callet', 'cockatrice', and 'common hackney' seem rare and unusual, located at a distance both from headwords and other privileged terms. Ironically, such relegation may signal greater precision in meaning: i.e. a sense that uncommon words encode rarefied, and therefore quite specific, connotations.[57]

[56] Cotgrave, *A Dictionarie of the French and English Tongves* (1611), sigs Ss3r, Mmm2r, Ppp4v, Ttt4v, Xxx[1]v.

[57] While I focus here on order of arrangement, it also worth noting that each of the first four terms are gendered feminine the French language, and that both *Gaultiere* and *Paillarde* possess masculine alternatives in *Gaultier* ('m[asculine]. A mad whor[e]son, mad wag, rakehell, good-fellow; also, a noddie, ninnie, goosecap, coxcomb, ideot; and, as *Garguille*') and *Palliard* ('m[asculine]. A lecher, wencher, whoremunger, whore-hunter; also, a knaue, rascall, varlet, scoundrel, filthie fellow'). See also *Paillarder*: 'To lecher; bitch-hunt it; haunt bawdie houses; also, to tumble in the straw'. The entry for *Putain* proves unique in its inclusion of short phrases or sayings, each of which are provided with a corresponding gloss (*Effronté en putain*: 'As bold, or brazen-faced, as a whore'; *Putain fait comme la corneille, plus se lave & plus noire est elle*: '*Pro.* A queane and Crow alike doe fare, the more they swash the fouler they are'. *Affez fait qui fortune passe, & plus encore qui putain chasse*: '*Pro.* as under *Fortune*'; *Fils de putain ne fit jamais bien*: '*Prov.* Never did sonne of a whore doe well'). While *Pimbesche* is presented without a masculine form, *Madam de rebut* appears as a subcategory of the masculine *Rebut*, which is defined as 'the refuse, of alls, outcasts, or leauings of better things; also, a foyle, repulse, reiecting, putting backe'. The entry then moves from this definition to the phrase *Brebis de rebut*

Such paradoxes permeate the lexicographic project. Although word order and citationality confer distinctions among Cotgrave's English terms, his definitional surpluses both expand the signifying field and complicate relations between terms that are linked in some entries only to be divorced in others: whereas 'whore', 'punk', and 'queane' subtend *Limax*, *Paillarde*, and *Putain*, for instance, only '(wilie) queane' appears in the definitional matrix for *Pimbesche*, where it is instead linked to 'subtile wench' and 'cunning drab' as well as, it would appear, an individual who 'can finely execute her Mistresses knauish deuises'. Such associations imbue 'queane' with a sense of cunning or subtlety, a link further supplemented by the loathsome, rascally, aged, and diseased inferences to which it is conjoined in the definitions offered for *Madame de rebut*. Yet where *Madame de rebut* reunites 'queane' with 'drab', 'punk', and 'whore', these terms unfold in a hierarchical order ('A loathsome queane, rascallie drab, ouerworne punke, pockie whore') which differs from that which governs the entries for *Gaultiere*, *Paillarde*, and *Putain*, each of which begin with the standard 'whore, punke, drab' sequence. As with *Pimbesche*, moreover, the addition of descriptive modifiers ascribes more specific, particularized meanings to the headword in question: '*Madame de rebut*' does not simply designate a 'queane', 'drab', 'punke', or 'whore', but a '*loathsome* queane', '*rascallie* drab', '*ouerworne* punke', and/or '*pockie* whore' (emphasis added). Longer lexicographic texts further amplify these lexical relations at both inter- and intralinguistic levels. Cotgrave's extensive *A Dictionarie of the French and English Tongves*, for example, associates eighty-nine French headwords and phrases with the English 'whore', while Florio deploys variations of that term in the entries for ninety-eight different Italian words and phrases in *Queen Anna's New World of Words*, where it is associated with foolish priests, secret lovers, women that commit fornication, garrulous housewives, witches, sex workers, promiscuous men, taverns, perceptions of filth, and the Catholic Church ('Whore of Babylon'). Both printed in 1611, these texts signal, in part, the expansion of the lexicographic enterprise as a whole; in doing so, they suggest a proliferation of sexual meanings in conjunction with this emergent textual-lexicographic project. Indeed, from a diachronic perspective the early modern 'whore' not

('Drapes, Cullings, or Kebbers; old, or diseased sheepe which be not worth keeping'), followed by *Madame de rebut* (sig. Xxx[1]v). A literal translation, therefore, might be 'a wasted woman'.

only proliferates lexicographically (i.e. appears with increasing frequency in succeeding dictionaries and lexicons) but increasingly relates terminologically and conceptually (i.e. is connected to a broader range of terms) to other facets of social life over the course of the sixteenth and early seventeenth centuries.

Terms of Early Modern Whoredom: An Archive in Motion

Adulteress
Alewife whore
Amazons
Amazonian trull
Ambulantrices
Ammunition whore
Angel
Ape
Ape-gentlewoman
Apple-john
Apple-squire
Apples of love
Apron mountant
Apron-squire
Arletta
Arrant whore
Aunt
Autem-mort
Babell publique prostitute
Backslider
Bad woman
Baggage
Barber's chair
Barbiera
Barren whore
Bartholomew-faire babe
Base beggarly queane
Base beggarly whore
Base queane
Base whore
Bastard-bearing whore
Bavo
Bawd[s]
Bawdstrot
Bawdy basket
Beagle
Beau
Bed-broker
Bed-swarver
Becco
Beef
Beggar's whore
Belswagger
Bird
Bird o'the game
Bitch
Bitch-fox
Bitch-whore
Bitched whore
Black ouzel
Blazing starre
Bloody queane
Blowzabellas
Blowzes
Bogs
Boiled stuff
Bold-fac'd queane[s]
Bold-fac'd whore
Bona roba
Bordel woman
Bordeler
Bouncing baggage
Bouncinge Nell
Boy-favourite
Boy-harlot
Brach
Brave whore
Brazen-faced queane
Brazen-faced whore
Bridewell baggage
Bridewell whore
Brigaille
Broker
Broker-between
Brothel
Brotheler
Brothel-monger

Brown Bess[ie]
Bugger[er]
Bully-back
Bunters
Burned-arse whore
Butter whore
Buttered buns
Callet
Caprae
Captain
Captain's wife
Captain's whore
Careful sisters
Carnival concupiscence
Car[r]ack
Carriage
Carrion whore
Carry-knave
Carted whore
Cat
Catamite
Cataracts of Nile
Causey-paiker
Chaste
Chattels
Cheapside dame
Choir of nuns
Chusherrel
Ci[e]fes
Cin[a]edo
Civel punckes
Cloth-o'-silver slut
Clyster-pipe
Cockatrice
Cock-bawd
Cockhorse
Committer
Commodity/ie
Common carted whore
Common cracks
Common customer
Common hedge whore
Common he-whore
Common housewife
Common loves
Common nightwalkers
Common queens
Common up-tail
Common whore
Common woman
Commoner
Community
Concubine
Concupiscence
Concupy
Cony/Coney
Copesmate
Cornuto
Cot-quean
Counterfeit
Counterfeit crank
Court jennet
Courtesan
Cousin
Cracks
Craftie wags
Creature
Creature of public use
Creature of sale
Cressid[a]
Crocodile
Croshabell
Crow
Cuckold
Cuckold-makers
Cunnus
Cunny berry
Cunny-fur
Curtain
Curtall[s]
Customer
Cut loaf
Cutpurse
Daffadown-dillies
Dainty
Damned whore
Daughter
Daughters of the game
Daughters of Whitefriars
Dear[e]
Delilah
Dell
Diabolares
Dick
Dipsas
Dirtheels
Dirty sow
Does
Dog-fish
Dogge
Doll
Doll-common
Doll Tearsheet
Dopye
Dove
Doxy
Drab

Drabber
Draggletaile
Driggle-draggle
Drivelling
Drunken bitch
whore
Droncken queane
Droncken whore
Duck[e]
Durty drabbe
Durty draggletaile
Ioane
Dutch Tanakin
Dutch widow
Easie-paced gennets
Encounterer
Engle/Ingle
English maddames
Englishman's whore
Fander[s]
Favo[u]rite
Fere
File
Filth
Filthy dirty slut
Filthy queane
Filthy sharking
punckes
Filthy whore
Fine light silken
whore
Fireships
Fish
Fitchew
Flap
Flax-wench
Flesh-monger
Fling-dust
Flirt
Flirt-gill
Flower-gentles
Florence
Follower
Fornicary
Fornicatress
Foul
Fowl
Frank frailty
Fricatrice
Frump
Gadding
Galled goose of
Winchester
Galloway nages
Gally Foist
Gamester
Ganimet/Ganymede
Gennet
Gentleman o'th'
smock
Gentleman usher
Gickesie
Giglets/Giglot
Gill/Gillottes
Gilliflower whore
Gill-flurts/Gilflirts
Girl
Gixie
Go-between
Gomorrhean
Good one
Good wench
Goose
Goshawke
Gossip
Gown
Grannam
Green gamesters
Green goose
Green women
Guest
Guinea bird
Guinea hen
Gypsee/Gipsie
Hackney
Hackney jade
Hackster
Hagerdlie
whore
Halfe a crowne
wench
Hare
Harlot[rie]
Harlotha
Hedge-bird
Hedge-whore
Heifer
He-lecher
Hell-moth
Hen
Hide
Hiren/Hyren/
Hyrin
Hoar/Hore
Hobby-horse
Holard
Hollow-tree whore
Honest
Honest polecat
Honest whore
Honysuckles
Honysuckles hound
Hore-cwen
Horn-maker

Horse
Horse-leech
Hospital whore
Hound
Horum
Hurry-whore
Huswife
Hyacinths
Idle wenches
Impudent queane
Instrument of fornication
Jade
Janet
Jay
Jelot
Jennet
Jesabel/Jezebel
Jill
Jilts
Jove's own page
Jumbler
Junt
Justice
Kate
Ken
Kept woman
Kind sister
Kitchen mort
Kitchen-stuffe slut
Kite
Knave
Lacedemonian
Laced-mutton
Lady of pleasure
Lady Vanity
Ladybird/Lady-birds
Laenis
Lambe
Land frigate
Land-pirates
Land-siren
Lasse
Laundress
Leageur-laundress
Leakinge vessayles
Lem[m]an
Lena
Leno
Lewd strumpet
Lewd woman
Libertine
Light
Light angell
Light gossip
Light horse
Light-hus-wife
Light woman
Light-taylde
Limax
Limmer
Lioness
Livers
Lombard whore
Loon[e]/Lown[e]
Lousy queane
Loue/Love
Love-broker
Love-monger
Lupa
Lyll
Mackerel[s]
Macrio
Mad wench
Madam[s]
Madam mackarell
Madam Mitigation
Madame de rebut
Maggie
Maggottie jade
Maggottie whore
Male bawd
Male varlet
Mandrake
Mangonist
Maquerela
Mare
Margerite
Marigold
Mar-tail
Masculine whore
Mauks
Mayden
Meat
Medlar
Meretrician
Meretrix
Mermaid
Micher
Migniard
Milk-white doe
Milke whore
Minion
Minion of the suburbs
Minx
Miss
Mistress
Mistress o' the game
Miswoman
Moll[s]

Money-creature
Monkey
Mort
Mother
Mother midnights
Mother of whore-
doms
Mouse
Movable chattel
Movables
Musk-cats
Mutton
Mutton-munger
My husband's whore
Nag
Naked boy
Naught-pack[s]
Nastie subtle queane
Naunt
Niece
Night-shade
Night trader
Nightwalker
Night-worm
Ningle
Noctiluces
Nun
Nuns of Stratford
Nuns of Venus
Nymph
Occupant
Old fore-ridden
jades
Old jade
Old ling
Old man's whore
Old whore
Open-arse
Overriden jade
Oyster whore
Oysterwife
Pad
Pad strumpets
Pagan
Painted lady
Painted queane
Painter
Pallaca
Palliard
Paltrocca
Pampered jades of
Asia
Pandar/Pander
Pandaregge
Panderous
Paphian
Paramour
Parcel-broker
Parnel
Partridge
Pathic
Pedlar's trull
Pellex
Pernel
Petronella
Petticoat
Phryne/Phrynia
Piece
Pilfering quean
Pimp
Pink[s]
Pinnace
Piskitching
Pissabed quean
Pissabed whore
Pitch
Play-fellow
Playhouse poultry
Plover
Plumbe muddy
whore
Pocky-faced jade
Pocky whore
Polecat
Poor
Poultry
Powdered-bawd
Presbyterian dog
Prevye whore
Priest's whore
Prim
Private whore
Privy queane
Privy whore
Procurer
Pronuba
Prostibula
Prostibule
Prostitute
Prostitute boy
Prostitutio
Prostitution
Proud Trull
Provoker
Prunella
Public commoner
Public courtesan
Public whore
Pucelle/Pussel/Puzel
Pug
Pull

Punchable nuns
Punk/Puncke
Punk device
Punk rampant
Punketees
Punketto
Punkling
Punter
Puritane whore
Putae
Putain/Putayne
Putanie
Pute
Putour
Putrer
Putyer
Pynk
Quail
Quean[e]
Queane punk
Rabbit/Rabbets
Ramp
Rampant cockatrice
Rampsman
Ranger
Rascal
Rascallie whore
Rearward
Retayling bodie-traffiquers
Ribaulde
Rig
Road
Roaring boy
Roaring girl
Roba
Rodophe
Rogue
Rome-mort
Roof
Rotten medlar
Rose
Ruffa
Ruffian[o]
Rumper
Runagate
Runagate whoore
Running bawds
Saddle-nosed queane
Same
Scorpions
Scortator
Scortillum
Scortum/Scorti
Scullion
Scurvie queane
Scurvy base whore
Scurvy whore
Sellary
Semiramus
She-beggar
She-goat
Shee apothecarie
Shee conny-catcher
Shee-diuels
Shee-minstrel
Sheep-biter
She-wolf
Short-heels
Shrimp
Silken strumpet
Silly poore whore
Simpler
Singlewoman
Siren/Syren
Sister
Sixpenny damnation
Sixe penny hackster
Skains-mates
Slattern
Slave
Slut
Smell-smocke
Smithfield nags
Smock-agent
Smock-rampant
Smocks
Smock-tearer
Smuts
Sodomite
Sodomitesse
Sparrows
Spinster
Spintry
Spittle whore
Spoil
Squal[l]
Squire
Squire of dames
Squire of entertainment
Squire of ladies
Squire of the placket
Squirrel[s]
Squirt
Stale
Stall
Stallion
Stallion ramp
Stew
Stewpot
Strange woman
Street walkers
Strong whore

Strumpet
Strumpet whore
Strumpetier
Subtle queane
Suburb-captain
Suburb curtizans
Suburban roarer
Suburb-roarer
Succubae
Sumner
Suppository
Surfeiter
Swaggering whore
Sweet-heart
Taffeta punk
Tale-bearers
Tapster
Tassitie queane
Tenant in tail
Thievish baggage
Tib
Tiger
Tilling
Tomb-haunting whores
Tomboy
Tongue pad whores
Toy
Traffic/Traffique
Trade
Tramp
Trash
Treadle
Trencher whore
Tribade
Trollop
Trot
Troth
Trout
Trug
Trugmoldies
Trull
Trully-bub
Tug-mutton
Turn-up
Tweak
Twigger
Ugly whore
Underputter
Unproved sluttery
Unruly woman
Vagabond
Vagrant whore
Varlet
Venture[r]
Venus-baths
Village whore
Villain
Virgin wagtails
Vulgar Tart
Wagtail[s]
Waistcoat[er]
Walking mort
Walk-street
Wanton
Wanton boies
Ware
Well
Welsh virgin
Welsh whore
Wench
Wencher
Wenches of the old religion
Whiblin
Whimsies
Whipper-ginnie
Whiskin
Witch whore
White apron
Whitefriars nation
Whitefriars nun
White-Friars puncke
White-friers queane
Whore
Whore gallant
Whoredomer
Whore-haunter
Whore-hunter
Whore-keeper
Whorer
Woman broker
Woman-louper
Whoremaster
Whoremasterly jack
Whoremasterly rogue
Whoreson
Whoreson cur
Whoreson rascally fellow
Whott tailed whore
Wiggletail
Winchester goose
Words
Wrestler
Wrimouthd jade
Wrymouthe queane
Yaud
Young man's whore
[...]

Archives, Impasses, and Open Works

Traditionally, an archive has designated a physical space in which historical materials are deposited for safe keeping and future study. While this definition has undergone a sea change over the last few decades—both as digital archives have flourished and as scholars increasingly have understood archives not simply as repositories for the traces of the past but as sites, whether virtual or material, that themselves shape epistemologies,[58] desires,[59] and political communities[60]—we can, at the very least, acknowledge that to create or even posit an archive is to argue, in the most basic sense, that something matters: that the materials gathered therein are worthy of preservation and analysis; that they possess historical relevance and utility; and that they might tell us something meaningful about the historical past, as well as the present moment(s) in which they are created, visited, or updated and the futures that they allow us to envision. The archive presented in the preceding section has been assembled by curating words and phrases used to define the early modern 'whore', or vice versa, in (a) the early modern lexicographic tradition;[61] (b) contemporary texts that posit definitions for these and related terms, including ballads and 'cant' dictionaries;[62] (c) modern editions of early modern texts;[63] (d) dictionaries, glossaries, and lexicons of early modern English, particularly those focused on 'bawdy' or 'sexual language';[64] (e) histories of sex, gender, and social

[58] Stoler, *Along the Archival Grain*; Arondekar, *For the Record*; Eichhorn, *The Archival Turn in Feminism*.

[59] Derrida, *Archive Fever*.

[60] Cvetkovitch, *An Archive of Feelings*; Love, *Feeling Backwards*.

[61] Especially *Lexicons of Early Modern English* (*LEME*): http://leme.library.utoronto.ca.

[62] See, for instance, Dekker, *The Belman of London* and *Lanthorne and Candle-light*; Greene, *A Notable Discouery of Coosnage*; Harman, *A Cavueat or Warening*. For ballads, see the extraordinary *English Broadside Ballad Archive*, available online at http://ebba.english.ucsb.edu.

[63] Alongside Arden, Bedford, Cambridge, Norton, Oxford, and Pelican editions of Shakespeare, these include the plays collected in *English Renaissance Drama* (ed. Bevington et al.), *Thomas Middleton: The Collection Works* (ed. Taylor and Lavagnino), as well as single play editions in the Revels Plays and Globe Quartos series, among others.

[64] These include, but are not limited to, Coleman, *Love, Sex, and Marriage*, esp. 302–331; Crystal and Crystal, *Shakespeare's Words*; Crystal, *Words in Time and Place*, esp. 149–168; Kiernan, *Filthy Shakespeare*; McMullan, *The Canting Crew*; Partridge, *Shakespeare's Bawdy*; Schmidt, *Shakespeare Lexicon and Quotation Dictionary*; Williams, *A Glossary of Shakespeare's Sexual Language*.

(dis)order in early modern England;[65] (f) literary-critical analyses of the representation of these and related issues, especially sexual commerce, in that historical culture;[66] and (g) studies which examine specific 'sexual' words, lexicons, and/or linguistic communities in early modern England.[67] As these broad parameters suggest, my goal in assembling this archive has been to curate rather than to adjudicate, to illuminate rather than to discriminate. It is neither definitive nor fixed.

What, therefore, is catalogued here? As I have already suggested, it is an archive of terms that have been connected to the early modern 'whore', either by language users in that historical culture or present-day scholars. But it is also an archive of relations: social, linguistic, discursive, sexual, historical. It is an archive of sexual-lexical creativity. It is an archive of glossarial praxes and the ideologies of early modern sex and sexual signification that underlie them. It is an archive of questions, impasses, and aporia, including those yet to be formulated or examined. It is an archive of possibilities. It is an archive of problems. Consider, for instance, the following terms, each of which are applied to Shakespeare's Juliet: 'baggage', 'minion', 'hilding'. In the first quarto of *Romeo and Juliet* (1597), Capulet critiques his daughter's 'headstrong selfewild harlotrie' and refers to her as 'greene sicknes baggage'.[68] This latter moniker appears twice in the play's second quarto,[69] where he also figures Juliet as a 'proud mistress minion' and a 'hilding'.[70] While

[65] I am particularly indebted to Capp, *When Gossips Meet*; Gowing, *Domestic Dangers*; Hair, *Before the Bawdy Court*; Hubbard, *City Women*; and Ingram, *Carnal Knowledge*.

[66] Salgado, *The Elizabethan Underworld*; Salkeld, *Shakespeare among the Courtesans*.

[67] Especially Bly, *Queer Virgins and Virgin Queans on the Early Modern Stage*; J. Higginbotham, 'Fair Maids and Golden Girls'; Panek, '"This Base Stallion Trade"'.

[68] *An Excellent conceited Tragedie OF Romeo and Iuliet*, i.e., *Q1*, TLN 2199, 2437.4. The first phrase is represented 'a peeuish selfewieldhar lottry' in *Q2* (TLN 2437) and 'a peeuish selfe-wild harlotry', in *F1* (TLN 2437). Most modern edition follow the follow in presenting the line as 'a peevish, self-willed harlotry'. See, for instance, *Romeo and Juliet* (ed. Weis), 4.2.14. The latter phrase appears as 'Out you greene sicknesse carrion, out of you baggage' in both *Q2* (TLN 2197) and *F1* (TLN 2197), and as 'Out, you green-sickness carrion! Out, you baggage', in *Romeo and Juliet* (ed. Weis), 3.5.156–157.

[69] *The Most Ex-cellent and Lamentable Tragedie, of Romeo and Iuliet*, i.e. *Q2*, TLN 2197, 2202. These variants underscore the subtle yet essential point that the terms of (Juliet's) whoredom assume a different shape and form in quarto 1 and quarto 2. For an insightful study of Juliet's differing figurations in the play's first two quartos, see H. James, *Ovid and the Library of Speech in Shakespeare's England*, 101–139.

[70] *The Most Ex-cellent and Lamentable Tragedie*, TLN 2193, 2210. Capulet's use of 'mistress' is also illuminating, recalling as it does Gainsford's deployment of that term alongside 'curtisan', 'queane', 'strumpet', 'puncke', etc., in the passage discussed at the out-

scholars might broadly agree that the first substantive, 'harlotrie', is a term of whoredom, how and whether the other appellations provided here—'baggage', 'minion', 'hilding'—should be included in our archive is less obvious. Yet at least one sixteenth-century dictionary links 'baggage' to 'whore',[71] a present-day glossary of 'Shakespeare's sexual language' hears 'paramour, whore' in 'minion',[72] and a recent edition of the play glosses 'hilding' as 'jade, hussy'.[73] While each thus qualify for inclusion under my terms, their primary utility as 'term of whoredom' may lie less in their semantic content than their capacity to channel attention to the glossarial practices and histories that produce such bonds in the first place.

Similar quandaries attend other terms. Take, for instance, the various sobriquets—'Choir of nuns', 'Milk-white doe', 'Easie-paced gennets', 'Cunny-fur'—that literary critic Duncan Salkeld parses as cognates for 'prostitute'.[74] On the one hand, such epithets powerfully reveal how early modern thinking about sex and gender was inextricably linked to, and animated by, contemporary discourses of race ('Milk-white doe'); religion ('Choirs of nuns'); husbandry, ethnicity, and nationality ('gennets/jennets' are Spanish horses); animality, criminality, and anatomy (a 'cunny/coney' is a rabbit, a criminal mark or victim, and a vagina).

set of this chapter. Where Gainsford thus suggests its status as contemporary term of whoredom, Eleanor Hubbard points out that 'mistress' was, alongside 'goodwife', one of the era's preeminent titles for respectable married women. See *City Women*, 111.

[71] See the entries for *Bagascia* ('a baggage wench, a harlot, a strumpet, a whore') and *Bagasciare* ('to play the baggage, harlot or whore') in Florio, *A Worlde of Wordes* (1598, sig. C6v). See also the entry of *Bagasse* ('A Baggage, Queane, Jyll, Punke, Flirt') in Cotgrave, *A Dictionarie of the French and English Tongves* (1611, sig. H3r). In his Arden 2 edition of the play, René Weis glosses 'baggage' as 'strumpet' (282n160), while Peter Holland and Dympna Callaghan offer 'worthless woman' (91n157) and 'good-for-nothing' (117n156), respectively, in their editions. The term goes unglossed in the editions by Gibbons (191–192), Greenblatt (952), and Levenson (295).

[72] Williams, *Shakespeare's Sexual Language*. For comparison, see the glosses provided by Weis ('spoiled little madam,' 281n151), Gibbons ('spoiled minx, hussy', 191n151), Greenblatt ('spoiled child', 952n151), Holland ('spoiled child', 90n152), Callaghan ('spoiled darling, minx', 116n151), and Levenson ('good-for-nothing woman', 295n150). Notably, none of these glosses address that term's status as one the period's preeminent signifiers of male homoeroticism. On the latter, see esp. DiGangi, *The Homoerotics of Early Modern Drama*, 100–133; Smith, *Homosexual Desire in Shakespeare's England*, 189–224.

[73] *Romeo and Juliet* (ed. Weis), 283n168. See also the editions by Gibbons ('jade', 192n168), Greenblatt ('hussy', 952n168), Holland ('worthless creature', 91n169), Callaghan ('worthless person', 117n168), and Levenson ('good-for-nothing woman', 296n167).

[74] *Shakespeare among the Courtesans*, 131–132.

Yet Salkeld's glosses are exceptionally context-specific: such terms, and the meanings he ascribes to them, are linked both to a specific event (the Gray's Inn Christmas revels of 1594) and to the persons (Lucy Negro, a reputed brothel owner, and her unnamed female companions) to whom they were, presumably, addressed. In these contexts, some appear to operate ironically ('Choirs of nuns', for instance), others analogically (the association of prostitutes and horses, common in the period, appears predicated on the notion that both could be 'ridden'). Some appear to work synecdochally ('Cunny-fur' as a body part that stands in for these women), others indexically ('Milk-white' as a reference to skin colour). Yet as this last example demonstrates, such linguistic operations are impossible to pin down—'Milk-white doe' might instead function ironically here, i.e. connoting what these women are not, whether in terms of their skin colour, gender presentation, moral character, and so on. As with Capulet's calumnies and the editorial glosses that append them, Salkeld's reading thus provides a useful reminder that sexual meanings are made and unmade through what Valerie Traub identifies as a highly fraught 'semiotic interplay of language, bodies, and acts' that unfolds in particular historical contexts and can be shaped by specific textual histories.[75]

With what remains, I wish to focus on how this archive helps to illuminate discursive differences that unsettle the hegemony of whore as the period's governing sexual signifier: preeminent in contemporary lexicographic texts, as well as the juridical archives favoured by social histories, it is supplanted by other terms in Shakespeare's oeuvre and the 'King James Bible' (i.e. *The Holy Bible*, 1611). Just as these usage patterns confound easy distinctions between history and literature, literal and figurative meanings, this archive also, as we shall see, destabilizes long-standing assumptions that the terms of whoredom are invariably illicit (versus licit), female (versus male), heteroerotic (versus homoerotic), transparent (versus opaque), and disciplinary (versus playful).

My analysis is supported by developments in modern-day technology that enable new vantage points from which to review potential

[75] It is this interplay, Traub argues, that distinguishes the instability of the 'sexual lexicon from the unreliability of all linguistic phenomena'. See *Thinking Sex with the Early Moderns*, 177.

relations—hierarchical, but also synchronic, diachronic, and discursive—between early modern terms of whoredom. Preeminent among these is *Lexicons of Early Modern English* (*LEME*), a website based out of the University of Toronto which incorporates 289 searchable lexicons, featuring over 542,000 entries and 60,000 English modern headwords.[76] In terms of the 'whore', *LEME* helps map a far more intricate field of relations. Table 1.1 illustrates the most common 'terms of whoredom' appearing in 133 English lexicographic texts from 1500 to 1650.[77] At the most basic level, the graph indicates that lexicographers

Table 1.1 Usage of select terms in English lexicographic texts, 1500–1650 (*LEME*).

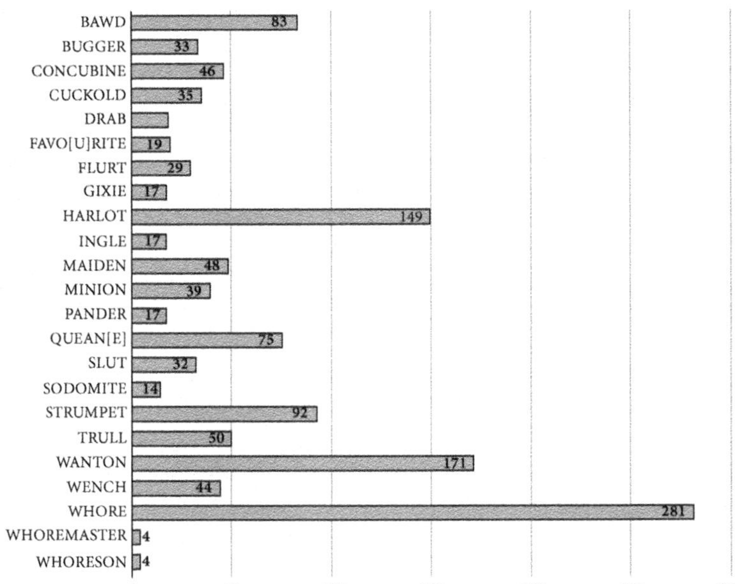

[76] In a devastating development for contemporary scholarship, *LEME*'s funding was rescinded in 2024, resulting in the discontinuation of its search engine and, it would appear, the broader project of uploading searchable early modern lexicons. As of August 2025, the website still provides access to 289 downloadable lexicons, as well as a bibliography of 1473 lexicons listed by date of publication. See https://leme.library.utoronto.ca/help/.

[77] My search parameters were defined by the texts available in the *LEME* as of April 2012. Citations were selected when associated with illicit sexual practices or states

favoured certain terms, including whore (281 citations), harlot (149), strumpet (92), and quean (75). The relative popularity of bawd (83), cuckold (35), and pander (17), moreover, supports the contention that the terms of whoredom encompass a wide range of social and sexual relations, including figures in proximity to, but not necessarily performing, sexual practices. Conferring notions of adjacency or contiguity to whoredom, these relational terms appear more frequently, for example, than punke (15), prostitute (13), minx (13), and doxy (6). Terms that scholars have associated with male homoeroticism—including bugger (33), ingle (17), and sodomite (14)[78]—also outweigh these latter terms and, in combination with minion (39), favourite (19), paramour (12), Ganymede (4), and catamite (3), reveal a rich lexicon for articulating such bonds. As terms frequently overlap, the boundaries, even among supposedly licit and illicit signifiers, or between supposedly 'male' and 'female' behaviours or identities, prove increasingly opaque. 'Wanton' reflects such diverse signifying potential: appearing 412 times in total, the term assumes sexual connotations—that is, it associates with other terms of whoredom or relates specifically to sexual practices—in just under half its entries (171). Citations include associations with 'minion boys' and 'ingles', as well as 'wenches', 'goddesses', and 'unchaste' women. As with Florio's 'whore', the lexicographic 'wanton' assumes a range of meanings, connoting, to varying degrees effeminacy, boyishness, delicacy, prodigality, lasciviousness, immodesty, love, gentleness, and playfulness.

If some terms predominate, others prove significant in their relative absence or seemingly unorthodox connotations. 'Courtesan', a privileged term in continental Europe at the time,[79] appears only eight times

(e.g. defloration, unchaste, etc.), or associated with other illicit terms. Given the focus of this chapter, I have excluded foreign terms from this graph, as well as those predominantly associated with 'licit' sexual categories, such as maiden (48) and virgin (108). Nonetheless, it is important to note that licit terms are often linked to those appearing in my graph, as with Bright's 'chaste|whore' (Fig. 1.8). Given the inchoate state of English orthography, terms also appear under a variety of different spellings. As noted in the main text, I have done my best to account for all entries, but my findings nonetheless are broadly representative rather than exact. For example, 'whore' (281) includes 'whoor, whoore', and hoore', while 'ingle' incorporates 'engle', etc. The most common foreign terms were, in order: *meretrix* (31), *leno* (13), *putain* (10), *succuba* (7), *pucelle* (6), *lupa* (7), and *lena* (5).

[78] For an important challenge to the presumptive gendering of early modern sodomy as male-male, see Daileader, 'Back Door Sex'.

[79] Storey, *Carnal Commerce in Counter-Reformation Rome*.

in these texts, while 'Doll'—a popular eponym on the early modern stage[80]—appears just twice. 'Tribade' and 'fricatrice', often linked to female homoeroticism,[81] do not appear in any of the *LEME*'s 133 texts. The phrase 'Winchester Goose', frequently glossed by textual editors as linking London prostitutes to the Bishops of Winchester,[82] emerges in these works as a cognate for venereal disease: it is 'a disease about the privie members', a 'cunt-botch', or a 'pockie sore'.[83] Even seemingly licit terms such as 'darling' (22), 'girle' (17), and 'lasse' (17), not to mention 'maiden' (48) and 'virgin' (108), appear in relation to, if not juxtaposition with, sexual terms or inferences. Such citations transcend the antonymic: 'maiden'—repeatedly conjoined with 'girle', 'lasse', and 'wench'—appears just one term removed from those bearing illicit connotations. Notions of proximity or substitution prove especially appropriate with homonymic terms such as 'queane' and 'huswife' (13), the latter of which assumed increasingly negative and sexual connotations heading into the seventeenth century: whereas earlier lexicographers define the term as a female head of house or 'goodwife',[84] Florio and Cotgrave associate it with gossiping, prattling, whoredom, sluttishness, and harlotry.[85]

[80] See, for instance, 'Doll Tearsheet', in *2 Henry IV*; 'Doll Williamson', in Munday et al., *Sir Thomas More*; 'Doll', in Dekker and Webster, *Northward Ho*; 'Dol Common', in Jonson, *The Alchemist*.

[81] Traub, *The Renaissance of Lesbianism in Early Modern England*, 188–228 and passim.

[82] Bonheim, 'Shakespeare's "Goose of Winchester"'; Kelly, 'Bishop, Prioress, and Bawd in the Stews of Southwark'.

[83] See, for instance, the entries for *Carolo* ('a moth or timber-worme. Also a cuntbotch or winchester goose. Also dust or powder of rotten timber vsed about yoong children against fleaing', sig. F1r), *Pannocchia* ('a cunt botch, a winchester goose, an impostume about the priuie members, a boile, a blane, a pocke, a plague sore, a knob, a bunch or wenne of flesh', sig. Y2v), *Pudendágra* ('a disease about the priuie parts like a winchester goose', sig. Cc1r), *Taróla* ('a cunt-botch or winchester goose', sig. Mm3r), and *Vaiólo, Vaiuólo* ('a pocke, a blane, a plague, a sore, a carbuncle, a botch, a winchester goose', sig. Oo3r) in Florio, *A Worlde of Wordes* (1598).

[84] Baret, *An Alvearie or Triple Dictionarie in Englishe, Latin, and French* (1574), sig. Jj6v. See also Huloet, *Abcedarium Anglico Latinum* (1552), sig. Q4r.

[85] See, for instance, Florio's entry for *Méscola* ('Also taken for a foolish idle huswife, a sluttish driggle draggle', sig. T4v), and Cotgrave's entry for *Putain* ('A whore, queane, punke, drab, flurt, strumpet, harlot, cockatrice, naughty pack, light huswife, common hackney', sig. Ttt4v). For an acute reading of the early modern 'h[o]usewife' and its deployment in poetry and drama of the period, see Crane, '"Players in Your Huswifery, and Huswives in Your Beds"'.

The meanings of 'nightwalker' also evolve over time, albeit in a different manner. As Paul Griffiths reveals, the term assumed a variety of differing connotations, depending upon locale and era, between the fourteenth and seventeenth centuries: predominantly associated with male thievery and vagrancy during the earlier period, it became increasingly feminized and sexualized by the end of the sixteenth century.[86] Where Griffiths's analysis depends almost exclusively upon legal documents, this example underscores potential differences according to textual format, medium, genre, chronology, and even the tendencies of specific writers involved in the production of early modern meanings: the term appears neither in the lexicographic texts assembled in the *Lexicon of Early Modern English* nor in Shakespeare's works.[87] This is not to argue that lexicographic texts bear correct or true meanings as opposed to poems, dramatic play-texts, sermons, bibles, or court records; rather, it encourages renewed attention to how early modern meaning-making—and unmaking—unfolds across a range of early modern discourses; the various textual and linguistic processes that (differentially) inform these semantic (de)constructions; and the epistemic privilege accorded to these sites of discursive negotiation by early modern subjects and by present-day scholars.

At the same time, the texts surveyed in this chapter remind us that the terms of English whoredom—and here it is useful to recall the multiple senses of 'terms' detailed in this chapter's introduction—vary both within and across a range of seemingly discrete early modern discourses. If 'whore', for instance, is the most common (i.e. appears with the most frequency) sexual signifier in the English lexicographic tradition, it is nevertheless clear that individual lexicographers favoured particular

[86] Griffiths, 'Meanings of Nightwalking in Early Modern London'.

[87] While concordances and digitized editions of Shakespeare provide scholars with valuable research tools, they are limited to the extent that they require a stable source text that, as such, must either eliminate or 'resolve' problems of textual variance. To account for this, all word searches have been cross-referenced in *The Oxford Shakespeare: The Complete Works*, which can be accessed via subscription at Proquest EBook Central; Spevack, *A Complete and Systematic Concordance to the Works of Shakespeare* (vol. 5), which uses the 1974 *The Riverside Shakespeare* as its source text; *OpenSource Shakespeare*, which, like *The Complete Works of Shakespeare* available at shakespeare.mit.edu, draws on the 1864 Globe Edition of the complete works as its source text; and the searchable full text edition of *M^{R}. WILLIAM SHAKESPEARES COMEDIES, HISTORIES, & TRAGEDIES* available at EEBO via Proquest. In what follows, I rely primarily on *The Oxford Shakespeare*, as it is the most recent searchable edition to which I have access.

terms, resulting in terminological fields, relations, and hierarchies that often shift depending upon the dictionary under analysis (Table 1.2): while Bright uses 'whore' almost exclusively in *Characterie* (1588), Thomas Elyot privileges 'harlot' in *The Dictionary of Syr Thomas Elyot knight* (1538), as does Thomas Cooper in *Thesaurus linguæ Romanæ & Britannicæ* (1578). Randle Cotgrave, for his part, features far more 'queane[s]' in his *Dictionarie of the French and English Tongves* (1611) than any of his contemporaries. Usage rates also shift over time: absent in *The Dictionary of Syr Thomas Elyot knight* (1538), 'whore' appears only eighteen times in Richard Huloet's *Abcedarium Anglico Latinum* (1552) and seventeen in Thomas Cooper's *Thesaurus linguæ Romanæ & Britannicæ* (1578)—numbers that pale in comparison to the term's seventy-five, eighty-nine, and ninety-eight appearances in John Florio's *A Worlde of Wordes* (1598), Cotgrave's *Dictionarie of the French and English Tongves* (1611), and Florio's *Queen Anna's New*

Table 1.2 Usage of select terms in prominent lexicographic texts, 1500–1650 (*LEME*).

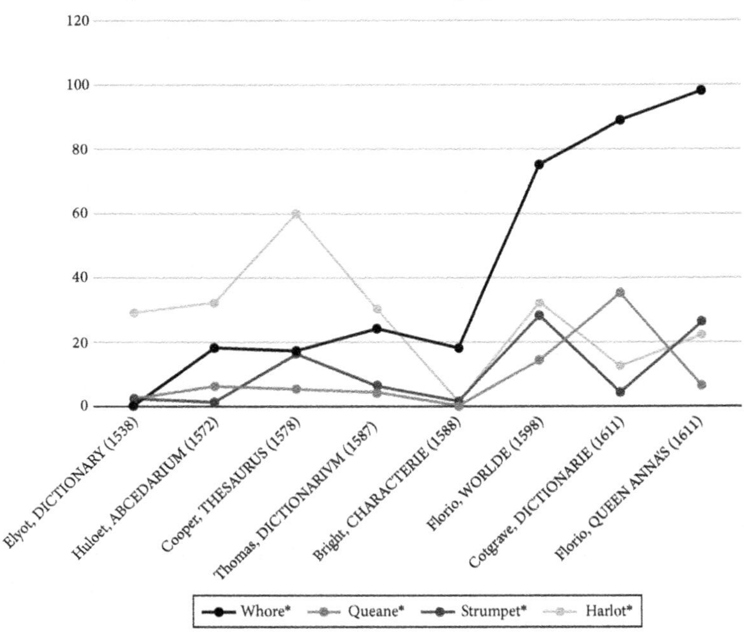

World of Words (1611), respectively. By way of contrast, 'harlot'—one of the more popular terms in the early and mid-sixteenth century—declines slightly over time: Florio reduces its presence from thirty-two to twenty-two appearances in his (admittedly abridged) second edition, while Cotgrave uses the term only twelve times in his 1611 dictionary. The record suggests these are not unrelated trajectories. Rather, a shifting lexical relationship between 'harlot' and 'whore' arises when one compares Rider's treatment of those terms to that of Huloet in his *Abcedarium Anglico Latinum* (1552), printed thirty-seven years before the *Bibliotheca Scholastica* (1589). In Rider's volume, as we may recall, readers looking to define 'A Harlot' are directed to 'see' (*vid.*) the entry for 'whore' instead (Fig. 1.7). Locating meaning in the latter term, Rider's lexical hierarchy inverts the harlot-whore dynamic proposed by Huloet, where readers seeking to know the meanings of 'Whore' are prompted to 'Loke in harlot' (Fig. 1.11). Indeed, whereas Rider will later position 'whore' as the primary site of semantic plenitude and variation for these and related terms (Figs 1.5–6), Huloet, in this earlier text, positions 'harlot' as the terminological node around which attributes and distinctions are clustered and conceptualized (Fig. 1.12).

As these examples reveal, the English lexicographic tradition was a central discursive engine through which the terms of whoredom were crafted and contested, made and unmade, throughout the sixteenth and seventeenth centuries. Of course, it was not the only discursive arena in which this cultural work was undertaken; as the four tables provided in this chapter reveal, the making and unmaking of these terms not only unfolded across a range of early modern discourses and textual corpora but often assumed differing forms and relations depending upon their discursive locale. While 'harlot' declines and 'whore' ascends as the lexicographic tradition heads into the seventeenth century, for instance, the former retains its dominant status in the so-called King James Bible

Whore. Loke in harlot.

FIGURE 1.11 'Whore. Loke in harlot', in Richard Huloet, *Abcedarium Anglico Latinum* (London: ex officina Gulielmi Riddel, 1552), sig. Lliiiir. Houghton Library Gen 13940. Harvard University Libraries.

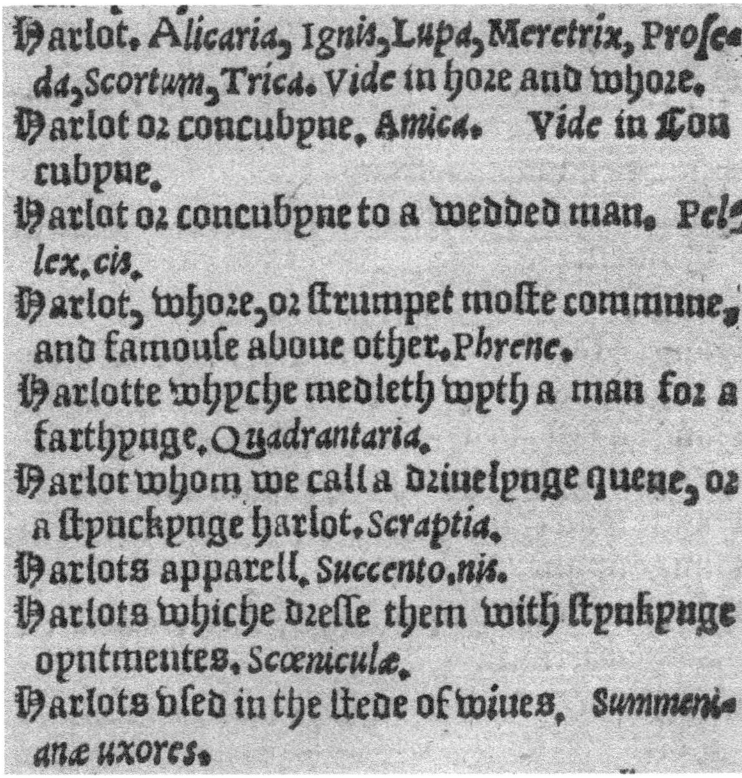
Harlot. Alicaria, Ignis, Lupa, Meretrix, Proſeda, Scortum, Trica. Vide in hore and whore.
Harlot or concubyne. Amica. Vide in Concubyne.
Harlot or concubyne to a wedded man. Pellex, cis.
Harlot, whore, or ſtrumpet moſte commune, and famouſe aboue other. Phrene.
Harlotte whyche medleth wyth a man for a farthynge. Quadrantaria.
Harlot whom we call a driuelynge quene, or a ſtynckynge harlot. Scraptia.
Harlots apparell. Succento, nis.
Harlots whiche dreſſe them with ſtynkynge oyntmentes. Scœniculæ.
Harlots vſed in the ſtede of wiues. Summenianæ uxores.

FIGURE 1.12 From 'Harlot' to 'Harlots used in the stede of wiues', in Richard Huloet, *Abcedarium Anglico Latinum* (London: ex officina Gulielmi Riddel, 1552), sig. Piiv. Houghton Library Gen 13940. Harvard University Libraries.

of 1611, where it appears fifty-seven times, as compared to nine uses of 'whore' (Table 1.3),[88] suggesting its continued purchase in contemporary religious discourse. The different set of terms emerge in *The Oxford Shakespeare* (Table 1.4), where 'wench' (94) far outweighs 'whore' (50),

[88] Variants of the broader term 'whoredome' appear sixty-six times in the 'King James Bible', suggesting that it is the *state or condition* of whoredom, rather than the *figure* of the whore, which is the primary point of emphasis in this bible. While such findings suggest differences of genre and discourse, it is worth noting that large portions of the KJV were likely derived from the 'Geneva Bible' (*The Bible and Holy Scriptvres Conteyned in the Olde and Newe Testament*, 1560) and the William Tyndale's *New Testament* (1538).

Table 1.3 Usage of select terms in the 'King James Bible' (*The Holy Bible*, 1611).

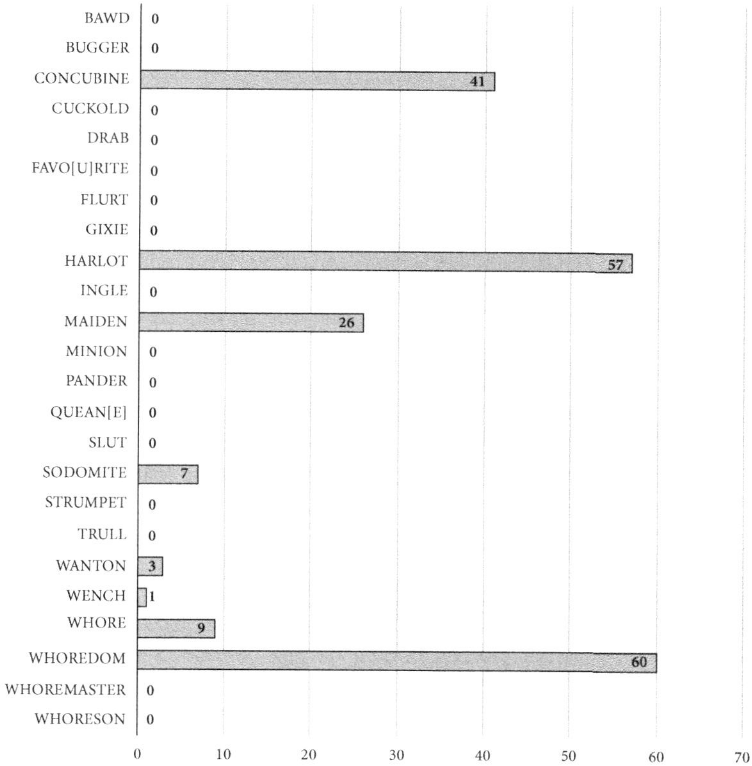

which appears at the nearly the same rate as 'bawd' (52), 'maiden' (59), and 'whoreson' (47). In contrast to the lexicographic tradition, moreover, terms such as 'bugger' (0), 'ingle' (0), 'sodomite' (0), 'fricatrice' (0), 'tribade' (0), and, most significantly for our purposes, 'whoredom' (0) are entirely absent in *The Oxford Shakespeare*, which instead favours 'minion' (24), 'Ganymede' (9), and 'favo[u]rite' (6), intimating a preference for suggestive, figurative, or euphemistic language at sites of polymorphous eroticisms.[89]

[89] As readers will surely note, these examples offer a pointed reminder that any terminological accounting depends upon parameters established by the critic in question and the edition(s) adopted for review. My decision to focus on nominal rather than verbal or

Table 1.4 Usage of select terms in *The Oxford Shakespeare* (1986).

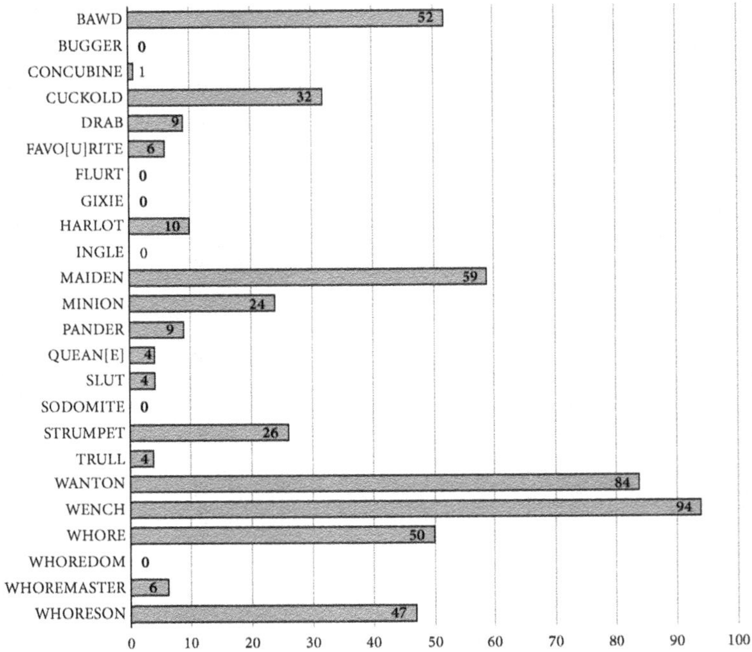

I will have more to say of the staging of these terms in the chapters to come. For now, I wish to note that this lexicographic analysis suggests how attending to the terms of English whoredom might reconfigure understandings of sexual-lexical meaning-making in early modern

adjectival forms, for instance, here results in the elision of York's suggestive allusion to 'ingling' in *King Henry VI, Part 1* (5.3.68). That this term/orthography appears in *The Oxford Shakespeare* yet is notably absent in the Riverside, MIT, and Opensource Shakespeare editions (which offer 'juggling' instead) further underscores the fluid textual foundations upon which any 'fixed' accounting depends. Similar consequences derive from my exclusion of compounds (such as 'whore-hunter'), stage directions, and speech headings: the presence of 'Ganymede', for instance, doubles—from six to twelve appearances—in *The Oxford Shakespeare* (1986) edition of *As You Like It* when these latter two categories are included, while the presence of 'bawd' (52) and 'pander' (9) in *The Oxford Shakespeare* (1986) version of *Pericles, Prince of Tyre* increases by roughly the same fold (55 and 22, respectively) when one includes speech prefixes.

England. If, as Peter Stallybrass has argued, it is the 'constant *conflation of signifiers* that characterizes Renaissance texts',[90] early modern lexicographers clearly navigated such relations through a variety of different means and to different ends. In his textual order, for instance, John Rider privileges acts over actors, whoremongers over whores, literal renderings over figurative connotations. When Timothy Bright pursues semantic precision by definitional reduction—positing direct, singular relations between headwords and meanings—he ironically amplifies the signifying capacities of his privileged definitions, including the capacious 'whore'. Seeking seemingly stable foundations for other hard words, Bright's 'whore' thus annexes a range of meanings that permeate multiple facets of social life. When Florio and Cotgrave, by contrast, seek precision in amplitude—as if striving to catalogue all possible significations for a given headword—they configure differing fields of terminological relation, suggesting degrees of both proximity and connotation. Amidst such plenitude, the terms of whoredom specialize and generalize: at times applicable to anybody, they appear, at others, restricted and particularized.

Just as these terms and texts illustrate the vast signifying potential of English whoredom, they also reveal the many ways in which these various and potential meanings were engaged, ordered, limited, or animated within an evolving print form. Exploring multiple fields of signification—linguistic, visual, mathematical, ideographic, cartographic—lexicographers grapple with relations not only textual and terminological but discursive, human, and social. In doing so, their texts represent sites of social reflection and creation. Codifying certain terms, many of which stabilize or define others, lexicographers balance precision and possibility. In their introductory epistles, some go so far as to suggest that the definitions provided within their texts are never final—and that 'judgement' thereof ultimately resides with readers and interlocutors, rather than the lexicographer who inscribes such meanings and relations. At the end of his introductory note, for instance, Rider comforts himself with the knowledge that 'learned reader[s]' will 'either with thy pen correct, or in courtesie conceale' the 'blemishes' they discover in his text.[91] A standard caveat, the digression nevertheless

90 Stallybrass, 'Shakespeare, the Individual, and the Text', 601; emphasis in the original.
91 Rider, 'To the Reader', *Bibliotheca Scholastica*, n.p.

suggests that lexicographers conceived of their texts, at least to a certain degree, as 'open works': as fields of exploration, relation, and interaction; of possibility as well as of reproduction and reiteration.[92] In (the) terms of whoredom, this emergent discourse allowed—even encouraged—readers to approach sexual meaning-making in a similar manner.

As with the aporia that surfaces for readers engaging the relationship between Rider's 'whore' and 'harlot', the 'open work' of early modern sexual signification encourages readers to look—'*vide*'—at sites of absence in these texts and to consider how such gaps are mediated by readers and other writers. Such cultural and semantic (un)making is palpably demonstrated—and rendered visible—when one compares the entries for 'whoredome' in two manuscript copies of Bright's *Characterie* (1588), which appeared in print just one year prior to Rider's *Bibliotheca Scholastica* (1589). Bright, as we may recall, offers 'whore' as the privileged definition for adulterer, baude, brothel, buggerie, chaste, concubine, defloure, gille, harlot, lemman, rauish, ribaude, stewes, strumpet, and vnchaste. Yet when readers seek a definition for this transcendental signifier in the edition printed by I. [John] Windet, they find not substance but absence: whoredome, not whore, appears in the table, and is presented without a corresponding definition (Fig. 1.13). Materializing absence, this manuscript palpably evokes another critical insight enabled by our archive of terms: that the very multiplicity of terms associated with whoredom signals an essential lack at the heart of whoredom—an absence that cannot be filled through the recovery of a proper term, name, or meaning.[93] To do so, I stress, is to deny neither the disciplinary force nor the political and gendered consequences of what Gowing has quite rightly figured as the

[92] Eco, *The Open Work*. As Wendy Wall notes in *The Imprint of Gender*, early modern readers 'were authorized to edit the poems as they read, to scribble answers in the blank white space of the page, and even to alter the poems themselves' (34). For a recent study of readerly inscriptions in early modern texts, see Orgel, *The Reader in the Book*.

[93] As J. Hillis Miller once put it, '[t]hat there are so many of these words, potentially a limitless number, indicates that no one of them is proper. What these words name has no proper name, only deferred, displaced, figurative, or improper names, that is, catachrestic labels.' Miller offers this description as a gloss on Derrida's 'iterability', which he figures as but one of many tropes that the latter animates to provide a temporary shape and form to the central (non-)concept that variously surfaces as '*différance*, hymen, supplement, *pharmakon*, dissemination, writing, margin, parergon, the gift, the secret, and so on' in his oeuvre. See *Speech Acts in Literature*, 78.

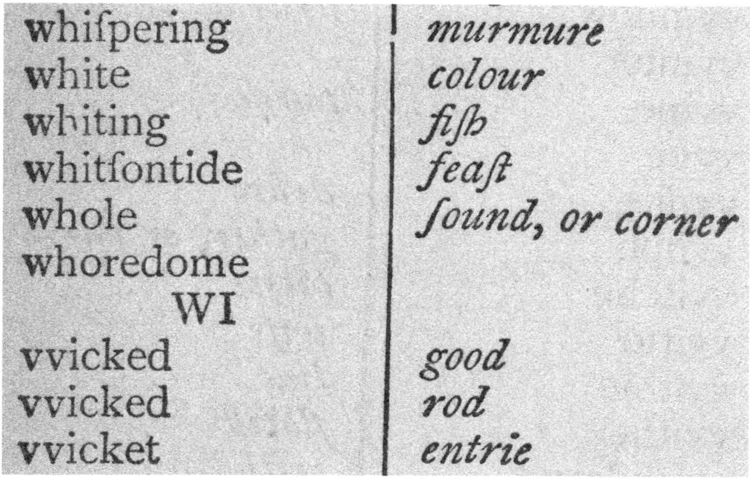

whiſpering	*murmure*
white	*colour*
whiting	*fiſh*
whitſontide	*feaſt*
whole	*ſound, or corner*
whoredome	
WI	
vvicked	*good*
vvicked	*rod*
vvicket	*entrie*

FIGURE 1.13 'Whoredome', in Timothy Bright, *CHARACTERIE* (London: I. Windet, 1588), n.p. BAC 601812. The Huntington Library, San Marino, California.

'idiom of abuse' in early modern England (59). It is, rather, to insist upon the materiality of that violence, its capacity to construct the very entity that it punishes, while concurrently resisting a metaphysical logic that links an individual's social and sexual practices to the character of their soul. Such a critical practice, as I argue throughout *Shakespeare and the Making of English Whoredom*, shifts attention from questions of ontology (what is a whore?) to those of epistemology (how does one know a whore?) and materiality (how are whores made?). It also allows us, as these two copies of Bright's manuscript so powerfully reveal, to focus on what emerges—what is written or inscribed—in the absences that structure the making of English whoredom.

If nothing stands behind Bright's 'whoredome' in manuscript 1, the marks and marginalia recorded in manuscript 2 (Fig. 1.14) reminds us that definitional absences are not only revealing but generative: encouraging others to alter the terms provided ('whoredom' is reduced to 'whore'); to contribute additional definitions or cognates ('wood' joins 'Rod' as a gloss for 'Wicker'); to pose questions (the inscriptions across from 'Whore' appear to say 'whose' and 'which'), and so on and so

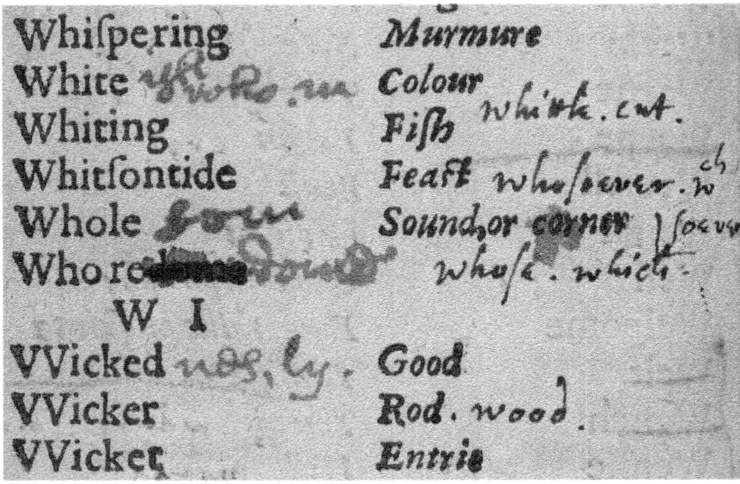

Whiſpering	*Murmure*
White	*Colour*
Whiting	*Fiſh*
Whitſontide	*Feaſt*
Whole	*Sound, or corner*
Whore[redacted]	
W I	
VVicked	*Good*
VVicker	*Rod.*
VVicket	*Entrie*

FIGURE 1.14 'Whore~~dome~~ (*whose. which.*)', in Timothy Bright, *CHARACTERIE* (London: by I. Windet, 1588), n.p. The Bodleian Libraries, University of Oxford, Weston Library, Deuce W 3.

forth. In so doing, they point to larger questions which persist into the modern era. Who gets to inscribe meanings within the open spaces and texts of early modern sex? What signifying practices appear when language—and/or definitional precision—fails? And finally, recalling the origins of lexicography, how do the terms of the margins relate to, define, or replace the central terms of the printed text?

In his own unique contribution to English lexicography, Bright encourages readers to consider an alternative sign system, subordinating his English lexicon to a system of 'characters' or ideograms. Here, it is an ideogram that both characterizes the 'whore' and configures its relationship to a series of 'related' terms (Fig. 1.15). In this lexical system, 'whore' is not only ideogrammatically connected to a series of interrogatives ('what', 'where', 'wherefore', 'which') but emerges—characteristically, we might say—as a species of (inverted) 'will'. Or, perhaps, it is the other way around. While Bright's text failed to achieve widespread acclaim, his novel system reflects both the creative spirit that animates early modern English lexicography and the possibility that readers and writers will discover yet news ways of imagining,

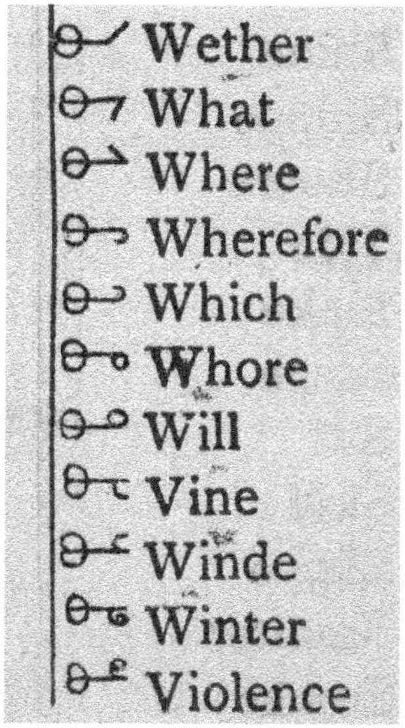

FIGURE 1.15 Alternative ideogrammatic system ('Wether-Violence') in Timothy Bright, *CHARACTERIE* (London: I. Windet, 1588), n.p. BAC 601812. The Huntington Library, San Marino, California.

organizing, textualizing, and visualizing not only the terms of their daily lives, but the various insights and possibilities that emerge when such terms—including the early modern 'whore'—are brought into relation with one another.

If the English lexicographic tradition suggests that the terms of whoredom are never fully fixed, and that we might therefore challenge the existing lexicons through which sex and its meanings have been adjudicated, the historical record nevertheless reminds us that unstable meaning are often sites of profound violence. In the chapters that follow, therefore, I attend closely to the interplay of possibility and foreclosure, agency and oppression, as both the conceptual category of whoredom and the epistemology that attends it in early modern England are made and unmade at the levels of language, textuality, and embodiment; sexual time and narrative knowing; history, memory, and affect. Building on the work begun here, the next chapter links the problems of signification and textuality revealed by lexicographic efforts to define the whore to questions of embodiment and agency. Reading three representations of 'Joan of Arc'—at her trial and execution in medieval Rouen, in Shakespeare's *The first Part of Henry the Sixth* (1591), and in scholarly accounts of that play—I reveal how 'heretic', 'witch', and 'whore' emerge, in historical succession, as operative terms for stabilizing her excess significance in medieval, early modern, and postmodern contexts. Reading the various forms of proclamation through which Joan's interlocutors have sought to render her legible, I focus upon who is served by these acts of proclamation, what is and is not known through such signifying practices, and how slanderous meanings have been materialized and contested. In so doing, I open onto how thinking embodiment-as-process, as a transitive and transformative action that brings the seemingly immaterial into the corporeal, enables new insights regarding the relations of bodies to discursive practices in medieval and early modern England.

Shakespeare and the Making of English Whoredom. Stephen Spiess, Oxford University Press.
 DOI: 10.1093/9780191851223.003.0002

2

Puzzling Embodiment

Proclamation, *La Pucelle*, and *The first Part of Henry the Sixth*

The Will to Proclaim

I begin with the voices of Jeanne la Pucelle.[1] Not those divine tongues heard by the young, fourteenth-century woman from Domrémy, but rather the cacophonous choruses that surround her, speak for her, and precede her many representations, including those on Shakespeare's stage. These voices span epochs and cultures, interpretations and ideologies, genres and genders. Some precede the historical figure herself; others speak to, within, and beyond our historical moment. A legend within her lifetime, Jeanne was mythically prophesied by Merlin, the Sybil, and the Venerable Bede; the narratives surrounding her multiplied as she traversed the battlefields of medieval France and Burgundy, witnessed the coronation of Charles VII at Rheims Cathedral, and burned at the stake in Rouen on 30 May 1431. Since then, she has been

[1] I use this name when referring to the woman born in Domrémy in 1412 and executed at the Old Market of Rouen on 30 May 1431, as it was the moniker by which she identified herself. See Warner, *Joan of Arc*. When referring to the role in *The first Part of Henry the Sixt*[*h*], I follow Edward Burns's Arden edition in using 'Joan de Puzel'. See *King Henry VI, Part 1*, esp. 25–27, 291–296.

condemned and canonized by the likes of Christine de Pizan, Voltaire [Françoise-Marie Arouet], David Hume, Friedrich Schiller, Jules Michelet, Pyotr Tchaikovsky, Mark Twain, George Bernard Shaw, Hélène Cixous, and Alain Badiou. There is, one might say, something uncanny about Jeanne—la Pucelle is a puzzle that generates a desire to proclaim both who she is and what her body means.[2]

This will-to-proclaim has produced a seemingly endless list of words and monikers by which Jeanne might be known and categorized. Edward Hall, in his famed 1584 English *Chronicle*,[3] catalogues Jeanne in a manner symptomatic of this larger cultural impetus to name her through profusion. She is, for him:

> mayd; monster; Ione the puzell; oracle; soothsaier; deuilishe wytche; sathanicall enchaunterese; sorceresse Ione (called the mayde, sent from GOD); wytch or manly woman; blotte...to the Frenche nacion; shephereds daughter; a chamberlain in an hostrie; beggers brat; an enchateresse; an orgayne of the deyill, sent from Sathan, to blind the people and bring them in vnbelife; supersticious sorceresse, and a diabolical blashemeresse of God; a persone scismatike and errone-ous, in the lawe of Iesu Christe; pevishe painted Puzel; Image or an Idole; false prophetisse, and seducer of the people.[4]

Maid and monster, oracle and false prophet, manly woman—Jeanne appears a paradox embodied: a 'persone scismatike' who incorporates terms of division into her physical substance. Or does she? Is there a body in this text? Hall implies that Jeanne's meanings partake of her body: of her speech, actions, and appearance, of her questionable femininity yet seemingly irrefutable womanhood. Like other writers, however, Hall describes this body in its material absence, one hundred years after it was consigned to ash; he never witnessed Jeanne embody, or fail to embody, his manifold terms. Hall's account demonstrates a definitional privilege: the power to proclaim Jeanne's bodily significance in

[2] On the homonymic play of 'pucelle' in medieval and early modern England, where the term could connote virgin (*pucelle*), whore (*puzel*), penis (*pizzle*), and/or puzzle, among other significations, see Warner, *Joan of Arc*, 22; Garber, *Shakespeare After All*, 95–96.

[3] Originally printed as *The vnion of the two noble and illustrious famelies of Lancastre & Yorke*....Citations here are drawn from the 1809 edition, retitled *Hall's Chronicle*, which retains the original orthography.

[4] Hall, *Chronicle*, 148–159.

English chronicle history. It also—in its verbal excess, in its mixtures of the material and abstract, the supernatural and everyday—belies the tight conceptual links between her demonic significance and lived human experience that his catalogue attempts to forge. One of many historical voices bespeaking Jeanne, Hall here proves emblematic rather than exceptional. A precursor to and influence for Shakespeare's *The first Part of Henry the Sixth*, his catalogue evokes relations of language, gender, and embodiment crucial to that play's dynamics, as well as to Jeanne's cultural legacies. Historicizing such relations, I contend, can re-form understandings of what, precisely, is at stake in proclaiming—and materializing—'Joan of Aire' (5.3.59).[5]

To illuminate these desires and processes, as well as provide a larger context for Shakespeare's work, I examine three historically situated representations of 'Joan of Arc': at her trial and execution in medieval Rouen, on Shakespeare's stage, and in scholarly accounts of that play. This triptych enables comparative understandings of how words materialize medieval and early modern bodies, as well as how attempts to proclaim Jeanne's embodied substance reflect historically contingent modes of knowing women who exceed culturally prescribed roles. Central to my methodology is the reading of various forms of proclamation: acts of naming, forced confession, public spectacle and execution, as well as dramatic representations and present-day literary critical practices. In this book's Introduction, I noted that 'proclamations' were official statements imbued with a particular form of authority—in that case, the rights and prerogatives of the crown—in Tudor England.[6] At the same time, I revealed that both the nature of that authority and its capacity to be enforced were active rather than settled questions in the period, and thus that proclamations instantiated not only relations of power but of knowledge, with the contours of the former often explicitly negotiated by way of the latter. To speak of 'proclamations' in early modern England, I therefore propose, is to recognize a yearning for the sovereign authority to impose one's preferred meanings through illocutionary speech—a desire I identify as the 'will to proclaim'. But it is also to acknowledge that while acts of proclamations possess perlocutionary

[5] Unless otherwise noted, all citations are drawn from Shakespeare, *King Henry VI, Part 1* (ed. Burns).

[6] See especially pp. 36–38.

force,[7] this force is neither absolute nor unidirectional but rather relational. Consequently, attempts to proclaim meanings can be scrutinized to reveal the nature and limitations of the proclaiming authority; their relations to the entity or entities being proclaimed; and the material and linguistic processes through which their preferred meanings are materialized or contested. With that in mind, I suggest that a rhetoric of proclamations can profitably be applied to the study of modern embodiment, in that it allows us to shift critical attention from the 'truth' of an individual's embodied meanings to the various relations of power and knowledge that emerge, often in striking relief, whenever such 'truth' is declared and contested. In what follows, I thus focus not on what Jeanne's body 'really means' in various historical contexts, but rather how her embodied meanings have been—and continue to be—proclaimed, by whom, and to what ends; how these acts of proclamation emerge, and often are explicitly figured, as responses to problems of knowledge that Jeanne appears to body forth; and how these acts therefore can be scrutinized to reveal some of the relational dynamics of early modern embodiment, the problems of knowledge that these relations index and incorporate, and the material consequences that attend their puzzling out.

As this overview suggests, my approach signals a departure from conventional understandings of embodiment in early modern studies. As a noun, 'embodiment' has come to indicate the varying ways in which the body was understood and experienced 'as embedded in a larger world with which it transacts' in early modern England.[8] In what follows, I shift our analytic lens to explore the concept in its verbal dimensions, to think embodiment as a transitive and transformative action that endlessly (re)negotiates the relationship between the seemingly immaterial—a word, idea, or discourse—and the corporeal.[9] Such a shift entails attention to language's performative properties, the capacity for specific words or utterances to produce tangible social,

[7] On the distinction between illocutionary and perlocutionary language, see especially Butler, *Excitable Speech*, esp. 1–41.

[8] Floyd-Wilson and Sullivan, *Environment and Embodiment in Early Modern England*, 2. See also Paster, *The Body Embarrassed* and *Humoring the Body*; Schoenfeldt, *Bodies and Selves in Early Modern England*.

[9] *Oxford English Dictionary Online*, s.v. 'embodiment | imbodiment' (*n.*), 2b: 'that in which (a principle, an abstract idea, etc.) is embodied, actualized, concretely expressed.'

material, and ideological effects, but does not presume that such acts are invariably successful or effective; rather, it situates them within a broader process of embodiment that is at once individual and social, material and discursive. This shift also turns attention to the relational dynamics that, I submit, attend both embodiment and epistemology in the era, linking them in ways we have yet to appreciate, and which inform the social and material consequences that attend their respective making but also the possibilities for agency and resistance.

Indeed, when viewed as action and process, embodiment raises important questions of discursive manifestation and individual contestation: how individuals negotiate socially circumscribed meanings. Jeanne's case proves instructive in this regard, as her trial and legacy reveal how empowered institutions and individuals have sought to manage (or mark) a dissident subject, including through practices that work to materialize the culturally inexplicable within a female body 'that can then be burned, murdered, blamed, reviled, contained, or simply eliminated'.[10] Yet by asking questions instead of providing answers, exposing contradictions, parodying faultlines in laws and logic, and playing with language, Jeanne not only contested the terms and practices through which others sought to know her at Rouen but in so doing underscored the cultural labour necessary to stabilize her excess significance. These discursive tactics, I argue, provide a template for analysing embodiment-as-process, especially the cultural work performed by this corporeal reckoning.

'To Remove any Doubt': Embodying *Fama Publica*

The voices of Jeanne's execution preserved in historical archives describe a spectacle so rich in its iconography, so stunning in its developments, and so unsettling in its affects as to beggar complete description. As with Hall's *Chronicle*, however, these accounts simultaneously overflow with words and bodies, as if attempting to bury the indescribable amidst

[10] Charnes, *Notorious Identity*, 176.

a mass of language. If such effects bespeak Jeanne's exceptional status, they also suggest the problems and paradoxes of proclaiming another's embodied meanings.

On 30 May 1431, Jeanne la Pucelle was led, for the second time in three days, from Rouen Castle to a plaster scaffold erected before the gathered public. As she progressed through the crowd, this 17-year-old peasant, anonymous only three years prior, bore the signs of her own condemnation. With her hair shorn to suggest penance, Jeanne wore a mitre: a bishop's headdress that traditionally signified male office and ecclesiastical authority. The headdress was, of course, a mockery, a derisive nod to Jeanne's claims of divine revelation. Its Latin embroidery—*Heretica, Relapsa, Apostata, Idolater*—augmented this parodic campaign, further marking the body beneath. As Jeanne passed through the crowd, those close to her might also have glimpsed three demonic figures on the cap—Belial, Satan, and Behemoth—intended to re-present Jeanne's guiding voices: the Archangel Michael, Saint Catherine, and Saint Margaret.[11] Distorting traditional signs of religious and gendered authority, the cap served two functions: it disclaimed Jeanne's voice, evacuating her claims to divine mandate by marking them as counterfeit, and proclaimed the body beneath as imitation, parody, and false sign.

Should viewers have missed the significance of such corporeal, sumptuary, and embroidered markers, Jeanne's execution tableau included additional visual and aural signs. Recording the scene in his diary, Clément de Fauquembergue noted:

> And on a placard in front of the fire in which she was placed were written these words: 'Joan who had named herself the Pucelle, liar, pernicious person, abuser of people, soothsayer, superstitious woman, blasphemer of God, presumptuous, unbeliever in the faith of Jesus Christ, boaster, idolater, cruel, dissolute, invoker of devils, apostate, schismatic, and heretic.'[12]

In all likelihood, Pierre Cauchon, Bishop of Beauvais and lead inquisitor, proclaimed these terms for the assembled audience, as sentences

[11] Warner, *Joan of Arc*, 117.

[12] *Journal of Clement de Fauquembergue* (June 1431), reprinted in Taylor, *Joan of Arc: La Pucelle*, 228. To avoid confusion, I hereafter refer to this text as C. Taylor, *La Pucelle*.

were traditionally read aloud prior to execution.[13] It is as if inquisitors sought to execute Jeanne in both words and body, to surround her with myriad signs of condemnation and char her name before they charred her flesh and bone. Perched above and below Jeanne, proclaimed for all to hear, such signs—invested with the authority of the church—were mobilized to legitimate her execution.

Where such excessive signifying practices imply anxieties on the inquisitors' part, they also underscore a concerted effort to divest Jeanne's verbal authority. The placard implies such concerns, charging that she 'had named herself the Pucelle'. Self-nomination implies self-assertion: an act that, in Jeanne's case, supplants male prerogative in a deeply patriarchal culture. The charge also, along with suggestions of her fraudulent speech, attacks the foundation of Jeanne's rhetorical agency; as codified by church fathers like Gregory of Nyssa, Ambrose, and Augustine, holy virginal women could, through the public renunciation of sexual relations, lay claim to a 'state of wholeness and perfection' that transcended masculine authority. In proclaiming this status, Jeanne surpassed strictures that traditionally 'delimit[ed] and define[d] her sex', including the right to public speech. She was, as François Meltzer demonstrates, an extraordinary and dangerous exception to the dominant orders of her era.[14] I am however less interested in the nature of Jeanne's authority than in how inquisitors negotiated her state of exception, particularly the ways in which they reestablished, or sought to reestablish, the right to proclaim the meanings of her material body.

Following the Fourth Lateran Council (1215), legal procedure demanded, as the basis for inquisition, what was known as *fama publica*: a collective, public sense of the accused's 'ill reputation'.[15] Inquisitors could arrest and charge individuals without evidence yet had to establish, retrospectively, the accused's 'public infamy' to legitimate the trial. This stipulation demanded creative, often coercive, legal manoeuvring: prosecutors would haul defendants into court to investigate *fama*,

[13] Extant accounts of the execution do not record Cauchon's words upon the scaffold, but it is likely, following inquisition procedure, that he read aloud the formal sentences, as decreed and printed by the court of inquisition. Jeanne was tried twice over the course of seven days, with an opinion issued on May 19, as well as verdicts on May 24 and May 30. Terms from the placard are drawn from a combination of these three accounts. See C. Taylor, *La Pucelle*, 213–224.

[14] Meltzer, *For Fear of the Fire*, 83.

[15] Kelly, 'The Right to Remain Silent'.

hoping the accused would make statements validating the initial charge. Trials thus depended upon a rhetorical paradox: to silence the accused, inquisitors had to let them speak. In a telling move, however, Jeanne's trial began not in dialogue but rather with a hymeneal inspection: prior to speech, her body was examined as evidence of, or witness to, her social and legal status. As the second occurrence of this procedural hierarchy—Jeanne also submitted to a virginity exam prior to meeting the Dauphin at Chinon—repetition here suggests how gender, sexual status, and the material body served as privileged sites for construing her embodied meanings. In both instances, she was 'found to be woman and virgin and *pucelle*'.[16]

When this body failed to provide the desired evidence, inquisitors sought proof by means of self-indictment. Enabling Jeanne's speech, Cauchon attempted to secure statements that would provide, in the trial transcripts, tangible evidence of heresy. To achieve this goal, he conducted six public and nine private interrogations, attended by as many as sixty-two male clerics. As Jeanne's statements accumulated in writing, inquisitors began to repeat questions, hoping she would contravene earlier statements. This strategy sought incrimination through heretical perjury: materializing her 'voice' in the court transcriptions,[17] inquisitors hoped to prove *fama publica* by documenting contradictory statements.

Fatigued and seemingly circumscribed by language, Jeanne nonetheless escaped Cauchon's rhetorical traps. The trial records reveal a range of discursive tactics through which she exposed and parodied fractures in her inquisitors' logic. When asked 'if she saw St Michael and the angels corporeally and really', Jeanne replied: 'I saw them with the eyes of my body, just as well as I see you.'[18] Shifting the corporeal object of Cauchon's interrogative, from the saints to herself, she evaded heretical inferences. When the Bishop implied her status as a false idol, noting that several Rheims women had touched her ring as if she were a papal prelate, Jeanne countered that 'many women touched my hands and my

[16] Meltzer, *For Fear of the Fire*, 93; italics in the original. The comment comes from the testimony of Jean Pasquerel, Jeanne's confessor.

[17] On problems of 'voice' and mediation in archival records, see especially Steedman, *Dust*.

[18] C. Taylor, *La Pucelle*, 153.

rings, but I do not know their thought or intention',[19] exposing conceptual distinctions between her acts, others' intentions, and thus the episode's potential significations. On other occasions, Jeanne demurred, claiming that 'she did not remember', 'will answer that another time', or would not speak 'without the permission of her voice'.[20] Such evasive responses suggest Jeanne's rhetorical insurgency at Rouen. When inquisitors asked 'in what form, size, appearance and clothing St Michael came to her', she responded 'that he was in the form of a very true and upright man, and that she would not say anything more about his clothing or other things'.[21] Forcing inquisitors to draw upon their own definitions or imaginative frameworks to evaluate her claims, Jeanne turned the interrogation back upon her interrogators. On other occasions, she explicitly inverted the subject of inquisition: when Cauchon probed potential divisions between 'our lord the pope' and 'whom she believed to be the true pope', Jeanne neither denied nor affirmed papal legitimacy, but instead asked 'if there were two of them'.[22] Cauchon moved to the next question.

Jeanne's tactical options, however, remained limited. Her apparent circumscription is perhaps best exemplified by a series of questions centred upon her willingness to submit to the Church Militant (the church as manifest on earth) as representative of the Church Triumphant (God's divine hierarchy). Although this line of inquiry broached a deeply contested theological issue,[23] inquisitors elided points of doctrinal disagreement and focused solely on Jeanne's submission to authority: would she submit to church patriarchs or to her divine voices? Jeanne again subverted the question: 'I submit myself to God who sent me, to the Blessed Mary and to all the saints of heaven. And it seems to me that God and the church are one, and no difficulty should be made about this. Why do you make difficulties about this?' In so doing, she pressed inquisitors to proclaim their own positions, then replied that she 'would not answer anything more for now'.[24]

[19] Ibid., 171.
[20] Ibid., 188, 181, 152.
[21] Ibid., 197.
[22] Ibid., 159.
[23] Warner, *Joan of Arc*, 128.
[24] C. Taylor, *La Pucelle*, 197–198.

Unable to secure Jeanne's conviction through self-incriminatory statements, the inquisitors again shifted strategies. On 23 May 1431, they declared Jeanne a heretic, schismatic, apostate, and witch, sentencing her to death by fire. Her only remaining option, it appeared, would be to recant her claims of divine mandate before the gathered public, an action that would publicly 'confirm' her *fama publica*. It was an ingenious double bind: Jeanne would either burn as an obstinate heretic unwilling to submit to church authority or proclaim herself as such and submit to that same authority. Once again, the desired evidence had to come from Jeanne, whether by confession or by silence.

Given her recalcitrance during inquisition, prosecutors perhaps expected Jeanne to remain defiant.[25] If so, they clearly misread her rhetorical tactics and underestimated her resolve to resist their snares. In place of confession or sacrilegious silence, Jeanne requested a direct appeal to the pope, a move that publicly undermined one of the charges levied against her: a refusal to submit to church authority. Moreover, by performing her own knowledge of, and adherence to, ecclesiastical law, Jeanne turned Cauchon's coercive binary back upon her inquisitors, who would either have to delay sentencing or, by denying her petition, violate the very laws upon which the trial depended. Choosing the latter, Cauchon unwittingly enabled the nullification of Jeanne's sentence in 1456.

These dissident tactics continued. When presented with a writ of abjuration moments later, Jeanne stunned witnesses by signing the document. The signature bore significant legal weight: in assenting, Jeanne accepted stipulations—including the rejection of male attire—whose breach would later authorize her execution. Yet even in this choice, Jeanne slipped the grip of her interrogators: when presented with the document, she did not pen her proper name but rather 'in a mocking guise...made a kind of circle'. As Larissa Juliet Taylor notes, 'even though [she] could not read or write, she *could* sign her name. That she did not do so is revealing.' Indeed, the notation may have represented another mark—'the cross in a circle'—that Jeanne used to 'tell her followers not to believe what she wrote'.[26] Rather than a sign of self-condemnation, therefore, the mark may have served as an anti-signature:

[25] L. Taylor, *The Virgin Warrior*, 154.
[26] Ibid., 159; emphasis in the original.

a signifier disclaiming denotation to encourage subversion. Here and elsewhere, Jeanne's actions both underscored the discursive labour necessary to secure her abjection and laid the groundwork for her posthumous retrial.

Accounts of Jeanne's execution pose many questions regarding her embodied and discursive statuses. According to court records, Jeanne returned to her cell after the abjuration, assumed female attire as ordered, and had her head shaved in penance. Three days later, Cauchon reported that she had resumed wearing masculine apparel and thus violated her signed writ. If she knew that donning her armour would put her life at risk, why did Jeanne change clothing? Taylor interprets the episode as the reclamation of Jeanne's knightly identity but notes another disturbing possibility: according to Martin Ladvenu, a Dominican friar, Jeanne alleged that she was 'forced to resume wearing men's clothes' after 'a great English lord...tried to rape her'. Another priest, Jean Massieu, offered a related account:

> One of the guards tore off the women's clothing she was wearing and...threw the male attire to her, ordering her to get up....She responded, 'You know that is forbidden to me. I will not put them on.' But they would not return the other clothes. This went on for about an hour until finally, out of necessity, she was constrained to get out of bed and put on the clothing.

Within this confined space, one fact appears indisputable: the means for Jeanne's self-incrimination had been placed at her disposal. As Taylor notes, 'if those around [Jeanne] wanted her to keep the promises she made on May 24, all male clothing would have been taken from her cell'.[27] Indeed, the possibility exists that Jeanne did not don that forbidden outfit, that her re-attiring instead emerged as a necessary and accepted fiction: a fabrication, scripted by her relentless prosecutors, now long cemented through historical and biographical reiteration. Whether adorned to proclaim an identity or to steel her flesh, forced upon her or cast aside in compliance with an imposed covenant, Jeanne's attire ultimately, and fatally, (re)aligned her body with the signs of heresy.

[27] Ibid., 160–161.

While Jeanne's persecutors carefully orchestrated her subsequent execution, they again failed to silence her. Even as she burned, la Pucelle contested the means by which others had proclaimed her meanings. Pronouncing her faithful service to God, Christ, the Holy Spirit, and the Virgin Mary, she reiterated her divine narrative and cast herself as a Christian martyr. These appeals, along with her spectacular suffering, moved witnesses to tears.[28] Jeanne's body continued to produce meanings postmortem and in absentia: moments after she fell silent:

> The fire was raked back, and her naked body was shown to all the people, with all the secrets that could or should belong to a woman, to remove any doubt from the people. When they had looked upon her as long as they wanted, her dead body bound to the stake, the executioner got a large fire going again under her poor carcass, which was promptly engulfed, and her bones and her flesh were reduced to ashes.[29]

It is an incredible image: this body subject to interrogation and speculation even in death. It is also a fantasy, one wherein Jeanne's 'naked' figure serves as the transcendental signifier of, and epistemological bedrock for, her social and religious meanings. Thus, even as this witness proclaims all 'secrets' exposed and 'doubt[s]' removed by the spectacle, his subsequent comments belie any such resolution: 'there were many people there, and elsewhere, who said that she had been martyred for her true lord. Others said that she was not, and that the one who looked after her for so long had acted evilly.'[30] Readers are left only to imagine that body of evidence—in its flesh, bone, and contested meanings—somewhere amidst those clamorous voices.

Staging 'Proof': Shakespeare's Joan de Puzel

Nearly one hundred and fifty years later, English playgoers would encounter a new incarnation of 'Joan de Puzel' on the London stage. In his famed spectator's account of *The first Part of Henry the*

[28] Ibid., 165–166.
[29] *Journal d'un Bourgeois de Paris, 1405–1449*, reprinted in C. Taylor, *La Pucelle*, 233.
[30] Ibid., 234.

Sixth, Thomas Nashe recalls the wonder with which audiences experienced the renaissance, the 'new birth',[31] of John Talbot in that 1592 production:

> How would it have joyed braue Talbot (the terror of the French) to thinke that after he had lyne two hundred yeares in his Tombe, hee should triumphe againe on the Stage, and have his bones newe embalmed with the teares of ten thousand spectators at least (at seueral times) who in the Tragedian that represents his person, imagine they behold him fresh bleeding.[32]

For Nashe, the spectacle suggests the imaginative and affective possibilities of late sixteenth-century English dramaturgy: players and companies can, he implies, reincarnate the heroic dead for contemporary audiences. Such embodied *exempla*, he further suggests, can inspire English masculine virtue: Talbot's triumphant 'bleeding' bodies offer sharp 'reproofe to these degenerate effeminate dayes of ours'.[33] Yet while Nashe celebrates Talbot's virile resurrection, he elides the simultaneous reincarnation of Joan de Puzel, Talbot's stage nemesis. How audiences received this 'English Scourge', returned to human form, goes unremarked (1.2.129).

Nashe's silence proves especially significant given that it is Joan, not Talbot, who largely triumphs onstage. French and English characters may incessantly proclaim Talbot's heroic status, but this 'scourge of France' (2.3.14) spends most of his reincarnation confused and 'fresh bleeding'. That he does so largely at Joan's hand, and by way of her rhetorical puissance, reflects a dialectical figuration central to the play's examination of embodiment-as-process. While scholars have long situated the pair in binary opposition, this approach uncritically reproduces a logic of embodied difference that the play queries. This governing ideology is given voice, and assumes theoretical form, in Talbot's famed distinctions of 'shadow' and 'substance'.[34] Speaking to the Countess, the English hero proclaims himself an idea or essence irreducible to

[31] 'Renaissance', in Cotgrave, *A DICTIONARIE OF THE FRENCH AND ENGLISH TONGVUES*, sig. yyy4v.

[32] Nashe, *Pierce Penilesse HIS SVPPLICATION to the Diuell*, sig. F3r.

[33] Ibid., sig. F3r. On gender and nationalism in Shakespeare's history plays, see especially Rackin, *Stages of History*; Howard and Rackin, *Engendering a Nation*.

[34] *King Henry VI, Part 1*, 2.3.35–62. On Talbot's 'shadow' and 'substance', see Mullaney, *The Reformation of Emotions in the Age of Shakespeare*, 94–143.

material embodiment: 'what you see', he tells her, referring to his physical body, 'is but the smallest part / And least proportion of humanity' (2.3.51–52). It is a metaphysical logic, if not also 'humanity', presented as foreign to the Countess and inapplicable to Joan. Yet while Talbot and his compatriots incessantly locate their French counterpart in terms of her mortal coil, how Joan does and does not confirm this logic fuels the play's historical and representational inquiries. Indeed, as *The first Part of Henry the Sixth* explores how bodies assume meanings and how meanings are embodied, Shakespeare's early modern Joan reveals how a different culture and media grappled with, and attempted to make sense of, this 'Excellent Puzel' (1.2.110).

Early in the second act, Burgundy gives voice to the play's central mystery: 'But what's that Puzel, whom they term so pure?' (2.1.20). His interrogative reviews Joan's early victories onstage, if not also a seemingly unimaginable chapter of English history wherein a peasant woman led Charles VII's armies to repeated victories over the forces of Saint George. Punning on puzzle/pucelle and the power to 'term', moreover, Burgundy discloses one of the play's dominant strategies for resolving Joan's puzzling status: 'they' will locate Joan in the 'term[s]' of her sexual and gendered substance. He speaks, presumably, of the French, whom playgoers have seen debate Joan's excess meanings. In that earlier episode, the Bastard of Orleans inaugurates the play's dominant *leitmotif* by proclaiming Joan's substance in—and as—profusion:

Bast: A holy maid hither with me I bring,
Which by a vision sent to her from heaven
Ordained is to raise this tedious siege
And drive the English forth the bounds of France.
The spirit of deep prophecy she hath,
Exceeding the nine sibyls of old Rome:
What's past and what's to come she can descry. (1.2.51–57)

However laudatory, the Bastard's description serves less to codify than to confound: a 'holy maid' who exceeds the 'nine sibyls of Rome', Joan is an 'ordained', martial, vocal, and prophetic woman. Her contradictions and allusions only proliferate as the scene continues: the Dauphin alone compares her to the Amazons, the biblical Deborah, Helen of Constantine, Mohammed, Venus, and Saint Philip's daughters (1.2.104–145). Male and female, mythical and biblical, maid and mother, daughter and wife: Joan emerges amidst a patchwork of names and absent bodies, figuring in language what the boy actor who played her would embody onstage: a surplus sign that incorporates the contradictions of purity, nubility, and sexual availability encoded in Burgundy's 'Puzel'. But does Joan incorporate such contradictions? If so, how and to what ends? The Bastard's proleptic figuration certainly channels attention towards Joan's staged body, but how she negotiates these corporeal and discursive selves, how her tactics unravel Talbot's metaphysical logic, and how the play attempts to stabilize this dissonance reveal what scholars have overlooked: that it is Joan in whom relations of shadow and substance achieve their fullest expression in the play, and through whom relations of language, body, and embodiment-as-process are puzzled out.

However broad and contradictory, the Bastard proposes an initial field of intelligibility for deciphering Joan's meanings. As if aware of these definitional desires, Joan immediately clouds the boundaries of legibility and inscrutability. She begins by ventriloquizing English critiques of her 'contemptible' origins, gender, and education: once 'black and swart', she has transcended a base and racialized estate solely through the blessing of 'Gods Mother' (1.2.75–84).[35] Now beautiful, chaste, and transparent ('Ask me what question thou canst... and I will answer unpremeditated', 1.2.87–88), Joan re-presents herself as the feminine ideal materialized: a conceptualization that encourages attention to, and comparison with, the perceived 'beauty' of 'her' sword-bearing body. Where this feminine aspect proves all the more complicated when Joan seemingly 'exceed[s]' her 'sex' in combat with the Dauphin, she immediately translates these actions in submissive terms: 'Christ's Mother helps me, else I were too weak' (1.2.86–106). Again ventriloquizing patriarchal rhetoric, she construes an identity less binary than labyrinthine by trafficking in the languages of expectation and the signs of exception.

[35] For a brief but incisive reading of Joan's 'newfound whiteness', see Little, Jr, 'Re-Historicizing Race, White Melancholia, and the Shakespearean Property', 90–91.

'Joan' is, of course, a fictional character conceived by English writers. I do not argue that her dissident tactics were intentionally written or even imagined at the time, but rather that these possibilities reflect that culture's difficulty in conceiving, articulating, and containing her significance—especially according to contemporary logics of gender and embodiment, and especially when given embodied form onstage. It is thus especially significant that a concurrent discourse emerges in this first scene, as Joan's interlocutors reconfigure her feats through the 'intelligible' logic of feminine lasciviousness and disorder. When she proclaims holy virginity, the Dauphin reads her as an erotic object: 'Impatiently I burn with thy desire' (1.2.108). When she negotiates with Charles, Alençon warns 'These women are shrewd tempters with their tongues' (1.2.123). When she routs English troops in battle, Talbot disparages her as a 'witch' and 'strumpet' (1.5.6–12). Much like Burgundy's proleptic description, this compulsive commentary seeks to stabilize Joan's excess significance through the repetition of terms and paradigms, a protracted strategy that depends less upon discrete illocutionary utterances than incessant perlocutionary proclamations, as if the English might smother her beneath the slanderous sediment.

However disparaging, this concurrent discourse amplifies Joan's substance early in the play; as the terms and voices surrounding her accrue, she appears less linguistically diminished than existentially expansive. As if the true embodiment of Talbot's metaphysical vision, she is body and discourse, partaking of both yet irreducible to neither. Rather, it is Talbot's substance that appears at risk when he faces this female potentate: 'Where', he vexes, 'is my strength, my valour and my force?' (1.5.1). Struggling to make sense of Joan, he hurls terms in her direction, only to be dismissed as if an overly imaginative child: 'Come, come', she chides, ''tis only I that must disgrace thee' (1.5.8). Scorning his 'strength' while displaying her own, Joan leaves a bewildered adversary in her wake. 'My thoughts are whirled like a potter's wheel', Talbot says, 'I know not where I am nor what I do' (1.5.19–20):

> A Witch by fear, not force, like Hannibal,
> Drives back our troops and conquers as she lists:
> So bees with smoke and doves with noisome stench
> Are from the hives and houses driven away.
> They called us, for our fierceness, English dogs;
> Now like to whelps we crying run away. (1.5.21–26)

Cognitively undone, Talbot spews metaphors that approach catachresis: a 'Witch ... like Hannibal' has achieved tangible victories. Conquering with apparent ease, Joan exposes Talbot's 'English dogs' as 'whelps', 'bees', and 'doves'. She appears less like 'Circe', as York later proclaims her (5.2.56), than 'smoke' itself: something simultaneously material and evasive, substantial and evanescent but poisonous nonetheless. As if extracting Talbot's virility, Joan scythes the English imagination and secures material results; she 'conquers', while he teeters on the brink of dissolution (1.5.2).

The next scene approaches the dangerous apex of allusive language in Elizabethan England. Having 'performed her word' in battle, Joan is recognized by the Dauphin as a female head of state: she is 'Astrea's Daughter', the emblem of a new golden age and, as the substitute for 'Saint *Dennis* [sic]', the heir apparent of church and state (1.5.42–68). As her unspeakable likeness to Elizabeth I lingers in the air,[36] English forces quickly reunite onstage, rallying to the '*Cry*, "S. George, a Talbot"' (2.1.38). Talbot furthermore appears both before and after Charles's uncanny allusions, as if bookending any disquieting resonances. Reiterating the terms of Joan's disobedience, moreover, he works to reassure audiences that this 'maid' will, ultimately, prove familiar in language. This strategy achieves sharper focus in the following scene, when Burgundy utters his pivotal inquiry:

Bur: But what's that Puzel, whom they term so pure?
Tal: A maid, they say.
Bed: A maid? And be so martial?
Bur: Pray God she prove not masculine ere long—
If underneath the standard of the French
She carry armour, as she hath begun.
Tal: Well, let them practise and converse with spirits.
God is our fortress, in whose conquering name
Let us resolve to scale their flinty bulwarks. (2.1.20–27)

As before, Joan disrupts English syntax: her dissonance manifest in Bedford's caesura, 'A maid? / And be so martial?'. Yet just as the men appear locked in their binary logic, hoping 'she prove not masculine ere

[36] Marcus, *Puzzling Shakespeare*, 51–105; Hodgdon, *The End Crowns All*, 44–99; Schwarz, *Tough Love*, 79–108.

long', Talbot begins to hone their interpretive paradigms, reiterating an earlier reference to witchcraft (1.5.5–6) that enables new forms of evidence to be materialized onstage.

Such evidence appears increasingly necessary, for while these rhetorical and conceptual moves appear to work—the men are quickly 'Agreed' and return to battle (2.1.33)—they do so in the absence of Joan's body. Their words thus appear less corporeal weapons or transcendental signifiers than cultural and conceptual tools that she must continually navigate. It is a laborious strategy, for both sides, as Joan proves more Teflon than 'trull' (2.2.28). Whereas the 'cry of Talbot' serves Englishmen like a 'sword' that hews Frenchmen on the fields of battle (2.1.78),[37] no singular term lacerates her substance; instead, Englishmen and Frenchmen alike hurl numerous slurs in her direction, proclaiming Joan:

> deceitful dame, witch, damned sorceress, vile fiend, shameless courtesan, foul fiend of France and hag of all despite, lustful, damsel, railing Hecate, Puzel, giglot wench, damsel of France, ugly witch, Fell banning hag, enchantress, miscreant, sorceress, Graceless, wicked and vile, cursed drab, Strumpet, foul accursed minister of hell.[38]

Such uncanny echoes of Hall, de Fauquembergue, and others, underscore the impossibility of fixing Joan in a single term and, as such, the need to smother her in terms of disparagement. They also raise new questions regarding the relations of signification and embodiment, especially where Joan's notorious final scenes appear to offer dramatic 'proof' of her 'accursed' status (5.2.28, 5.3.91).

Prior to her summoning and condemnation, the semantic field encircling Joan accrues in marked tension with her expansive puissance. After she confounds Talbot, Joan oversees victories at Rouen and Bordeaux, the deaths of Talbot and his son, and the defection of Burgundy, a rhetorical victory that highlights her command of affective language. Submitting to Joan's entreaty, Burgundy confesses 'these haughty words of hers / Haue battered me like roaring cannon-shot' (3.3.78). Such verbal authority contrasts with English linguistic impotence; when Lucy eulogizes Talbot as the 'great Alcides of the field', Joan

[37] I am indebted to Andrew Bozio for this insight.

[38] 2.1.50, 3.2.37–119; 4.4.153, 5.2.51–65, 5.3.1–91. See also the many 'positive' monikers applied to Joan, with presumed irony, by Joan's persecutors in Act 5, scene 3: 'maid', 'holy maid with child', 'girl', and 'virgin pure' (5.3.55–83).

juxtaposes his 'silly stately style' with the body that 'Stinking and fly-blown lies here at our feet' (4.4.172–188). English playgoers like Nashe may remember, and reiterate, Lucy's proclaimed meanings, but above this 'Stinking and fly-blown' corpse, Shakespeare places Joan.

Joan's dissidence underscores Lucy's blindness: his inability to see the messy, once living human body that lies before him. But her mockery also poses a threat: one that scorns a patriarchal illogic which celebrates a disembodied Talbot while insisting that Joan be reduced to a base, material body of evidence. Indeed, just as Lucy attempts to transform Talbot into pure discourse, the play seeks resolution in the material proof of Joan's maleficence. This strategy, which begins with Talbot's allusion to witchcraft, is further enacted in the famed summoning scene, where, according to the Folio stage directions,[39] Joan's 'familiar spirits' materialize onstage yet fail to do her bidding (5.2.31). For Joan, their 'speedy and quick appearance argues proof / Of [their] accustomed diligence to me' (5.2.29–30). For London playgoers, their 'appearance' is offered as 'proof' of Joan's demonic status. As she goes on to offer her 'body, soul, and all' for assistance (5.2.43), the scene further dramatizes the type of incriminatory self-proclamation desired by Rouen's clerics. Yet just as this staging works to codify Joan's excess meanings in 'familiar' terms, it secures such knowledge by way of obvious paradoxes. First, and as at Rouen, the exchange affirms Joan's linguistic authority in the very processes of evacuating it. Second, it secures her abjection by violating a central tenet of Protestant reform: the evidence presented onstage—the very materiality of Joan's 'spirits'—'argues proof' precarious for Protestants playgoers to accept.[40]

These unsettling contradictions help explain Joan's subsequent denigration at the hands of the English court. Already 'condemned to burn' as a 'sorceress' (5.3.217), why is she subjected to further condemnation? Without precedent in the source materials, this dramatic censure includes an especially strange encounter with Joan's supposed father, a *pater-ex-machina* to whom she must 'Kneel down and take [his] blessing' (5.3.43). A French shepherd working in collusion with the English nobility, he makes sense only as a symbolic figure, whose subsequent

[39] Shakespeare, *The first Part of Henry the Sixt[h]*, TLN 2433.

[40] On ghosts and demons on the Protestant stage, see especially Greenblatt, *Hamlet in Purgatory*. Should Joan's fiends not materialize in a given adaptation, as is often the case in contemporary representations, such an absence further underscores the problematic relations of evidence and indictment examined throughout the play.

denial by Joan—'Thou art no father, nor no friend of mine'—provides, according to York, further proof of her 'Wicked and vile' nature (5.3.9–16). Having materialized her familiars, bartered her soul, and performed daughterly disobedience, it would appear that Joan finally can be excised. As if settling her ambiguities, this 'father' goes on to link Joan's discursive and corporeal selves, associating paternal disobedience with sexual incontinence to demand an end to her puzzling body: 'Dost thou deny thy father, cursed drab? / O burn her, burn her, hanging is too good' (5.3.33–34).

By way of response, Joan immediately inverts the subject(s) of inquisition, turning this paternal rhetoric of feminine incontinence back upon her persecutors. Reasserting a right to self-proclamation ('First let me tell you whom you have condemned'), she castigates an English imaginary that insistently sexualizes her body and cannot envision her authority 'but by help of devils':

> But you, that are polluted with your lusts
> ...
> Corrupt and tainted with a thousand vices,
> Because you want the grace that others have,
> You judge it straight a thing impossible
> To compass wonders but by help of devils.
> No—misconceived, Joan of Aire hath been
> A virgin from her tender infancy,
> Chaste and immaculate in very thought,
> Whose maiden-blood, thus rigorously effused,
> Will cry for vengeance at the gates of heaven. (5.3.36–53)

As if reflecting back upon her own reception throughout the play, Joan acknowledges the discourses that have preceded and followed her but tactically reverses the terms of sexual transgression: it is 'you' who are stained, lustful, and graceless, 'you' who possess a 'polluted' imaginary that reads her as impossible, permeable, feminine, and demonic. Moments after the signs of witchcraft materialize onstage, Joan unsettles the play's own interpretive practices: what, exactly, have playgoers seen? What have they 'misconceived?'

The associations of witchery and whoredom are especially important given that scholars have overwhelmingly represented Shakespeare's

Joan as a 'diabolic whore'.[41] Yet if the early modern stage could materialize her demonic shades, what then demonic shades, what then of her sexual substance? How does this portrait of whoredom materialize? At Rouen, inquisitors examined Jeanne's hymen and executed her as a heretic. On the London stage, Joan offers 'body, soul, and all' to secure French 'glory', only to be refused. When York demands her 'execution' (5.3.54), she redefines herself in his terms: recognizing her entrapment, she draws upon the terms figuring her circumscription to plead for life. While such statements appear to configure her as intelligible, Jeanne leverages them in a manner that her implicates her oppressors in the very conceptual work—in whoredom as a knowledge relation—necessary to puzzle out her confounding status. Appealing for mercy, Joan stresses her feminine 'infirmity', and then requests the 'privilege' of pregnant recusal as 'warranteth by Law'. When both are denied, she claims the status of an elite mistress (5.3.60–78).[42] By interpellating herself according to the contradictory dictates of early modern femininity, that is, Joan traps her English oppressors in a series of double binds: if playgoers believe her female infirmity, her claims support the accusation that her persecutors possess 'unrelenting hearts'; if they assume her promiscuity, her claims to pregnancy bear some validity—and thus her execution represents a violation of religious and secular 'law'; if they suppose her virginity, the dialogic exchange exposes a strategic interpretive practice that can only fantasize and abject Joan in sexualized terms. As York himself declares, 'She and the Dolphin have been ingling. / I did *imagine* that would be her refuge' (5.2.68–69, emphasis added).

Often taken as a reference to sodomy,[43] York's 'ingling' juggles multiple resonances,[44] queering the English sexual imaginary.[45] But it also

[41] H. Bloom, *Shakespeare*, 45.

[42] As Kay Stanton (See 'A Presentist Analysis of Joan, La Pucelle', 113) notes, Joan's potential sexual partners occupy successively higher positions in the social hierarchy: a progression that, in my terms, suggests tactical alterations throughout Joan's final moments.

[43] Burns, *King Henry VI, Part 1*, 275–276 (5.3.68 n.); see also Bray, *Homosexuality in Renaissance England*, 53–55.

[44] On the play of 'ingles', 'enghles', 'angles', and 'English' in the period, see Parker, *Shakespeare from the Margins*, 143–147. As Burns notes *King Henry VI, Part 1*, 275 n. 68), the term appears as iugling ('juggling') in the First Folio.

[45] The phrase's queer inflections remind us, moreover, that sodomitical allusions encompassed a range of possible relations and pleasures in the period, including, but not

suggests how Joan's imagined embodiment incessantly puzzles the very terms through which she has been proclaimed. Early in the play, Joan proclaims 'Glory is like a circle in the water, / Which never ceaseth to enlarge itself / Till by broad spreading it disperse to nought'. A metonym for reputation or substance or language or puissance, 'Glory' refers as much to Joan as to the 'English circle' she subsequently identifies (1.2.133–136). It is a fitting image for Joan's ephemeral authority but also for an embodied self that, in its shadow and substance, suggests what cannot be fully codified, contained, or excised in either language or body. Talbot claims that his substance transcends the corporeal yet dies onstage and is forgotten as the tetralogy proceeds. Joan persists beyond the frame of the play, not only as a potential phoenix reborn in Margaret,[46] but as a figure for tactical manoeuvre, self-proclamation, and resistance within a constricted cultural imaginary. Proclaiming her own exit from the drama ('Then lead me hence'), she leaves a portentous 'curse' in her wake (5.3.86), words that linger in place of an absent body. Where Joan's representation in *Henry the Sixth* thus depicts the cultural labour necessary to 'argue proof' of gendered embodiment in early modern England, it likewise queries just what is materialized—or made known—through such practices, and how such knowledge itself depends upon a series of fraught relations between the terms, bodies, and processes through which disparate historical cultures attempt to out her 'substance'.

Proclaiming the 'Slut Underneath': Joan and the Critical Imaginary

Students are often surprised to encounter Joan de Puzel in *The first Part of Henry the Sixth*, unaware that Shakespeare participated in shaping her extended historical legacy. Far less familiar than Juliet or Cleopatra, less notorious than Lady Macbeth, she is a puzzling figure for them: why haven't they heard of Shakespeare's Joan? This conundrum may reflect Joan's reception within the scholarly and performance traditions: neither

limited to, those of male homoeroticism. On the 'critical tendency to speak of sodomy when one means *andro*sodomy' (306), and evidence for 'gynosodomitical' arrangements in early modern texts, see Daileader, 'Back Door Sex'.

[46] Hodgdon, *The End Crowns All*, 56–59.

one of 'Shakespeare's Heroines' nor his 'Unruly Women',[47] her dramatic representation has been read as a 'virtual parody';[48] an obscene archetype;[49] the 'caricatured' foil for the English Talbot;[50] the sign of women's 'promiscuous sexuality'[51] and Renaissance 'antifeminism';[52] a 'composite portrait of the ways women are dangerous to men';[53] and a 'smudgy cartoon'.[54] Where terminological plenitude signals charactero-logical lack, Joan proves too full of words and too empty of substance.

Yet while scholars critique Shakespeare's Joan as at once too excessive and too empty, they almost universally imagine and proclaim her illicit sexual status in the play. Echoing her assertion—voiced as she begs for life—that she bears the child of Charles, Alençon, or Reignier, scholars declare that Joan 'sleeps with the Dauphin';[55] that the 'reiterated innu-endo of sexual misconduct is made utterly explicit in her confession';[56] and that her 'sexuality is not only demonic but obsessive in its promis-cuity and seeming insatiability'.[57] She is 'a vixen of monstrous preten-sions and ingratitude',[58] as well as a 'polluted...and self-proclaimed harlot'.[59] Although 'an outwardly immaculate virgin', Joan 'turns out to be a slut underneath'.[60] Such imagined sexual plenitude—one scholar cites her 'many lovers',[61] another asserts that she is 'is extremely active in the sheets',[62] and two others suggest that Joan 'claims to have engaged in illicit sexual liaisons with *virtually every member* of the French court'

[47] Jameson, *Shakespeare's Heroines*; Ziegler, *Shakespeare's Unruly Women*.
[48] Riggs, *Shakespeare's Heroical Histories*, 22.
[49] Fiedler, *The Stranger in Shakespeare*, esp. 43–84.
[50] Leggatt, *Shakespeare's Political Drama*, 7.
[51] French, *Shakespeare's Division of Experience*, 39.
[52] Bevington, 'The Domineering Female in *1 Henry VI*', 51.
[53] Kahn, *Man's Estate*, 55.
[54] H. Bloom, *Shakespeare*, 46.
[55] Leggatt, *Shakespeare's Political Drama*, 7.
[56] Riggs, *Shakespeare's Heroical Histories*, 107.
[57] *The Complete Works of Shakespeare*, ed. Bevington, 496.
[58] Saccio, *Shakespeare's English Kings*, 110.
[59] Tricomi, 'Joan La Pucelle and the Inverted Saints Play in *1 Henry VI*', 22.
[60] Marcus, *Puzzling Shakespeare*, 70; see also Nancy A. Gutierrez, who argues that 'Joan's construction as whore...a construction *ever obvious* to the viewing audience', is solidified by the end of the playtext: 'what had heretofore been artifice *becomes reality*' (185, emphasis added), in 'Gender and Value in *1 Henry VI*'.
[61] Fiedler, *The Stranger in Shakespeare*, 64.
[62] Jankowski, *Pure Resistance*, 6.

(emphasis added)[63]—permeates the critical tradition, captivating even queer and feminist critics who have sought to reevaluate this dramatic representation.[64]

The first Part of Henry the Sixth offers clues to how this happens, in part by dramatizing what, following Judith Butler,[65] I call 'strategies of sedimentation': the reiteration and reapplication of slanderous terms to dissonant bodies until they assume some semblance of stability. While the concept of sedimentation acknowledges the possibility for dissident tactics, it stresses the weight of empowered proclamations and the difficulty of navigating one's own embodied meanings, especially when occupying a culturally marginal position. The three 'bodies' discussed above certainly encourage attention to the ways, means, and effects of cultural proclamation, whether by utterance, legal transcript, dramatic playtext, or literary criticism. They also reveal how specific terms ('heretic', 'witch', and 'whore') have performed related cultural work in different cultural contexts, in part by providing medieval, early modern, and even postmodern subjects with familiar paradigms that work to bypass contemporary problems of signification, evidence, and knowledge.

Who proclaims embodied meanings, and to what effects? When viewed as transitive action and cultural process, 'embodiment' encourages reconsideration of the languages, bodies, and discursive practices in medieval and early modern England, but also of our contemporary scholarly lexicons. In his Arden edition of *Henry VI, Part I*, for example, Edward Burns reads Shakespeare's Joan as a 'kind of optical paradox as well as an embodied word-play, as a trick of point of view, like the anamorphic figure that can be read one way as a young woman, the other as a hag'.[66] The claim encourages approaching Joan from oblique or alternative perspectives, yet remains grounded in the very binary thinking that Burns seemingly critiques: describing Joan as 'a summation of binary categories normally seen as discrete—saint/witch,

[63] Howard and Rackin, *Engendering a Nation*, 52; see also Jankowski, who argues that such sexual incontinence likewise indexes Joan's mendaciousness: 'Not only does her claim of pregnancy belie her former claims of virginity, but the shifting list of fathers suggests that Joan has slept with the entire French chain of command' (*Pure Resistance*, 3).

[64] For notable exceptions to this trend, see Schwarz, *Tough Love*, and Jackson, 'Topical Ideology'.

[65] See especially *Bodies That Matter*.

[66] Burns, *King Henry VI, Part 1*, 27.

peasant/gentry, villain/hero, man/woman, virgin/whore', he simply alters the terms of the lexicon, seeing her as an aggregation of binaries rather than a figure who disrupts binary thinking altogether. Such paradoxes suggest an ongoing need or desire to codify Joan in familiar terms: 'the critical controversies surrounding the depiction of Jeanne as Joan Puzel', Burns claims, 'can perhaps be contained if we see the figure' as by parts 'young woman' and 'hag'.[67]

Jeanne's discursive tactics at Rouen encourage an alternative approach, one that attends less to the 'substance' of historical figures and their varying representations than to the cultural terms and processes through which embodied meanings are materialized and contested. Rather than lamenting, as Burns does, that Joan 'cannot be read as a substantive realist character, a unified subject with a coherent single identity',[68] we might see her bodies and selves as querying precisely those needs—historical, cultural, and epistemological—served by proclaiming such 'coherence' in the first place. What is at stake in the puzzling out of Jeanne la Pucelle? The voices of Rouen, *The first Part of Henry the Sixth*, and scholarly accounts of Shakespeare's play suggest not simply the work inherent to the production of 'identity' and 'character', but also that of embodiment and epistemology: the ongoing, exhaustive labour necessary to press the culturally inexplicable into resolution, into familiar terms and bodies that purport to bypass the 'puzzles'—the interpretive impasses[69]—that non-normative lives represent to governing regimes of intelligibility, and by which the latter's contingency can be revealed and their hegemony contested.

As she departs the stage of Shakespeare's history, Joan de Puzel is again trailed by language, York's portentous curse lingering in her wake as if filling the space absented by her troubling body: 'Break thou in pieces, and consume to ashes, / Thou foul accursed minister of hell' (5.3.92–93). As this staged body disappears from view, ever moving beyond language that seeks to contain it, we are left to consider how—in what terms and bodies and guises, through what practices and acts of proclamation—she will be put back together again.

Shakespeare and the Making of English Whoredom. Stephen Spiess, Oxford University Press.
 DOI: 10.1093/9780191851223.003.0003

[67] Ibid., 26–27.
[68] Ibid., 26.
[69] see *OED*, *puzzle*, *verb*, 2a.

3

The Times of Whoredom

> There is nothing contrary to the mercifulness of truth, or inconsistent with Christian faith, in a harlot leaving fornication, and becoming a chaste wife.
>
> Saint Augustine, *Contra Faustum* (*c*.400)[1]

> *Bellafront*: A woman honest first and then turn whore,
> Is, as with me, common to thousands more;
> But from a strumpet to turn chaste: that sound,
> Has oft bin heard, that woman hardly found.
>
> *The Honest Whore, With, the Humours of the Patient Man, and the Longing Wife (1604)*[2]

In 1589, Ursula Shepherd appeared on the steps of Saint Mary Wollchurch, London, to repent her whoredom. 'Good people', she began:

> I doe here before God and yow all confesse that whereas I have been a marryed wife unto Henry Shepherd for the space of twentie yeres I (forgetting god and my dutye unto my husbande) have committed adultery and playde the harlott with one Richard Mathewe my servant nowe of late tyme And for the same I am by order of law devorced from my husband and enjoyned to do this my pennance And therefore I desire yow all to take example of me and I doe promise herafter to lead a chaste life.[3]

Shepherd's story putatively ends here: this public confession represents the last, indeed only, trace of her lived existence. In this, her tale proves

[1] *Contra Faustum*, XXII.80.

[2] Dekker and Middleton, *The Patient Man and the Honest Whore* (ed. Mulholland), 9.206–210.

[3] Gowing, *Domestic Dangers*, 40.

emblematic rather than exceptional; as with most lives documented in London's ecclesiastical court records, Shepherd surfaces only briefly, then disappears from view.[4] We might say that her narrative ends in chastity: we know nothing of her life after whoredom. Yet her tale discloses several aspects central to what I have called the making (and unmaking) of English whoredom: the ongoing cultural and discursive labour through which a specific social formation worked to craft and sustain an epistemology of the whore. Some of these facets are well known, but worth repeating. First, these episodes reflect the decidedly *public* nature of women's sexual reputation in early modern England: whether an aristocrat or commoner, a woman's 'honesty' in matters of sex was an issue of public concern and adjudication.[5] From shaming spectacles like carting, parading, pillorying, and whipping to acts of public confession and penance,[6] Londoners employed a variety of formal and informal mechanisms for rendering visible and 'known' the sexually transgressive woman.[7] As the Shepherd spectacle suggests, the inverse also held true: efforts to reclaim one's honourable or licit sexual status required both careful staging and the solicitation of communal assent.

Second, Shepherd's case displays the inherently *dramatic* component of early modern whoredom. By this, I mean not only that the terms of whoredom possessed significant social and symbolic weight, but that their application to individual bodies was perceived and adjudicated through a range of theatrical terms, tropes, and practices. As historian Laura Gowing argues, the 'power of slander lay in the social drama of speaking about sex on the street': to proclaim someone a 'whore'—and, in so doing, to position oneself as an agent of moral authority—required

[4] Ibid., passim. As Susan Amussen points out, any early modern women 'about whom we have more than fragmentary evidence' qualifies, from an historiographic perspective, as an exception to the rule ('Elizabeth I', 200).

[5] In addition to Gowing, *Domestic Dangers*, see Amussen, *An Ordered Society*, esp. 95–134; Capp, *When Gossips Meet*; Jardine, '"Why Should He Call Her Whore?"'.

[6] The literature on shaming spectacles in early modern England is vast. For historical studies of punishments related to illicit sexual behaviour, see especially Gowing, *Domestic Dangers*; 'The Freedom of the Streets'; Walker, *Crime, Gender, and Social Order*; Ingram, *Church Courts, Sex, and Marriage*; 'The Reformation of Manners'; and *Carnal Knowledge*; Ungerer, 'Prostitution in Late Elizabethan London'.

[7] I do not mean to suggest that such meanings were inevitably accepted. While acknowledging the symbolic force and material realities of such rituals, Foucault reminds us that even (and perhaps especially) the most violent of signifying practices cannot ensure what knowledge gets produced through the expressions and inscriptions of power. See especially *Discipline and Punish* See also the responses to Jeanne la Pucelle's public execution, which I discuss on page 118.

a stage and audience.[8] From the streets and doorsteps to the churches and courtrooms of early modern London, efforts to define an individual's sexual status were often carefully orchestrated performances, designed to maximize the symbolic force of public denomination.[9] Appearing before her church during a Sunday service, Shepherd confesses to having 'playde the harlotte', presents herself as an 'example' of wayward conduct, and closes by extending a promise to, and soliciting assent from, an audience of neighbours. The gesture reminds us that conversion, whether religious or sexual, is not simply an individual act or state of being but rather, as with the processes of embodiment reviewing in the preceding chapter, critically relational, in that they require some form of recognition or ratification by others.

Shepherd's penitential drama was also carefully scripted, bespeaking a third and fundamentally *narrative* dimension of early modern whoredom. Derived from the Latin *narrāre* ('to relate, to tell') and *gnārus* ('knowing', 'skilled'), narrative itself incorporates an epistemological relation between telling and knowing, the recounting of tales and the possession of knowledge. To narrate something is to transform seemingly disparate matter—events, experiences, sensations, etc.—into a coherent structure whereby each component part accrues significance in relation to a broader whole to which it contributes. Narrative thus operates as a privileged mechanism through which human experiences are organized and rendered meaningful, often by situating them within

[8] Gowing, *Domestic Dangers*, 71. As Gowing notes, it was women 'most of all, who hunted out whores and called for their punishments' (101), a fact that speaks to one of the many double binds that informed and restricted women's agency within the patriarchal hegemony of early modern England, i.e., critiquing other women was one of the primary means through which women could claim vocal and moral authority. Significantly, Gowing goes on to note that such insults rarely pertained to sexual practices: '[t]he words of slander, ostensibly about sex, turn out to be about almost everything else. The sexual insult of women absorbed and refracted almost every kind of female transgression' (118). On the gender dynamics of sexual defamation in early modern England, see also Boose, 'The Priest, the Slanderer, the Historian, and the Feminist'; Capp, *When Gossips Meet* (esp. 197–200); Orlin, 'Women on the Threshold'; Walker, *Crime, Gender, and Social Order*, 99–112.

[9] See, for example, the case of Ann Symes, who, when accusing a priest of sexual misconduct in 1586, chose to use 'his church as her stage and his congregation as her audience' (Gowing, *Domestic Dangers*, 72–73). On the theatricalism of commercial sex in early modern England, including choreographed presentations before potential clients and acts of voyeurism, see Ungerer, 'Prostitution in Late Elizabethan London'. On conceptual overlaps between theatre and prostitution in the era, see Lenz, 'Base Trade'; Mullaney, *The Place of the Stage*, 135–151.

a preexisting framework through which they can be recognized, apprehended, and 'known' by historical subjects.[10] Shepherd's confession is emblematic in this regard: modified only in the names of those implicated, it follows a common template prescribed for such occasions.[11] Absent are details which might add texture and nuance to her story: the contours of Shepherd's daily life, the character of her relations with Henry and Richard, the quality of her marriage, the nature of her struggles and yearnings, the essence of her pleasures and frustrations. In their place, neighbours are presented with a familiar tale, populated by recognizable figures and established tropes: the wayward wife, the unwitting cuckold, an illicit liaison between mistress and servant, an analogous betrayal of God and husband, a divorce at once literal and symbolic. Shepherd's confession subsumes the personal to the conventional, rendering her experience intelligible to audiences as the manifestation of a common sexual plot. Echoing the narrative techniques adopted by deponents as they strove to shape and contest sexual meanings in London's ecclesiastical courts,[12] it reminds us that epistemological purchase of early modern whore narratives may reside less in their sexual content per se—e.g. the various acts, practices, desires, and identities embedded within the available repertoire of relevant scripts—than in the formal structure(s) through which such content is organized, emplotted, and unfolded in narrative time.

These repeated and conventional aspects of whore narratives disclose an equally critical but as yet underexamined *temporal* aspect of early modern whoredom. As public and dramatic narratives, Shepherd's confession reveals how particular temporalities emerge and conflict at sites of early modern sexual knowing. By temporalities, I refer to the various ways in which individuals and cultures perceive, experience, and record

[10] Polkinghorne, *Narrative Knowing and the Human Sciences*; White, 'The Value of Narrativity in the Representation of Reality.' For a recent collection of essays exploring the intersections of narrative and epistemology, see Warhol and Lanser (eds), *Narrative Theory Unbound*. For a provocative study of the epistemological imbrications of narrative and sexuality in contemporary society, see Roof, *Come As You Are*.

[11] Gowing, *Domestic Dangers*, 40–41.

[12] Ibid., passim. From the deployment of familiar literary and dramatic *topoi*, tropes, and motifs—locked rooms, thin walls, the adoption of disguises, acts of spying, scenes of discovery, absent husbands, lustful wives, treacherous servants, etc.—to the considered selection, ordering, and elision of details, Gowing reveals how records of the bawdy courts were shaped by themes, plots, dramatic conventions, and narrative practices derived from contemporary popular culture.

time: not only as synchronic and diachronic, sequential and progressive, but teleological, recursive, perverse, atemporal, and hybrid, among other temporal orientations. Time moves forward, but this does not entail that our experience of it is inherently sequential (i.e. with each moment logically leading to the next) or episodic (i.e. with each moment equal in value or meaning). Rather, we might find an event meaningful precisely to the extent that it evokes or anticipates a specific endpoint (teleology); repeats, recalls, or turns back towards prior experiences or sensations (recursivity); swerves from or inverts an expected sequence (perversity); appears to suspend or exist outside of time altogether (atemporality); brings together or mingles several temporal orientations at once (temporal hybridity); and so on. As queer and postcolonial critics have argued, how we perceive and ascribe value to the temporal dimensions of a given event, narrative, or culture directly informs the knowledge produced in relation to that object of inquiry.[13]

At the most basic level, the episode described above took remarkably little time: at most, it spanned a few minutes.[14] Such brevity conspicuously contravenes the protracted period that preceded the event: some 'twentie yeres' through which prior meanings had accrued. Thus, while the potential success or failure of Shepherd's narrative revision reflects in part the performative force of a particular cultural practice—public confession—it also speaks to deeper culture beliefs regarding how one's sexual status is or can be known in relation to specific temporalities. For example, does a single, brief event 'make' an early modern whore, cancelling out a long period of sexual fidelity? Conversely, can a moment of

[13] For a useful overview of the turn toward time in queer studies, see Freeman, 'Introduction', and the essays included in *GLQ* 13.2–3 (2007). For an acute analysis of the teleological debate in queer approaches to early modern studies, see Friedlander, 'Introduction'. The paradigmatic study of postcolonial time remains Fabian, *Time and the Other*. On the mixed temporalities of early modern England more broadly, see Harris, *Untimely Matter in the Time of Shakespeare*.

[14] I focus here on the act of confession but acknowledge that Shepherd's penitential performance, broadly speaking, may have taken more time: she may have been required, for instance, to stand before the congregation for the entirety of the church service. It is also possible that she had to perform this penance on multiple occasions. When Shakespeare's son-in-law, Thomas Quiney, 'confessed to having had carnal copulation with [Margaret] Wheeler' in 1616, he was 'sentenced to perform open penance in a white sheet, according to custom, in the church on three successive Sundays before the whole congregation'. Yet as Samuel Schoenbaum notes, this penalty was ultimately reduced to a 5*s* fine. It is therefore possible that Quiney did not perform this public act of penance. See *William Shakespeare*, 293–294.

penance 'unmake' that sexual status, turning a whore back into a chaste wife? Or does duration matter—can an extended period of either chastity or whoredom, for instance, solidify that sexual status, thereby making it harder to undo or cast doubt upon?

In narratives of repentant whoredom, such questions of duration (how much time is taken or passes), emplotment (when specific acts or events occur), frequency (how often these acts repeat or reoccur), and ideological weight (the value accorded to these acts respectively and in tandem) are further informed by contemporary logics of sexual sequence (the potential syntactical arrangements through which acts, desires, meanings, and identities might be organized to create coherent sexual meanings in a given culture),[15] teleology (the sexual statuses or 'endpoints' towards which one could, conceivably, advance, as well as how such endpoints reframe, retrospectively, prior meanings and know-ledges), directionality (how and whether one might return to a prior sexual state or condition), and object choice (toward what or whom one's erotic energies could be redirected). Can chastity follow whoredom? Can an individual 'turn back' the sexual clock, so to speak, and become chaste?

Even if Shepherd was successfully 'turned chaste', her conversion remains animated by a temporal paradox: it undoes the putatively rigid teleologic that underwrites women's sexual status in early modern England, wherein whoredom prefigures social, religious, and corporeal death.[16] In place of such expected ends, her narrative turns towards new possibilities, meanings, and knowledge-relations: from degradation to respectability, from incontinence to virtue, from whoredom to chastity. Rewriting the ends of whoredom, it reveals the fiction that such endpoints are fixed or inevitable. Enacting a kind of sexual re-turn,

[15] My thinking here is indebted to Valerie Traub, who demonstrates how approaching sequence as 'a matter of syntactical form... enables access to the construction of meaning, not only through the displacement and substitution of content and tropes, but through temporal and spatial relations'. See *Thinking Sex*, 229–265; citation 256.

[16] In using 'teleologic' (teleo-logic), rather than the more conventional teleology, I aim to foreground the epistemological dimensions of time in its various manifestations and modalities. As a preliminary step, I propose that we reframe these modalities as chronologics: as varying logics—and illogics—of time that circulate within and across specific cultural formations. These logics may prove coincident with, or contradict, other chronologics; they may span multiple discourses and textual domains or prove restricted to specific sites and conditions of possibility; they may work differently across different domains, including those of religion, sexuality, and historiography. They may align with or trouble hegemonic narratives of sex, gender, race, religion, and class.

it progresses backwards from whoredom towards an assumedly prior state of sexual being. As my first epigraph suggests, such transformations were conceivable, at least from a theological perspective: Saint Augustine finds 'nothing contrary to the mercifulness of truth, or inconsistent with Christian faith, in a harlot leaving fornication, and becoming a chaste wife'. And yet, as the literary character Bellafront proposes in my second epigraph from *The Honest Whore*, the conceivable and the probable do not always align: while stories of such conversions, she suggests, have 'oft been heard', such a 'woman [is] hardly found'. Indeed, when Bellafront attempts to 'turn chaste' in this early Jacobean play, Matheo, her former client and future husband, rejects this conversion as a temporal impossibility:

> *Matheo*: Is't possible, to be impossible: an honest whore? I have heard many honest wenches turn strumpets with a wet finger; but for a harlot to turn honest is one of Hercules' labours. It was more easy for him in one night to make fifty queans than to make one of them honest again in fifty years.[17] (9.104–109)

Figuring women's sexual status in time, Matheo ascribes divergent timeframes to the practices of turning honest and turning whore. Whereas a single action or somatic response—'wet finger' here indexes the digital stimulation of the vagina, penile ejaculation, and vaginal lubrication, among other possibilities[18]—instantaneously transforms the honest woman into a strumpet,[19] the inverse trajectory is construed as a Herculean task, necessitating a half-century's labour. Bellafront

[17] According to legend, Hercules made love to all fifty daughters of Thespius in a single night, each of whom bore him a son. See Bate, *How the Classics Made Shakespeare*, 216. In *ΓUNAIKEION*, Thomas Heywood provides a slightly different account of tale, arguing 'hee lay with fiftie daughters of *Lycomedes* in one night and got them all with child with forty nine boyes, onely fayling in the last for that prooued a guirle' [sic] (sig. Q2r/172). See also Mammon's desire, in Jonson's *The Alchemist* (1612), that he prove 'as tough / as Hercules, to encounter fifty a night' (2.2.39–40).

[18] As Paul Mulholland notes, additional possibilities include the licking of one's finger, either as a 'come on' or in preparation for insertion into a bodily orifice. See Dekker and Middleton, *The Patient Man and the Honest Whore*, 288.

[19] Bellafront herself advances this logic, decrying, earlier in the play, 'that *minute*—for it was no more, / So soon a maid is changed into a whore— / Wherein I first fell' (6.179–181). See also *MICHAELMAS Terme*, where the Country Wench's Father, upon learning that she has absconded to London, laments 'how soone Maides are to their Ruins won / One minute, and aeternally vndone' (sig. C3v).

thus appears to Matheo a practical impossibility: betraying not only the laws of ontology but those of sexual time.

Struggling to conceptualize an 'honest whore', Matheo conjoins ideologies of sexual time to problems of sexual knowing. We will see how this fraught conjunction is puzzled in *The Honest Whore* in the second half of this two-part analysis. But first, I draw upon Matheo's insight to inaugurate a discussion of the 'times of whoredom': the often-conflicting temporal orientations that underwrite the governing paradigms through which early modern whoredom has been brought into clarity, both in that era and our own. From 'the necessary evil', 'life cycles', 'characters, persons, & types' and 'the fallen woman' to, by way of binary opposition, 'virginity' and 'chastity', early moderns possessed a variety of interpretive frameworks for apprehending the whore's meanings by describing their socio-sexual function, identifying them as a kind of person, situating them in a narrative trajectory, or describing what they are not. Attending to these frameworks, however, reveals tensions and contradictions among the temporal orientations subtending discourses of whoredom. While many narratives, for instance, present the whore as locked in a trajectory of inexorable degradation with death as its telos, other whore narratives reveal cyclical patterns, privilege sudden reversals, and/or place whoredom outside human time altogether. These chrono-logics can diverge from or contradict one another; at other times, they overlap with, borrow from, and/or reinforce one another. Rather than evacuating their cultural purchase, the unrationalized coexistence of mixed temporalities that underlie these frames are essential to their cultural and explanatory appeal, affording multiple methods of securing whoredom's meanings in lieu of any fixed or stable essence.[20] In other words, this chapter unfolds the process by which whoredom's temporal complexity creates the terms both for its discursive making and unmaking.

As with the ever-proliferating 'terms of whoredom' charted in Chapter 1, and the manifold practices of proclamation traced out in Chapter 2, this conglomeration of explanatory frameworks reflects the exhaustive discursive labour necessary to demarcate the early modern

[20] My thinking about the 'unrationalized coexistence' of contradictory logics is indebted to Sedgwick, *Epistemology of the Closet*, 47 and passim, and Friedlander, *Rogue Sexuality in Early Modern English Literature*, esp. 11.

whore, as well as the various fissures and contradictions upon which any such knowledge depends. But it also, by channelling attention to the often-explicit temporal considerations that inform early modern thinking about whoredom, reveals an animating tension between sexual narrativity and sexual time: just as narrative depends upon a theory (or theories) of sexual temporalities, the latter's labile and shifting nature threatens to undo the conceptual stability that narrative traditionally aims to secure.

The Necessary Evil

Derived primarily from the writing of Saint Augustine, developed by Saint Thomas Aquinas, and debated well into the seventeenth century, the 'necessary evil' is a socio-sexual illogic that concomitantly condemns and legitimates prostitution as a practice essential to the maintenance of a sexually healthy polity.[21] Construing male lust as irrepressible and thus as a never-ending threat to social order, it concurrently figures that desire within a cyclical framework of accretion and release—one whose organic, almost rhythmic temporal character, as we shall see, diverges markedly from the teleologic that governs the sexual time of honourable women as well as the atemporality that the necessary evil ascribes to the figure of the whore. As receptacles or 'sewers' into which disorderly male lust can be deposited,[22] the latter figures are positioned outside of human time altogether: always present, fully degraded, they simply persist in a state of non-being. While similar ideologies can be traced back to antiquity,[23] the logic is crisply formulated by Augustine in *De Ordine* (*c*.386):

[21] Bailey, *Sexual Relation in Christian Thought*; Bullough and Brundage, *Sexual Practices & the Medieval Church*; Dever, 'Aquinas and the Practice of Prostitution'. In her analysis of sexual commerce in counter-Reformation Rome, Storey offers an important reminder that 'Prostitution was not just the necessary evil portrayed by city regulations…it was also a convenient source of revenue' (*Carnal Commerce*, 63). As scholars have long noted, the necessary evil was also deployed in defences of usury and theatre. On the former, see Shapiro, *Shakespeare and the Jews*, 99–100; on the latter, see Barish, *The Antitheatrical Prejudice*, 43. Henceforth, subsequent usages of each conceptual logic—unless drawn directly from source materials—will be presented without quotation marks. I adhere to this practice in each remaining section.

[22] Ptolemy of Lucca, *On the Government of Rulers*, 253.

[23] David Halperin, for instance, argues that 'contemporary moralists, both philosophers and comic poets' in classical Athens positioned "(female) prostitution" as a preferable

> What is filthier, uglier, and more disgraceful than whores, procurers, and such-like plagues of humanity? Remove prostitutes from the social order, however, and lust will destroy it. Let them rise to the same status as married women, and you will dishonor matrimony with an unseemly stain.[24]

While Augustine would later attenuate this position,[25] the basic logic introduced here—that prostitution, however 'sordid', helps to ensure a stable sexual polity—would have a long afterlife.

Aquinas plays a pivotal role in this history, both recuperating the Augustinian formulation and extending its cultural and theological purchase. In the *Summa Theologica* (c.1265-1274), Aquinas draws upon Augustine's remark to buttress a broader argument for limited toleration of prostitution, predicated upon a notion of divine sanction for 'certain evils' that operate as bulwarks against greater iniquity:

> [God] allows certain evils to take place in the universe, which He might prevent, lest, without them, greater goods might be forfeited, or greater evils ensue. Accordingly in human government also, those who are in authority, rightly tolerate certain evils, lest certain goods be lost, or certain greater evils be incurred: thus Augustine says (*De Ordine* ii, 4): 'If you do away with harlots, the world will be convulsed with lust.' Hence, though unbelievers sin in their rites, they may be tolerated.[26]

As with his predecessor, Aquinas would elsewhere proffer statements that appear to temper, if not contradict, the logic introduced here.[27] Nevertheless, the notion of a necessary evil—and its conceptual association with these renowned theologians—would prove durable: the 'Augustinian justification' governed a range of state and ecclesiastical

alternative' to 'consenting but unauthorized sex with any female under the legal guardianship of a citizen'. See 'The Democratic Body', 92.

[24] *On Order [De Ordine]*, 65.

[25] Some fourteen years later, Augustine would insist that 'prostitution of women merely for the gratification of sinful passion...is condemned by the divine and eternal law' (*Contra Faustum*, XXII.61).

[26] *Summa Theologica* II-II.Q10.11.

[27] Ibid., II-II.Q32.7, Q62.5, Q87.2, Q118.8. See also *De Perfectione* (*c*.1225–1274), where Aquinas, in a section on male chastity, urges young men to 'chiefly avoid gazing at women, and especially at young ones, lest he be caught by the eyes of a harlot, and lest beauty of form lead him on to unlawful embraces'.

approaches to prostitution in the European middle ages, facilitating its sanction in various jurisdictions.[28]

Such pervasiveness intimates the logic's conceptual appeal: something about the necessary evil gained purchase across a range of cultures. Perhaps this was due to its metaphorical and imagistic dynamism: the vivid language through which it encourages subjects to apprehend the functions and meanings of whoredom. By the turn of the fourteenth century, for instance, one finds Ptolemy of Lucca re-presenting the necessary evil by way of an infamous simile:

> Augustine says that a whore acts in the world as the bilge in a ship or the sewer in a palace: 'Remove the sewer, and you will fill the palace with a stench.' Similarly, concerning the bilge, he says: 'Take away whores from the world, and you will fill it with sodomy.' For this reason, Augustine says that the earthly city made the use of harlots a licit foulness.[29]

The memorable analogy—in its coarse materiality, its fetid inflections—would prove irresistible to early modern writers, many of whom would go on to figure prostitutes, courtesans, and whores as 'but sincks and priuies to swallow in mens filth',[30] 'places of evacuation',[31] a 'Mire, where worse th[a]n Swine doe wallow in.'[32]

But these rhetorical dimensions, for all their force, threaten to elide other kinds of work performed by the necessary evil, including how it situates gendered subjects in sexual time. Significantly, these figurations

[28] Norberg, 'The Body of the Prostitute', 394. See also Karras, 'The Regulation of Brothels in Later Medieval England'; Bullough, 'The Prostitute in the Early Middle Ages'.

[29] *On the Government of Rulers*, 253–254. While Aquinas composed Book I, and apparently contributed to Book II, the final two sections—including Book IV, from which this passage is drawn—have been attributed to Ptolemy. As Ruth Mazo Karras argues, while Ptolemy 'attributes the analogy to Augustine', the trope itself 'is found in none of the latter's works' (*Sexuality in Medieval Europe*, 166 n. 29).

[30] Nashe, *Christs Teares over Iervsalem* (1593), 78.

[31] Coryat, *Coryats Crudities* (1611), 264–265.

[32] Taylor, *A Common Whore*, sig. A3v. As historian Lyndal Roper suggests, it is precisely the dynamism of such imagery that, ironically enough, helped to smooth over the conceptual dissonance that underlies this theo-logic of toleration: 'The tradition of toleration derived from Augustine and Aquinas justified the need for prostitutes in vivid analogy as well, comparing them to a cesspit for a palace. Though dirty in themselves, it was their function to purify a town—without them it would soon become corrupt. The image equated prostitutes with what was dirty and evil, while making men's sexuality appear an uncomplicated urge' (*The Holy Household*, 101). On the cultural and conceptual work performed by rhetorics of pollution, see Douglas, *Purity and Danger*.

do not always correspond to the gender binary but rather produce distinctions that are both intra-categorical (i.e. between respectable women and prostitutes) and inter-categorical (between men and prostitutes).[33] In the Augustinian formulation, for instance, 'prostitutes, procurers, and other pests of that sort' emerge as counterparts necessary to preserve the status and intelligibility of respectable womanhood. The necessary evil thus serves an important epistemological function, enacting and reproducing a diacritical distinction between the licit and illicit woman. At the same time, this distinction is linked to the management of disorderly (male) 'lusts', which must be siphoned off to preserve female chastity. In so doing, the logic distinguishes between (at least) three sexual temporalities: those ascribed to respectable women, to men, and to prostitutes. In terms of the former, the necessary evil thus reinforces what is commonly known as the woman's life cycle of maid, wife and widow, which I address in the next section.

But first, we must note that the necessary evil is predicated upon the assumption assumes that men will pursue premarital, extramarital, and/or non-procreative sexual relations if not provided with an appropriate 'outlet' for their lusts.[34] Whereas medieval and early modern writers elsewhere code lustfulness as an intrinsically female trait and sin, by contrast, the necessary evil implicitly figures lust as intrinsically male.[35] In so doing, it evinces what historian Ruth Mazo Karras has characterized—by way of her own formidable metaphor—as a 'hydraulic model of masculine sexuality', wherein the 'male sex drive' is figured as akin to 'a damned-up river' which 'would build up until it burst its bounds, leading men to seduce or rape the respectable wives of the city', were it not periodically released by recourse to prostitutes. Licensed prostitution thus emerges as a 'logical' solution: a safety valve that allows

[33] Such a template, of course, operates on the presumptive gendering of prostitutes as female—a governing ideological figuration in early modern England that must be acknowledged but not essentialized. Indeed, as the passages by Aquinas and Ptolemy of Lucca suggest, the necessary evil certainly encompasses the possibility of male 'harlots' or 'whores', and thus male-male homoeroticism. As Jennifer Panek suggests, the presence of early modern 'He-whores' intimates a related distinction between 'patriarchal' and 'anti-patriarchal masculinity'. To the extent that the former is associated with erotic moderation and self-mastery, and the latter with sexual stamina and the capacity of repeated ejaculations, such masculinities suggest a related sexual-temporal orientation that necessitates further inquiry. See '"This Base Stallion Trade"'.

[34] Roper, *The Holy Household*, 32.

[35] Rossiaud, *Medieval Prostitution*, 81.

for the periodic release of sexual energies that might otherwise imperil the socio-sexual order.[36]

The necessarily evil therefore envisions male sexual practices as differing in kind—and in time—from those ascribed to respectable women. Figuring sex with prostitutes as a common bodily practice, it situates men within a cyclical sexual temporality. It understands male sexual time, in other words, as patterned, rhythmic, periodic. To the extent that this framework appears compatible with the male subject's (teleological) progression towards licit conjugality, the necessary evil accommodates a sexual-temporal hybridity that affords early modern men greater latitude in their pre- and extra-conjugal sexual practices than their female counterparts.[37] Just as the necessary evil affords multiple temporal frames within which to comprehend male sexual appetites, it positions the prostitute in a different time(line) than her licit counterparts, male and female alike. Divorced from the life cycle trajectory (maid, wife, widow) associated with honourable women as well as the hybrid time ascribed to respectable men, prostitutes in this conceptual frame appear divorced from human time altogether: as cesspools, 'Iakes' [toilets],[38] and 'filthy dripping-pan[s]',[39] they are repositories for male lust, containers into which sin itself might be siphoned off. Always present, inhuman, immutable: they simply persist, locked in their own state of non-being.[40]

[36] Karras, 'Prostitution in Medieval Europe', 245. On the persistence of such thinking well into the twentieth century, see Davis, 'The Sociology of Prostitution'. For an incisive history of the 'safety valve' as an applied interpretive logic, see Stallybrass, 'The World Turned Upside Down'.

[37] One could argue that the formulation ascribes a particular teleology to elite men, wherein premarital, non-procreative sex (but not sodomy) is figured as part of a normative progression towards licit conjugality, which then ceases upon marriage. Yet as the scholarship on the necessary evil makes abundantly clear, the logic was intended not simply as a premarital measure—that is, to protect unmarried women, and to salve the irrepressible lust of unmarried men—but as a prophylactic that syphoned male lust away from the marital bed as well. It also corresponded with a broader misogynist logic which figured women as 'at best but necessary evils', 'necessary harmes', 'needful evils', and 'necessary ill[s]'. These phrases appear in Mendelson and Crawford, *Women in Early Modern England*, 60, and Gainsford, 'Woman,' in *The Rich Cabinet*, Y3r.

[38] Lenton, 'A Prostitute or Common Whore' (in *Characterismi*, 1631), sig. E6. The passage is worth citing at greater length: '[she] may be compar'd to a Iakes, which euery rogue vseth for necessity, and then abhorres it.'

[39] Gainsford, 'A Whore,' in *The Rich Cabinet*, sig. Y6r.

[40] This atemporal figuration may reflect, at least in part, the unique contours of the necessary evil as a socio-sexual logic that channels attention to the toleration of commercial

If the necessary evil thus positioned the whore within a certain atemporality, as outside of time altogether, the cultural logic of the necessary evil itself would prove far more contingent. A central axis of social and religious differentiation in the Protestant Reformation, it would emerge for Martin Luther as a central emblem of Catholic licentiousness and heresy, fit to be abolished.[41] As Luther puts it in *Lectures on Genesis* (1539):

> [O]nce a young man who associates with prostitutes has surrendered his modesty, he will, when the occasion arises, keep away neither from married women nor from virgins. Therefore, lust is increased rather than cured by this means, and it becomes a warrant to sin for those who otherwise would be continent if this opportunity had been denied them. Other and better remedies have been pointed and commanded by God, namely, marriage. Therefore a government which tolerates houses of ill fame should be regarded as heathenish.[42]

Catalysing a lust that cannot fully be satiated, Luther's prostitute traps men in a recursive cycle of incontinence: bound by immodest desires, they cannot progress to towards their 'proper' social and sexual ends. As a remedy, Luther positions marriage as a licit telos for male sexual desire, thereby (re)locating men within a teleologic similar to that which governed women's sexual time.[43]

sex rather than the figure of the whore per se. Allusions to the whore in this model thus tend towards a brief reference or 'snapshot', rather than a diachronic figuration, which—in conjunction with these dehumanizing metaphors—amplifies this sense of atemporal stasis or fixity.

[41] As Susan C. Karant-Nunn and Merry E. Wiesner-Hanks note, Luther 'discusses prostitution in almost every type of writing—lectures, sermons, letters, table talk' that he produced (*Luther on Women*, 138). On the centrality of sex, gender, and marriage to Reformation theology, see Crowther, 'Sexual Difference'; Hull, *Sexuality, State, and Civil Society in Germany*, 17–29; and Roper, *The Holy Household*. On whoredom as a privileged means of articulating religious difference in the period, see Dolan, *Whores of Babylon*; Norberg, 'The Body of the Prostitute'.

[42] Reprinted in *Luther on Women*, 157. See also Luther's earlier *Letter to the German Nobility* (1520): 'Is it not a lamentable thing that we Christians maintain open and common brothels among us, when we are all baptized into chastity? I certainly know what some say about this, that it is not simply the custom of one people and that it would be difficult to end it, that it is better to have such [houses] than to bring married women or maidens or even more honourable people to dishonour. But should not the temporal and Christian government recognize that such evil is not to be prevented in this heathen way?' (ibid., 156).

[43] For a useful overview of Luther's writings on marriage and sexuality, with particular emphasis on its gendered inflections, see *Luther on Women*, 88–170.

Luther's marriage plot neither erased prostitution nor the persecution of those involved in such practices. Nor did it dissolve the temporal differences ascribed to such persons. As Lyndal Roper points out, Luther's moral campaign—by re-narrating relations of sex, pleasure, and marriage—enhanced the marginalization and demonization of prostitutes: no longer licensed, no longer necessary, they came to embody evil itself.[44] For Roper, such a shift facilitated an emergent 'typology of sinners', whereby those who committed certain acts began to be seen as fatally flawed by that sin.[45] As I will argue, a similar kind of typological thinking circulated in early modern England, providing contemporaries with yet another interpretive frame for 'knowing' illicit sex and those who practice it. Indeed, even as Luther pointedly rejects the necessary evil, his language concurrently reiterates its ontological and sempiternal inflections: 'scabby, scratchy, stinking, nasty, and syphilitic', prostitutes are, for him, nothing more than 'poisonous dung-heap[s]' sent by the 'devil' to infect 'good people' each year.[46] Recurring, reappearing, persisting over time: prostitutes remain for Luther, as with Augustine and Aquinas, locked within their own iniquitous (a)temporality.

By the turn of the seventeenth century, English readers were most likely to encounter the necessary evil in anti-Catholic discourses, where it figured prominently to reveal papal iniquity and to forge religious distinctions. From John Jewel,[47] John Bale,[48] Andrew Willett,[49] William Vaughn,[50] and John Downame[51] to Thomas Tuke,[52] Robert Burton,[53]

[44] *The Holy Household*, esp. 89–131. Although Roper is interested in how Reformation ideas about gender, sex, and domesticity altered civic and social life in early modern Augsburg, her analyses of prostitution, I would suggest, bear much in common with the cultural dynamics of Reformation England.

[45] Ibid., 68.

[46] *Luther on Women*, 157–158; see also Luther's ghastly claim that '[i]f I were a judge, I would have such a poisonous syphilitic whore tortured by being broken on the wheel and having her veins lacerated, for it is not to be denied what damage such a filthy whore does to young blood, so that it is unspeakably damaged before it is even fully grown and destroyed in the blood [e.g. poisoned]', 158.

[47] *An Apologie* (1562), sigs F3v–G1r.

[48] *THE IMAGE of both Churches* (1570), sigs Aaa2r, Ccc1v; *The Actes of Englyshe Votaries* (1546), sigs D5r, F7r, H3v.

[49] *AN ANTILOGUE OR Counterplea* (1603), sig. Ii2r.

[50] *The Golden-Groue* (1608), sig. P2r–v.

[51] *A TREATISE AGAINST FORNICATION AND ADULTERIE* (1609), sigs S1r–v, S3r.

[52] *A DISCOVRSE Against Painting and Tincturing of WOMEN* (see WC 275) (1616), sig. H1v.

[53] *THE ANATOMY OF MELANCHOLY* (1628), sig. Cccc4r.

Richard Cooke,[54] and William Camden,[55] writers working across a range of genres and discourses would castigate the papacy's most 'permissiue and toleratiue lawes, for houses of prostitution'.[56] For many, the ongoing toleration of sexual commerce aptly disclosed the church and/or pope's status as the biblical Whore of Babylon. A popular trope, which 'persistently associate[es] the Roman church with fallen women',[57] the Whore of Babylon annexes a teleologic of social and sexual decline associated with feminine errancy. In other words, it draws a metaphorical link between the decline of the Catholic Church and the degeneration of the sexually illicit woman: a paradigm, as we shall see, that assumes a particular shape and form in the figure of the 'fallen woman'. But it also bodies forth an eschatological orientation that encouraged early moderns to perceive and experience their historical present in prophetic and apocalyptic terms. As Victoria Brownlee notes:

> The prominence afforded to the Whore of Babylon in reformed thought emerged as part of a broader commitment to apocalyptic theology, which advocated viewing present circumstances through an eschatological lens.... [I]t was generally accepted that in the final days of history, Satan would persecute the faithful through earthly representatives, such as the Antichrist and Whore of Babylon, until Christ returned and inaugurated the eternal reign of truth.[58]

While irreducible to the necessary evil alone, this conceptual structure and the temporalities that attended it were augmented by contemporary beliefs that the papacy, as Robert Burton puts it, not only 'tolerate[d] and wink[ed] at...Brothel-houses and Stews', but filled their coffers with profits derived from 'Colleges of Courtesans', and then defended such practices as lawful, necessary, and beyond reproach.[59] For many, such audacious 'corruption' offered undeniable proof that the 'Prostitute-Pope' should be perceived not simply as an iniquitous prelate but the embodied 'sign of the impending apocalypse'.[60]

[54] *A White Sheete, Or A Warning for Whoremongers* (1629), sigs E2v–E3r.
[55] *CAMDENS BRITANNIA* (1695), sig. X1r.
[56] Sheldon, *THE MOTIVES of Richard Sheldon* (1612), sig. V4r.
[57] Dolan, *Whores of Babylon*, 52; see also McEachern, '"A Whore at First Blush Seemeth Only a Woman"'.
[58] Brownlee, 'Imagining the Enemy', 214.
[59] *ANATOMY*, III.3.4.2.
[60] Roper, *The Holy Household*, 109.

The necessary evil thus offered medieval and early modern subjects a framework for understanding prostitution and its meanings, one whose conceptual appeal was amplified by the various temporalities attending its governing logic[s], and whose popular association with the papacy rendered it as a central site of reformist critique. Responding to a cyclical or recursive male sexual temporality, it provides a logical 'outlet' for lusts that might otherwise threaten the social and marital order.[61] Figuring prostitutes as the inhuman receptacles for this periodic discharge, it positions them within an inhuman atemporality. As a paragon of Catholic iniquity, it annexes an apocalyptic temporality associated with the biblical Whore of Babylon.

But cultural logics lead curious lives, rarely allowing for such neat and tidy distinctions. Critiques of Catholic toleration of sexual commerce also carried with them the possibility, even the likelihood, of recalling England's own notorious license: the official sanction of prostitution in London until 1546, when the practice was suppressed by royal proclamation. To excoriate the 'baudy house[s] in Rome', William Vaughn confesses, is to remember that 'the stewes of London... [once] were innumerable'.[62] All the more troubling, John Taylor suggests, it is to acknowledge that they remain so, albeit in altered terms:

> The Stewes in *England* bore a beastly sway,
> Till the eight *Henry* banish'd them away,
> And since those co[m]mon *Whores* were quite put downe,
> A damned crew of priuate *Whores* are growne,
> So that the deuill will be doing still,
> Either with publique or with priuate ill.[63]

Laws and ideologies may change, Taylor contends, but whoredom will persist—growing, evolving, reappearing in new shapes and forms. His perspective echoes that offered by Shakespeare's Pompey, who, upon learning that Vienna's suburban brothels have been suppressed by proclamation in *Measure for Measure*, counsels Mistress Overdone to 'fear... not' the demise of her profession: 'good counsellors', he stresses,

[61] Ibid., 32.

[62] *The Golden-Groue*, P3r.

[63] *A Common Whore* (1622), B3r. While framing the Henrician suppression as a partial failure, Taylor nevertheless deploys it to differentiate English and Roman approaches to prostitution. Positioning sexual commerce as a 'Pagan' practice, he notes that 'Christian gouernments these things forbid', except 'where the Pope is Landlord of the game' (B3r).

will 'lack no clients. Though you change your place, you need not change your Trade.'[64] When the constable Elbow mis-labels Pompey and Froth as 'notorious benefactors' just a few scenes later (2.1.49), playgoers may well have conceded the aptness of a malapropism that brilliantly encapsulates the tangled affective legacies of legalized prostitution.[65] They may have agreed with Elbow's uncanny (il)logic, or shared Lucio's conviction that such a 'vice' would be 'impossible to extirp', for it was as common to the human condition as 'eating and drinking' (3.1.365–366).

As these works suggest, English writers and historians would continue to grapple with the necessary evil—both its conceptual appeal and historical relevance—for decades. One finds Thomas Fuller, some forty years later, methodically working through the Augustinian-Thomistic position in *The Church-History of Britain* (1655). In a section addressing the suppression of the '*Stews*' by royal proclamation under Henry VIII, Fuller begins by reckoning with England's own history of 'toleration': 'such filthy persons and practices', he acknowledges, had been 'publicly permitted by the *State*'.[66] Reproducing a section from Stow's *Svrvay of London* (1598), Fuller revisits laws passed during the reign of Henry II aimed at demarcating and regulating practices of sexual commerce in medieval London. Yet where Stow simply notes 'these and many more orders were to be observed upon great payne and punishment',[67] Fuller excavates their underlying logic: such sanction, he contends, was intended to delineate the sex trade from other 'honest' professions, in part to prevent 'simple' labourers from accidently stumbling into the wrong shop and finding themselves 'inveigled into sin'. Lest readers mistake his stance on the official 'toleration of sin', Fuller concludes by pointedly rejecting the necessary evil:

> For though Naturall poysons may by Art be so qualified and corrected as to make them not onely not noxious, but in some cases (as wisely applied) cordial. Yet Morall poysons, I mean, things sinfull of

[64] Shakespeare, *Measure for Measure* (ed. Bawcutt), 1.2.98–107.

[65] In a similar vein, Cocledemoy cites Mary Faugh as a 'necessary damnation' in *The Dutch Courtesan*, 1.2.25–26, while Freevill figures 'common house[s] of lascivious entertainment' as 'most necessary buildings' (1.1.60–62).

[66] Fuller, *The Church-History of Britain* (1655), 239–241. Italics in the original, both here and in all subsequent citations.

[67] Stow, *A Svrvay of London* (1598), 332.

> themselves can never be so ordered and regulated, but that still they will remain pernitious [sic] and unlawfull. The onely way to order and amend, being to *remove* and extirpate them.

One cannot eradicate sin, Fuller contends, by persisting in sin. The necessary evil is for him a pretended necessity concocted by 'bad men' who 'ende[a]voured with arguments to maintain... the necessity, but more the conveniency of such *Brothel-houses*'. Fuller is careful here; he doesn't name specific individuals, nor does he locate the logic within his own historical moment. Rather, he endorses the Lutheran solution, arguing that a 'malady *cannot be accounted* a remedy: *For whilest* Matrimony *is appointed and blessed by God* to cool the heat of *Lust*, Whoredome *doth double the* drought *thereof*'. In so doing, Fuller figures the necessary evil *as* history: as firmly fixed in England's religious and sexual past. Noting that the 'Paramount Whore', i.e. the Roman church, continues to '*tolerate* Whores' in the present historical moment, he stresses that this 'branch *of* popery'—i.e. the official sanction of prostitution as a necessary evil—is '*now banished* [in] England'. For Fuller, English intolerance of sexual commerce marks the nation's spiritual progress: '*more honour it is for us to go before forraign* Nations *in* Reformation, *than to follow them in their* Corruptions.' In its sexual politics, Fuller suggests, England leads the charge to a Christian future.

Yet Fuller's analytical labours belie any such easy chronological distinctions. Not only do his careful refutations intimate the logic's ongoing appeal—particularly as he addresses multiple points 'in favour' of the necessary evil—but as he draws to a close, Fuller confesses that the very distinction between popish toleration and English suppression upon which his argument rests resides more in law than practice. Addressing the contention that '[*t*]*he suppressing of* Stewes *would not make men more chaste, but more close; not more sincerely honest, but secretly wanton*', Fuller admits that such an '*undeniable truth is sadly granted*'. Echoing Taylor, Fuller acknowledges not only that English sexual commerce persisted beyond the royal suppression, but that the very elision of licensed prostitution may have facilitated its growth: '*Perchance there may be now be mo*[*r*]*e* English-folk adulterers' than before.[68] Just as Fuller works to fix the necessary evil in English history, he concedes that

[68] Fuller, *The Church-History of Britain* (1655), 239–241.

the very desires and practices that subtend it likely persist in the present, albeit in new shapes, forms, names, and meanings.

Life Cycles

Augustine and Luther. Aquinas and Fuller. If the voices of the preceding section present opposing perspectives on the necessary evil, they nevertheless are united in the general conviction that the sexual integrity of female virgins and married women must be protected. This shared axiom discloses another prominent conceptual template for apprehending the relations of sex, gender, and embodiment in early modern England. Conventionally known as 'life cycles', these sequential frameworks situate men and women within chronological schemas of successive social identities. Informed by such seemingly incontrovertible factors as age, gender, conjugality, professional status, and reproductive capacity, they offer another common structure for apprehending a subject's socio-sexual identity in and across time. Like the necessary evil, early modern life cycles both differentiate between male and female sexual time and, by positioning whoredom outside the sequential logic of licit femininity, facilitate understandings of the whore (and other abject women) as occupying or existing within a temporal void, outside the ebb and flow of daily life. But they also accommodate other temporal possibilities, including one that figures whoredom less as a definite break from sequential femininity than as a deviation or swerve from the proper order of things that retains the possibility of one's return to normative time. We might call this, following the work of queer critics like Jonathan Dollimore and Valerie Traub,[69] the perverse temporality of early modern whoredom. Governed neither by linearity nor atemporality per se but rather by (the possibility of) movement from the latter to the former, this temporal orientation, as we shall see, sheds new light on the prescriptive force of sequential femininity by

[69] Dollimore, *Sexual Dissidence*; Traub, 'The Perversion of Lesbian Desire'. I adopt the modifier 'perverse', as opposed to the more capacious and un-pathologizing 'queer', both to highlight a specific genealogical debt to the formulations advanced by these two critics and to acknowledge the disciplinary inflections that attended this temporal frame within the early modern period. I am using the term, like they did, in the spirit of reclamation and depathologization. See also Eve Kosofsky Sedgwick's practice of 'perverse reading' (*Tendencies*, 4).

disclosing a kind of temporal stick-and-carrot that associates dissident sexual behaviour with abjection yet promises restoration, so long as the whore in question (re)submits to sequential femininity through marriage. Here as elsewhere, attention to the temporalities of English whoredom helps to reveal the contingency, lability, and gender specificity of prominent cultural logics, but also the disciplinary processes through which such instabilities could be shored up.

In the 1980s and early 1990s, feminist literary critics and social historians drew attention to a sequential logic that situated early modern women within, it was argued, one of three identity categories: maid, wife, or widow. This progressive sequence defined and categorized women in terms of their reproductive capacity, conjugality, and relationships to men.[70] It offered a powerful example of patriarchal ideology, whereby the complexities of women's lives were reduced to a socially restrictive trajectory characterized by sexual status. Those who did not fit within or deviated from this sequential logic—adulterers, prostitutes, and unmarried mothers—were figured as transgressors and subject to various forms of social discipline.[71] For historians and literary critics, the paradigm helped to illuminate a range of ritual, social, and familial practices; revealed governing ideologies of marriage and licit femininity; channelled attention towards those figures, both literary and historical, who troubled easy categorical distinction; and offered traction on the various cultural mechanisms through which such transgressions were adjudicated, punished, and/or allowed to pass.[72] For literary critics, it

[70] For a recent survey on the scholarship of early modern life cycles, see Toulalan, 'Age to Great, or to Little, Doeth let Conception'.

[71] Traub, *Thinking Sex with the Early Moderns*, 112–113. For an important study that challenges the hegemony of the maid/wife/widow paradigm, see Dowd, *Women's Work in Early Modern Literature and Culture*.

[72] Representative historical studies during this first wave of scholarship include Amussen, *An Ordered Society*; Cressy, *Birth, Marriage, and Death*; A. Erickson, *Women and Property in Early Modern England*; and King, *Women of the Renaissance*. Influential works by literary critics can be found in Lenz et al., *The Woman's Part*; Woodbridge, *Women and the English Renaissance*; Neely, *Broken Nuptials in Shakespeare's Plays*; and Jardine, *Still Harping on Daughters*. Important early modern texts are reprinted, with extensive commentary, in Henderson and McManus, *Half Humankind*, Klein, *Daughters, Wives, and Widows*, and Tilney, *The Flower of Friendship*.

Probing homologies and fissures between social prescription and lived reality, scholars have revisited early modern women's life cycles from a variety of productive angles. These include studies that explore alternative temporal categories and frameworks in the period, such as girlhood, childhood, adolescence, menarche, youth, courtship, maternity, menopause, and old age (Higginbotham and Johnson, *Queering Childhood in Early Modern*

provided a lexicon for analysing representations of women, parsing relations between historical reality and literary representation, and theorizing the gender politics of Shakespeare and other playwrights.[73]

Even as the maid-wife-widow triad helps bring certain identities into focus and connects those identities to presumed sexual statuses, early modern marriage contracts, or espousals, suggest how even a putatively rigid framework could accommodate additional temporal orientations. Under English common law, persons interested in marrying could enact a state of conditional matrimony through one of two speech acts: *sponsalia per verba de praesenti* (betrothal by words regarding the present) or *sponsalia per verba de futuro* (betrothal by words regarding the future). The former, when spoken aloud, signalled a shared intention to wed at the present moment; while the marriage would be consecrated in church at a later time, such words were considered legally binding, allowing licit conjugal relations between the couple. The latter phrase, when uttered, indicated a shared intention to marry at a future time and thus remained contingent: it could be broken either by mutual consent or just reason (failure to materialize a dowry, infidelity, disease, etc.). Yet should the couple 'occupy' one another, to adopt a contemporary idiom, *futuro* became *praesenti*—from a legal standpoint, at least, such contracts were

English Drama and Culture; Preiss and Williams, *Childhood, Education, and the Stage in Early Modern England*; Cohen and Reeves, *The Youth of Early Modern Women*; Mendelson and Crawford, *Women in Early Modern England*; Toulalan, 'Age to Great'); trace how the meanings of particular categories, and/or the relations between them, shifted over time (J. Higginbotham, 'Fair Maids'); attend to the lives of single women, servants, and midwives (Froide, *Never Married*; Korda, 'Singlewomen and the Properties of Poverty in *Measure for Measure*'; Dowd, *Women's Work*); map women's alliances within and across identitarian lines (Frye and Robertson, *Maids and Mistresses*); and grapple with the threats posed by desirous widows and adulterous wives (Panek, *Widows and Suitors in Early Modern English Comedy*; Todd, 'The Remarrying Widow'; A. Erickson, *Women and Property in Early Modern England*, esp. 166–222). Others channel attention to the lability of these prescriptive categories (Howard, *Theater of a City*); parse relations between men's and women's life cycles (Cohen and Reeves, 'Introduction', in *The Youth of Early Modern Women*; Wiesner-Hanks, *Gendered Temporalities in the Early Modern World*; Mendelson and Crawford, *Women in Early Modern England*; J. Higginbotham, 'Fair Maids'); and identify alternative paradigms circulating in the period (Menchi, 'The Girl and the Hourglass'; essays by Cohen, Hardwick, and Hubbard in Cohen and Reeves, *The Youth of Early Modern Women*).

[73] On the early modern stage as a privileged venue for troubling the licit-illicit binary and for probing contradictions in patriarchal ideology, see especially Howard, *The Stage and Social Struggle in Early Modern England*. Prominent voices in the 'patriarchal versus feminist bard' debate include Dusinberre, *Shakespeare and the Nature of Women*; McLuskie, 'The Patriarchal Bard'; and P. Erickson, *Patriarchal Structures in Shakespeare's Drama*. On other playwrights, and with special attention paid to representations of prostitutes, see Haselkorn, *Prostitution in Elizabethan and Jacobean Comedy*.

presumed 'sealed' by sexual intercourse.[74] Espousals thus offer fascinating insights into how early moderns navigated the life cycle paradigm in lived time: in some communities, premarital sex was tolerated so long as marriage appeared imminent.[75] Put differently, the tight conjunctions between sexual status and women's approved social identities were somewhat malleable so long as the proper relational, sexual, and identitarian teloi remained intact: that is, as long as young women moved from maidenhood to marriage with the same man and then into widowhood or sometimes into marriage with another man. Exactly when they began to have sex with their intended partner often mattered less than the fact that this sequence was maintained.

Premarital sex nevertheless remained a fundamentally precarious undertaking, especially for early modern women.[76] As Leah Marcus notes, the customary license noted above was not universally recognized, and even couples who intended to marry could find themselves prosecuted for premarital incontinence.[77] Furthermore, while espousal logics suggest that intercourse would instantaneously materialize the marital bond, reality proved far more complicated. Many women who 'became pregnant having assumed that marriage would take place'[78] found themselves neither maid nor wife: their contracts denied, their reputation besmirched, their child declared a bastard. Where men could always deny paternity (or the existence of the verbal contract itself, unless it had been overheard in public), espousals—especially *de future*—could hold different futures for men and women. Certainly, espoused men could be shamed and persecuted for premarital incontinence, but the

[74] Gowing, *Domestic*, 143. See also Ingram, *Church Courts, Sex, and Marriage*, 132–134, 189–219; Cressy, *Birth, Marriage, and Death*, 267–281.

[75] In the ecclesiastical court records reprinted in Hair (*Before the Bawdy Court*), for instance, one finds punishments ranging from the levying of minor fines and performances of public penance to court-compelled marriage and, in cases wherein the accused fail to appear, excommunication. At the same time, several such cases are dismissed due to lack of evidence and/or testimony on behalf of the accused's good character. Some records go so far as to note that, even though premarital fornication has been confirmed, the court will dismiss the charges once the couple gets married.

[76] For examples of contested *sponsalia*, wherein one deponent alleges that 'words of intent' preceded an act of 'carnal connection', but the other denies this charge, see Hair, *Before the Bawdy Court*, entries 344, 414, and 574; citation 142.

[77] Marcus, *Puzzling Shakespeare*, 171–173. See also, Cressy, *Birth, Marriage, and Death*, 277; Hair, *Before the Bawdy Court*, passim.

[78] Ben-Amos, *Adolescence and Youth in Early Modern England.*

consequences for such practices, especially should they result in pregnancy, were significantly higher for women.

Whereas women's life cycles were conspicuously organized around reproductive conjugality, the various 'ages of man' paradigms circulating in the period were governed by a progression from misrule to 'reason, discretion, self-government, moderation, strength, self-sufficiency, and honesty'.[79] In other words, where licit femininity was governed by a sexual teleology, licit masculinity was governed by a behavioural teleology that could accommodate, indeed even incorporate, illicit sexual practices into its sequential logic. Figuring proper male behaviour as learned and honed over time, these paradigms implicitly depict male youth as intemperate, unruly, indiscrete, and sexually licentious.[80] In *Micro-cosmographie* (1628), for instance, John Earle characterizes a 'Young-man' as one who 'conceiues his Youth as the season of his Lust, and the Houre wherein hee ought to bee bad: and because he would not lose his time, spends it',[81] while Francis Lenton, in *Characterismi* (1631), describes 'A Bachelour' as one governed by 'Concupiscence': 'Hee courts each handsome obiect, his veines being full of *Venus*, and his heart of *Cupids* darts'. Significantly, such pursuits do not derail the bachelor's marital prospects: 'ere long, he salutes *Hymen*, and proues an honest man.'[82] As these descriptions suggest, male incontinence could be defended or explained away as a 'pastime, a dalliance... a touch of youth'.[83] It could also, as Ezra Horbury details, be interpreted by recourse to biblical narratives of male prodigality.[84] Thus, while virginity was the necessary precondition for a woman's progression from maid to wife in early modern England, the ages of man could accommodate illicit sexual practices prior to respectable manhood. For men, a season of Lust could preface an age of Honesty. Crucially,

[79] Shepard, *Meanings of Manhood in Early Modern England*, 49. Drawing primarily on medical texts, Shepard identifies six paradigms circulating in the period, ranging between four and seven stages of manhood. See pp. 54–58.

[80] In addition to Shepard, see Fletcher, *Gender, Sex and Subordination in England 1500–1880*; Bailey and Hentschell, *Masculinity and the Metropolis of Vice*. The early sixteenth-century ballad *A most excellent Godly New Ballad* (c.1615) figures whoredom within such a limited temporal frame: 'Whoredom is counted a youthfull sport, / greatly pleasing the letcherous sort, / Not caring whither their soules shall resort'. See *English Broadside Ballad Archive*, entry 36012.

[81] Earle, *Micro-cosmographie*, '31. A Young-Man', n.p.

[82] Lenton, *Characterismi*, sigs. G2–3.

[83] Fletcher, *Gender, Sex, and Subordination in England*, 93.

[84] Horbury, *Prodigality in Early Modern Drama*, esp. 221–256.

however, this progression neither entailed nor necessitated an altered theory of male sexual time; rather, male life cycles remained grounded in a cyclical theory of male sexual time, differing from the necessary evil only to the extent that they associate mature masculinity with a heightened capacity to moderate or govern one's desires.

Women who fall outside of sequential femininity in early modern life cycle discourse are often difficult to locate in space and time. Defined by negation, they emerge in a temporal void: frozen or suspended in a manner that reflects the broader categorical impasses that they body forth. Shakespeare's Mariana (*Measure for Measure*) is emblematic in this regard. Abandoned by her fiancé (Angelo), Mariana slips out of the progression that would see her move smoothly from maid to wife. The victim of a failed *sponsalia*,[85] she exists in a kind of spatial and temporal limbo, passing her days in a 'moated grange' somewhere near Vienna (3.1.265).[86] A musical and melancholic world seemingly far removed from the play's urban centre, this nebulous locale reinforces the notion that Mariana is not only stuck in grief but suspended in space and time. It is as if she cannot exist in Vienna until the Duke (Vincentio) can find a way to restore her to sequential femininity. As is well known, the play resolves this categorical and temporal impasse through a bed-trick: when Angelo demands that Isabella, an aspiring nun, sleep with him, Mariana takes her place, thereby concretizing the prior *sponsalia*. The bed-trick thus not only protects Isabella but allows Mariana to be restored to normative female time by play's end.[87] Significantly, Vincentio

[85] Mariana and Angelo previously had exchanged oaths, which the latter subsequently denied on account of a lost dowry (3.1.215–225). Significantly, Vincentio stresses the temporal gap between oath and marriage when relaying Mariana's story: 'She should this Angelo have married; was affianced to her oath, and the nuptial appointed. *Between which time of the contract and the limit of the* solemnity, her brother Frederick was wrecked at sea, having in that perished vessel the dowry of his sister'.(3.1.215–219, emphasis added). All citations drawn from Shakespeare, *Measure for Measure* (ed. Bawcutt).

[86] While the dialogue situates the grange outside (what appears to be) a local church, 'Saint Lukes' (3.1.264–265), its precise location vis-à-vis the city of Vienna is never established. Her (re)appearance at the city gates in the dénouement suggests that the grange is located either outside or just along the city boundary, further reinforcing her liminal status.

[87] It also underscores how sexual intercourse, when recognized by the 'proper' authorities, can resolve the sexual-temporal opacities of the *sponsalia* discourse and facilitate the transition from maid to wife. As Jennifer Higginbotham points out, however, Mariana's status remains 'complex and liminal; she is a wife and not a wife, and the categories "maid", "wife", and "widow" are insufficient to describe her status' ('Fair Maids', 178).

sanctions this sexual traffic by insisting that it simply concretizes a marriage that already exists: Angelo, he stresses, 'is your husband on a pre-contract' (4.1.70). From the Duke's perspective, therefore, Mariana's abjection is a problem of social rather than sexual time: a 'wronged maid' (3.1.251), she has retained her sexual integrity yet still fallen out of sequence. It is a telling phrase. Struggling to identify Mariana in a manner that protects both her reputation and the tripartite sequence from which she has been expelled, Vincentio creates an adjacent category ('wronged maid') that reveals the limitations of the maid-wife-widow paradigm yet remains wedded to it. Like the moated grange that both is and is not a part of Vienna, the moniker at once reflects and stands outside a structure of sequential femininity.

While Vincentio labours to defend Mariana, other characters remind audiences that her nonsequential status renders her vulnerable—regardless of her actual sexual history—to charges of whoredom. These include Lucio, a local gallant, but also the elusive Kate Keepdown: another abandoned woman who exists beyond the play's social and temporal order and who, like Mariana, is restored to sequential femininity by ducal fiat in the dénouement. Figured as a 'whore' and 'punk' at the precise moment that she (officially) becomes a wife (5.1.518–525), Kate suggests that the ambiguities and opacities of early modern life cycle discourse are not as easily ironed out as Vincentio would have us believe. The Duke's investment in sequential femininity, and its implications for women who fall outside this progressive structure, is first articulated midway through Act 5, as he begins to stage-manage Mariana's return to the socio-temporal order. Disguised as Friar Lodowick, he introduces her to Viennese society by querying her status within the maid-wife-widow taxonomy. When Mariana confesses that she does not fit within (t)his sequence, 'Lodowick' emphasizes the social costs of this categorical lapse: 'Why', he notes, 'you are nothing then' (5.1.177). It is a clearly strategic exchange: as readers and playgoers well know, Vincentio is aware of Mariana's socio-temporal ambiguity. His questions, therefore, reflect not an act of inquiry but an exercise of power that aims to underscore both his privileged paradigm and unique capacity to author[ize] her transition from 'nothing[ness]' to licit femininity. Before he can do so, however, Lucio intercedes to remind audiences that the Duke's tripartite sequence implicitly produces a fourth, abject category: 'My Lord, she may be a punk, for many of them are neither maid, widow, nor wife' (5.1.179–180). Figuring whoredom as the anti-type or catchall for those who trouble—or exist beyond—the boundaries of licit femininity, he aligns Mariana with the sign of whoredom, thereby unsettling the purported ease of her impending restoration. But Lucio's deconstructive logic also, and more importantly for our purposes, illuminates the whore's (a)temporal position in the Duke's life cycle paradigm. Defined by negation ('neither maid, widow, nor wife'), the 'punk' emerges not only out of sequence but out of time: possessing no time of its own, whoredom is implicitly figured within a temporal void or vacuum.

The atemporality of whoredom complicates understandings of Mariana's 'moated grange'. On the one hand, this temporal condition helps to explain how and why this space and the scenes in which it is depicted feel so strangely out of joint with the rest of the play. Within the temporal order of Vienna, Lucio suggests, Mariana is a 'punk'. It is therefore imperative, given that the Duke wants to defend her 'wronged' status, that she reside somewhere else—outside the city, but also beyond its socio-temporal order—until she can safely be restored to sequence. On the other hand, however, the timelessness and nebulousness of the grange foreground Mariana's social and temporal abjection, thereby heightening her proximity to whoredom. It is all the more meaningful that it is the Duke who enters this space of ambiguity and suspension, proclaims Mariana's status as a 'wronged maid' (rather than a 'punk'), and shepherds her back from this timeless void into sequential femininity in the play's closing moments. It is a restoration, the play insists, that can only be authorized by the city's most powerful figure.

Yet even as Vincentio forcefully distinguishes the 'wronged maid' from the 'whore', his marriage plot discloses an additional temporality that further sutures these figures together. Marrying Mariana to Angelo, her former fiancé, the Duke seemingly solidifies her return to sequential femininity: in the play's final moments, this 'wronged maid' becomes the 'wife' that, Vincentio insists, she already is (5.1.500). In so doing, however, Mariana's socio-temporal abjection is reconfigured as a temporary condition—not as a telos in itself but as a swerve or deviation from sequential femininity that can be rectified. Her experience of time in the play, therefore, is not simply atemporal but also perverse: characterized by a movement between the very antitheses (licit femininity and 'nothing[ness]', maid and whore, sequence and atemporality) that the Duke-as-Friar wants to erect, and upon which his social order depends.

While Vincentio, as noted, works to suppress this dissonance by locating Mariana in the 'moated grange', aligning the bed-trick with her prior *sponsalia*, and insisting upon her status as a 'wronged maid', his concurrent restoration of Kate Keepdown discloses a kinship between the two women that undermines both the distinction that Vincentio draws between them and the purported ease of their return to sequential femininity. Like Mariana, Kate has been abandoned by a lover who 'promised her marriage' (3.1.457), and with whom she is ultimately reunited in the dénouement. Yet, where Mariana is ushered from the grange back into Viennese society, Kate remains a dislocated and disembodied figure, even as the Duke 'Proclaim[s]' her restoration-by-marriage to Lucio (5.1.511–515). Famously absent from the scene, her ambiguities only multiply as the play draws to a close. At the precise moment that she becomes a wife, Kate's husband reiterates her status as a 'whore' and 'punk', reminding audiences that her divergence from sequential femininity is not so easily forgotten (5.1.518-525). Rather than defending Kate, as with Mariana, however, the Duke implicitly acknowledges Lucio's claim by figuring their marriage as a just punishment for the latter's dissident behaviour. Intimating that this marriage will soon be 'executed' in 'prison' (5.1.523–524), moreover, Vincentio concludes this plotline in decidedly ominous fashion. The point, it would appear, is to distinguish a Mariana from a Kate, an Angelo from a Lucio. To the extent that the play compels us to rationalize this distinction, the answer appears to lie in the fact that Kate has borne a 'child' out of wedlock. Almost a 'year and a quarter old', the unnamed child troubles the purported ease of the Duke's sequential restorations (3.1.458); as a living reminder of Kate's nonsequential past, the child would continue to unsettle the categorical and temporal distinctions upon which Vincentio's tripartite paradigm depends. Perhaps this is why Kate is denied a grange of her own, as well as why her abjection extends beyond the (time)frame of the play: as with the (absent) child that she has borne into the play-world of *Measure for Measure*, she so powerfully (dis)embodies the ambiguities and opacities of the Duke's life cycle discourse, especially as related to the figure of the whore, that she must remain out of sight and out of time.

The capacity for whoredom to disrupt normative life cycle templates is perhaps best exemplified in a misogynist paradigm proffered by Piedmontese jurist Giovanni Nevizano in *Sylva nuptialis* (1526), a sixteenth-century compendium of Italian marriage law:

> Some enumerate female activities by dividing them into woman's ages, seven years each. In the first seven years she's a procuress, for her mother uses her, a child uncapable of understanding evil, to go summon her lover. In the next seven years she's a virgin. Between fourteen and twenty-one she's the prey of love. In the following seven years, from twenty-one to twenty-eight, she's a whore. From twenty-eight to thirty-five she's a heifer or sow. In the next seven-year period she's a whore again. Between forty-two and forty-nine she's a junk dealer. From forty-nine to fifty-six she goes around begging wine with a jug. In the next seven years she becomes a witch. She ends up burned.[88]

Mimicking licit sequential logics circulating elsewhere,[89] Nevizano twists and turns sexual time: implicated in bawdry as a child, his female archetype cycles through various sexual identities, from 'procuress' to 'virgin' to 'whore' to 'whore again', all while 'progressing' towards complete social, economic, and religious degradation. The vision is at once teleological and recursive: the witch ends, ironically, where the child begins: implicated in evil. The only difference, it would seem, is that the 'witch' presumably understands her profane status, and how she arrived at such corrupted 'ends'. Throughout, however, Nevizano unsettles easy distinctions between licit and illicit status: underscoring the child's innocence in stage one ('uncapable of understanding evil'), he nevertheless figures her as a 'procuress' or a critical intermediary in her mother's sexual traffic. From ages seven to twenty-one, her status then largely mirrors that of a licit maid, albeit with greater emphasis placed on her position as a hunted object. Turning 'whore' next, she departs from the licit sequential femininity yet remains locked in sequence, albeit one progressing towards a different telos. In so doing, Nevizano's whore doesn't so much fall out of sequence as occupy a parodic parallel sequence, one in which she subsequently progresses—like her married counterpart, the licit wife—through a period of sustained childbearing. Rather than 'progressing' to widowhood, however, she next returns to 'whore[dom]', cycling back to an earlier identity even as she 'progresses' forward. Her final years are then characterized by her increased social, economic, and spiritual degradation, all leading to the 'logical' endpoint for a life lived

[88] Reprinted in Menchi, 'The Girl and the Hourglass', 43.

[89] Focusing on continental models, Menchi locates several seven-stage paradigms for women's life cycles in the premodern era.

in whoredom: execution at the stake. Figuring the sequence as applicable to all women, Nevizano presents a universalizing vision of women's sexual degradation in and over time.[90] While strongly teleological, the paradigm is also pointedly recursive: not only do women return to whoredom at various stage in their lives, but they reproduce the cycle itself by enlisting their own daughters in this sexual traffic at an early age.

While it is unclear whether Nevizano's text was available to English readers in the early modern period,[91] its interplay of teleology and recursivity was echoed by a range of Elizabethan and Jacobean writers. These include those interested in demarcating specific 'social characters, persons, or types', as well as those who traced the trajectories of 'fallen women'. I address these categories separately, in order to home in on the particular temporal inflections and quandaries which accompany each. Nevertheless, both exemplify a paradox: just as each situates whoredom within a logic of progressive degradation, the very rigidity of this identarian sequence produces additional temporalities that belie the categorical stability and social intelligibility such narratives aim to provide. Moreover, this degenerative teleologic resurfaces as a governing trope in texts that undo the fixity of that temporal orientation, especially as the magnitude of the whore's sinful estate renders them a privileged figure for conversion.

Characters, Persons, and Types

'A Whoore', declares Sir Thomas Overbury, 'is a hie way to the Diuell, hee that lookes vpon her with desire, begins his voiage'. One of many London personae vividly rendered in *New and Choise Characters* (1615)—an enormously popular work which, following the Theophrastian tradition, succinctly describes common social

[90] This is not to suggest that Nevizano's vision governed contemporary Italian thought, nor that it represents a striking outlier; rather, it is to recall, as Eve Kosofsky Sedgwick reminded us long ago, that universalizing and minoritizing discourses often not only coexist but work in tandem to produce culturally-specific epistemologies of sex. See especially *Epistemology of the Closet*.

[91] A Latin version of the text was printed in Paris in 1521, followed by several more editions over the sixteenth and seventeenth centuries (1524, 1526, 1545, 1559, 1570, 1572, 1585, 1647).

types—the illicit sexual woman is here depicted as a common thoroughfare that facilitates men's passage to ignominious 'end[s]'.[92]

It is a telos, Overbury suggests, that the whore already embodies. Envenomed by sin and disease, she is 'dead' to God yet 'liues a Reprobate, like *Cain*, stil[l] branded, finding no habitation but her feares' (E2v). The living embodiment of sinful futurity, Overbury's whore conjoins past sins to future punishments. She is prolepsis incarnate. Or perhaps autotelic: always already the embodiment of their presumed goal or endpoint. As the text makes clear, such temporal figurations are explicitly and differentially gendered: having already reached her end(s), Overbury's whore operates as an omen, portending the destination which awaits male sinners should they pursue illicit 'desire(s)'.[93]

Caustic and captivating, Overbury's figuration is also conventional. In *Characterismi* (1631), Lenton portrays the '*Prostitute or Common Whore*' as both a walking catalogue of sin and an animate portent of divine punishment: '[s]he is the very Compendium and abstract of al[l] baseness....She is hell it selfe whilst she liues vpon earth, and her fire burnes as hot as Etna; to whose flames none can approach without either scorching or consuming.'[94] In *The Rich Cabinet* (1616), Thomas Gainsford compares '*a Whore*' to an extinguished candle whose 'lifes-flame quencht...like a snuffe doeth stincke', as well as to smoldering 'coales taken out of the fire, which either burne a man or besmeere him' (sig. Y5v).

Dead yet living. Extinguished yet smouldering. The whore's bi-temporal, proleptic figuration may be familiar to readers of early modern literature, but how these mixed temporalities inform and impede the work of reading, identifying, and/or knowing whores remains underexamined.[95] These temporal inflections are especially significant in the context of an early modern character-writing project seemingly

[92] Ouerburie, *New and Choise Characters* (1615), sig. E2r. Similar claims appear in Cooke, *A White Sheete* (1629): 'the house of an whore is the way to hell going downe to the chambers of death', 30; and Taylor, *A Common Whore* (1622): '*Whores* are the Hackneyes which men ride to Hell', sig. A4.

[93] Ouerburie, *New and Choise Characters* (1615), sig. E3r.

[94] *Characterismi*, sig. E6. See also Breton, who figures the 'Wanton Woman' as a 'kinde of Diuell', in *The Good and the Badde* (1616), sig. E3.

[95] The discursive linkages between whoredom, physical decay, and spiritual degradation have been discussed primarily in studies of early modern syphilis and its stage representations. See especially Harris, '(Po)X Marks the Spot'.

predicated upon the assumption that certain kinds of individuals can be aptly described and known.[96] Such typological thinking intimates a certain synchronic fixity: whether reiterating or troubling the meanings of early modern 'characters', 'social persons', or 'sexual types', typology promotes a putatively stable ideological template against which individual manifestations can be cognitively and socially processed. Thus, even if select figurations appear to challenge or demystify the 'disciplinary ideologies' that frame their appearance,[97] the taxonomic impulse that underlies these projects works to reinforce the putative stabilities—synchronic, conceptual, and ideological—of early modern characters. The sketches above encourage us now to ask how the cultural and epistemological work of characterization is informed by the various temporalities within which such specific figures are emplotted. How, for instance, do the mixed temporalities described above inform or unsettle the whore's status as an 'easily recognizable figure'?[98]

On route to addressing these questions, we must note another temporal inflection ascribed to these figures in the early modern character project. Just as Overbury presents the whore as a fixed endpoint or 'dead end', the narrator currently (re)situates this figure within a sequence of corrosive decline, one palpably figured through an extended analogy between hawk and whore:

> The first yeare of her trade she is an Eyesse [a fledgling bird or hawk], scratches and cries to draw on more, affection: the second Soare [a hawk in its second year]: the third a Ramage [wild, untamed, violent] whoore: the fourth and fifth, she's an intermewer [molting hawk], preies for her selfe, and ruffles all she reaches; from thence to tenne shee beares the name of white whoore, for then her bloud forsakes her with salt Rheumes, and now shee has mewd three coates; Now

[96] It is worth noting that the texts which comprise this minor genre overwhelmingly eschew explicit description, much less theorization, of the project(s) which they pursue. Overbury, for his part, alludes simply to his work as providing 'Wittie descriptions of the properties of sundry Persons', sig. B8. While early modern writers generally identify Overbury as the catalyst for a resurgent character project, Thomas Harman's *A Caueat For Commen Cvrsetors Vvlgarely Called Vagabones* (1567) can be seen to pursue a similar function and precedes Overbury's work by four decades. As with the text reviewed here, Harman's work, albeit more explicitly, foregrounds the difficulty of identifying such figures.

[97] DiGangi, *Sexual Types*, 4.

[98] Ibid., 4.

> shee growes weary and diseas'd together, fauours her wing, checkes little, but lies for it, bathes for her health, & scoures to keepe her coole, yet still she takes in stones, she fires her selfe else: the next remoue is Haggard [a wild, female hawk caught when in her adult plumage], stil more cunning; and if my art deceiue mee not, more crazie. All cares and cures are doubled now vpon her, and line her perch, or now she mews her pounces, at all these yeares shee flies at fooles and kils too: the next is Bussard Bawde, and there I leaue her.[99]

The falconry metaphor advances a relatively conventional image of the whore as animalistic, deceptive, cunning, metamorphic, murderous, and either physically or mentally unsound.[100] It is a figuration that approaches ontology: as with the decrepit prostitutes and bawds depicted on the London stage, Overbury's hawk-whore appears corrupt in essence, polluted to the marrow. Yet by emphasizing progressive decline, Overbury privileges sequence over fixity, teleology over immutability. This hawk-whore '*growes* weary and diseas'd', her madness and violence amplifying as 'yeares' pass (emphasis added). Penning a bestial analogue to the gendered life cycles described above, Overbury not only suggests that whores [d]evolve over time but links these metamorphoses to the acquisition of new names, concerns, and practices.

It is a progression so powerful as to challenge the taxonomic thinking that underlies the early modern character project. As Overbury's concluding clause suggests, the whore's progress does not terminate in Haggard-ness; rather, and as other early modern writers frequently surmise, young whores become old bawds.[101] In a later character sketch entitled '*A Maquerela, in plain English, a Bawd*', Overbury picks up where this prior entry leaves off, channelling attention to the aged sexual woman.[102] As beauty withers and diseases fester, such a figure transitions from prostitution to bawdry: like 'old *Char-cole*, that hath beene burnt her selfe', she fuels the degradation of others, leading them toward her own, already 'rotten', estate. Thus, just as Overbury and his peers characterize the whore as living-in-death, they concurrently foreground—and

[99] Ouerburie, *New and Choise Characters*, sigs E2v–E3r. Interlineated definitions drawn from the *Oxford English Dictionary* entries for 'eyas', n. (*c.*1486); 'soare', n. 2 (*c.*1596), 'ramage', adj. (*c.*1300), and 'intermewer', n. (*c.*1575).

[100] See *OED*, *crazie*, *adj.*

[101] See, for example, Erasmus, 'Of the Yong man and the *euill disposed woman*' (in *A modest meane to Mariage*); Gainsford, 'A Whore,' in *The Rich Cabinet*, sig. Y6r.

[102] Ouerburie, *New and Choise Characters*, sig. G3v.

appear fascinated by—her progressive decay: just how profane, they ask, can such a figure become? John Taylor, for instance, describes an 'olde *Whore*' who 'Falls at the last, the obiect of mens loathing, / Scorn'd and vnpittied, and to finish all, / Dyes in Ditch, or in an Hospitall',[103] while Lenton encourages readers to envision '*an Old Bawd*' as:

> a menstruous beast, engendred of diuers most filthy excrements, by the stench of whose breath the Ayre is so infected, that her presence is an ineuitable contagion, her eyes more poysonous than the Basilisk; her nose (if any) most pestilently pocky, her tongue more subtile than the Hyena, who stil howles in some fained voyce for the deuouring of innocents.[104]

This degenerative teleologic captivated the imagination of such writers, spurring them to envision ends that stretched the bounds of decrepitude.

Such descriptions appear to confirm the whore's socio-sexual legibility. How could one overlook such a demonic figure? How could one fail to apprehend death personified? Implicitly aligning temporality to epistemology, they suggest that the whore can and will be known by a telos always already inscribed on their body. At the same time, however, such legibility is belied by other factors and attributes. First, and as Alan Bray has argued, apocalyptic rhetorics facilitate imperceptibility as much as intelligibility: it can be hard to reconcile the cataclysmic monsters of discourse with the bodies and persons one encounters in everyday life.[105] Second, Overbury and his peers repeatedly stress that such figures are not what they appear to be: '*A Very Whoore*', he alleges, baits men 'with a million of prostitute countenances and enticements';[106] '*A Bawd*', Lenton claims, traffics in 'Adulterate beauties, and counterfeit complexions';[107] '*A Wanton Woman*', Nicholas Breton suggests, is 'an illusion' embodied.[108] Thus, just as early modern character books figure whores as (a) always already embodying their future damnation, and (b) perpetually becoming more degraded, they concurrently insist that, by way

103 Taylor, *A Common Whore*, sig. B8r.

104 *Characterismi*, sigs C3r–C4v. See also Breton's *A Bawde*, in *The Good and the Badde*, sig. E4v.

105 Bray, *Homosexuality in Renaissance England*, 9.

106 *New and Choise Characters*, sig. E3r.

107 *Characterismi*, sig. C4r.

108 *The Good and the Badde*, sig. E2v.

of their deceptive practices, whores often are not discernible as 'whores'—and therefore are able, for a time at least, to (c) swerve back into the sexual temporalities associated with licit femininity. These descriptions reinforce what I have termed the 'counterfeit ontology' of early modern whoredom: figured as definitionally fixed and socially legible, whores concurrently operate as privileged emblems of artifice, changeability, counterfeit, dissimulation, falsehood, impurity, and inauthenticity. But they also connect this broader paradox to the specific problems of sexual knowing: in their capacity to pass as respectable women—and thereby to insert themselves into a licit timeline or trajectory—whores unsettle the tight conceptual linkages between sexual time, bodily status, and narrative knowing that such catalogues aim to secure.[109]

These tensions bear resonance with the scholarship on early modern social and sexual types, as well as the literature and drama of the period more broadly. While studies of London city comedy, for instance, have long queried the stability (and putative intelligibility) of the stage whore,[110] the conspicuous temporal thinking evinced here suggests a need to further scrutinize how, when, and where ideologies of sexual time emerge not only within these plays—including instances in which sexual temporalities are explicitly addressed or thematized—but in other genres and discourses as well. As throughout, I aim less to demonstrate the whore's instability per se than the cultural and discursive labour necessary to navigate what Breton implicitly figures as her social, temporal, and epistemological 'abuse': 'She is Youths plague,

[109] My reference to three putatively different types—'very whore', 'bawd', and 'wanton women'—is also revealing; just as Overbury's entries trouble rather than resolve a strict sexual taxonomy, comparisons across these various works reveal the elasticity of these typological distinctions. In so doing, they suggest—much like the emergent lexicographic project examined in Chapter 1—that it is porosity, lability, and experimentation, rather than fixity and distinction, which best characterize the early modern character-writing project.

[110] Leggatt, *Citizen Comedy in the Age of Shakespeare*; Haselkorn, *Prostitution in Elizabethan and Jacobean Comedy*; Kahn, 'Whores and Wives in Jacobean Drama'; Singh, 'Narratives of Sexuality'; Newman, *Fashioning Femininity and English Renaissance Drama*, 131–143; Howard, 'Mastering Difference in *The Dutch Courtesan*'; Twyning, *London Dispossessed*; Howard, *Theater of a City*, 114–161.

and Ages Purgatory, Times abuse, and Reasons trouble.'[111] In particular, I am interested in the culturally specific mechanisms, practices, and strategies (narrative, textual, hermeneutic, etc.) that emerge to resolve such problems of knowledge and knowability, and/or to press early modern whoredom into a kind of legibility. The next section explores one such practice—confessional self-narration—that works to relocate whores in narrative time. Significantly, this counter-logic emerges in texts that foreground the otherwise adamantine fixity of the whore's sexual and spiritual degradation. In so doing, it further discloses the contingency of this teleologic and the sexual knowledge-relations that it purportedly secures.

The Fallen Woman

Of the various logics explored thus far, the 'fallen woman' perhaps most conspicuously yokes the whore's meanings to a teleologic of corrosive decline, functioning as both a literary motif and a recognizable cultural script. Yet even as these narratives imply that the ends of whoredom are always already fixed, their investment in the whore's multiple 'turns'—rising and falling fortunes, certainly, but also returns to 'virginity', multiple sexual encounters, and attempted conversions—disclose a recursive temporality that emerges in tension with this governing teleological orientation. Gervase Markham's *The Famovs Whore, or Noble Curtizan* (1609) presents a useful case study. A lyric poem in the tradition of the female complaint, the tale follows Paulina, a young woman born into a wealthy and noble family who, upon the death of her father, pursues her sensual 'appetite[s]' to ignominious ends. Progressing from 'voluptuous idleness' to drunken revelry, she soon commits her first sexual transgression: granting, at age thirteen, her 'maiden flower' to 'one of the meanest and basest drudges of her mothers house' (sigs B1v–B2r).

[111] Breton, *The Good and the Badde*, sig. E2v. It is unclear what Breton means here: he may be signalling the wanton woman's own degradation in youth and old age, that she corrupts others positioned within these temporal frames, a combination of the two, or something else altogether. Such opacity, I suggest, is precisely the point: the wanton woman is characterized precisely by the trouble she presents to such categorical distinctions.

Spiralling into poverty, mother and daughter move to Rome, where the former presses the latter into the sex trade. Able to re-present herself as a 'pure virgin' in this new locale, Paulina first sells (and resells) her fictive maidenhead to various and 'sundry' youths. '[M]ade anewe' as a Cardinal's concubine, she then circulates among the Roman elite and establishes herself as a 'starre' in that courtly universe (sigs B2v–B4v). Growing restless, she hatches a plan to secure her transition from clerical concubine to 'honest wife' and, with the Cardinal's help, quickly ensnares an 'innocent yong man', who, unacquainted with the 'sly deceits / Of *Romish Curtezans* nor their sweete baites', believes himself fortunate in the match. Quickly disabused of that notion, he nevertheless proves corrupted by the alliance: having 'taste[d] a poisoned dish', this hapless husband turns scheming parasite. Dissembling affection for Paulina, he drains her savings and absconds to France (where he dies in battle), leaving her on the brink of destitution (sigs B4v–C1v).

Even in the early stages of her narrative, therefore, Paulina does not so much occupy a single sexual temporality as she mixes multiple temporal orientations. Rising as she falls, returning to 'virginity' time and again, sliding from whore to concubine to wife: the course of Paulina's degradation turns backwards and forwards, time and again, even as she implicitly proceeds towards her ultimate destination. When she enters the next stage of her life, Paulina describes her experience by reference to two additional—and pointedly contradictory—temporalities in immutability and ephemerality. To restore her fortune(s) following her husband's death, Paulina re-enters the sexual market and quickly ascends to the pinnacle of Roman society, proving 'of all the curtezans the most renound' (sig. C1r). She frames this period as a collision of competing temporalities: 'Seauen yeares at least this golden time did last / (Whilst youth and beauty swiftly from me past)' (sig. D1r). Enlisting a golden age *topos* characterized both by immutability and ephemerality, Paulina couples this framework with a parenthetical reminder that the body possesses its own temporal logics. Thus, even and perhaps especially as her luxuries appear endless and her power indissoluble, the foundations upon which Paulina's reign depend—her 'youth and beautie' (sig. E2v)—inexorably decay. These tensions between the lived experience of time and the body's own chronologics disclose a broader temporal conflict that governs the poem as a whole: just as the narrative proceeds chronologically, tracking Paulina's life-in-sequence, its status as a (retrospective) lament allows the speaker to reframe specific actions in light of her final ends. While Paulina declares that 'No life may with the curtezans compare, / Whilst she holds fast the glorie of her faire', she follows this statement with a proleptic warning: 'But when her rose and lillies are decaid, / No life so base, so abiect or dismaid' (sig. D3r).

To a limited degree, Paulina apprehends this prescribed trajectory within the lived time of the poem itself. Even as her body deteriorates—a process accelerated by the emergence of various and 'foule diseases' (sig. D4r)—she attempts to rewrite her narrative ends. To do so, she embraces the cultural logic of conversion:

> Meaning to mend what *I* had done amisse,
> Making my selfe a Metamorphosis.
> My wanton life *I* chang'd and mine attire,
> Becomming new in bodie and desire.
> *Rome* stood amazd at her new conuertite,
> Seeing me giue my goods away in sight,
> To Monastaries and religious places,
> As holy creatures wont in such like cases.[112]

Performing conversion, Paulina confesses that these outer gestures belie a true, inner *metanoia*: 'altred more in habite then in minde', she finds herself 'repenting that I so repented had' (sigs D3r–v). Turning and returning, she situates herself within a recursive temporality that not only evokes misogynist figurations of women as intrinsically fickle but underscores broader epistemological concerns regarding how one can know the sexual and conversional status of another person: all of '*Rome*', Paulina implies, readily accepts the 'conuertite' status that she herself calls into question. Returning to the courtesan's life, Paulina falls in love with a younger man but proves unable to gain his affection. Exhausting her finances in pursuit of this impossible love, she finally arrives at the expected destination(s): diseased, disgraced, and exiled, she concludes her tale by living a kind of death, able only to caution others from pursuing her ignoble path.

[112] In this dispersal of worldly goods, Paulina's actions mimic those of Pelagia and Thais, two well-known repentant whores whose narratives circulated broadly in the period.

The Famovs Whore thus figures the whore's decline as inevitable and unalterable. Despite repeated efforts to escape this rigid teleologic, Paulina appears irrevocably bound to a profane end. At the same time, however, the work unfolds a more complex vision of the whore's status in and across sexual time. Paulina's repeated performances of 'pure virgin[ity]', for instance, figure a division between socio-sexual status and inner substance, while her extended reign atop the Roman social hierarchy suggests that the clever whore can swerve from the predicted course of degradation and the linear temporality it implies. Paulina's narrative is less unidirectional than undulating and recursive: characterized by massive fluctuations in her social, economic, and (perceived) sexual statuses, and characterized by abrupt and sharp reversals in direction. Her degradation emerges in tension with the unrealized prospect of a penitential return.

Even in its disavowal, the thematization of repentant whoredom is significant. As Margaret Soltan has argued, the fallen woman operates as part of a broader cultural and religious discourse of female errancy that stretches back to biblical tropes of 'womanly vagrancy'.[113] It is also one structured upon a governing paradox: the woman's fall from licit sociality often emerges in relation to, and at times prefigures, the possibility of return and reincorporation. As Soltan writes, 'while [the fallen woman] might seem lost to the spiritual and civic body, her real role was to be forgiven and returned to the fold. Reformed, she became a permanent embodiment of penance, a Magdalene. She also became, more importantly, an emblem of cultural survival, for to bring the errant back was to demonstrate the ability of culture to maintain its integrity.'[114]

Abject yet laden with emancipatory value, the fallen woman's conversional potential—including, in our terms, her capacity to return to normative sexual time—sustains a Christian world-order. Even as Paulina finds herself at the logical 'end' of a life spent in whoredom, she annexes this teleologic to encourage others to 'mend' their ways before too much time has passed:

[113] Soltan, 'Night Errantry', 109.

[114] Ibid., 109. Crucially, Soltan argues that this paradox appears only in particular cultural formations. The nineteenth-century rise of 'new-Darwin criminology', she goes on to note, shifted the prostitute from a figure whose reincorporation reflected the transformative power of religious grace to one of 'contagion' who had to be eradicated by the 'instruments of science' (110-111).

Though the beginning's sweete, the end is sad,
O leaue off then whilst you haue youth and time,
For earely sorrow purges our worst crime.
Looke vp to heauen before your sins be growne,
And aske for mercie ere your faults be knowne. (sig. F2v)

Should the sinner request 'mercie' at a proper time in their narrative, Paulina suggests, they can rewrite its ends and meanings. In this, Markham's tale gestures towards a temporal irony that underlies many early modern England whore narratives: the teleological character of such lives often is given voice precisely in texts that challenge or undo the fixity of that narrative endpoint. Thus, while Paulina presents a cautionary tale—referencing not her own salvation but the potential for others to pursue honest (re)turns—a range of contemporary works situate similar acts of confessional self-narration as practices essential to catalysing one's conversional (re)turn to chastity. Indeed, articulating one's status within a teleologic of whoredom operates in such works as a requisite step towards escaping that temporal bind. It is also a practice, as we shall see in Chapter 4, that evokes additional temporal and epistemological concerns.

Virginity and Chastity

The various transgressions catalogued in *The Famovs Whore* extend far beyond Paulina, encompassing a range of social actors—from permissive mothers, libidinous servants, and crafty bawds to licentious popes and decadent patricians—who are figured as complicit in her degradation. These include the Cardinal Hipolito: that wealthy prelate who procures Paulina on condition of her (fraudulent) virginity, retains her as a concubine for three years, then facilitates her transition to 'honest wife' by testifying on behalf of her (counterfeit) chastity. At once a dupe and a collaborator in Paulina's sexual fictions,[115] he is a fulcrum

[115] While Paulina offers a sympathetic take on the Cardinal, praising his 'loue' and 'admiration' (sig. B2v), the unnamed commentator who provides marginal glosses in the 1609 edition leaves no doubt as to how readers should interpret Hipolito's actions: 'The Cardinal first bought her of her mother for money and after gaue money to mary her honestly from him' (sig. B4v).

who helps leverage her narrative revisions. Emplotted between two falsehoods, Hipolito also foregrounds the utility—and conspicuous instability—of 'virginity' and 'chastity' as privileged conceptual frameworks through which early moderns sought to know sex in narrative time.[116] Frequently defined as antithetical to whoredom, premodern virginity and chastity concurrently worked to structure—by way of this oppositional logic—both the category of whoredom itself and the epistemology through which it might be recognized and known. As I have argued throughout this chapter, such categorical and epistemological work concurrently produces, and depends upon, theories of sexual time: to know early modern whoredom, especially by way of the interpretive logics detailed here, is to accept a series of propositions regarding how it is oriented, and accrues meanings, in and over time. The same holds true for virginity and chastity, which are riven with their own temporal multiplicities and contradictions in the period but nevertheless reinforce understandings of whoredom as at once teleological (rather than anterior), perverse (rather than sequential), and atemporal (rather than ephemeral, perpetual, and diachronic), as we will see. But they also open onto a variety of temporal ironies that unsettle precisely the conceptual clarity that such binary oppositions aim to secure.

[116] The epistemological problematics of virginity and chastity were a mainstay of the early modern theatre. Even the most cursory of engagements with the extant drama reveals a wellspring of desires and anxieties associated with these fugitive knowledges, as well as a plethora of strategies—from bed-tricks, bedsheets, and blushes to dead bodies, dreams, false wares, handkerchiefs, potions, puns, relics, riddles, rings, speech acts, spying scenes, and even *dei ex machina*—through which they could be mediated onstage. Whether framed as comedy or tragedy, such dramatic negotiations bespeak an enormous cultural investment in apprehending women's chaste and virginal bodies. Reading these and related representations alongside contemporary medical, juridical, political, economic, religious, and colonial discourses, scholars have long demonstrated both the lability (historical, definitional, tropological) of these oft-conflated paradigms and the gravity—the very real social implications and effects—of their perceived verisimilitude. On the challenges of representing, performing, and proving women's virginity and chastity in the era, see especially Ferguson, 'Hymeneal Instruction'; Schwarz, 'The Wrong Question'; Kelly, *Performing Virginity and Testing Chastity in the Middle Ages*; Jankowski, *Pure Resistance*; Kelly and Leslie, *Menacing Virgins*; Loughlin, *Hymeneutics*; Berry, *Of Chastity and Power*. On chastity as an ideological veil which can work as a 'cover for erotic activity that, if publicly expressed in repudiation of reproductive ideology, would have invited censure' (35), see Traub, 'Perversion'. For an acute analysis of scholarly assumptions about, and desires for, the chastity of a specific literary character, see Stockton, 'Chasing Chastity'.

Difficult to substantiate yet laden with significance: it is no surprise that virginity and chastity figured as prominent metaphors in the period, and that writers sought to manage their conceptual dissonance by recourse to sequential logics. Frequently, these figurations align with the life cycle paradigms outlined above, with marital chastity neatly supplanting maidenly virginity. It easy to understand the appeal of this successional reasoning. At the most basic level, succession supports categorical distinction: in this instance, differences that can be mapped along axes of relationality, social identity, and/or physiological status. One category comes before, the other after. Such progressive emplotment furthermore enables threshold rituals, whereby additional signs can be introduced to situate bodies and statuses in sexual time.[117] Finally, and perhaps most importantly, this sequential modality affords conceptual differentiation while concurrently producing a potent analogical relation: where marital chastity proves at once virginity's licit *telos* and its socio-spiritual reincarnation, its destination and discursive double, succession figures seemingly disparate categories as two sides of the same socio-sexual coin. This contiguity has several advantages: it supports smooth conceptual transitions; it allows subjects to draw upon one category when attempting to define or comprehend the other; and, by enabling a series of powerful metonymies—between bodily intactness, sexual fidelity, cognitive purity, and spiritual devotion—it broadens the symbolic parameters of virginity and chastity.

Virginity presents a logical starting point for this analysis, as the category itself is characterized by a kind of anteriority when described by premodern writers and theologians: a primal condition, virginity always comes first. This temporal orientation partly reflects an anatomical style of reasoning within which an intact hymen serves as the sign and synecdoche of a woman's integrity more broadly.[118] Freighted with

[117] Weddings, of course, represents only one aspect of a broader symbolic economy which could also include proleptic utterances (espousals), social, material, corporeal, and sumptuary practices (announcing of banns, exchange of rings, binding of hair, payment of dowries); spatial arrangements (cohabitation, church seating, domestic practices); and so on.

[118] By 'anatomical style of reasoning' I neither suggest nor refer to an epistemology of virginity produced and disseminated within a discrete scientific discourse that operated in isolation from, if not opposition to, a similarly distinct theological discourse. Rather, and as historian Joan Cadden points out, 'to emphasize a disjunction between science and medicine on the one hand, and theology and ethics of the other, is to misrepresent

significance, the so-called maidenhead operates as an epistemological fetish-object of sorts: a desired entity that appears to promise, through the material evidence associated with its rupture, irrefutable sexual knowledge.[119] One thus finds the physician Thomas Chamberlayne figuring the 'gushing forth of some quantity of blood' during intercourse as 'an evident sign of [a woman's] virginitie' while concurrently noting that an absence thereof incurs 'suspition of a former *deflowring*'.[120] So tethered to an anatomical referent, women's virginity appears easily legible (even if it is never seen) and demonstrably provable—albeit solely, and ironically, at the very moment of its dissolution.[121] The precise moment of 'defloration' thus emerges as a privileged scene of sexual knowing, one whose epistemological purchase derives from the bifold promise of ocular proof and narrative clarity: channelling attention towards a singular and putatively unrepeatable event, virginity-as-hymeneal-integrity enables the charting of a fixed plot-point in a woman's life narrative, operating as a narrative hinge that marks a transition between distinct socio-sexual categories. Crucially, it is a micro-logic predicated upon a theory of irreversibility: virginity brooks no returns. One is born virgin; one cannot become one. To the extent that virginity's meanings are informed by this orientation towards, and desire to preserve, a primal state or condition of sexual purity, it possesses an anterior temporality that is both denied to the whore and diverges from the teleologic of social and sexual decline with which the latter is often associated.

Innate, incarnate, emplotable, irretrievable: virginity-as-hymeneal-integrity appears well suited to fostering social, sexual, and narrative intelligibility. In place of categorical fluidity, it promises conceptual fixity and anatomical clarity. In lieu of chronological malleability, it presents itself as unconditionally anterior, affording no possibility of recurrence

the late-medieval'—and, I would suggest, early modern—'situation'. See 'Medieval Scientific and Medical Views of Sexuality', 162. Among the many works that attend to the hymen's semiotic dimensions, my thinking is especially indebted to Kelly, who famously describes virginity as 'an abstract idea residing in an anatomical metonym' (*Performing Virginity*, 7); Peterson, 'The Ring's the Thing'; and Schwarz, 'The Wrong Question'. On early modern constructions of 'physical virginity' and its implications for women's health, particular in older women, see Peterson, 'Elizabeth I's Virginity and the Body of Evidence'.

[119] On the epistemology of the hymen, see especially Ferguson, 'Hymeneal Instruction'.

[120] *The Complete Midwifes Practice* (1658), sig. C7v. Emphasis in the original.

[121] A variety of scholars have explored this evidentiary and epistemology paradox. In addition to Ferguson, 'Hymeneal Instruction', see Loughlin, *Hymeneutics*; Derrida, *Dissemination*, esp. 187–316; and Meltzer, *For Fear of the Fire*, esp. 79–118.

or return. The non-virgin may become many things—a chaste spouse, an adulterer, a widow, a *senex amans*, even a repentant whore—but never, presumably, '(re)turn virgin'. Stability in this regard provides ballast to other sexual categories, including whoredom, that can then be defined differentially vis-à-vis virginity, both in terms of anatomical difference and posterior emplotment. It thus comes as no surprise that references to virginity in the literatures of the period frequently denote past estates rather than present conditions, framing a character's current sexual status by identifying what they are *no more*. When Paulina, for instance, describes her 'maiden flower, my virgin honoured tree', she deploys such tropes retrospectively rather than referentially, coupling their citation with an immediate acknowledgement of loss: '[these] I gaue to stealth and hatefull luxurie' (sig. B1r). As a marker of a present absence, 'virgin[ity]' here harkens back, framing Paulina's sexual present—and future—through the remembrance of things past.

And yet, as Chamberlayne's 'suspition' suggests, premodern writers were well aware that hymeneal 'integrity' ensured neither the sexual nor narrative clarity with which it was invested. From Saints Ambrose, Augustine, and Aquinas to the famed sixteenth-century barber-surgeon Ambrose Paré, prominent figures had long troubled the fixed metonymic logic upon which strictly anatomical understandings of virginity depend. In an oft-cited passage from *Of the Citie of God* (circulating in London via translation by 1610), Augustine acknowledges that hymeneal ruptures can occur for a variety of reasons, including accidental perforations during the procedures that aim to verify the 'integritie of the Virginall part'.[122] Noting that it would be 'foolish', in such cases, to suggest that the 'virgin' in question had 'lost any part of her bodily sanctitie', he privileges volitional continence over corporeal intactness as virginity's *sine quo non*. So long as the subject's 'intent of the minde stand[s] firme, (which firmnesse it is that sanctifies the body) the violence of anothers lust cannot depriue so much as the body of this sanctity'.[123] As Aquinas would put it, in a concise paraphrase authored

[122] S^T. AVGVSTINE, *OF THE CITIE OF GOD*, I.17, sig. D3v. Similar examples appear in John Florio's edition of Montaigne's *Essaies* (1613), 487; *Aristotles Masterpiece* (1684), 94; and Sharp, *THE MIDWIVES BOOK* (1671), sigs D8r–Ev.

[123] S^T. AVGVSTINE, *OF THE CITIE OF GOD*, sigs D3v–r. As Melissa Sanchez points out, Augustine's position should not be taken to evince a proto-feminist understanding of sexual assault. Turning to the (in)famous honour-suicide of Lucretia, for instance,

some eight centuries later: '[t]herefore virginity does not consist in incorruption of the flesh.'[124] Rather, it betokens a state of mental, spiritual, and affective purity that may be reflected in, yet is irreducible to, the materiality of that 'bodily organ' with which it is most frequently associated. In this theological genealogy, 'virginity' emerges as a condition characterized less by anatomical presence than affective absence: by (erotic) sensations that the subject does not feel, rather than the integrity of a membrane that they do possess. It is a dematerialization of virginity that, as we shall see, activates a sexual temporality perhaps more readily discernible in contemporary discussions of chastity: a sempiternal orientation that aims to preserve a given state in perpetuity.

This is not to diminish the intricate reasoning often attending patristic writings on virginity: the divergences and disputations, the caveats and nuances, the complex parsing of literal and figurative meanings.[125] Nor, for that matter, do I suggest that a majority—or even a significant minority—of medieval and early modern subjects devalued the presence (or absence) of hymeneal blood during intercourse as a privileged signifier of women's virginity. To the contrary, the hymen and its traces remain laden with significance well into the seventeenth century and beyond.[126] Such persistence reflects the social and conceptual utility of anatomical virginity, particularly as a means of 'resolving' an otherwise intractable epistemological problem. By way of contrast, one might

Augustine intimates that her affective response to the violation—and subsequent self-'murder'—may bespeak complicity in her rape. Examining various positions on this potential culpability, he presses towards an interpretive aporia: 'What if it were so, *which none could know but herselfe*, that thou Tarquinius son offered her force, yet she her self gaue a lustfull consent, & after did so greeue at that, that she held it worthy to be punished with death?' (sig. D3v, emphasis added). As Sanchez notes, the judicial force of this interrogative is further amplified by Juan Luis Vives, who, in his 1610 edition of *Citie of God*, glosses the passage by noting: 'For who can tell who whether she gave consent by the touch of some incited pleasure?' (sig. D4v). Pressing undecidability into complicity, Augustine and Vives enact an interpretive praxis which continues to inform, and haunt, ideologies of rape into the modern era. See *Erotic Subjects*, 93–94.

[124] *The Summa Theologiae of St. Thomas Aquinas*, II.ii.Q152.

[125] In addition to works already cited, see Atkinson, 'Precious Balsam'; Brown, *The Body and Society;* Payer, *The Bridling of Desire.*

[126] As Atkinson notes, such persistence is extraordinary given the church's broad authority in matters pertaining to sex and its meanings: 'the physiological definition survived in spite of the power and influence of the moral and spiritual interpretation of virginity, and in spite of the enormous regard for humility as the "true" virginity best exemplified by the virgin Mary.' See 'Precious Balsam', 138.

consider the various hermeneutic quandaries that accompany a predominantly spiritualized approach to virginity. If virginity is not (fully) anatomy, how does one differentiate the virgin from the non-virgin? In the absence of a stable material referent invested with the authority to demarcate the sexual before and after, how can one ascertain, know, and/or demonstrate a (prior) virginal condition? How does one prove an unsullied mind and soul—that they have never, as Aquinas memorably puts it, been 'parched by excessive heat?'[127] As these questions imply, a spiritualized conceptualization alters not only the semiotics of virginity but how, when, and in whom it is—or can be—perceived, materialized, confirmed, reiterated, and known in time. Across these same vectors, it destabilizes the semiotics and epistemology of early modern whoredom.

These altered temporalities and their discontents help to explain the novel taxonomy of virginities traced out by Albertus Magnus, a Dominican friar writing in the mid-thirteenth century. Seeking greater categorical precision, Albert posits four virginities:

> first, the innate virginity of infants before the age of reason; second, the virginity of individuals who have not taken a religious vow of chastity; third, virginity that is dedicated to God through a vow or firm proposal; and fourth, that of foolish virgins (those whose behavior is too extreme or their dress inappropriate).[128]

As Pierre Payer notes, the list addresses a range of quandaries that had long troubled the epistemology of virginity in Christian theology. These include: (1) what to do in cases, such as rape, in which a hymen is broken but one would not want to claim a corresponding loss of virginity; (2) how to characterize women who engage in illicit activities yet retain their hymeneal integrity; (3) the role played by, and effect of, religious vows of continence; (4) the relationship between virginity and chastity; and, albeit implicitly, (5) how to apprehend male virginity, which lacks a corresponding anatomical referent.[129] Perhaps most significantly, Albert's four-tiered taxonomy expands—by channelling attention to behavioural and performative practices—the semiotic and

[127] Aquinas, *Summa*, II.ii.Q152.

[128] Beattie, *Medieval Single Women*, 19. The paradigm is also addressed in Kelly, *Performing Virginity*, 6; Payer, *Bridling*, 162–164.

[129] Payer, *Bridling*, 162.

temporal frames through which virginity might be perceived, materialized, and known. Rather than a precise moment of anatomical 'revelation', virginity for women emerges as a condition of ongoing and ritualistic embodiment: an amalgamation of discrete social acts and ongoing bodily performances.[130] Its meanings, in other words, are informed by a sempiternal temporal orientation which privileges stability and maintenance across time.

This is not to suggest that Albert eschews virginity's anterior dimensions. As his first category implies, virginity remains for him a primal ('innate') orientation, one implicitly figured as proximate to the divine and, subsequently, a state from which one invariably drifts through the acquisition of 'reason'.[131] To dedicate oneself to God by means of a 'vow or firm proposal', i.e. category two, is to reorient oneself (back) towards a prior condition and (re)commit oneself to approaching a (lost) prelapsarian purity. Where this speech act thus looks back, it concurrently encodes additional temporal dimensions: as a testament or a declaration of one's present condition, it annexes the precise moment of its articulation; as a covenant or a binding promise to God, it operates proleptically, anticipating a future life of 'perpetual continence'.[132] As Peter Brown notes, it is precisely this sempiternal character that elevates, for some early Christian writers, the avowed virginal woman above other consecrated persons, including male priests: 'to her male admirers, the consecrated virgin stood for continuity in its most pure

[130] In this, Magnus demonstrates how one might apprehend, and adjudicate, what Saint Ambrose once referred to as 'virginity made manifest by works of character rather than in the body's enclosure'. See *Saint Ambrose: Letters*, 159.

[131] As a popular metonym for purity, integrity, continence, innocence, wholeness, and/or holiness in the period, virginity thus evokes, in the premodern texts which have come to us, a certain metaphysical intactness—a union of mind, body, and divinity—perceived always already under threat, if not irrevocably lost, upon one's entrance into a fallen world.

[132] See, for instance, the mixed temporalities ascribed to the virginal woman in Juan Luis Vives's *De Intitutione Feminae Christianae* (1523/4), translated into English by Richard Hyrde as *A very frutefull and pleasant boke called the Instructio[n] of a Christen woma[n]* in 1529. In a section entitled 'Of Virginite', Vives urges Christian women to 'shutte vp bothe bodye and mynde / and seale them with those seales that none can open / but he that hath the keye of Dauid, / that is thy spouse: whiche resteth so in the[e], / as in a temple most clene and goodlye' (sig. F4r). Anticipating (re)union with a divine 'spouse' who always already 'resteth' within, Vives's virginal woman here proves at once anterior and anticipatory, primal and proleptic: she looks forward to a condition she already embodies.

state ... she was the one human being who could convincingly be spoken of as having remained as she had first been created.'[133] A living testament to and embodiment of sacral 'continuity' from creation to the cultural present, such women are described in select early Christian treatises as if existing in a different temporal realm altogether, their 'bodies withdrawn in perpetuity from the normal ebb and flow of marital strategies' navigated by the general laity.[134]

Albert, of course, wrote within a theological tradition that predated the Protestant Reformation. For women living in Protestant countries, the elimination of life-long virginity as a prospective career path meant that marital chastity emerged—with few exceptions—as the sole legitimate 'end[point] or *telos* for maidenly virginity'.[135] As Katherine Gillen notes, this change amplified perceptions of maidenly virginity as an inherently 'transitional rather than an absolute state'.[136] Such ineluctable ephemerality—what two modern critics have called the 'limited shelf-life' of maidenly virginity[137]—captivated the imagination of early modern writers, perhaps most notably in a revived *carpe diem* tradition that figured the cultural and erotic value of maidenly virginity by direct appeal to its imminent loss. The ominous prolepses that underwrite the various entreaties of Herrick, Jonson, Marvell, and Carew thus can be seen to bespeak, at least in part,[138] the unique temporal contours of maidenly virginity in an age of Protestant reformations: the sense that, as Margaret Ferguson has argued, the maiden's 'cultural value lies in the fact that [she] has *not yet* been used', that her social and erotic authority

[133] Brown, *The Body and Society*, 271. As Brown suggests, the exemplary nature of avowed female virginity is underwritten by a pervasive misogyny that perceives women as inherently disorderly and incontinent.

[134] Ibid., 262. As Helen Hackett notes, it is precisely through logics of exceptionality that female empowerment is both afforded and circumscribed with patriarchal societies: 'One way to accommodate a powerful woman, without disrupting a predominant cultural framework which regards women as inferiors and subordinates, is to represent her as a wonder and a miracle, an 'exceptional woman' whose marvellous gifts stand out in contrast to the general fallibility or even depravity of her sex'. See *Virgin Mother, Maiden Queen*, 239.

[135] Ferguson, 'Foreward', 8.

[136] Gillen, *Chaste Value*, 75. See also J. Higginbotham, 'Girls and Sexuality in Seventeenth-Century Love Lyrics', 154.

[137] Kelly and Leslie, *Menacing Virgins*, 21.

[138] For an alternative account of the temporal dimensions of the *carpe diem* tradition, see Hyman, *Impossible Desires and the Limits of Knowledge in Renaissance Poetry.*

is not only temporally circumscribed but enhanced by 'the specter of an imminent or eventual use, consumption, or violation'.[139]

Anterior and proleptic, perpetual and ephemeral: premodern virginity encoded a variety of temporal orientations that informed the cultural, political, theological, sectarian, gendered, and erotic stakes of the virginal body. These mixed temporalities at once (a) reflect the conspicuously troubled epistemology of a privileged conceptual framework through which early moderns sought to know, emplot, and articulate the meanings of sex in their life narratives; and (b) emerge as a direct consequence of the ongoing discursive labour necessary to produce and sustain female 'virginity' as a stable and apprehensible category of sexual knowledge in early modern England—one that, by way of binary opposition, concurrently structures an epistemology of the whore. Where virginity looks back to and aims to preserve a primal condition, whoredom is characterized by its orientation towards, and presumed tendency to embody, a decrepit endpoint. Such a framework affords narrative and conceptual clarity in place of the manifold quandaries—evidentiary, hermeneutic, temporal, theological, etc.—detailed here. It also figures whoredom as atemporal or perverse, i.e. out of sequence but also, under certain circumstances, capable of returning to normative sexual time.

Yet even these tidy distinctions belie the fact that, for many premodern writers, virginity was chastity. When Robert Greene, writing in the early 1590s, argues that the famed '*Vestall* [V]irgins' of antiquity 'were not reuerenced of the Senators for their curious clothing, but for their chastitie',[140] he is not making a category error. Rather, what may appear a conflation of terms is instead a conventional logic—one that stretches as far back as the writings of Cicero and Macrobius, if not Aristotle[141]—that positions virginity as a subspecies of chastity: as one of three stages, along with marital conjugality and continent widowhood, that comprised the broader category of women's chastity.[142] Within this

[139] Ferguson, 'Foreward', 7; emphasis in the original. Lest one assume that such ideologies have been consigned to the distant past, the contemporary term 'nubile' suggests that a similar temporal dialectic continues to inform the eroticization of young women. See *OED*, *nubile*, adj.1.

[140] *A Dispvtation* (1592), sig. D3r.

[141] Payer, *Bridling*, 141–153.

[142] Or more: as with virginity, multiple taxonomies of chastity were posited in the premodern period, including the seven-branched 'tree of chastity' that appeared in the fourteenth-century *Book of Vices and Virtues*. See Payer, *Bridling*, 160.

framework, phrases like 'virginal chastity' or 'chastest virgine' appear less tautological than taxonomic, less as superfluous idioms than as markers of intra-categorical relationality.[143] It is no surprise, therefore, that as Greene goes on to describe how 'men iudge of Maydens rarenesse', he offers an almost textbook description of what we might today call the epistemology of chastity in early modern England, whereby a woman's 'inward good quality' is adjudged by 'the modestie of their rayment', their disinclination 'to iet abroade, or to frequent too much company', and their 'Sylence' (sig. D3r). Forging tight metonymic links between various forms of female constraint—of apparel, movement, behaviour, speech, and sexual practice—Greene's advances an epistemology that appears indistinguishable from the broader figuration of women's chastity as a marriage of 'seeming' and 'being'. As Thomas Tuke (in)famously put it:

> It is not enough to be good, but she that is good, must seeme good: she that is chast, must seeme chast: shee that is humble, must seeme humble: shee that is modest, must seeme to bee so, and not plaister her face, that she cannot blush vpō any occasiō (tho she would) so as to be discerned of another.... It is not enough for Christian chastitie that it be, but that it be also seene.[144]

In this book's Introduction, I suggested that this relationship of seeming and being, one of the period's central epistemological conundrums, assumed particular shape and resonance in the discourse of English whoredom, where the presumed whore's capacity to perform chastity, beauty, humility, and modesty—to seem what they were not—defined

[143] Aquinas attributes the phase 'virginal chastity' to Ambrose. See *Summa Theologica* II-II.Q152.1. The phrase 'chastest virgine' appears in John Lyly's *Gallathea*, sig. B1v.

[144] Tuke, *A Discovrse Against Painting and Tincturing of Women*, 16. See also Dorothy Leigh, *The Mothers Blessing* (1627): 'Some of the fathers have written, that it is not inough for a woman to bee chaste, but even so to behaver her selfe, that no man may thinke or deeme her to be unchast.' Cited in Gowing, *Domestic Dangers*, 86. Whereas Leigh gestures towards the prescription's status as a patriarchal construction, the speaker of 'Shall I, like a hermit, dwell', a poem occasionally ascribed to Sir Walter Ralegih, offers a far more laconic construction: 'If she seem not chaste to me, / What care I how chaste she be?' See *The Poems of Sir Walter Raleigh*, 82. And even more ominous version appears in Joseph Swetnam's *The araignment of leuud, idle, froward, and vnconstant women*, wherein the narrator implies that a woman's failure to maintain (the perception of) chaste embodiment would render her culpable for any sexual assault to follow: 'therefore it behooueth euery woman to behaue her selfe so sober and chaste in countenance and speech, that no man may bee so bold as to assayle her' (55).

their 'counterfeit ontology'. This foundational irony helps to explain the often-palpable anxieties that attend figurations of female chastity in the era, as well as the demand, here voiced by Greene and Tuke, that a woman's internal substance be manifest on their bodily exterior: that their daily habitus materialize what lies beneath. But it also reveals a temporal orientation that unfolds less in terms of anteriority, prolepsis, or teleology than what we might call, to borrow a Spenserian formulation, the 'endlesse worke' of appearing always the same.

To apprehend these temporal contours, we must first recall that the discourse of early modern chastity emerged against the backdrop of a broader misogynist ideology that figured all women as innately sensual, inconstant, and duplicitous.[145] To be a 'chaste, silent, and obedient' woman therefore was to overcome—or more precisely, to *chastise*—an intrinsic openness, garrulity, and obstinacy.[146] Understood thus, female chastity appears neither an inborn condition towards which one intuitively inclines nor an anatomical 'fact' to be preserved, both of which would align it with an anterior temporal orientation, but an ongoing and contestatory process: the day-to-day, moment-to-moment work of chastening—of correcting, curbing, disciplining, policing, restraining—one's (supposedly) natural tendencies.[147] To understand premodern chastity as an embodied process is not to suggest ipso facto that it is a sedimentary process: that chastity naturally accrues weight and stability over time, that it becomes more secure, more stable, and less vulnerable with each passing moment. On the contrary, what is most striking about premodern chastity is its conspicuously provisional character: the sense that no matter how hard—and for how long—one has laboured to protect it, one's chaste condition/reputation can disappear at any moment. If such contingency was part and parcel of the culture's broader misogyny,

[145] See, for instance, the critiques of women reprinted in Henderson and McManus, *Half Humankind*.

[146] Indeed, to the extent that the governing terms associated with premodern chastity—continence, continuity, constancy, commitment, fidelity, stability, etc.—directly contravene what we might call, broadly speaking, the ontological portrait of women advanced in the prescriptive literature, the phrase 'chaste woman' emerges, ironically enough, as a kind of catachresis. Useful overviews of early modern prescriptive literature, along with documentary examples, include Hull, *Chaste, Silent, and Obedient*, and Klein, *Daughters, Wives, and Widows*.

[147] Aquinas draws an explicit link between 'chastity' and 'chastisement' in *Summa Theologica* II-II.Q151.11.

it also, I want to suggest, bespeaks narrative and epistemological quandaries unique to chastity as an early modern sexual logic. At once synchronic and diachronic (i.e. a moment-to-moment disciplining of the self that extends without end), this 'chastising process' is—as Matheo's allusion to a 'wet finger' in *The Honest Whore* reminds us—both defined in opposition to and always at risk of termination by the presumed instantaneity of whoredom. Whether or not individual women accepted this oppressive logic,[148] the immense cultural investment in chaste female bodies, and the disciplinary apparatuses that reinforced a woman's literal and symbolic value, rendered the maintenance of chaste embodiment a practical requirement for even the most exceptional of early modern women: even Queen Elizabeth herself was repeatedly forced to defend—at times, with force—the corporeal and characterological constancy proclaimed by her adopted motto, *semper eadem* ('always the same').[149] In a cultural system in which an improper outfit or indiscreet glance or imprudent laugh or untimely blush or unseemly gesture could unsettle a long-established reputation, female chastity was the never-ending work of maintaining one's social, sexual, religious, and corporeal constancy in a world sceptical of its very possibility.

The challenges of premodern chastity, both of its maintenance and adjudication, were further amplified by the demands of licit conjugality. How does one have sex and remain chaste? When is it (in)appropriate to have sex in marriage? On what days, at what times, how often, and for how long? What should conjugal intercourse aim towards, and how might such aims inflect how one's marital coition is perceived and experienced, both 'in the moment' and in relation to broader narratives of social, sexual, and marital life? If such questions illuminate how temporal considerations always already inform the meanings of premodern sex, marital or otherwise, they also remind us that the primary dividing line between virginity and post-virginal chastity in premodern Europe centred on the capacity of the latter to accommodate—indeed, to sanction and render licit—sex in marriage. Or, more aptly, certain kinds of sex,

[148] On women as among the most vociferous supporters of early modern patriarchal ideology, see n. 8 supra. As Valerie Traub reminds us, however, 'the prescriptive power of patriarchal doctrine...fails to capture the ways that women asserted their desires and will—their agency—within such ideological constraints.' See 'Gender and Sexuality in Shakespeare', 101.

[149] Berry, *Of Chastity and Power*; Levin, *The Heart and Stomach of a King*.

for certain reasons, at certain times, and under certain conditions. From the early days of the Christian church through the era of Scholasticism and into the age of Reformations, the discourse of marriage in Western Christianity repeatedly returned to the highly fraught question(s) of sex-in-marriage: of how to define, defend, and delimit an act that would, in any other context, constitute a venial or mortal sin.[150]

Central to such debates were questions of sexual time, timing, and temporality: not only when sex could take place, but how conjugal intercourse should be understood, experienced, and emplotted within broader narratives of social, religious, and domestic life. Certainly, reproductive teleology loomed large: the belief that sex must aim towards procreation was the governing axiom in most conceptualizations of marital coition in pre-Reformation theology. But teleology was not only the only temporal dimension associated with or ascribed to licit conjugality by the theologians and canonists who debated its contours well before Luther arrived in Wittenberg. Rather, and as Pierre Payer has shown in a detailed study of thirteenth and fourteenth century theological struggle, biological reproduction was but one of four potential *causae*—legitimate reasons or intentions—examined by Scholastic writers as they laboured to define and defend the 'moral legitimacy [of] sexual relations in marriage' (62). The other three *causae* argued the validity of marital sex on the grounds that it provided a sanctioned means of (a) fulfilling the marital debt, (b) avoiding fornication, and (c) satisfying lust and/or for the sake of pleasure. Far more controversial than the procreative mandate, these supplemental logics opened onto larger quandaries—particularly regarding the role or function of sexual pleasure—that resisted tidy resolution.[151] They also open onto alternative understandings of how marital chastity was figured and experienced in lived time: less as a teleological phenomenon governed by a singular aim or endpoint than an aspect of daily life informed by a complex interplay of responsibilities, desires, prescriptions, and practices. At the most basic level, these included a series of calendrical prohibitions: married couples were expected to

[150] As Payer puts it, 'sex was not peripheral to the subject of marriage; it was central to almost every facet of marriage' (*Bridling*, 63). Payer attends primarily to the age of Scholasticism, roughly spanning the thirteenth and fourteenth centuries. On sex and marriage in early Christian thought, see Brown, *The Body and Society*.

[151] Payer, *Bridling*, esp. 61–131.

abstain during times of prayer, penance, and menstruation; on holy days and other times associated with the liturgical calendar; on the days preceding childbirth, before and after receiving communion; and, in some traditions, for several days following their nuptials (98–101). Whether or not such proscriptions were honoured in practice, this 'conjugal calendar' offered spouses a tangible means of emplotting sexual practices in calendrical time—and thereby knowing their chaste or unchaste status.

Far more difficult to navigate were the questions of conjugal obligation, libidinal management, and affective moderation embedded within these additional *causae*. Consider, for instance, some of the temporal contradictions and opacities that attend the so-called marital debt, a seemingly straightforward logic that ascribes to each spouse 'the right to ask for sex and the duty to pay the debt when asked' (91). Building on the questions noted above, we might ask: in a cultural system that differentiates between male and female desire, and which associates chastity with the 'bridling of desire', how does a couple achieve an equitable mean? What constitutes the appropriate amount of sex—and for whom?[152] How can a wife request her sexual due and yet remain 'chaste, silent, and obedient?' Who is responsible when a spouse fails to satiate their partner's needs or desires?[153] What happens when a spouse falls ill, proves impotent, or otherwise is unable to fulfil their sexual obligations?[154] Behind each lies the spectre of whoredom, wherein the wife whose desires exceed social expectation (and the vagaries and double binds

[152] As Jennifer Panek notes, while historian Patricia Crawford has suggested that 'moderate' intercourse likely 'meant about three times a month', a broader analysis of contemporary medical and marriage texts reveals 'that the "right" amount of sex was understood to depend very much on the nature of the individual' in question. See '"This Base Stallion Trade"', 367–368. It is also worth noting that whereas contemporary ideologies of gender distinguished between male and female desire, figuring the latter as far more libidinal, the logic the marital debt is, in the contexts of Renaissance England, always already fractured to the extent that it suggests that the possibility of meeting the needs of wives and husbands alike.

[153] See the mid-twelfth-century *Decretum Gratiani*: 'if you abstain without your wife's agreement you give to her a license to fornicate and her sin will be attributed to your abstinence' (reprinted in Payer, 95).

[154] See Luther, 'The Estate of Marriage. 1522': 'Notice that St. Paul forbids either party to deprive the other, for by the marriage vow each submits his body to the other in conjugal duty. When one resists the other and refuses the conjugal duty she is robbing the other of the body she had bestowed upon him. This is really contrary to marriage, and dissolves marriage' (34).

that attend it) can be aligned with the whore who is defined, in part, by a supposedly insatiable desire for sex. Subject to ongoing debate in the period, such quandaries only amplified the challenges of living, maintaining, navigating, and knowing marital chastity even before Protestant reformers began to rethink the contours and meanings of sex in marriage.[155]

If I have here focused on pre-Reformation ideologies of chastity, I have done so for several reasons. First, such an approach aims to avoid the simplistic binary distinction between putatively stable sexual epistemes: a pre-Reformation culture of chastity that refused to countenance any form of intercourse beyond the procreative mandate and a Reformation movement that suddenly and radically reconfigured the meanings of both chastity and marital intercourse. Rather, the questions of chastity—including and perhaps especially how it was perceived and experienced in lived time—presented not only a theological problem that persisted across seemingly disparate historical periods and religious cultures, but a problem of practice and knowledge in quotidian life. Second, such insights recall the various and unstable metonymies that—by linking women's sexual status to their use of language, apparel, comportment, spatial practices, and so forth—buttressed a semiotic system that worked to address the tangled epistemologies of virginity, chastity, and whoredom in early modern England. These were not simply linguistic or academic conjunctions but conceptual bonds that had to be materialized and rematerialized on a day-to-day, even moment-to-moment basis. Third, the long histories of chastity underscore the epistemological implications of a Protestant affirmation of marital sex and pleasure that (officially) encouraged conjugal intercourse as a means of fostering marital and domestic harmony.

As I hope to have suggested, discussions of premodern virginity and chastity concurrently worked to structure, by way of binary opposition, an epistemology of whoredom: where virginity is anatomical presence, whoredom is hymeneal absence; where virginity evokes a certain prelapsarian perfection, whoredom is grounded in a postlapsarian world;

[155] Recalling the proliferation of virginities authored by Albert Magnus, the various quandaries associated with marital chastity generated ongoing efforts to clarify different stages or states of chastity, including the four marital chastities—of spirit, prevention, bed, and body—posited by Daniel Rogers in 1642's *Matrimonial Honour*, sig. Z2r. On this, see Stockton, 'Chasing Chastity', 203–204.

where virginal and marital chastity are materialized through specific acts, practices, or modes of restraint, whoredom is marked by their transgression or violation; where virginity and chastity are characterized by restraint and enclosure, whoredom is typified by errancy, mobility, volubility; where marital chastity follows virginity, whoredom represents a narrative break or deviation—a falling out from the accepted sequence of things. Throughout, I have foregrounded a critical link between temporal and categorical dissonance, stressing how the mixed temporalities of virginity and chastity not only elicit significant cultural labour to resolve the problems (conceptual, definitional, hermeneutic, epistemological, etc.) that they body forth, but concurrently how they produce and frame whoredom by way of conceptual and temporal opposition. At the same time, any such clarity was conspicuously unsettled by two competing ideologies. First, by an ontological construction that foregrounded the whore's ability to pass as a pure virgin or chaste wife—to reposition themselves within a licit narrative sequence by successfully imitating their virgin-chaste counterparts. They do so, writers stress, by mastering the arts of seeming: dressing as respectable women to mask their true social standing; using cosmetics to conceal their age or decrepitude; by inserting 'the bladders of fishes, or galles of beasts filled full of blood' into their vaginas to mimic hymeneal rupture; shedding 'crocodiles teares' to imply 'that the act of generation is very painefull and grievous unto them.'[156] Seemingly able to slip and slide out of roles, relations, and identities at will, to arouse desires and to counterfeit their attachments, it is no surprise that 'whores' emerged as privileged emblems for the manifold dangers—social, spiritual, ontological, epistemological—ascribed to the Renaissance stage by contemporary antitheatrical writers. Second, any notion of an irreconcilable opposition between whoredom and its virginal/chaste antitheses was unsettled by a cultural logic of conversion that incorporated 'honest' or 'repentant

[156] Paré, *The Workes* (1634), sig. Kkkk2r. See also the contemporary ballad, The pedlar opening his pack (*c.*1620): 'A water [that] can restore / a Maydenhead that's vanisht, / You'le say she is no whoore, / Although that it were banish / long before.' Reprinted in *A Pepysian Garland*, 116–120; stanza 12. As Monica H. Green notes, the notion that women might 'restore' their virginity through various 'remedies' long preceded the English Renaissance. The second section (De Curis Mulierum / 'On Treatments for Women') of the composite twelfth-century text known as the *Trotula*, for instance, includes five recipes for, in Green's phrase, 'virginal simulation', including the use of tinctures and the insertion of leeches into the ruff to stimulate blood flow. See *The Trotula*, 42, 103–104.

whores' into its conceptual repertoire, thereby affording a narrative framework through which these previously abject figures could rewrite their socio-sexual ends.

In this chapter, I have explored the various ways in which Ursula Shepherd's story, with which I began, evokes the temporal complexities of early modern whoredom. I have also demonstrated how these complexities augment and unsettle some of the available paradigms through which her sexual narrative may have been understood by those who witnessed her confession at Saint Mary Wollchurch. Finally, I have gestured toward the complexities that underlie her concluding 'promise herafter to lead a chaste life'. If whoredom is at once unchanging and sequential, proleptic and recursive, teleological and atemporal, it is also and therefore a category whose temporal contours encompass all conceivable turns and trajectories, heightening the inherent challenge of ever escaping its narrative and disciplinary grasp. Such an insight points to the significance of all that we do not know about Shepherd's life after whoredom. Did she remarry, pursue new desires, move from the city, or reintegrate herself into the community? How did family members, friends, and neighbours respond to her proclaimed chastity, her return from harlotry? Were they able to reconcile or rethink the relations between her sexual past and chaste present-future? If these questions remain unanswerable, contemporary works like *The Honest Whore* and THE FAMOVS *Whore* remind us that early moderns possessed at least one template for conceptualizing a (re)turn from whoredom to chastity: a long-standing narrative tradition centred on the honest whore or converted courtesan as a repentant sinner *par excellence*. In the second half of this two-part analysis, therefore, we will (re)turn to the period's most memorable and sustained depiction of repentant whoredom: *The Honest Whore*. Representing Bellafront's life both during and after whoredom, the play not only thematizes her sexual status as a (fraught) knowledge relation but actively dramatizes how her narrative and embodied meanings are crafted and contested, made and unmade, in and over time, including by recourse to the temporal logics detailed above. In so doing, the play helps to illuminate some of the unique affordances of the London stage—particularly its capacity to enlist audiences in the conceptual work of sense-making that it depicts onstage—as a medium for exploring how sexual knowledge is made and unmade in early modern England.

Shakespeare and the Making of English Whoredom. Stephen Spiess, Oxford University Press.
 DOI: 10.1093/9780191851223.003.0004

4

Making and Unmaking Whoredom

Turning Chaste in *The Honest Whore*

Ursula Shepherd's implicit promise to 'turn chaste', with which we concluded the preceding chapter, was only one of many early modern narratives that used the repentant whore to invert the normative one-way temporal orientation of a woman's passage from chastity to unchastity. From Jacobus de Voragine's *Legenda Aurea* (trans. 1483), the Digby *Mary Magdalene* (*c.*1515–1525), and Desiderius Erasmus's *A Pithy Dialogue between a Harlot and a godly yong man* (1523) to Robert Greene's 'The conversion of an English Courtizan' (1592), Edward Sharpham's *The Fleire* (1607), and Thomas Cranley's *Amanda, or, The Reformed Whore* (1635), the repentant whore emerged as a privileged figure through which medieval and early modern writers could explore not only the social, linguistic, and corporeal processes necessary to enact and sustain shifts in sexual meanings, but the tensile dynamic between sexual time and narrative knowing.[1] As I detailed in Chapter 3,

[1] To posit a repentant whore 'canon', of course, raises problems of definition similar to those explored throughout this monograph. In addition to those listed above, texts that might be incorporated into any such canon include, but are not limited to, Lewis Wager, *A new enterlude, neuer before this tyme imprinted, entreating of the life and repentaunce of Marie Magdalene* (1566); I.C., *Saint Marie Magdalens Conversion* (1603); Gervase Markham, *The Famovs Whore* (1609); Anon., *The Costlie Whore* (1620–1633); Thomas Heywood, 'Loosenesse of life first conuerted, and the conuersion rewarded, in a home-bred

by turning from incontinence to virtue, degradation to respectability, repentant whores challenge the normative temporal logic that insists whoredom leads inexorably to death and damnation. Disclosing the fiction that such endpoints are fixed, they help to illuminate the varying ways in which non-linear sexual temporalities, including recursive and perverse temporal orientations, inform early modern thinking about sexual status, particularly how it is or can be known as a product of narrative time. But they also, as the fictional tales of Bellafront (*The Honest Whore*) and Paulina (*The Famovs Whore*) reveal, animate additional conceptual and interpretive conundrums, especially in their capacity to evoke an ontological construction (what I have called the 'counterfeit ontology') wherein the very act of 'turning'—and the recursive temporality that it activates—emerges as a preeminent sign by which whoredom is revealed and known. This epistemological double bind both fuels contemporary representations of repentant whoredom and, in so doing, renders whores privileged sites for exploring the narrative and temporal dimensions of early modern sexual knowledge-making.

The early modern stage plays a pivotal role in this conceptual history. While stories of repentant whoredom circulated across a variety of genres and mediums in the period, the unique possibilities and affordances of theatrical representation could be leveraged in ways that encouraged playgoers to examine—even, I will argue, to experience—the epistemological conundrums of repentant whoredom, and the processes through which they might be puzzled out, in performance. Three features are vital here. The first is the theatre's capacity to explore the making and

Historie', in *Γυναικειον* (1624), 458–460; and Thomas Dekker, *The Second Part of the Honest Whore, with the Hvmors of the Patient Men, the Impatient wife: the Honest Whore, perswaded by strong Arguments to turne Curtizan again. her braue refuting those Arguments* (1630). Erasmus's dialogue was printed in a variety of different collections between 1523 and 1637, alternatively entitled '*Adolescenti et Sorti*' ['The Young Man and the Prostitute'], 'Of the Yong man and the *euill disposed woman*', and 'A Pithy Dialogue betweene a Harlot and a godly yong man: shewing how shee going about to catch him in her snares, was (by his forcible persuasions) caught herselfe, and converted to an honest woman'. Nicholas Leigh delivered the first English translation of the dialogue in *A modest meane to Marriage*' (1568). The title adopted here comes from *Seven Dialogves Both Pithie and profitable (1606)*, trans. William Burton. For a contemporary sermon that figures Mary Magdalene as the archetype of human sin and repentance, see Harim White, *The Ready Way to Trve Repentance* (1618).

unmaking of bodily meanings through the staging of real bodies before live audiences. By way of this essential property, theatre affords consideration of what I have called embodiment-as-process on at least two levels: at the level of thematization, whereby select plays depict characters who shape and defend their embodied meanings within the space and time of the fictional world represented onstage; and at the level of mimesis, whereby spectators watch actors embodying roles and can scrutinize how the former become the latter. In Chapter 2, I detailed how this dynamic rendered the early modern stage an especially useful site for exploring how words materialize bodies, what is and is not known through these perlocutionary practices, and how individuals might contest the terms through which they are proclaimed and 'known' by others. But early modern sexual knowledge, as I argued in Chapter 3, is not simply a matter of words and bodies; it is also crafted and contested by recourse to narrative logics and theories of sexual time. Again, the stage offers unique traction on these relations and processes. As with embodiment, theatrical thinking about sexual narrativity and sexual time is animated by an implicit double consciousness that can be deployed in ways that not only channel attention to the problems and processes of sexual knowledge-making depicted onstage but that actively enlist playgoers in this conceptual work. This mode of theatrical interpellation proceeds through the indexing of familiar terms, categories, narratives, and sexual temporalities, and exploring their applicability to staged bodies in the compressed time of performance. Where these structural and temporal binds naturally place such processes under (often conscpicuous) pressure, they also can be animated through the deployment of theatrical conventions and devices that work to foreground the conceptual labour necessary to know and unknow the sexual status of others. To these dual capacities, the staging of (repentant) whoredom and its epistemological quandaries is further enlivened, as we shall see, by a metatheatrical dimension which derives from the whore's status as a privilege emblem of artifice, changeability, and mimesis in the period.

In the early modern period, no work leveraged these meta-epistemological capacities to greater effect than the play I briefly discussed in the preceding chapter: Thomas Dekker and Thomas Middleton's *The Honest Whore, With, the Humours of the Patient Man, and the Longing*

Wife.[2] First performed at the Fortune Playhouse in 1604, the play was printed twice in quarto that year, reprinted four additional times by 1635, and fostered a sequel, *THE SECOND PART OF THE HONEST WHORE*, penned by Dekker and performed onstage by 1608.[3] Collectively, the two plays deliver the period's most prominent and sustained treatment of repentant whoredom. Depicting Bellafront's life during and 'after' whoredom, the plays jointly figure 'turning chaste' to be an ongoing and contestatory process whose dizzying spirals of (un)meaning elicit both a range of powerful affects—including anger, confusion, and erotic desire—and recourse to the narrative and temporal logics detailed in the preceding chapter. In so doing, the duology offers unique analytical traction on the problems of knowing and unknowing (honest) whoredom, the narrative and corporeal strategies through which such problems might be mediated, and the powerful affects to which they might give rise. But the plays also, as I have already begun to suggest, incorporate audiences into these fraught sexual knowledge relations. To detail how this happens, I offer an extended close reading of Bellafront's narrative (un)making in the first play, followed by a brief discussion of her return to the stage in its sequel. Central to my methodology is an analysis of how the play's formal dimensions—from title, emplotment, and stage directions to euphemistic dialogue and uses of dramatic irony—not only channel attention to problems of sexual knowledge but enlist audiences in the very conceptual work being depicted onstage. In so doing, *The Honest Whore* underscores the relational dynamics that, I have argued throughout this book, are essential to understanding the making and unmaking of English

[2] In his diary, Philip Henslowe records a payment of £5 to 'Thomas dekkers & Midleton in earnest of ther playe Called the pasyent man & the onest hore'. For a succinct overview of the authorship debate, see Daalder, 'Dates and Authorship'. Unless otherwise noted, all citations are drawn from Dekker and Middleton, *The Patient Man and the Honest Whore* (ed. Mulholland).

[3] Entered into the Stationers' register on 29 April 1608, the play did not appear in print until 1630. The full title is worth noting: *THE SECOND PART OF THE HONEST WHORE. WITH, THE HVMOURS of the Patient Man, the Impatient Wife: the Honest Whore, perswaded by strong Arguments to turne Curtizan again: her braue refuting of those Arguments.* Cyrus Hoy and Joost Daalder have argued that *THE SECOND PART* may have been written as early as autumn 1604, following immediately upon the success of the first instalment. See Hoy, *Introductions, Notes, and Commentaries to texts in 'The Dramatic Works of Thomas Dekker' Edited by Fredson Bowers*, 68; and Daalder, 'Dates and Authorship'.

whoredom. Both whoredom and turning chaste, the play reveals, are not individual acts but rather knowledge relations and material processes.

To show how this happens, I begin with a plot summary. A hybrid production—by parts romance, London city comedy, and morality play—*The Honest Whore* pursues three interlocking plotlines.[4] In the first, we follow Hippolito and Infelice, young lovers whose desired union is opposed by the latter's father, the powerful Duke of Milan. Putatively conventional, this narrative—which inaugurates the play—begins at an apparent end, as Infelice's seemingly lifeless body is paraded through the streets of Milan en route to interment. The spectacle, audiences soon learn, is a ruse: Infelice's meddling father has drugged her with a sleeping potion and choreographed this 'counterfeit' procession to stymie the relationship and preserve his daughter's chaste estate (13.81). From the outset, Milanese sexual time is out of joint. When a disconsolate Hippolito pledges fidelity to 'her that's dead' (1.137), his rakish companion, Matteo, promises to test this vow by immersing his counterpart in the local sex trade. The primary conflict thus centres not on the prospect of romantic reunion but on the possibility of chaste masculine devotion: how and whether a young gallant can remain honest and faithful in the absence of his (presumably dead) beloved and in the presence of other erotic temptations.

Where Hippolito's journey queries the nature and naturalness of masculine fidelity, the play's second plotline examines a putatively unnatural figure in Candido, a citizen and linen draper whose excessive tranquillity exasperates his wife, Viola. Stretching the bounds of masculine intelligibility, this placid, imperturbable, and seemingly impotent husband proves an unsettling force: a 'patient man' whose gender trouble elicits a range of violent responses from friends and customers alike. These include three young men who enter his shop and test his temperament by making outrageous demands, destroying wares, and absconding with goods. They also extend to Viola, the play's 'longing wife', who hires her dissolute brother, Fustigo, to stir her spouse to wrath and awake his virility through a series of carefully planned sexual and economic offenses: he brazenly steals goods in the shopkeeper's presence, then openly gropes his sister. Crucially, these efforts fail: as Candido proves immutable, it is ultimately this 'longing

[4] Given our interest in the shaping power of interpretive categories, we might also note that the play could also be categorized as a humours play, a shrew play/taming play, and a conversion play, among other possibilities.

wife' who emerges transformed by play's end, undone by her husband's enduring and inexplicable patience.[5]

As a disorderly woman chastened by her male love object, Viola bears a certain kinship to Bellafront,[6] a Milanese sex worker. Spurred by love for Hippolito, Bellafront pledges to reform her ways and convert to an honest life. As we shall see, this conversion takes place early in the play, leaving three full acts—eight, should one include its sequel—to examine her transition, including how others perceive her reformed sexual status over time.[7] Thus, where the dramas of Hippolito and Candido examine how and whether certain kinds of men can remain constant in the face of taunts and temptations, the play's third plotline, cantered on Bellafront, dramatizes an inconstant woman's efforts to become constant, then defend this condition from sceptics and seducers alike. Throughout,

[5] For an acute reading of the economic benefits of Candido's extreme patience, see D. Higginbotham, 'Effete and Elite'.

[6] Frequently overlooked by critics, Viola appears ill-suited to inclusion in the play's title: not only is her role much smaller than that of Candido and Bellafront, but whereas her appellation ('longing wife') broadly aligns with contemporary misogynist constructions of women as insatiable, impassioned, and shrewish, it differs in kind from those applied to her titular counterparts, 'patient man' and 'honest whore', which signal the kinds of social and gendered 'impossibility' that these figures will body forth onstage. In his 2009 edition, Paul Mulholland 'corrects' this imbalance by eliding Viola from the play's title, arguing that *The Patient Man and the Honest Whore* 'restores the balance of the play, giving a unified double paradox where the editorially conventional title provides a single paradox and a consequent sense of incompleteness' (280). Mulholland here presumably is referring to Cyrus Hoy's earlier edition of the play and its sequel), which went by the abbreviated titles *The Honest Whore, Part 1* and *The Honest Whore, Part 2*. Yet if Mulholland is broadly correct at the level of dramatic structure, in that Candido and Bellafront operate as (relatively equal) anchors around which the play's plotlines can be ordered, such an elision discourages consideration of important thematic linkages between Viola and Bellafront, both of whom are, as we shall see, ultimately converted—and chastened—by their male counterparts, in contrast to a figure in Candido whom, we might say, remains ever the same (*semper eadem*).

[7] In so doing, the play encourages attention to how and where other early modern plays emplot a conversional turn, metanoia, practice, or proclamation. Where turns to apostasy, for instance, often occur either early in or prior to the narrative time of works like Daborne's *A Christian Turned Turk* (1612), turns to Christianity often conclude a convert's narrative arc: Corcut (*Selimus, Emperor of the Turks*, 1594), Shylock and Jessica (*The Merchant of Venice* (c.1596–1598), Quisara (*The Island Princess*, c.1619–1621), and Donusa (*The Renegado*, 1630), for instance, all disappear from their textual worlds following conversion. Certainly, this teleological structure governs some repentant whore narratives, such as those by Erasmus and Cranley, which conclude either upon or soon after a desired turn. Yet others devote significant narrative attention to the whore's life after their initial metanoia. In some cases, such as THE FAMOVS *Whore* (1609), these afterlives foreground the fictionality or inauthenticity of the harlot's proclaimed penance.

The Honest Whore channels attention to figures who defy or unfix the social, sexual, and gendered narratives within which they might otherwise be conscripted, as well as to the often powerful affects that emerge in response to the categorical trouble that they elicit and body forth.

Significantly, the play links these fraught knowledge relations to 'madness',[8] a critical keyword and motif that designates not only a cognitive condition, state of affective arousal, and trio of eponymous characters in the play, but ultimately its narrative and spatial telos: in *The Honest Whore*, all plotlines lead to 'Bedlam/Bethlem', the local hospital/madhouse/prison, where the dénouement unfolds.[9] It is an appropriately ironic endpoint for a play so invested in exploring how certain sexual and gendered subjects, to build on Matheo's suggestive formulation, 'be[come] impossible': how, that is, they assume and sustain embodied meanings that defy normative categories of social intelligibility. To do so, the play argues, is to subject oneself to the endless work of becoming otherwise than one has been: the day-to-day, moment-to-moment processes of (re)materializing, (re)narrating, and (re)defining the self. It is also, as we shall see, to navigate the manifold desires and violence that such work elicits in and from others. In *The Honest Whore*, this undertaking takes the shape and form of a 'chastising process': a particular mode of sexual and gendered becoming whose performative requirements, as we shall see, can be leveraged to scrutinize contemporary ideological structures of sex, gender, race, religion, and their complex intersections. Because this process is most explicitly detailed and thematized in and through the figure of Bellafront, I focus primarily

[8] Variations on 'mad' ('horn-mad', 'madcap', 'madman', 'madwoman', &c.) appear eighty-five times in Quarto 1 (1604), permeating the play's rhetorical fabric. Significantly, this rhetoric of madness reaches its apogee in the dénouement, where forty-three discrete utterances create a powerful—and conspicuous—verbal echo. This sense of saturation is only heightened in the playtext, where speech headings and stage directions, particularly those associated with the eponymous 1 MADMAN, 2 MADMAN, and 3 MADMAN, further enhance the verbal and visual presence of madness in Bedlam. At the same time, it is important to note that these eponymous figures are never denominated as 'mad' in the dialogue itself; thus, where these speech headings work to stabilize and materialize these characters' cognitive and social status for readers, playgoing audiences must draw on other forms of evidence—speech, gesture, costume, spatial context, etc.—to discern any such condition.

[9] An infamous London institution translocated to Milan, 'Bethlem/Bedlam' (characters identify the site by both names in Quarto 1) provides an apt habitation and name for the telos of a play so conspicuously invested in category confusion, blurring the boundaries between the play's fictive world and the urban locale in which was initially staged. On the play's 'English Milan', see Howard, 'Civic Institutions and Precarious Masculinity'.

on her narrative in what follows, albeit with the acknowledgement that her plotline intersects in meaningful ways with a range of other characters whose narrative and temporal transgressions appear inexorably to lead to the play's Milanese (London) house of madness.

My argument has three parts. First, I demonstrate how the play's introductory figurations of Bellafront, both prior to her materialization onstage and in her initial scene, work to heighten audience awareness of their own interpretive practices, especially as it aligns her body with nearly every imaginable signifier of Renaissance whoredom. Second, I examine both the play's extraordinary rendering of her chastising process and the temporal irony that underlies it: to prove her newfound chastity, Bellafront must incessantly reiterate her prior whoredom. Suturing her sexual past to her present and future meanings, this performative practice (re)animates the very narrative and temporal ambiguities that the chastising process aims to resolve. In so doing, it creates an interminable feedback loop whereby Bellafront's social, spiritual, and identitarian 'progress' is endlessly undone by the analepses upon which it depends. In the chapter's final section, I connect these spirals of narrative and temporal (un)knowing to *The Honest Whore*'s 'mad' teleology, whereby the play both locates resolution in the city's madhouse and, in the case of Bellafront, figures heterosexual marriage as a pointedly ironic endpoint for a life lived in whoredom. Significantly, Bellafront's narrative does not end when the play draws to close. In this final section, I therefore briefly describe her return to the London stage in *The Second Part of the Honest Whore*, where this now chaste wife finds herself entreated—both by her husband, Matheo, and the agent of her conversion, Hippolito—to 'turne Curtizan again'.[10] Patterned closely on its predecessor, the sequel not only rekindles the epistemological work of its predecessor but also, in its structural and thematic echoes of this prior work, enacts the temporal recursivity that the duology associates with 'honest whoredom'.

Querying the (Honest) Whore

To begin thinking about Bellafront as a problem of sexual and narrative knowing requires turning to a time before the play begins. As we learn

[10] See the play's subtitle: *the Honest Whore, perswaded by strong Arguments to turne Curtizan again: her braue refuting of those Arguments.*

more about theatrical publication in early modern England, it has become increasingly apparent that Londoners could begin thinking about—perhaps even thinking with—a given play before arriving at the theatre. Whether hearing local actors 'crying' the title of an upcoming production in the local streets and thoroughfares or spotting one of the many playbills that graced the 'walls, doors, and doorposts' of city homes and other civic spaces, prospective playgoers—and even those uninterested in such pursuits—may have encountered a given performance prior to its materialization onstage.[11] Some titles may have aroused interest by referencing a well-known figure or personage (*Edward II*, *Selimus*, *Julius Caesar*, *Sir Thomas More*), inviting bystanders to imagine how a new version of an old tale might unfold onstage. Others marketed the representation of a recent history or event (*Arden of Faversham*, *The Massacre at Paris*, *Hollands Leaguer*); a local custom, venue, or trade (*The Shoemaker's Holiday*, *Bartholomew Fair*, *The Alchemist*); or a foreign land, culture, and people (*The Dutch Courtesan*, *The Merchant of Venice*, *The Duchess of Malfi*). But some plays clearly appealed to customers on the basis of a perplexing premise or putative impossibility that—their titles seem to promise—would be puzzled out onstage: *A Woman Killed with Kindness*. *A New Wonder, A Woman Never Vexed*. *Epicœne, or The Silent Woman*. *A Christian Turned Turke*. *A Chaste Maid in Cheapside*. And, of course, *The Honest Whore, With, the Humours of the Patient Man, and the Longing Wife*.

Both similar to and different from 'patient man', 'honest whore' presents a contradiction in terms: a catachresis or, in the contexts of stage drama, an embodied paradox.[12] Even at the level of noun and modifier, the phrase proves conceptually and temporally elusive. To put a few such aporias in motion: does it designate an individual candid or straightforward about their sexual status—someone 'honest', that is, about their (present? past? perpetual? occasional?) 'whoredom?' Does it narrate a history of identity, signalling a progressive movement from whoredom to honesty? Does it operate dialectically, holding past and present meanings in intimate conjunction, suggesting a necessary interplay between seemingly opposed states of sexual being? Is it therefore a noun phrase that betokens neither 'honesty' nor 'whore' per se but rather an identitarian amalgam irreducible to these component parts?

[11] Stern, *Documents of Performance*, 36, 51.
[12] Ure, 'Patient Madman and Honest Whore'; Howard, *Theater of a City*, 114–161.

A semantic aporia that encodes broader questions of sexual ontology and narrative temporality, the phrase 'honest whore' names one of the play's central quandaries.[13] In conjunction with this titular enigma, the structure of the play's opening scenes invites audiences into the work of imagining the sexual status of the characters onstage. Indeed, as Bellafront's appearance onstage is postponed until the sixth scene (and where a similar delay attends the presentation of Candido, the titular 'patient man'),[14] the play's title and dramatic structure work in tandem to heighten audience awareness of our own interpretive practices: how we read the gender and sexual status of the characters who appear before us onstage, and how we categorize each vis-à-vis these titular appellations. Who is (not) whom? How does one know?

Modern editions do some of this conceptual work for us. In their respective editions of *The Honest Whore*, for instance, Fredson Bowers and Paul Mulholland identify Bellafront as the 'honest whore' in character lists that appear just before the play's first scene,[15] thereby foreclosing the moniker's applicability to a range of characters—including Infelice, Viola, and Matheo—who precede her onstage. Consider, for instance, how the word 'honest' circulates in these early scenes. First introduced as an allegorical figure—Matheo, lamenting Hippolito's fidelity to (the supposedly dead) Infelice, argues that a 'strange monster,

[13] These category questions are further amplified by the play's textual history. Configured as an *The Honest Whore* on the title page of Quarto 1 (1604), Bellafront is re-presented as *The Converted Curtezan* in Quarto 2, printed that very same year, only to re-turn to her prior appellation by Quarto 3, printed in 1605. Turning and returning: even in manuscript form, Bellafront slides in and out and between categories of intelligibility, troubling systems of classification. Lest we dismiss such textual oscillations as mere circumstance, Thomas Cranley's 1635 prose pamphlet, *Amanda: or, The Reformed Whore*, reiterates this categorical instability, as its second quarto, printed in 1639, is retitled *The Converted Courtezan, or the Reformed Whore*. Where such movement can be read as mere synonymy, with 'honest' and 'converted', 'whore' and 'curtezan' operating interchangeably, the play's ongoing investment in doubleness, as I argue throughout this chapter, suggests the importance of querying, rather than glossing over, this logic of smooth substitution.

[14] In modern editions of the play, Candido first appears Act 1, scene 5, followed by Bellafront in Act 2, scene 1. See Dekker and Middleton, *The Patient Man and the Honest Whore*; Dekker and Middleton, *The Honest Whore, Part I (Modern)*.

[15] Dekker, *The Honest Whore, Part I*, 20; Dekker and Middleton, *The Patient Man and the Honest Whore*, 285. Similar work is performed by the playbills or *dramatis personae* which circulate in advance of modern performances.

honesty' resides within his counterpart's 'belly' (1.143–144)—the term subsequently is used to describe: the 'honest porter' who greets Fustigo at his sister's door (2.27); Candido, whom Fustigo figures as an 'honester citizen' than the average man (2.107); 'good honest George', a journeyman who works in Candido's shop (5.164); and 'honest Roger', Bellafront's pander, whose relation to the term I address at greater length below (6.30). By the time 'honest' finally is applied to Bellafront, therefore, it already yokes together a multiplicity of characters whose relationship to the modifier range from the (seemingly) authentic to the (potentially) ironic. Far from being resolved, this play of 'honest' is only amplified when Fleullo identifies Bellafront as 'the prettiest, kindest, sweetest, most bewitching honest ape under the pole', after which Matheo cites his brothel-going compatriots as 'honest gallants', and Bellafront figures Hippolito as an 'honest fellow' (6.209–210, 245, 261).[16] This is not to suggest that modern readers and playgoers fail to scrutinize the behaviours and identities of various characters as they appear onstage, nor that they contemplate how such figures do and do not align with the play's titular categories. To the contrary, it is to argue that the play encourages precisely such conceptual work, and that this work is delimited by editorial conventions which augment—we might even say speed up—these interpretive processes: equipped with character lists such as those provided by Bowers and Mulholland, audiences are encouraged to disarticulate a potential conjunction between an onstage character and the 'honest whore' as soon as they hear the former's name uttered aloud (or see their speech prefix).[17] More specifically, these pre-textual and pre-theatrical identifications alter the conceptual parameters of the play's early scenes by shifting from an interrogative to identificatory framework: instead of querying who is or might be the 'honest whore', playgoers are encouraged to locate Bellafront, a figure who always already is attached to this pivotal moniker.[18] In so doing, modern

[16] The term's promiscuous circulation continues throughout the remainder of the play, annexing as well: 1 Prentice ('thou'rt an honest lad', 7.136–137), Crambo and Poh ('they are honest men', 12.113), the Duke ('Honest lord', 14.123), and the Sweeper ('how now, honest fellow', 15.104).

[17] In other words, this conceptual work is especially restricted on the page, where speech headings identify characters often long before their names are uttered onstage.

[18] By contrast, Bowers and Mulholland both identify Candido as 'a linen-draper', rather than 'the patient man', in their respective character lists, thereby enabling the conceptual work that they foreclose in the case of Bellafront. Pauline Kiernan's report on a

editions—however unintentionally—curb the conceptual dynamism of the play's first act, where the identity of the honest whore remains a mystery for six scenes.

Such questions are seemingly laid to rest when Bellafront finally arrives onstage, some thirty minutes into the production, surrounded by nearly every conceivable signifier of early modern whoredom: cosmetics, ruffs, and pokers; mirrors, wines, and tobaccos; bawdy puns and dissolute interlocutors; references to maidenheads, punks, prentices, poisons, pomatums, prices, devils, diseases, gallows, cony catching, and, as one character intimates, more than five hundred sexual partners.[19] It is as if, after withholding the 'honest whore' and the questions that this epithet incorporates—thereby allowing the moniker to circulate across a range of bodies and potential attachments—the play must suddenly and decisively arrest such movement and affix (at least part of) this appellation to a single, identifiable body. As this catalogue suggests, the work of materializing Bellafront's sexual status partakes of multiple sign systems and signifying practices, ranging from dialogue and deictic markers to the non-verbal languages of the early modern stage. All six of the play's seventeenth-century quartos, for instance, feature an unusually explicit set of stage directions preceding Bellafront's entrance,[20] referencing specific props, costumes, and gestures that work

1998 Globe production of the *The Honest Whore* duology suggests a similar bifurcation: while Bellafront is identified as 'the honest whore' in the play's 'persons', Candido appears as a 'line draper'. Mistress Fingerlock, moreover, is identified as 'a bawd', while Roger appears as 'servant to Bellafront'. This tendency to address sexual statuses is replicated in the persons list for the Globe's production of Part II, where Bots ('a pander'), Mistress Horseleach ('a Bawd'), Penelope Whore-hound ('A Whore'), and Catryna Bountinall ('A Whore') are all figured vis-à-vis their roles in Milan's sexual economy. See Kiernan, 'The Honest Whore'. See also the online description for the 2014 Red Bull Theater production of *Dekker & Middleton's The Honest Whore*, which describes Bellafront as a 'lusty prostitute'.

[19] Each of these signifiers appear either in the dialogue or stage directions in Quarto 1: select productions, of course, may alter this polyvalent semiotic economy. Emblematic of the scene's allusive elusiveness, the reference to Bellafront's sexual partners is pointedly suggestive rather than concrete: when she asks Roger, 'how many gentlemen hast thou served thus?', he replies, 'None but fiue hundred, besides prentices and servingmen' (6.164–166).

[20] Such prescriptive work is further amplified in Mulholland's 1999 edition of the play, which interpolates an additional thirty stage directions in this scene alone. On the interpretive foreclosures performed by such 'editorial choreography' (101), see Hodgdon, 'Who is Performing "In" These Texts?'.

to mark to her, and the social space in which she first appears, as recognizably illicit:

> *Enter* Roger *with a stool, cushion, looking-glass and chafing-dish; those being set down, he pulls out of his pocket a vial with white colour in it, and two boxes, one with white, another red, painting. He places all things in order and a candle by them, singing with the ends of old ballads as he does it. At last Bellafront, as he rubs his cheek with the colours, whistles within.*[21]
>
> ...
>
> *Enter Bellafront not full ready, without a gown. She sits down, with her bodkin curls her hair, colours her lips.* (TLN 757–758)

It is a seductive introduction. Bringing audiences into the boudoir and offering a tantalizing glimpse of the 'mistress' beneath her applied 'complexions' (6.35, 9), the *mise-en-scène* conjures an aura of authenticity that encourages us to believe that we are encountering an 'honest' portrait of the figure(s) residing therein. As Bellafront trades barbs with her servant (Roger), warbles a suggestive tune ('Cupid is a god, / As naked as my nail; / I'll whip him with a rod, / if he my true love fail', 6.25–28), and repeatedly calls for her mirror, the scene further aligns her with the signs of whoredom.

Yet just as this introduction presses towards characterological disclosure, it concurrently channels attention to the various kinds of evidence—and interpretive processes—upon which such sexual knowledge depends. It is useful here to think about theatrical time: while the stage directions take only a few seconds to read, the scene might stretch out over several minutes in performance, with Roger leisurely 'assembling' the space for audience as he croons, whistles, and colours his cheeks, followed by Bellafront slowly 'making herself up' with curlers and cosmetics. In performance, the scene can unfold in ways that encourage audiences to contemplate the various non-verbal cues through which this space and its inhabitants are marked. Significantly, it does so not through the terms of whoredom laid out in Chapter 1, but rather the objects of whoredom's significations: its material signatures. Bespeaking whoredom before the characters themselves speak, the *mise-en-scène*

[21] Dekker and Middleton, *The Patient Man and Honest Whore*, 296. These stage directions closely align with those that appear in Quarto 1. See *The Honest Whore, With, The Humours of the Patient Man, and the Longing Wife*, sig. C3v.

hails audiences into an interpretive practice that queries the sexual significance of everyday objects (stools, mirrors, cosmetics, lipstick, etc.) and practices (singing, dressing, curling one's hair, etc.). When and how, the play asks, do we 'know' that this is the space of (honest?) whoredom? And, again, who is this 'honest whore?' As the stage directions reveal, it is Roger—not Bellafront—who initially appears within this space and who paints himself, both literally and figurately, with its cosmetic 'colours'. In the absence of prefatory materials that pre-emptively affix the titular phrase to Bellafront, the scene encourages scrutiny, however briefly, of Roger's candidacy for this moniker. Identified as 'a panderly sixpenny rascal' (6.41), soon thereafter, he seems to be a sexual facilitator, i.e. one who provides access to professional sex workers, rather than a sex worker himself. But even this description is laden with ambiguities: while the first modifier appears to cement his status as a pander, the second modifier and noun, by affixing a price ('sixpenny') commonly associated with whoredom to his 'rascal[ness]', blurs any simple distinction between sexual facilitator and sex worker.[22] As the scene proceeds, moreover, Roger appears less a corrupt procurer than a loyal servant who apprehends his mistress's moral degradation and, as we shall see momentarily, offers this insight up for recognition through several quibbles. Trafficking in allusion, euphemism, and double entendre, he emerges in this early scene as a kind of ironic truth-teller—'honest Roger', Bellafront calls him (6.30)—who, like these rhetorical devices, himself seems to oscillate between multiple meanings, introducing questions about his role that the play never fully resolves.[23]

Such ambiguities, and the questions of sexual knowledge that they encode, incorporate Bellafront as well. Revealed in the very process of 'making herself up', she is presented initially to audiences as a performer *par excellence*: a figure whose very essence lies, in both senses of that

[22] It is an ambiguity aptly reflected in the sexual meanings of 'rascal' in the period. See, for instance, Randle Cotgrave's definitions for the French 'paillard' in *A Dictionarie of the French and English Tongves* (1611): 'm[asculine]. *A lecher, wencher, whoremunger, whore-hunter; also, a knaue, rascall, varlet, scoundrell, filthy fellow*'—a cluster of meanings that Cotgrave distinguishes from 'Paillarde', which he defines as 'f[eminine]. *A whore, punke, drab, strumpet, harlot, queane, courtezan, callet*' (sig. Mmm2r).

[23] Compare, for instance, Roger's role in this scene with his figuration in scene 8 (Act 3, scene 2, in modern editions), where he laments his loss of income following Bellafront's 'turn' and is subjected to an extended critique—along with 'Madonna Fingerlock', her 'poisonous bawd'—by this former 'mistress' (8.1–93).

word (i.e. it both 'resides within' and 'is a falsehood'), in her cosmetic re-presentations. Enacting a dance between seeming and being, artifice and authenticity, her introductory figuration activates a thematic doubleness that will redound throughout the remainder of the scene and play, raising questions of interpretation that evade resolution. By intimating Bellafront's sexual status through a series of euphemisms and double entendres, it implicates readers and playgoers in its conceptual work. Take, for instance, the following exchange:

Ro. There's your ruffe. Shall I poke it?
Bel. Yes, honest Roger—no, stay; prithee, good boy, hold here.
[*Roger holds looking-glass and candle*]
[*She sings*]
Down, down, down, down, I fall
Down, and arise I never shall.
Ro. Troth, mistress, then leave the trade if you shall never rise.
Bell. What trade, Goodman Abram?
Ro. Why, that of down and arise, or the falling trade.
Bell. I'll fall with you by and by.
Ro. If you do, I know who shall smart for't...
...
Bell. So poke my ruff now.—My gown, my gown; have I my fall?
Where's my fall, Roger?
Ro. Your fall, forsooth, is behind. (6.29–60)

What is conveyed here? At the most basic level, we have a servant helping his mistress get dressed. He references a piece of her apparel (a 'ruff', or frill worn around the neck), then offers to animate it with an accoutrement (a 'poker', or object used to stiffen pleats). Concurrently, he activates a series of (potential) double entendres—ruff as vagina, poker as penis, poking as sexual penetration—whose signifying capacities depend upon audience knowledge of these embedded meanings and/or upon onstage actions that press them into visibility.[24] She then croons a contemporary song, which Roger parses as a gloss on her trade and moral condition: she will never be saved (i.e. 'rise') if she doesn't

[24] On euphemism and double entendre as knowledge relations, see Traub, *Thinking Sex with the Early Moderns*, 171–226. We must stress, moreover, that gestures and other non-verbal modes of theatrical meaning-making—an actor thrusting their pelvis forward, for instance—may not signify clearly or univocally to all playgoers.

leave her (as yet unspecified) 'trade'. Failing to follow his drift (or ignoring it), she draws on contemporary cant discourse—a niche lexicon associated with the criminal underworld—to figure him as a 'Goodman Abram', i.e. a beggar who feigns madness to avoid work. When he attempts to clarify his comment by suggesting that she trades in bodies that (literally) rise and fall, and/or participates in a (metaphorically) fallen trade, she threatens to hit him: 'I'll fall with you by and by', which Mulholland glosses 'assail with blows; settle with'.[25] Or, she intimates that she'll have sex with him, i.e. 'fall' into bed with him. Should she 'do' so (strike him? Have sex with him?), Roger replies, he knows who will pay for it. It is a knowledge withheld from audiences, as the dialogue shifts in another direction without further explication. When Bellafront searches for another piece of apparel (her 'fall', or lace collar) moments later, she reanimates the double entendres (arguably) implicit in Roger's opening query—'poke my ruff now'—and introduces another (potential) pun in 'fall', which may also connote a fall from grace. Indeed, both senses of the term remain active in Roger's response, where he locates Bellafront's lace collar and/or moral lapse 'behind' her, i.e. spatially located to her posterior or chronologically located in her historical past. Laden with multiplicities, the exchange aptly figures the problems of sexual knowledge that attend Bellafront's introductory figuration: who understands what here? What do the characters know about the meanings, sexual or otherwise, to which they give voice? How does this knowledge compare to, or contrast with, what audiences (presumably) learn about them and their sexual statuses by way of such language?

Bellafront's song is also instructive in this regard. As Roger suggests, the lyrics—'Down, down, down, down, I fall / Down, and arise I never shall'—operate as a kind of theatrical confession, clarifying Bellafront's fallen condition and the teleologic to which it presumably is tethered: she 'never shall…arise' from such an abject position. To the extent that she appears unable or unwilling to apprehend such inflections, moreover, the exchange offers additional narrative and identitarian coordinates: fully immersed in a cosmetic, euphemistic, and polyvalent world, Bellafront does not—perhaps cannot—(yet) apprehend the 'true' meanings of her narrative. She is, in other words, not (yet) an 'honest' whore but rather a woman still falling 'down, down, down'.

[25] *The Patient Man and the Honest Whore*, 297 n. 38.

In the context of a conspicuously allusive scene, the song offers a certain narrative and conceptual ballast, illuminating Bellafront's standing for audiences by situating her within a recognizable narrative trajectory. Articulated in her own voice, it foregrounds the epistemological purchase of self-critique, previewing the central role that confession will play in her later conversional turn. But as a confession, the song is riven with ironies. First, if Bellafront here proclaims her fallen condition, she does so not in her words but by way of another's language.[26] Second, if these lyrics annex a teleologic that fixes her narrative trajectory, they contravene Roger's subsequent intimation that, should she 'leave the trade', she might reverse this moral and narrative decline—as well as the play's own dramatic trajectory. Third, and in so doing, the song foreshadows the structural irony that underwrites her later turn to chastity: to 'arise' and return to honesty, Bellafront must incessantly revisit her 'fallen' condition.

Emblematic rather than exceptional, the exchange discloses a broader play of revelation and evasion that both suffuses Bellafront's introductory moments and implicates audiences in its epistemological work. Incessantly proffering evidence of her illicit sexual status by way of words and signs that quite conspicuously can mean otherwise—that are pointedly allusive, suggestive, and playful rather than concrete or referential—the scene thematizes sexual status as a knowledge relation: as constituted, that is, through a highly fraught interplay of signifying processes, material bodies, social histories, narrative logics, and, as Valerie Traub has argued, 'implicit understandings of what counts as knowledge and what eludes or baffles as ignorance'.[27] Hailing audiences into a series of interpretive quandaries—does 'ruff' connote 'vagina'? What 'trade' does Bellafront practice? Does the song disclose a fallen condition? How do these verbal signifiers correspond with the nonverbal evidence proffered onstage?—it asks them to annex the sexual knowledges and assumptions that they bring to the theatre in order to make sense of what appears before their eyes. And it is a kind of cognitive work shaped by the unique temporal pressures of performance, where playgoers cannot simply freeze time to check an editorial gloss or

[26] Mulholland (*The Patient Man and the Honest Whore*, 297 nn. 32–33) identifies the lyrics as a refrain from a contemporary song, 'Sorrow, Sorrow, Stay', printed in John Downland's *Second Book of Songs or Ayres* (1600).

[27] *Thinking Sex with the Early Moderns*, 5.

look up unfamiliar terms in the dictionary. This work, of course, is also informed by the scene's implicit voyeurism, which offers audiences a privileged glimpse into the boudoir and its illicit inhabitants. As Bellafront's metatheatrical entrance reminds us, moreover, stage drama is a representational medium especially well suited to leveraging differences of insight and understanding, not only between characters onstage but between characters and playgoing audiences. Dramatic irony, in other words, can operate as a tool for epistemological inquiry: channelling attention to what is offered, accepted, overlooked, and rejected as evidence and/or knowledge, as well as to terms, narrative logics, and interpretive strategies that work to bypass or resolve these epistemological quandaries.

Additional ironies structure Bellafront's theatrical introduction and the questions of sexual (un)knowability encoded therein. The first is perhaps so obvious as to escape notice: even as the dialogue and *mise-en-scène* submerge Bellafront and audiences within a sea of signifiers that intimate her illicit status, the term 'whore' is conspicuously withheld from the scene's discursive economy. Over the first 278 lines, she is identified as [a/an/the]:

> mistress (×11); devil; pug; coz (×3); sweet acquaintance (×2); little marmoset; good pretty rogue; light angel; acquaintance (×5); wench (×3); my little pretty mistress, sweet Bellafront; lady (×3); sweet; a poor gentlewoman, of passing good carriage; a captain's wife; the prettiest, kindest, sweetest, most bewitching honest ape under the pole; sale courtesan; good wench (×2); sweet Jew; sirrah Bellafront; punk (×2); waspishest ape; like a madwoman; like every common hackney that steals out at the back gate of her sweet knight's lodging. (6.1–278)

Mingling the honorific and affectionate (sweet, lady, mistress, gentlewoman) with the derogatory and dehumanizing (devil, wench, ape, punk), such monikers oscillate among seemingly incommensurate identities and meanings. Riven with puns (sweet acquaintance, light angel) and oxymorons (good…rogue, sweet Jew),[28] they render in

[28] I here follow Traub's insight that historically contingent puns and euphemisms activate questions of sexual knowledge that enlist audiences, both past and present, into the play's conceptual work. Does 'acquaintance', for instance, suggest that such characters are familiar with Bellafront's 'quaint/cunt'? See *Thinking Sex*, esp. 171–226. On 'rogues' as figures that unsettle some of the basic binaries (illicit/illicit, elite/base) through which

linguistic form the broader thematic doubleness that suffuses the scene and unsettles its signifying economy. Finally, and by encouraging audiences to perceive the 'lady' in the 'punk', and the 'sale courtesan' in the 'sweet acquaintance', they loosen some of the binary oppositions upon which whore discourse depends. It comes as little surprise, therefore, that when the term 'whore' finally enters the scene, it is not applied to this polyvalent figure but rather to (the absent) Infelice—Hippolito's supposedly dead/chaste beloved, whom Bellafront cites as '[s]ome whore!' (6.153). Laden with irony, the utterance aptly foreshadows Bellafront's ironic declaration, some one hundred lines later, that she will 'prove an honest whore' (6.363).[29]

As should be clear, I am not arguing that the play introduces Bellafront as a pure or chaste woman, nor that audiences fail to perceive her illicit sexual status in the scene. Indeed, the play's structure—and Bellafront's conversion in particular—depends precisely upon establishing this abject condition in order that it subsequently can be undone. In both religious and theatrical terms, such extreme depravity enhances the drama of Bellafront's attempted conversion. What I wish to stress, however, is the extraordinary elusiveness of the scene: the manner in which it incessantly offers and withdraws sexual knowledge; how it surrounds Bellafront with nearly every signifier of early modern whoredom yet pointedly resists aligning the term 'whore' with her body until the precise moment that she turns away from it; how its semiotic excess belies the purported ease of distinguishing between women chaste and wanton, suggesting just how many cues are needed to render Bellafront as a stable and intelligible object of sexual knowledge; how, in so doing, it encourages attention to additional terms, tropes, narrative logics, and material practices that emerge to 'fix' her place in sexual and narrative time; how even these are beset by ironies and aporias that, as with Bellafront's initial figuration, intimate an intrinsic doubleness that appears destined to haunt her own—and the play's—narrative gambit;

early modern society has been brought into clarity by scholars, see Friedlander, *Rogue Sexuality in Early Modern English Literature*.

[29] In addition to the obvious (i.e. Bellafront, who is 'really' a whore, slanders Infelice, who is 'really' chaste), the first utterance establishes an unexpected kinship between these seemingly disparate figures, both of whom transition from 'death' to 'life' and, for the majority of the play, are attached to the same love object in Hippolito. The latter utterance, of course, is ironic in that Bellafront acknowledges her 'whoredom' precisely in the act of undoing it.

and how, finally, such dizzying spirals of meaning implicate audiences in what I have called the making of English whoredom.

The play further interpellates its audiences by teaching them to read Bellafront ironically. The primary instructors here are Matheo and Hippolito, who enter midway through this introductory scene. First, Matheo provides her with a proper name: 'Bellafront' (6.173).[30] A cross-linguistic portmanteau that marries the Italian *Bella-* ('pretty', 'beautiful') to the English *front*, the name is a fitting synecdoche for the play's cultural double vision. But it also, and more important for our purposes, is an interpretive clue that cues playgoers to perceive a disjunction between Bellafront's external appearance and her inner substance. Intimating both that she is beautiful and that this beauty 'could be a superficial façade',[31] in other words, the name encourages audiences to distrust (some of) the evidence that appears before their eyes. The point is further underscored during Hippolito's initial exchange with Bellafront. As elsewhere, the dialogue is animated by an implicit metatheatricality. Introduced to audiences as a 'stranger' unacquainted with 'the fashions o'th' house' (6.189–190), Hippolito operates as a kind of surrogate for 'honest' playgoers: as we watch him take the measure of this house and its inhabitants, navigate its bawdy lexicon, ask questions, and work towards understanding, he models a kind of sense making amidst this world of playful allusion. What he does *not* do is immediately proclaim Bellafront's illicit status, thereby giving the lie to the notion that whoredom is readily legible on the body and/or easily perceptible to 'honest fellow[s]' (6.261). To the contrary, Hippolito twice refers to her as a 'lady' (6.185, 200), reinforcing the notion that—at 'face value'—she is indistinguishable from her licit counterparts. He does not stop there. Rather, and after thanking Bellafront for inviting him to sit, he turns to one of her 'acquaintances', Fluello, and gives voice to the scene's central enigma: 'What may this lady be whom you call coz?' What follows is an act of analysis so succinct as to approach the didactic:

[30] As with 'whore', this moniker is withheld for an extended period of time: 173 lines in the scene, 891 lines in the play as a whole.

[31] Brunning, '"Thou Art Damned for Alt'ring Thy Religion"', 155. For a broader of Bellafront as a figure of cosmopolitan hybridity, see Fox, 'Cosmopolitan Desire and Profitable Performance in *The Dutch Courtesan*'.

Flu. Faith, sir, a poor gentlewoman, of passing good carriage; one that has some suits in law, and lies here in an attorney's house.
Hipo. Is she married?
Flu. Ha, as all your punks are; a captain's wife, or so.—Never saw her before, my Lord?
Hipo. Never; trust me, a goodly creature.
Flu. By gad, when you know her as we do, you'll swear she is the prettiest, kindest, sweetest, most bewitching honest ape under the pole. A skin—your satin is not more soft, nor lawn whiter.
Hipo. Belike, then, she's some sale courtesan.
Flu. Troth, as all your best faces are, a good wench.
Hipo. Great pity that she's a good wench. (6.201–214)

Swatting aside Fluello's euphemisms, Hippolito cuts to the quick: 'is she married?' As if rejecting all that come before—the circuitous allusions, the manifold ironies, the teasing play of identifications, and so forth—he privileges conjugal status as the conceptual anchor that will ground his interpretive practice. It doesn't matter, in other words, what Fluello calls her ('a poor gentlewoman'), or why she is here (she 'has some suits in law'), or even where 'here' is ('an attorney's house'); what matters, Hippolito implies, is her marital status. It is the departure point for his style of reasoning, the condition upon which his hermeneutic practice seems to hinge. But when Fluello blurs rather than clarifies this condition—intimating that, like other 'punks', Bellafront will veil herself under the cloak of marriage by claiming a husband-at-sea—and persists in figuring her metaphorically, Hippolito shifts gears. Converting from a hermeneutics of authenticity to one of irony, he finds meaning in Bellafront's metaphoricity itself. In so doing, he is able—and quickly—to perceive the 'sale courtesan' in the 'good wench'.

The insight aptly captures the abyssal nature of Bellafront's proclaimed meanings and the interpretive binds that it places upon audiences. How, in a scene and play that incessantly ironizes meaning, can we take any word or statement applied to this dissonant figure—much less her subsequent declaration that she will 'become pure-honest' (6.483)—at face value? The answer, it would appear, is three-fold: first, the play requires the emergence of an 'honest' speaker, i.e. Hippolito, whom audiences can take at their word;

second, this figure must narrate Bellafront's sexual meanings—past, present, and future—at such length as to leave little doubt regarding her illicit status; and third, she must recognize herself, both in his terms and the interpretive logics to which they give voice. Only in so doing, the play's structure intimates, can she invert her narrative trajectory and turn chaste. It is neither an instantaneous act nor progressive sequence but rather an interminable process of chastisement that stimulates additional ironies, ambiguities, and desires through the very practices that aim to clarify Bellafront's sexual meanings in narrative time.

'I Am Not as I Was': Sexual Time, Narrative Knowing, and the Chastising Process

Bellafront's turn to chastity begins with a counterfeit vision of her conjugal future. After briefly departing, Hippolito returns to find himself alone with her. Sharing his intuition that 'my friend [Matheo] / Is old in your acquaintance', he inquires whether she would 'let [him] play Matheo's part...embrace you, dally with you, kiss [you]' (6.300–308). It is a shocking query. Configured as the scene's only 'honest' broker moments earlier, Hippolito suddenly appears to have succumbed to the seductions of the house; or to be a false coin himself; or to be playing an ironic game that seeks truth (i.e. Bellafront's real character) by way of the lie (i.e. Hippolito's desire for her). Before audiences have time to parse these possibilities, he further muddies the scene by encouraging her—and us—to envision their potential future together:

Hipo. Faith, tell me, will you leave him, and love me?
Bell. I am in bonds to no man, sir.
Hipo. Why then,
You're free for any man; if any, me.
But I must tell you, lady, were you mine,
You should be all mine: I could brook no sharers;
I should be covetous, and sweep up all.
I should be pleasure's usurer; faith, I should.
Bell. O fate! (6.309–316)

As Bellafront's apostrophe suggests, it is Hippolito's vision of monogamous coupledom that first kindles her metanoia—a 'change of spirit or mind' often translated, in theological discourses, as 'repentance' or 'penitence'.[32] Lamenting that it 'has never been my fortune yet to single / Out that one man whose love could fellow mine, / As I have ever wished it', she responds to Hippolito's conditional with her own counterfactual, insisting had she 'but met with one kind gentleman / That would have purchased sin alone to himself / For his own private use', she would have been as 'true' and 'loyal' to him as 'ever a poor gentlewoman could be' (6.317–328). Blurring the boundaries between licit monogamy and illicit sex work, the statement brilliantly figures metanoia less as an instantaneous transition between opposed states of being than a confusing process that brings perceived opposites (wife and kept woman) into unsettling proximity. It is also, as Hippolito quickly points out, a claim nearly impossible to accept: 'This were well now, to one but newly fledged, / And scarce a day old in this subtle world: / 'Twere pretty art, good birdlime, cunning net' (6.329–331). Reading her ironically, he reminds audiences that it is precisely through such deceptive 'art[s]' that 'cunning' whores 'net' naïve men. Lest they miss the point, he puts it even more succinctly moments later: 'I know you feign / All that you speak; ay, for a mingled harlot / Is true in nothing but in being false' (6.365–367). Evoking what I have called the 'counterfeit ontology' of early modern whoredom, Hippolito's illuminates the conceptual impasse being staged for audiences at this very moment: just as Bellafront insists upon the 'truth' of her testament, promises to 'swear' by it, and declares that she will 'prove an honest whore, / In being true to [him] and to no more' (6.362–363, 343), he insists that the only truth to be derived from such language is its—and her—inherent falseness.

The only way out of this aporia, the scene goes on to suggest, is to saturate Bellafront in yet more language. What follows is an act of chastisement both extraordinary in length and breathtaking in its virulence. Where such excess is *to the point*, I reprint the majority of passage, then parse its most salient characteristics:

Hipo. Lend me your silence, and attention.—
You have no soul;
That makes you weigh so light; heaven's treasure bought it,

[32] Murray, *The Poetics of Conversion in Early Modern English Literature*, 7–8.

And half a crown hath sold it. For your body,
It's like the common shore, that still receives
All the town's filth. The sin of many men
Is within you; and thus much, I suppose,
That if all your committers stood in rank,
They'd make a lane, in which your shame might dwell,
And with their spaces reach from hence to hell.
Nay, shall I urge it more? There has been known
As many by one harlot maimed and dismembered
As would ha' stuffed an hospital; this I might
Apply to you, and perhaps do you right.
O, you're as base as any beast that bears;
Your body is e'en hired, and so are theirs.
For gold and sparkling jewels, if he can,
You'll let a Jew get you with Christian.
Be he a Moor, a Tartar, though his face
Look uglier than a dead man's skull,
Could the devil put on a human shape,
If his purse shake out crowns, up then he gets:
Whores will be rid to hell with golden bits.
So that you're crueller than Turks, for they
Sell Christians only; you sell yourselves away.
Why, those that love you, hate you, and will term you
Lickerish damnation; wish themselves half sunk
After the sin is laid out, and e'en curse
Their fruitless riot—for what one begets
Another poisons; lust and murder hit.
A tree being often shook, what fruit can knit?

Bell. O me unhappy!

Hip. I can vex you more.
A harlot is like Dunkirk, true to none,
Swallows both English, Spanish, fulsome Dutch,
Back-doored Italian, last of all the French;
And he sticks to you ,faith, gives you your diet,
Brings you acquainted first with Monsieur Doctor,
And then you know what follows.

Bell. Misery.
Rank, stinking, and most loathsome misery.

Hip. Methinks a toad is happier than a whore.
That with one poison swells, with thousands more
The other stocks her veins.—Harlot? Fie, fie!

You are the miserablest creatures breathin,
The very slaves of nature. Mark me else:
You put on rich attires, others' eyes wear them;
You eat but to supply your blood with sin,
And this strange curse e'en haunts you to your graves:
From fools you get, and spend it upon slaves.
Like bears and apes you're baited and show tricks
For money, but your bawd the sweetness licks.
Indeed, you are their journeywomen, and do
All base and damned works they list set you to;
So that you ne'er are rich—for do but show me,
In present memory or in ages past,
The fairest and most famous courtesan,
Whose flesh was dear'st, that raised the price of sin
And held it up, to whose intemperate bosom
Princes, earls, lords—the worst has been a knight,
The mean'st a gentleman—have offered up
Whole hecatombs of sighs, and rained in showers
Handfuls of gold; yet for all this, at last
Diseases sucked her marrow, then grew so poor
That she has begged, e'en at a beggar's door.
And—wherein heaven has a finger—when this idol
From coast to coast has leaped on foreign shores,
And had more worship than th' outlandish whores,
When several nations have gone over her,
When for each several city she has seen
Her maidenhead has been new and been sold dear,
Did live well there, and might have died unknown
And undefamed, back comes she to her own;
And there both miserably lives and dies,
Scorned even of those that once adored her eyes;
As if her fatal-circled life thus ran:
Her pride should end there where it first began.
What, do you weep to hear your story read?
Nay, if you spoil your cheeks, I'll read no more.

Bel. O yes, I pray proceed:
Indeed, 'twill do me good to weep indeed.

Hip. To give those tears a relish, this I add:
You're like the Jews, scattered, in no place certain;
Your days are tedious, your hours burdensome,
And were't not for full suppers, midnight revels,

Dancing, wine, riotous meetings, which do drown
And bury quite in you all virtuous thoughts,
And on your eyelids hang so heavily
They have no power to look so high as heaven,
You'd sit and muse on nothing but despair,
Curse that devil Lust, that so burns up your blood,
And in ten thousand shivers break your glass
For his temptation. Say you taste delight
To have a golden gull from rise to set,
To mete you in his hot luxurious arms;
Yet your nights pay for all: I know you dream
Of warrants, whips, and beadles, and then start
At a door's windy creak, think every weasel
To be a constable, and every rat
A long-tailed officer. Are you now not slaves?
O, you have damnation without pleasure for it!
Such is the state of harlots. To conclude,
When you are old, and can well paint no more,
You turn bawd and are then worse than before.
Make use of this; farewell. (6.373–474)

Almost one hundred lines, Hippolito's chastisement is a theatrical set piece: a rhetorical tour de force that, were it not for Bellafront's brief interjections, would rank among the longest declamations on the early modern stage.[33] Framed as a didactic tool through which he will 'teach

[33] Excepting Bellafront's interjections, Hippolito's speech is exactly one hundred lines in Quarto 1 (TLN 1082-1187). By comparison, Don Andrea's opening soliloquy in *The Spanish Tragedy* clocks in at eighty-five lines (1.1.1–85), as does Ulysses' oration on 'degree' in *Troilus and Cressida* (Quarto 1, TLN 513–597). Edward's portion of the deposition speech in *Edward the Second* is eighty-two lines (5.1.5–89), while Berowne's 'affections men' speech in *Love's Labours' Lost* is seventy-seven lines (Quarto 1, TLN 1639–1716). Morocco and Arragon's casket speeches in *The Merchant of Venice*, excepting Portia's interjections, are seventy-one and sixty-five lines in Folio 1 (TLN 976–1051, 1121–1191, respectively, while the introductory and concluding soliloquies in *Doctor Faustus* are sixty-four and fifty-two lines (1.1.1–66, 5.3.133–185, A-Text). Francisco's recollection of, and encounter with, Isabella's ghost in *The White Devil* is sixty-five lines (4.1.74–139); *Hamlet*'s 'rogue' soliloquy is fifty-seven lines (Quarto 2, TLN 1589–1646); Marcus's reading of Lavinia in *Titus Andronicus* is forty-six lines (Quarto 1, TLN 1084–1130); Kate's 'a woman moved' speech in *The Taming of the Shrew* is forty-three lines (Folio 1, TLN 2694–2737); John of Gaunt's 'blessed plot' speech in *Richard II* is thirty-seven lines (Folio 1, TLN 672–709); and Juliet's 'gallop apace' soliloquy is a rather concise thirty-five lines (Quarto 2, TLN 1645–80). Herod's concluding speech in the closet drama *The Tragedy of Mariam*, among the longest I have found, clocks in at 105 uninterrupted lines (5.1.153–258).

[Bellafront] how to loathe' herself (6.368), his invective is both time-consuming and, as such, a critical component of Bellafront's chastising process: turning chaste, the play argues, is to submit oneself precisely to such seemingly endless acts of castigation. While Bellafront will soon internalize and self-administer this chastisement, the scene here foregrounds the importance of an initial castigator: an external figure—invariably male[34]—whose 'thunder oaths' can 'pierce [the harlot's] soul...with horror and amazement' (6.340–343). Hippolito's lacerating language, in other words, is an important catalyst for Bellafront's metanoia-in-process.

In addition to its astonishing vitriol, the speech encourages audiences to 'know' Bellafront's illicit status by annexing several of the interpretive paradigms detailed in Chapter 3. Echoing Augustine and Aquinas, Hippolito figures Bellafront as a repository for 'All the town's filth'. Like Luther, he paints her as a parasite envenomed with disease. Like Gainsford, Lenton, and Overbury, he delineates her present 'damnation' and predicts her further degradation. Like Markham, he claims that she has sold her 'maidenhead' time and again, thereby corrupting the life cycle paradigm, then prophecies her eventual impoverishment and imprisonment. To these logics Hippolito adds his own formidable metaphors, the most striking of which figures her body as a seaport ('Dunkirk') that 'swallows' men of all religions (Jew, Christian, Moor, Tartar, Turk) and ethnicities (English, Spanish, Dutch, Italian). Figuring her as sexually indiscriminate, the trope annexes another contemporary stereotype: the whore as 'open' to all men. It also, albeit more subtly, opens onto another motif that courses through Hippolito's discourse: a fascination with, and fixation upon, the multiplicity of men whose 'sin', he insists, remains 'within [her]'. First, he conjures a striking image of her paramours standing in a line that stretches 'from hence to hell'. Organized hierarchically (by 'rank') and oriented vertically and teleologically (descending to her implied destination), the projection powerfully figures the breadth, depth, and consequence of Bellafront's sexual degradation. It also insists upon the present significance—we might even say the present 'presence'—of these men to her sexual meanings.

[34] In Thomas Cranley's *Amanda, or, The Reformed Whore* (1635), for instance, the title character first recognizes her profane status when the narrator sends her a vitriolic letter detailing 'the legend of [her] wicked life' (29).

A similar trajectory subtends Hippolito's seaport analogy, which comes moments later and declines from lovers 'English, Spanish, [and] fulsome Dutch' to the 'Back-doored Italian, [and] last of all the French'. Together, these sequences recall Hippolito's earlier inference that, should he 'but [step] o'er your threshold', i.e. enter Bellafront's house/body, he would immediately be followed by 'a next man / And after him a next, and then a fourth' (6.346–347). In their striking interplay of hierarchy and mixture, aggregation and individuation, the images raise fascinating questions about Hippolito's sexual imaginary. They also reiterate the importance of conceptualizing Bellafront's sexual meanings in and across time: historically, sequentially, and proleptically. To know herself, Hippolito insists, Bellafront must narrate the present and future significance of her sexual past. Just as Bellafront's introductory scenes dramatize the manifold processes through which an individual can be aligned with the sign of whoredom, Hippolito's extraordinary chastisement demonstrates how the mixed temporalities that subtend early modern whore discourse work, even by way of their apparent contradictions and paradoxes, to secure Bellafront's meaning in lieu of a fixed or stable essence: not simply through their sheer denunciatory force, but by offering audiences multiple methods for apprehending her sexual meanings in narrative time.

Time-consciousness remains a point of emphasis even as Hippolito exits the scene. Noting that 'time hath barred [him]' from remaining in place, he eschews Bellafront's entreaty to 'Stay yet a little longer!' (6.476–478). In his wake, she immediately revisits her own sexual history, cursing 'that minute—for it was no more. / So soon a maid is changed into a whore—/ Wherein I first fell, be it for ever black' (6.479–481). Anticipating Matheo's later claim that 'many honest wenches turn strumpets with a wet finger' (9.106), the recollection both underscores the speed of her transition from 'maid' to 'whore' and signals an emerging self-consciousness grounded in a narrative understanding of her sexual past and its temporal dimensions. But it also invites audiences into the sexual-conceptual work being depicted onstage: juxtaposing this momentous 'minute' in her sexual past with her newfound 'love' for Hippolito, Bellafront turns this temporal (il)logic on its head moments later. Asking 'Am I not fair?' (6.485), she forces audiences to contemplate the (im)possibility of an equally quick transition in the opposite direction. If maids can become whores in under a minute, she queries, why can't she become 'pure-honest' with similar speed (6.483)?

Easily addressed to playgoing audiences, Bellafront's inquiry underscores one of the many ways in which her chastisement can be performed in ways that enlist audiences into the play's sexual-conceptual work. When Hippolito interpellates Bellafront, for instance, insisting that she recognize herself in his terms, his declamation can be delivered in ways that facilitate audience participation. By this, I don't simply mean that playgoers are encouraged to accept his framing of Bellafront's embodied meanings, the narrative and temporal logics that he annexes, the misogyny that underpins his argument; to a certain extent, the structure of the repentant whore plot requires such acceptance, even as it discloses the contradictions and ambiguities upon which such knowledge depends. Rather, Hippolito can chastise playgoers alongside Bellafront. 'Lend me your silence, and attention': much like a pastor preaching from the pulpit, the actor playing Hippolito might begin with a direct appeal to audiences, suggesting that they too must submit to his chastening invective. Such a move would reinforce his didactic function, noted above, wherein he operates as the play's preeminent instructor in the arts of reading and knowing whoredom. But it would also, and even more provocatively, emphasize a potential kinship between Bellafront and her offstage audiences, wherein both are figured as sinners requiring moral rectification. Such a possibility aligns with the discursive figuration of early modern playgoers advanced in contemporary antitheatrical literature, which placed considerable emphasis on the theatre as a site of sexual commerce. At the same time, however, the very force of Hippolito's denunciation, and the extremity of his discursive figuration, allows audiences to critique his perlocutionary practice in ways unavailable to Bellafront.

It is therefore unsurprising that, as her narrative unfolds, the play foregrounds not only the material and linguistic practices through which Bellafront attempts to prove her newfound condition but also her counterparts' inability—or unwillingness—to imagine or accept her on such terms. As noted, she first signals her metanoia-in-process by embracing Hippolito's vision of patriarchal monogamy and submitting to his chastisement. Voicing a desire for further castigation, she then reflects on her own sexual narrative and, as such, begins to recognize herself in Hippolito's terms. Oscillating between her 'fair' and 'foul' condition(s), she moves to purge the 'Harlot' within (6.485–495), figuring it as a material stain that might be excised through bloodletting, only to jettison this idea and the material-temporal logic that subtends it upon Hippolito's return. Rejecting her request that he love or kill her, Hippolito augments her chastening by treating her with voiceless 'disdain' (6.504). In the scenes that follow, Bellafront further performs her reformation through a variety of means. Changing her apparel, she re-presents herself to audiences as a licit woman (8.30). Weeping, blushing, and lowering her head in shame, she materializes her metanoia through a range of affective responses that are discerned and described by her onstage counterparts (6.448–449, 9.23–24). Eschewing the bawdy rhetoric of Matheo, Castruccio, Fluello, and Pioratto, she adopts a language of 'pray[er]' and 'soul', further intimating her altered consciousness (9.35–66). Echoing Hippolito's 'poison[ous]' language, she begins to supplant him as the play's preeminent castigator: a scourge whose unflinching chastisement narrates the long-term consequences of illicit sex and thereby aims to 'persuade' others to reform their ways (9.52). It is an endless practice, the play argues, necessary to batten down the ever-present prospect that Bellafront's manifold alterations—her change of apparel, her capacity to weep and repent, her purified speech—are not authentic signifiers of a newfound honesty but rather counterfeit signs of her enduring whoredom.

Such paradoxes remind us that, no matter how much Bellafront might echo Hippolito, she is not him. Speaking as an 'honest whore', that is, her chastisements are uniquely inflected by a sexual history that makes self-reflexivity inevitable. As speech acts, her proclamations of reform establish her newfound virtue upon the 'honest' acknowledgement of her total abjection. This foundational irony, and the conceptual contradictions and aporias that subtend it, is most palpably figured when Bellafront challenges her former clients to accept her altered condition:

Bell. Let this suffice: I am not as I was.
Flu. 'I am not what I was!'—No, I'll be sworn thou art not. For thou wert honest at five, and now th'art a puncke at fifteen. Thou wert yesterday a simple whore, and now th'art a cunning, cony-catching baggage today.
Bell. I'll say I'm worse; I pray forsake me then.
I do desire you leave me, gentlemen,

And leave yourselves. O, be not what you are—
Spendthrifts of soul and body.
Let me persuade you to forsake all harlots:
Worse than the deadliest poisons, they are worse,
For o're their souls hangs an eternal curse.
In being slaves to slaves, their labours perish.
They're seldom blest with fruit, for ere it blossoms,
Many a worm confounds it.
They have no issue but foul ugly ones
That run along with them, even to their graves;
For 'stead of children, they breed rank diseases,
And all you gallants can bestow on them
Is that French infant, which ne'er acts but speaks.
What shallow son and heir, then, foolish gallants,
Would waste all his inheritance to purchase
A filthy, loathed disease, and pawn his body
To a dry evil? (9.41–65)

'I am not as I was': moments after Matheo greets her as a 'goody punk', '*subaudi* Cockatrice', and 'sweet whore' (9.20–21)—suggesting that these 'gallants' continue to perceive in her such terms, regardless of her changes to apparel and appearance—Bellafront sharply distinguishes between her past and present being, urging them to think of her otherwise than she has been. In response, Fluello dismisses this refashioning as a narrative impossibility: whores only get worse, he argues, not better. They are locked in a one-way trajectory of progressive decline. Parsing her claim as evidence of this growing degradation, he augments this teleologic by reminding audiences that 'cunning, cony-catching baggage[s]' entrap men precisely through such dissimulations.

Rather than rejecting this characterization, Bellafront leans into Fluello's interpretive frames. Amplifying his degrading figuration ('I'll say I'm worse'), she positions herself as 'foul', 'ugly', 'rank', 'filthy', 'loathed', and 'diseased'. Urging the men to 'forsake all harlots' in the future, she insists that they are—and, by implication, that she is—'eternal[ly] curse[d]'. Arguing that such women 'breed' death and disease rather than 'son[s] and heir[s]', she encourages her male counterparts to envision an alternative sexual teleology—wherein sex undoes rather than ensures their lineage—that threatens their own physical, economic, and reproductive futurity. Raising their time-consciousness, she challenges them to re-view their own narrative trajectories: 'leave me, gentlemen. / And leave yourselves. O be not what you are— / Spendthrifts of soul and body' (9.48–50). By abandoning their recursive returns to whoredom, she contends, they can return to respectability. Extending the parameters of chastisement beyond herself, Bellafront begins to embrace the ironic position that she will occupy, with ever increasing authority, throughout the remainder of the play: by virtue of her sexual past, she emerges as the individual best suited to chastising Milanese corruption writ large—and, even more provocatively, to resolving its thorniest relational impasses, including her own.

This is not to suggest that *The Honest Whore* resolves the conceptual conundrums that Bellafront bodies forth. Instead, it repeatedly channels attention to the various ways in which her onstage counterparts respond to—and attempt to re-narrate—her proclaimed meanings. Fluello, for instance, responds with feeling. Simultaneously befuddled and enraged by Bellafront's provocations, he immediately threatens her with violence: 'What's here? Instructions, admonitions, and caveats? Come out, you scabbard of vengeance' (9.70–71). Where this hostility fosters an immediate confrontation with Matteo, who moves to defend his 'punk' (9.73), the scene links conceptual disorientation to increased misogyny and masculine aggressivity. It also highlights an immediate recourse to familiar categories, as well as the narrative and temporal logics that subtend them: as Fluello departs, he pointedly reiterates Bellafront's status as recognizably profane, a practice then echoed by his companions:

Flu: Adieu, damnation.
Cast: Cockatrice, farewell.
Pi: There's more deceit in women than in hell. (9.88–89)

These are revealing slurs. On the one hand, they are pointedly analeptic: just as Bellafront proclaims her newfound condition ('I am not as I was'), they insist upon the present significance of her sexual past. She remains in their eyes a dishonest whore. On the other hand, they are conspicuously proleptic, figuring her as the present embodiment of sinful futurity: she is the very 'damnation' to which all sinners proceed. Once again, audiences must discern between this discursive figuration and the evidence that appears before their eyes, as well as her preceding claim that 'all harlots' are damned in perpetuity. In so doing, the play incessantly queries its own narrative gambit: how and whether, as Matheo puts it, it is 'possible, to be impossible'.

Left alone with Bellafront, Matteo proves wedded to the same interpretive frame as his compatriots, albeit in a different affective register. Framing her chastisement in reference to past encounters, he reads the scene as a counterfeit performance, the very emblem of a whore's duplicity: ''Sfoot, she gulls 'em the best! This is always her fashion, when she would be rid of any company that she cares not for, to enjoy mine alone' (9.67–69). But when Bellafront insists 'In troth, I have no part of harlot in me', he turns befuddled: 'How this?' In response, Bellafront revisits their sexual past, foregrounding his complicity in her sudden and seemingly irreversible fall: 'you were the first / Gave money for my soul. You brake the ice / Which after turned a puddle; I was led / By your temptation to be miserable' (9.98–101). It is this act of chastisement, and the sexual history that it re-narrates, that prompts Matheo's mind-bending reflection upon the (im)possibility of Bellafront's honest whoredom, which we addressed briefly in the previous chapter: 'Is't possible, to be impossible: an honest whore? I have heard many honest wenches turn strumpets with a wet finger, but for a harlot to turn honest is one of Hercules' labours' (9.104–107). Extending the Herculean metaphor, which memorably juxtaposes the making of fifty queans in one night with the fifty years' labour necessary to undo whoredom, Matheo concludes by suggesting that she must be joking. Insisting that she is not, Bellafront urges Hippolito to think in the broader temporal frame of eternity: ''Tis time to leave off jesting', she notes, 'I had almost / Jested away salvation' (9.110–111). Following up with a paradoxical prolepsis ('I shall love you / If you will soon forsake me'), she encourages him to imagine a conjugal future in which he atones for his past wrongs by marrying her (9.111–112). When Matheo rejects this proposal by insisting upon her illicit status ('How, marry with a punk, a cockatrice, a harlot?'), she follows with a blistering critique: 'Why, la, these are your oaths. You love to undo us, / To put heaven from us, whilst our best hours waste; / You love to make us lewd, but never chaste' (9.119–123). It is an extraordinary passage. *You*, she charges, participate in my undoing. *You* revel in my degradation. *You* insist that I cannot turn chaste. *You* refuse to think chastity after whoredom. Bellafront presumably speaks to Matheo, but such provocations can easily be seen to incorporate readers and playgoers who likewise are challenged to reconsider their own investments in witnessing Bellafront's degradation, as well as their own capacities to reimagine her in other terms. What, she seems to ask, is the role of readers and playgoers in the making and unmaking of English whoredom?

It is a question that the play belabours rather than resolves. Where the next scene finds Bellafront penetrating Hippolito's chamber and attempting to woo him in the guise of a young (male) 'parson',[35] audiences again must parse not only the evidence before their eyes but the competing claims of the figures onstage. Presenting herself as a text to be interpreted by Hippolito—a pointedly ironic trial, given her counterfeit appearance as a '*page*'[36]—she challenges him to recognize her altered condition, only to find herself re-presented by him as a 'devil' and 'plague' whose presence has 'infected' his 'chamber' (10.127–137). When she subsequently begs him to love her, lest she fall back into sin, he presents her a skull—a *memento mori*—and urges her to:

> Ask counsel of this head what's to be done;
> He'll strike it dead, that 'tis damnation
> If you turn Turk again. Oh do it not!
> Though heaven cannot allure you to do well,
> From doing ill let hell fright you, and learn this:
> The soul whose bosom lust did never touch,
> Is God's fair bride, and maidens' souls are such;
> The soul that, leaving chastity's white shore,
> Swims in hot sensual streams, is the devil's whore. (10.180–189)

Striking in its religious, terrestrial, and racializing imagery, such prophetic 'counsel' offers a murky vision of Bellafront's present status. Intimating that she will be damned if she 'turn[s] Turk again', Hippolito appears to recognize her present movement away from this debased condition. Yet by annexing one of the period's preeminent tropes for feminine inconsistency—the misogynist perception, famously given voice by Othello, that women will 'turn and turn, and yet go on / And

[35] Mulholland adopts 'person' in his edition (10.92, 94), Daalder follows the Quarto in using 'parson' (TLN 1793), which seems more appropriate given that the subsequent lines query whether this figure's status as a vicar (10.95–96; TLN 1794–1795).

[36] The description, reprinted in Mulholland (10.115), appears as Quarto 1 stage directions (sig. G3r).

turn again'[37]—he concurrently implies her inevitable '[re]turn' to 'damnation'. Insisting that she can never reclaim a 'maiden's soul' he concludes with a vivid terrestrial-aquatic metaphor that not only augments the play's racialization of (un)chastity but, in so doing, underscores the unlikelihood—if not impossibility—of her returning to 'chastity's white shore'.[38]

(Im)possibility, as I have argued throughout, is the conceptual and thematic engine that propels Bellafront's ironic narrative in *The Honest Whore*, and which incessantly enlists audiences into the play's conceptual work. Bound by a conversional structure that insists upon the present significance of her sexual past, her ongoing chastisement requires that audiences incessantly recall her past meanings, question her present motives, and, by recalling commonplace figurations of women as intrinsically inconstant, predict how and whether she will '[re]turn' to whoredom in the future. Implicating us in its conceptual work, the play figures 'turning chaste' not only as a highly fraught, ongoing, and contestatory process but as a knowledge-relation that unfolds within the mind of the convert but also in the minds of their external audiences. Such an insight allows us to understand the inconsistencies and contradictions that arise as Bellafront attempts to 'become pure-honest'. What audiences are watching, in other words, is her becoming-in-time. To the extent that the play figures 'turning chaste' as the endless work of 'becom[ing]' otherwise than one has been, it is a process that remains bounded in *The Honest Whore* by the teleologics that underpin both drama-in-performance and early modern stage comedy. The play must, in other words, work towards a kind of resolution that is intrinsically at odds with the interminable temporality that underwrites the chastising process.

It is therefore unsurprising that, after Hippolito again departs the scene, Bellafront identifies two additional actions through which she plans to enact and materialize her honest condition: she will 'fly / From this undoing city, and with tears / Wash off all anger from my father's brow' (10.202–204). By returning to her past, atoning for her sins, and

[37] *Othello*, 4.1.250–251. See also Anthony's reference to Cleopatra as a 'Triple-turned whore' (*Antony and Cleopatra*, 4.13.13) and Joan de Puzel's assertion that Burgundy will, like an effeminate Frenchman, 'turn and turn again' (*King Henry VI, Part I*, 3.4.85).

[38] On the race-making work of early modern chastity tropes, see especially Bovilsky, *Barbarous Play*; Gillen, *Chaste Value*; and Hall, *Things of Darkness*.

resubmitting to patriarchal authority, she hopes to be seen—by her father, at least—as a woman 'new born' (10.205–206). If audiences are not privy to this familial re-naissance, which occurs offstage, Bellafront's proposal nevertheless intimates an incremental reincorporation into the social and patriarchal order that will culminate, in the play's final scene, with her marriage to Matheo. As elsewhere on the early modern stage, a heterosexual and a notionally chaste marriage thus emerges as the pointedly (il)logical endpoint for a life lived in whoredom.[39]

Prostitution Ends in Marriage: Madness, Teleology, and the Afterlives of (Honest) Whoredom

At the outset of this chapter, I argued that Bellafront's trajectory in *The Honest Whore* cannot be understood in isolation from the play's other plotlines. Candido is a patient man who resists all attempts to stir his placid humours. Hippolito is a gallant who remains devoted to his (supposedly) deceased beloved, even when alone with a sex worker. Bellafront is a sex worker who inverts her fallen condition and turns chaste. As the play progresses, it draws these seemingly disparate characters into symbolic alignment as models of unexpected constancy in the face of multiple temptations and provocations. Constancy is an explicitly diachronic trait: one that, in these cases, describes a mode of characterological stability or fixedness that defies contemporary sexual and gender expectations. But constancy is also, at the level of dramatic structure and climactic action, a problem of sorts. How does one conclude a play in which each of its major characters is defined by their unchangeability? What needs to be resolved when it is precisely this immutability that the play celebrates? In *The Honest Whore*, these quandaries are further complicated by the generic convention that comedies end in marriage: Candido, we must recall, is already married, and while Infelice's revivification enables her (somewhat) conventional

[39] In addition to *Measure for Measure* (1604), which I address in Chapter 5, see *inter alia Eastward Ho* (1605), *Northward Ho* (1607), *The Woman Hater* (1607), *The Fleire* (1609), *Ram Alley* (1611), *The Costlie Whore* (1620/33), and *A Chaste Maid in Cheapside* (1630).

reunion with Hippolito, the simultaneous marriage of Bellafront to Matheo, her former client, not only necessitates her rapid transition from '(honest) whore' to 'wife' but fosters a conspicuous conceptual linkage between prostitution and marriage. With these dizzying inversions and ironies in mind, it is no surprise that *The Honest Whore* locates dramatic closure, both spatially and thematically, in an urban madhouse. Bedlam/Bethlem, in other words, provides a perfectly ironic telos for a play that so incessantly queries the conceptual (im) possibilities of rewriting one's social, sexual, and gendered narratives, as well as the often powerful affects that attend this narrative undoing in and over time.

Unsurprisingly, the dénouement pointedly thematizes its temporal and affective contours. The scene begins, conventionally enough, with the lovers Hippolito and Infelice, accompanied by Matheo and Father Anselmo, arriving at Bedlam/Bethlem in the hopes of concretizing their marital bond. When the latter declares that he is ready to proceed, however, Hippolito defers 'till the evening' (15.17), a postponement that makes little sense except at the level of plot: i.e. as a means of allowing the play's other major characters to arrive, facilitating a disguise narrative, and enabling an extended, and pointedly metatheatrical, narrative dilation. Indeed, upon hearing of the Duke's approach, the lovers agree to cloak themselves as friars. When the Duke enters accompanied by several gallants (including Fluello, Castruccio, and Pioratto), he and his men—concluding that they have arrived too early—decide to pass the 'interim hours' touring the madhouse (15.101). Following a brief exchange with the house's 'honest' sweeper, who pointedly notes that madness in Milan is not restricted to the asylum, these gentlemen-voyeurs interact with three unnamed 'madmen' (15.159): a citizen 'undone' by the loss of investments at sea (15.237); another driven to madness by the death of a beloved 'maiden' (16.265); and a third who, having married a 'fair' and 'very virtuous wife', is overcome by the 'jealous' notion that she has slept with all the men around him: 'All these are whoremongers, and lay with my wife: / whore, whore, whore, whore, whore' (15.269–272). It is a striking moment, both syntactically and thematically, that doubles back upon playgoing audiences: as we observe the Duke and his compatriots observing the pernicious effects of a mind fully entangled in whoredom—one that can only perceive the world and its inhabitants through such terms—this 'mad' man's propulsive asyndeton ('whore, whore, whore, whore, whore') encourages us, like him, to see whores everywhere. Here as elsewhere, the scene implicates audiences in another interpretive impasse: does the madman's ranting imply that whoredom causes madness, or does it suggest that his vision of a world populated by whores is a species of madness?

As the scene devolves into chaos, with two of the madmen attacking each other and Friar Anselmo threatening to whip them both, Bellafront emerges as a 'mad' fortune-teller who, by predicting the future, begins to script Milan's social and sexual restoration.[40] Recognizing Infelice, she predicts that this 'friar' will marry a 'friar' who is 'no friar, nor no friars son' (i.e. Hippolito), and thus, despite her evident holiness, will 'not die a maid' (15.362–369). She then '*discovers*' both lovers moments later,[41] catalysing their union and reconciliation with the Duke, who soon 'yield[s] unto [their] happinesse' (15.421). Praised by the Duke as a 'pretty soul' (15.428), Bellafront subsequently directs her own marriage to Matheo. It is an act, significantly, that she figures as at once a narrative reiteration, revision, reckoning, and rebirth. She begins by insisting upon her present decrepitude ('I am mutton', 15.439), an assertion that augments her chastened condition by rejecting the Duke's positive figuration only moments earlier. Turning to her sexual past, she then revises her narrative fall, figuring it less as a reflection of her own lust or hubris than an act of thievery: 'I had a fine jewel once, a very fine jewel, and that naughty man [i.e. Matheo] stole it away from me' (15.439–40). Bespeaking the logic of a singular 'maidenhead' (15.445), and therefore a counterpart who has taken it, she spurs the Duke to demand her narrative restoration: 'Had he thy maidenhead? / He shall make thee amends and marry thee' (15.446–7). When Matheo balks at this proposal, the Duke reiterates this conventional telos (marriage) as just compensation for Bellafront's undoing: 'you see the wrong / Has

[40] Bellafront's 'mad' condition is first signalled in the stage directions: '*Enter Bellafront mad*' (Quarto 1, sig. K1v), which appears between lines 15.326 and 15.327 in Mulholland's edition. Significantly, whereas Pioratto and Matteo present Bellafront as a 'punk' and 'mad whore' to the Duke (15.331, 349), thereby reiterating her prior status, Father Anselmo, who oversees the asylum, respond to the Duke's inquiry, 'Father, what's she, I pray?', by simply noting, 'As yet I know not; / She came but in this day, talks little idly, / And therefore has the freedom of the house' (15.332–334). Bellafront later reveals that her 'mad' condition was a ruse: 'I am not mad, but put on this disguise' (15.466–467).

[41] Again, this '*discover[y]*' appears in the Quarto 1 stage directions (sig. K2v / lines 15.381–2 in Mulholland).

led her spirits into a lunacy' (15.453–4). Discovering herself, Bellafront concludes by positioning the marriage as a '[re]turn' that is also a rebirth: 'Mattheo, thou first mad'st me black, now make me / White as before; I vow to thee, I'm now / As chaste as infancy, pure as Cynthia's brow' (15.470–2). Annexing contemporary rhetorics of racial impossibility, Bellafront frames the recovery of her chastity as impossibly sudden as its prior loss had been.[42] But she also, and in so doing, alters the temporal contours of chastity itself, shifting from an ongoing process of (self-)chastisement to a teleological progress that aims towards, and is made whole by, her restoration in marriage: 'now', she insists, Matheo can 'make white as before', implying that marriage actualizes the purity—and, implicitly, honesty—towards which she had previously been labouring.

It is an appropriately ironic end to Bellafront's ironic narrative. Securing chastity through a deceptive performance, she reanimates the spectre of whoredom that, the play insists, always already haunts her newfound honesty. Thus, even as Hippolito, the play's honest speaker, immediately affirms her proclaimed 'chast[ity]', Matheo reminds audiences of the ironic double bind that has just been staged: 'Cony-catched, gulled! Must I sail in your fly-boat / Because I helped to rear your main-mast first?' (15.472–475). Repositioning himself as a victim of a whore's cunning (and subtly evoking that figure's sexual-gender dissonance), he encourages audiences to reconsider what they have just witnessed. He then concludes their narrative with the audacious claim that 'it's better / To take a common wench, and make her good, / Than one that simpers and at first will scarce / Be tempted forth over the threshold door, / Yet in one [week], zounds, turns arrant whore' (15.479–483). Turning the epistemological screw on his audiences, he argues that it is better to marry a known whore than an honest woman, because the latter will invariably—and quickly—turn whore.

In *The Honest Whore*, Matheo's provocation operates proleptically, encouraging audiences to look beyond the play and envision what lies ahead for his whore-turned-wife—if not also their own wives, husbands, friends, and future selves. They would not have to wait long. Some four years later, Bellafront would return to the London stage in

[42] On rhetorics of racial impossibility in the period, see Akhimie, *Shakespeare and the Cultivation of Difference*, esp. 1–49.

The Second Part of the Honest Whore, where this now chaste wife finds herself entreated—both by her husband, Matheo, and the agent of her conversion, Hippolito—to 'turn courtesan again'.[43] Inverting the figure(s) of conversion, the sequel ironizes and undoes some of the gendered logics that govern its predecessor. At the same time, it further underscores the insight that, for women like Bellafront, turning chaste is not only an ongoing and contestatory process but a knowledge relation whose performative requirements proliferate the very desires that they might otherwise seek to contain: in *The Second Part of the Honest Whore*, the more Bellafront proclaims her past whoredom to prove her present honesty, the more she finds herself, yet again, positioned and pursued as an erotic object. To the extent that the play neither posits a way out of this double bind nor anticipates a conceivable endpoint to Bellafront's chastising process, what lingers in the wake *The Honest Whore* duology is not the impossibility of proving an honest whore but rather our own inability to reckon with the madness of whoredom, and to imagine a world in which such a term no longer applies.

Shakespeare and the Making of English Whoredom. Stephen Spiess, Oxford University Press.
 DOI: 10.1093/9780191851223.003.0005

[43] *The Second Part of the Honest Whore*. While the play was officially entered into the Stationers' register on 29 April 1608, Hoy (*Introductions* II.68) argues that 'it seems likely that Part Two had been conceived before Part One was completed'.

5

The Measure of Sexual Memory

Duke: You were not bid to speak.
Lucio: No, my good lord,
Nor wished to hold my peace.

Measure for Measure (5.1.77–79)[1]

In the dizzying, chaotic finale of *Measure for Measure*—moments before Lucio unwittingly discovers the Duke, catalysing a famously unsettling resolution—the play's dramatic energy intensifies during a sharp repartee between Vienna's most prominent male figures. Fuelled by the disguised Duke's 'presence-in-absence',[2] the dialogue draws energy from the tensions inherent within competing memory narratives: those of Lucio and the Duke, but also of Escalus, Angelo, their fellow citizens, and even play-going audiences. Dramatic irony reaches its apogee, however, neither in Escalus's torturous threats nor the Duke-as-Friar's critique of Viennese corruption but rather by way of a basic memorial inquiry:

Lucio: Come hither, goodman baldpate. Do you know me?
Duke: I remember you, sir, by the sound of your voice. I met you at the prison, in the absence of the duke.
Lucio: O, did you so? And do you remember what you said of the Duke?
Duke: Most notedly, sir.
Lucio: Do you so, sir? And was the Duke a fleshmonger, a fool, and a coward, as you then reported him to be?
Duke: You must, sir, change persons with me, ere you make that my report. You indeed so spoke of him, and much more, much worse. (5.1.330–336)

[1] Unless otherwise noted, all citations are drawn from Shakespeare, *Measure for Measure* (ed. Bawcutt).
[2] Goldberg, *James I and the Politics of Literature*, 235.

Punning upon absence and substitution, dominant motifs throughout the play, the dialogue pulls *Measure for Measure*'s dramatic past into its immediate present: as the two characters debate previous roles, they replay the humorous inequality of their situational understanding—Lucio knows not to whom he speaks. Yet irony here derives not simply from Lucio's ignorance, nor solely his memorial reconstructions, but also the memory work of playgoing audiences, who presumably recall that Lucio 'so spoke' of the Duke's alleged sexual histories and desires. And while playgoers likely perceive the friar's true identity, the characters within the play remain, at this moment, oblivious to the immense power imbalance between the two interlocutors. Before the Duke reveals himself, Viennese citizens hear competing recollections, either of which could prove valid. Escalus and Angelo, the Duke's avatars, take neither side on this aspect of the debate, responding instead to the 'Friar's' preceding comments: his 'Slander to the State!' (5.1.320). The central contention of the Lucio-Duke exchange—the latter's status as a fleshmonger, fool, and coward—falls into silence.

Lucio's charges of sexual immorality, intellectual impotence, and masculine incapacity disappear, at least rhetorically, as the play concludes. Imbued with social and political authority, the Duke goes on to identify subjects, order social and sexual relations, and organize the play's dramatic narrative in relation to his personal recollections: he remembers Lucio's slanders, Marina's virtuous confessions, Escalus's 'goodness' and the Provost's 'care and secrecy' (5.1.531–533). His memory, quite literally, matters: these recollections provide the bases for Vienna's official narrative and—conjoined as well to questions of torture, imprisonment, execution, and enforced marriage—are inscribed upon Viennese bodies. Having encouraged Friar Thomas to 'throw away [the] thought' of an alleged sexual past (1.3.1), the Duke furthermore aligns memory production with processes of forgetting, whether natural or enforced.[3] Throughout, he works to dissociate his bodies natural and politic from the very 'thought' of sexual practice or desire. The only character who explicitly challenges this official narrative—Lucio, who remembers the Duke as 'One of all luxury, an ass, a

[3] On the politics of forgetting in early modern England, see especially Wilder, *Shakespeare's Memory Theater*; Holland, ed., *Shakespeare, Memory and Performance*; Sullivan, *Memory and Forgetting in English Renaissance Drama*; Baldo, 'Wars of Memory in Henry V'.

madman'—is subjected to public discipline and forcibly married to a 'whore' (5.1.504–518).

If such practices enable an ordered resolution, the call to memory evokes that which has been sacrificed to achieve social, sexual, familial, and dramatic coherence in Shakespeare's Vienna. Indeed, where the dénouement stages the labour of memorial production, it construes memory not simply as an individual and cognitive phenomenon but also as an ongoing, collaborative, and contestatory process. By associating the Duke's authority with his control—or lack thereof—of sexual memory, the play encourages consideration of how cultures remember and forget their sexual histories, including practices, such as prostitution, once licensed by state authority.

As Foucault argues, battles over cultural memory disclose relations of power but also questions of signification and knowledge production.[4] 'Do you know me?', Lucio asks, to which the Duke-as-Friar replies, 'I remember you, sir, by the sound of your voice'. What are the relations of memory and knowledge in *Measure for Measure*, and how are they informed by alleged sexual statuses or practices? As noted, the Duke's recalls the sound of Lucio's voice but also the content of his slanders: his allegations that the former had 'some feeling of the sport' and 'his use was to put a ducat in her clack-dish' (5.1.381–388); that he would 'eat mutton on Fridays' and 'mouth with a beggar' (5.1.439–440). What is recollected in such claims? How do they signify, to whom, and to what effects? To pose such questions seeks neither to know nor concretize the Duke's—or any other character's—sexual practices or desires; rather, I argue that *Measure for Measure* renders them significant precisely in their epistemological opacity. Indeed, by pursuing questions of memory, signification, and knowledge rather than those of 'sexuality',[5] I demonstrate how the queer epistemological method adopted throughout this study enables new insights onto the relations of history and memory, authority and resistance, health and sex, marriage and prostitution in Shakespeare's play. To do so, I examine acts of sexual remembrance and forgetting as they span four interrelated registers: in scholarly studies of the *ars memoria*, in *Measure for Measure*, in modern editorial practices, and in other early modern textual practices including

[4] See especially 'Nietzsche, Genealogy, History' and 'Film and Popular Memory'.
[5] Cf. C. Brown, 'The Homoeroticism of Duke Vincentio'.

English chorography, chronicle history, and state proclamation. In each, I discover not only vital linkages between memory, whoredom, and the workings of power but between these relations and broader problems of sexual knowledge. I therefore argue that *Measure for Measure* is not simply an exemplary anatomy of how state power works through discourses of sex, but also and more specifically of how power works through the problems of sexual knowledge that subtend these discourses; of how these problems encode—and therefore can be leveraged to disclose—the character and contingency of these power-knowledge relations, as well as some of the material processes through which they are configured and contested; and of how the complex materiality and epistemology of English whoredom can put to dramatic use in ways that enable an interrogation of the social and conceptual costs of the shifting historical relation between law and prostitution in early modern England.

Forgotten Memories

In her analyses of the classical, medieval, and early modern arts of memory, Frances Yates describes a remarkable, if strikingly grotesque, mnemonic promoted by the Franciscan priest John Ridevall. To recall the sin of Idolatry, preachers should, Ridevall argues, construct a deformed prostitute in their minds—her face painted and disfigured, her ears mutilated, and her body conspicuously diseased.[6] As with exceptionally beautiful recollections, such ghastly images, it was believed, would impress themselves upon a practitioner's brain, ensuring their preservation and effortless recollection. This affective intensity might inspire socially sanctioned behaviour, stirring the memory artist to virtuous conduct or, at the very least, away from lascivious comportment. Even the horrific 'similitude' served a pedagogic function: the recollection of vices and virtues, it was hoped, would induce a 'moral habit ... used to remember past things with a view to prudent conduct in the present, and prudent looking forward in the future'.[7]

[6] Yates, *The Art of Memory*, 96–97. For a fuller account of Ridevall's career and works, see Smalley, *English Friars and Antiquity in the Early Fourteenth Century*, 109–132.
[7] Yates, *The Art of Memory*, 62.

Ridevall's imagined harlot(-Idolatry) was thus a moral mnemonic, derived from the social and characterized by the sexual, that sustained and reproduced contemporary gendered and sexual ideologies: this 'strikingly hideous' figure is conspicuously female, a common woman who embodies a specific sin.[8]

Although there is little evidence to suggest that Ridevall's treatise was well known in late Elizabethan and early Jacobean England, the text proves interesting for its emphases on prosopopoeia as mnemonic practice. Indeed, the use of personae—especially those marked by sexual practices or reputations—as mnemonics has been overlooked in modern scholarly accounts regarding the classical arts of memory, which have tended to foreground spaces, clothing, material objects, rituals and iconography.[9] While scholars have rightly noted the centrality of memory to medieval and early modern European cultures, relations of memory and sexual practice—especially at the cultural level—remain underexplored.[10] Yet traces of Ridevall's practice, wherein individual types serve as embodied mnemonics with social, sexual, and religious meaning, persist well into the sixteenth century, ranging across a variety of cultural forms. These include, of course, medieval morality and mystery plays, where audiences were encouraged to remember cardinal virtues and deadly sins by ritualistically observing eponymous characters who personified specific traits, but also an array of sixteenth-century printed texts,[11] such as Peter of Ravenna's *The Art of Memory* (1548), that likewise incorporated sexually personified mnemonics. In this extraordinarily popular text, Ravenna proffered 'maydens and vyrgyns' as especially effective moral and sexual mnemonics,[12] and even encouraged practitioners to model these constructions after individuals known personally to the memory artist. If not a dominant trope in the medieval

[8] Ibid., 96.

[9] Greenblatt, *Hamlet in Purgatory*; Jones and Stallybrass, *Renaissance Clothing and the Materials of Memory*; Duffy, *The Stripping of the Altars*; Cressy, *Bonfires and Bells*; Marshall, *Beliefs and the Dead in Reformation England.*

[10] For a notable exception, see the essays collected in Garrison and Pivetti, eds., *Sexuality and Memory in Early Modern England*, esp. Fleck, 'Exemplarity and Its Discontents in Michael Drayton's *Englands Heroical Epistles*', and Garrison, 'Marlowe's Helen and the Erotics of Cultural Memory'.

[11] In addition to Yates and Smalley, see Carruthers, *The Book of Memory.*

[12] Cited in Wilder, *Shakespeare's Memory Theater*, 36. On the erotics of chastity and virginity in the period, see inter alia Berry, *Of Chastity and Power*; Jankowski, *Pure Resistance*; Lochrie, *Heterosyncrasies*; Traub, 'The Perversion of Lesbian Desire'.

and early modern arts of memory, the Ridevall harlot(-Idolatry)—and its virginal/chaste correlatives in Ravenna—nonetheless suggests how the *ars memoria* participated in, and drew energy from, contemporary sexual ideologies and cultures.

Among the most striking aspects of Ridevall's harlot(-Idolatry) is its combined social and individual characteristics. Lacking a proper name and body, she functions as an abstraction, the personification of a general vice: whereas—in accordance with the scholastic memory tradition—the text lacks a visual image, the memory artist must therefore draw from a rhetorical description to produce this harlot in their mind, around whom they then cluster various attributes and meanings associated with the sin of idolatry. While it is unclear whether Ridevall's preachers directly transmitted this mnemonic to parishioners—that is, encouraged them to use it in their everyday lives—the image clearly draws upon a collective social typology in the pursuit of an explicitly communal objective.[13] Figuring the harlot(-Idolatry) as a visibly diseased woman, it also proposes specific interpretive cues through which parishioners might, conceivably, recognize and 'know' the harlots (-idolators) among them. At the same time, and in its striking mixtures of the extraordinary and the common, the abstract and the particular, the allegorical and the referential, the historical past and the imagined future, Ridevall's harlotry(-Idolatry) seems as likely to confound as to clarify an epistemology of the whore, promulgating as it does a figure so exceptional as to belie any easy alignment with one's everyday counterparts.

Of course, page and pulpit were not the only discursive arenas through which early moderns could access, recall, and imagine the bodies of English prostitution. By the turn of the seventeenth century, prostitutes, harlots, whores, and an array of related figures saturated the scripts and stages of London dramaturgy. Such figures encouraged playgoers to contemplate their own desires and anxieties,[14] as well as the gender, politics, and prices of early modern sexual commerce,[15] but also, in the case of Shakespeare's *Measure for Measure*, to consider how the histories of English prostitution itself have been—and might be—shaped, remembered, and forgotten.

[13] Cf. DiGangi, *Sexual Types*.
[14] Traub, *Desire and Anxiety*, esp. 71–87; Lenz, 'Base Trade'.
[15] Singh, 'The Interventions of History'; Howard, *Theater of a City*, esp. 114–161.

The Authority of Memory in *Measure for Measure*

Traces of illicit sex permeate the social and corporeal landscapes of Shakespeare's Vienna. Written across its citizen's bodies, inscribed in the laws of the land, enshrined within buildings razed or repurposed, present and absent in the bawdy languages of its subjects, sexual memory saturates the contours of Viennese life. Although criminality, sexual transgression, and authority in *Measure for Measure* have received ample scholarly attention,[16] their relations to cultural memory have gone unnoticed. The play, however, both begins and concludes at sites of remembrance, constructing the Duke's memory practices as the manifestation of his social authority. He opens by praising the deputy Escalus, noting that 'The nature of our people, / Our city's institutions, and the terms / For common justice, you're as pregnant in / As art and practice hath enrichèd any / *That we remember*' (1.1.10–14, emphasis added). Locating in his counterpart those 'qualities essential to the office of ruling',[17] the Duke qualifies this praise by stressing that Escalus's authority depends upon, and indeed emerges from, the parameters of official memory, the boundaries of the Duke's recollection.

This caveat sheds light upon the passage's otherwise enigmatic concluding sentiment: 'There is our Commission', the Duke goes on to note, 'From which, we would not have you warp' (1.1.14–15). What, exactly, is this commission, and how does it relate to the 'no more... But that' (1.17–18) which Escalus has been entrusted to perform? The question turns upon an obscure editorial crux, yet one that centres precisely upon the acknowledgement—or elision—of memory as a central

[16] On criminality, transgression, and authority in the play, see especially Singh, 'The Interventions of History'; Dollimore, 'Transgression and Surveillance in *Measure for Measure*'; Mullaney, *The Place of the Stage*, 88–115; Goldberg, *James I and the Politics of Literature*, 230–239. More recently, scholars have approached the play's representation of power through the discourses of sovereignty and political theology. See especially Shuger, *Political Theologies in Shakespeare's England*; Lupton, *Citizen-Saints: Shakespeare and Political Theology*, 125–158. For an overview of political theology and various readings attuned to this play, see Rust, 'Political Theology and Shakespeare Studies', esp. 175–179.

[17] The gloss comes from J. W. Lever's Arden2 edition of the play, 3.

category in *Measure for Measure*. Here is the passage in full, with the 1623 First Folio alongside the 1986 Oxford edition, with emphasis added:

Folio (1623)	*Oxford* (1986
Of Gouernment, the properties to vn-(fold),	Of government the properties to unfold
Would seeme in me t'affect speech & discourse,	Would seem in me t'affect speech and discourse;
Since I am put to know, **that** your Science	Since I am put to know that your owne science
Exceedes (in **that**) the lists of all aduice	Exceeds in that the lists of all advice
My strength can giue you: Then no more remaines	My strength can give you. Then no more remains,
But **that**, to your sufficiency, as your worth is able	But **this**: to your sufficiency, as your worth is able,
And let them worke: The nature of our People,	And let them work. The nature of our people,
Our *Citties Institutions*, and the Termes	Our city's institutions and the terms
For Common Iustice, y'are as pregnant in	For common justice, you're as pregnant in
As Art, and practise, that inriched any	As art and practice hath enriched any
That we remember: There is our Commission	That we remember. There is our commission,
From which, we would not haue you warpe. (TLN 6–17)	From which we would not have you warp. (1.1.3–14)

In both versions, the stated 'commission' delineates Escalus's cognitive authority: his advanced understanding of the nature, institutions, and terms of Viennese life. It also hearkens back to the Duke's earlier, seemingly inscrutable assertion that 'no more remains but **this**: to your sufficiency, as your worth is able, and let them work' (*Oxford*, 1.1.5–7). This lineation emends the Folio's 'Then no more remaines / But **that**, to your sufficiency, as your worth is able, / And let them worke'. The pronoun shift proves critical. In the Oxford construction, the clause looks forward, functioning as instruction: Escalus must go to or rely on his 'sufficiency', letting 'them work'. His commission, as it were, is to use this knowledge to the best of his abilities—an obtuse charge at best. The emendation generates further problems: object (sufficiency) and pronoun (them) fail to agree, and the command disrupts the balance of the speech; the Duke's subsequent lines prove unnecessary (quite literally, no more 'remains'—only a retrospective inventory of Escalus's 'science') and the passage loses a critical verbal echo.

Editions drawn from the Folio retain this overlooked rhetorical device and produce—by way of the pronoun 'that'—a commission directly connected to Escalus's memory practices. In the Folio, the pronoun refers not forwards but backwards—to the Lord's 'owne Science', a knowledge base that 'exceedes (in that), the lists of all aduice / My strength can giue you'. The term's second citation, positioned parenthetically in the Folio, moves even further back, remembering the 'properties' identified in the speech's first line. A restored Folio construction has the Duke offer an entirely different commission, summarized thus: 'it would appear vain of me to expound upon the properties of Viennese governance, as I am aware that your knowledge (in this particular realm) exceeds mine own; nothing more do you possess, so use these faculties to the best of your ability. *This* knowledge—regarding the nature of our people, our institutions, and the codes of our legal system—is as deep and thorough as that possessed by any person in my memory. *That* is your commission—to understand how the state functions—from which you must not deviate.' Escalus thus possesses no official powers beyond a unique capacity to know, acknowledge, and remember how power operates in the Duke's Vienna. 'Pregnant' in this capacity, he is a repository of state memory, embodying its critical interrelations with authority and power in Vienna. Such an understanding proves invaluable in its own right, as other citizens will learn to their benefit or detriment: one's status and livelihood, the savvy Escalus knows, depends upon 'that' which 'we'—the state—'remembers'. In forgetting the Folio, the Oxford edition elides memory itself.

Angelo's election only reiterates the potent and capricious nature of official memory in Vienna. Turning to this alternative deputy, the Duke declares 'There is a kind of character in thy life / That to the observer doth thy history / Fully unfold' (1.1.28–29). The statement may appear benign, coming only moments after Escalus affirms Angelo's honourable reputation, but the Duke's assertion rings a discordant note: based upon conspicuously vague evidence—a 'kind of character' observed—he declares his counterpart a capable and qualified ruler. Angelo himself immediately challenges this memorial construction; noting his own lack of experience, he responds 'Let there be some more test made of my mettle, / Before so noble and so great a figure / Be stamped upon it' (1.1.49–51). The Duke pithily discards this self-history: 'No more evasion, / We have with a leavened and preparèd choice / Proceeded to you' (1.1.51–53). While the stately proclamation, with its emphases upon prudence and circumspection, appears to settle the case, the Duke's haste unsettles his declared discretion. Two scenes later, the conceptual framework for Angelo's election—that he possesses the proper character to oversee Vienna—crumbles when the Duke acknowledges, to Friar Thomas, that he does not know whether Angelo will govern responsibly: 'Hence shall we see / If power change purpose, what our seemers be' (1.3.53–54). Angelo's 'history fully unfold' thus unfolds not the deputy's histories—his past, present, or future—but those of the Duke and Vienna, one wherein the state produces and enforces certain memory narratives, to pointedly material consequences: Claudio, Juliet, Pompey, and Froth are all detained or imprisoned under Angelo's reign, while Mistress Overdone stresses its potential effects upon her trade and livelihood.

Measuring the material effects of official memory, *Measure for Measure* exposes the labour necessary to reproduce dominant social narratives. But it also encourages audiences to consider what exactly the Duke wants to forget—and why. Indeed, this memory work begins not only with chosen recollections but also conspicuous ellipses. Amidst the haste and clamour of the play's first scene, the Duke offers a significant, if easily overlooked, aside to his newly appointed deputy: 'Our haste from hence', he declares, 'is of so quick condition / That it prefers itself, and leaves unquestioned / Matters of needful value' (1.1.54–56). A seemingly casual digression, the comment barely registers in light of the scene's momentous actions: just prior, the Duke announced his intentions to abscond from the state and transfer full authority ('Mortality and Mercy in Vienna', 1.1.45) to an untested deputy, bypassing the more experienced Escalus. Plunged into chaos, the Duke's audiences—Escalus, Angelo, readers, and playgoers alike—struggle to synthesize an abruptly disordered state of affairs, to locate a thread of stability in a world suddenly gone awry. In such a situation, 'unquestioned Matters' appear trivial; as a ruler rushes away, the scene produces a powerful impetus to focus upon what remains visible, upon what materializes onstage rather than offhand occlusions. Yet the Duke's aside offers a haunting reminder that matters of 'needful value' have been pointedly omitted. Far from trivial, the comment identifies a central narrative omission. If, at first glance, the Duke appears to overlook the parameters of Angelo's commission or the 'scope' of his authority as substitute ruler, he addresses these issues moments later by ordering the deputy 'to enforce or qualify the laws / As to your soul seems good' (1.1.65–67). A troubling assertion—granting Angelo powers *carte blanche* in his absence—the claim nonetheless broadly defines the deputy's mandate. The Duke's aside thus suggests another omission, some other casualty to the imperatives of haste: amidst harried departures and substitutions, what the Duke 'leaves unquestioned' are the very grounds for his withdrawal.

The Duke addresses these motives in the play's third scene, acknowledging to Friar Thomas that he has forgotten—or failed—to enforce the 'strict statutes and most biting laws.... Which for this fourteen years we have let slip' (1.3.19–21). These claims echo those of Claudio who, in the preceding scene, suffers under a 'drowsy and neglected act' and cites his persecution as an expression of 'tyranny' (1.2.168, 161), thereby associating capricious enforcement with despotism. The Duke, in part, agrees: 'Sith 'twas my fault' he confesses to the Friar, ''Twould be my tyranny to strike and gall them / For what I bid them do' (1.3.31–33). The elected Angelo stands in his place. By this substitution, the Duke displaces his forgetting—and the responsibilities inherent to remembering—onto his deputy. The ruse works: the Viennese subjects never question what the Duke 'bid them do' but rather focus upon the actions of Angelo, who 'for a name' (1.2.167), they believe, resurrects the forgotten law.

Placing Angelo in his stead, the Duke elides his relations to the sexual politics of contemporary Vienna, a displacement further enacted by the play's chronology: the Duke defers explanation until meeting with the Friar (Act 1, scene 3, in modern editions), and therefore it is the citizens who first articulate the 'diseased' sexual state of Vienna (Act 1, scene 2). By the time the Duke—disguised and thus further dissociated from his official position—admits that he has 'seen corruption boil and bubble / Till it o'errun the stew' (5.1.320–321), such corruptions already have been associated with, and embodied by, his subjects. Through such deferrals, he works to forget—or, more precisely, to dissociate himself and the official narrative from—Viennese sexual 'corruption': that which 'o'errun[s]' sanctioned boundaries, desires, or practices.

The Duke's denial—or elision—of his own desires mirrors these sexual politics. In conversation with Friar Thomas, the Duke notes:

> No, holy father, throw away that thought.
> Believe not that the dribbling dart of love
> Can pierce a complete bosom. Why, I desire thee
> To give me secret harbour hath a purpose
> More grave and wrinkled than the aims and ends
> Of burning youth. (1.3.1–6)

Actively repudiating 'love' and erotic desire, he instructs the Friar to 'Believe not' that the Duke possesses the 'aims and ends / Of burning youth'. Yet, just as Viennese sexual commerce persists beyond the frame of the play—as Leah Marcus notes, 'despite all the initial talk about the rigid enforcement of law, the Viennese statute punishing fornication with death is forgotten'[18]—the Duke's own desires return with force in the dénouement, when he shockingly expresses an intention to wed Isabella. The play thus associates forgetting not with oblivion but rather with persistence and the possibility of return. Indeed, just as the Duke attempts to contain the sexual and social memories of Vienna, his actions simultaneously reveal and encounter sites of (sexual) memory beyond his authoritarian grasp, including mnemonics that shift, transfer, reside elsewhere, and even—much like the Duke himself—assume a certain disguise in other names, spaces, and bodies.

Sexual Geographies, Urban Palimpsests

Literary historians seeking to date and localize *Measure for Measure* often turn to the play's second scene, including Pompey's reference to a state 'proclamation' that demands the razing of 'All houses in the

[18] Marcus, *Puzzling Shakespeare*, 178.

suburbs of Vienna' (1.2.94). Scholars have long read this citation—in conjunction with Mistress Overdone's references to the 'war', 'sweat', 'gallows', and 'poverty' (1.2.80–82)—as an allusion to events contemporary to the play's first known performance before the court of King James I on 26 December 1604. These include J. W. Lever, who famously links Pompey's proclamation to a contemporary Stuart Royal Proclamation, issued 16 September 1603, that 'called for the pulling down of houses and rooms in the suburbs of London as a precaution against the spread of plague by "dissolute and idle persons"', and which, Lever argues, 'bore heavily on the numerous brothels and gaming houses which proliferated on the outskirts of the city'.[19] For Lever, in other words, Pompey's 'proclamation' operates not simply an allusion but a mnemonic: a verbal cue that, in its original contexts, would have prompted playgoers to recall the issuance of a recent royal decree and thereby to interpret the events unfolding onstage in relation to that memory. In this, I would suggest, Lever gets it both right and wrong: undoubtedly, the play and scene are invested in English sexual memory, including those relating to the histories of prostitution. But this memory work, as we shall see, is far less stable or predictable than Lever would have us believe. Rather than tethering audiences to a specific memory or referent, *Measure for Measure* enacts a 'measure' of sexual memory itself: an accounting not only of how the sexual past is remembered and forgotten, by whom, and through what cues and practices, but of the knowledge relations that this memory work incorporates and reveals. As I have already begun to demonstrate, such relations are centrally configured around questions of signification and knowledge: of what is or can be known through terms, such as Pompey's 'proclamation', that point in more than one direction, and which therefore can facilitate alternative understandings of the memories and meanings of sex in Shakespeare's Vienna. As we shall see, these knowledge relations are placed under particular strain in the play's second scene, to which we will soon return. But first, I want to propose another narrative—one that, *pace* Lever, focuses less on the play's topical resonance(s) than on the memorial and geographic presence of past prostitutions in the city

[19] *Measure for Measure* (ed. Lever), xxxii–iii. Further discussion of the 1603 proclamation and its relevance to the play can be found in editions overseen by Bawcutt (2–3), as well as Braunmuller and Watson (116–117).

that played the stage for *Measure for Measure* at the onset of the seventeenth century. To do so, I turn to London's famed chronicler of urban memory, John Stow.

As is well known, Stow's *A SVRVAY OF LONDON* (1598) constructs an early modern city in and of memory, wherein present buildings, geographies, and edifices 'stand as monumental signposts to a community, a culture, a history defined and embodied by the traces it has left behind'.[20] Yet scholars have overlooked the manner in which Stow describes commercial sex both in absence and as memory—an approach invoked, in part, by a shift in verb tenses as he perambulates through the present spaces of London's sexual past.[21] Stow begins in the present, noting 'I **am** now to crosse over the said Riuer into the Borough of Southwarke', where 'There **be** also these fiue prisons or gaoles'. He soon declares that the 'Houses most notable **be** these', including 'The Stewes on the banke of the Thames', yet abruptly shift tenses when entering this latter geography:

> Next on this banke **was sometime** the *Bordello* (or Stewes) a place so called, of certaine stewhouses priuiledged there, for the repaire of incontinent men to the like women.... These allowed stewhouses **had** signes on their fronts, towardes the Thames, not hanged out, but painted on the walles, as a Beares Head, the Crosse Keyes, the Gunne, the Castle, the Crane, the Cardinals Hatte, the Bell, the Swanne, &c. **I haue heard** auncient men, of good credit report, that these single women **were** forbidden the rightes of the Church, so long as they continued that sinfull life, and **were** excluded from Christian burial, if they **were** not reconciled before their death. And therefore there **was** a plot of ground, (called the single woman's Churchyard) appointed for them farre from the church. / In the year of Christ 1546. the 37. of *Henry* the eight, this row of stewes in Southwarke **was** put down by the kings commandement, which **was** proclaymed by sounde of trumpet, no more to be priueleged, and vsed as a common Bordell

Moving to the next location, Stow returns to the present tense ('next **is** the Clinke, a Gayle or prison for the trespassers in those parts'), but

[20] Mullaney, *The Place of the Stage*, 6; On Stow's SVRVAY as emblematic of a growing nostalgia for a 'lost London' in an era of urban change, see Griffiths, *Lost Londons*, 3–4. On London as urban palimpsest, see Rubright, *Doppelgänger Dilemmas*, 162–188.

[21] All citations from Stow, *A SVRVAY OF LONDON*, 331–332. My use of bold font highlights Stow's verbal shifts.

even these present constructions incorporate the traces of past prostitutions: an existing jail had served 'in old time' to house the rabble who might 'breake the peace' in 'the Brothell houses' and '**were** straightly imprisoned'. Moving forward, he again returns to the present tense: 'Next **is** the Bishoppe of *Winchesters* house.'

Within this peripatetic memory narrative, where Stow walks readers through the present spaces of London's sexual past, these brothels assume an absent materiality. Whereas other buildings are present, this section of the bankside exists as a type of cartographic lacuna, a gap filled solely with memory narratives centred upon the suppression and persistence of commercial sex in early modern London. If the material spaces of prostitution have been razed from the face of London, these buildings remain a ghostly presence—urban palimpsests occupying the gap between hospital and jail; erased but not gone in Stow's narrative, the 'Stewes on the banke of the Thames' remain present in his earlier inventory of 'Houses most notable' that '**be**' in Southwark. Whereas Steven Mullaney has argued that early modern London was haunted by the 'traces of a past whose outlines were daily growing more tenuous',[22] Stow's brothels appear as a curious exception—a durable, even interminable, urban memory.[23]

I rehearse Stow's memorial journeys less to ascribe causal links between texts and contexts than to illustrate four points: first, to note how material records participate in the reproduction and dissemination of English sexual memory; second, to foreground Stow's reference to the official suppression of prostitution—previously 'priuiledged' and 'allowed'—under Henry VIII; third, to highlight his emphases on visibility and erasure; and fourth, to stress his configuration of prostitution as a present-absence haunting the early modern city. While I do not suggest that *Measure for Measure*—including the play's 'seedy' second scene[24]—reflects such memories, it does participate in the memorial

[22] Mullaney, *The Place of the Stage*, 15.

[23] See, for example, *CAMDENS BRITANNIA*, 322. Fuller, *THE CHURCH-HISTORY OF BRITAIN*, 2.V.39–41.

[24] In a telling editorial move, Gary Taylor and Stanley Wells isolate Act 1, scene 2, to suggest that 'someone—perhaps Thomas Middleton, to judge by the style—seem to have supplied a new, seedy opening' to the scene (*The Oxford Shakespeare*, 843). Such a practice replicates the very displacements enacted by the 'playwright'-Duke of Vienna, shifting responsibility for sexual content from the privileged figure of Shakespeare to an alternative writer.

cultures of English sexual practices. It also construes sexual memory as simultaneously contested and opaque, as a persistent if evasive cultural form that continually disrupts the dominant memory narratives of state authority.

As noted, the proclamation of Act 1, scene 2, arguably invited playgoers to recall a Stuart Royal Proclamation, issued 16 September 1603, that called for the dissolution of plague-ridden buildings in the city and suburbs of London. Upon closer examination, however, the alleged reference proves a surprisingly imprecise match for the play, testifying less to prostitution than to plague, less to topicality than to persistence—an extended royal campaign, spanning the entirety of the Tudor monarchy, focused upon the unsuccessful suppression of undesirable diseases, spaces, and persons: 'excessive numbers of idle, indigent, dissolute, and dangerous persons... in the Citie of London, and in about the Suburbes', it alleges, 'have bene one of the chiefest occasions of the greate Plague and mortality'. As such, 'His Majestie... to avoide the continuance or renewing of such mortalitie... doth straightly prohibite and forbid, That no new Tenant or Inmate, or other person or persons, be admitted to inhabite or reside in any such house or place in the saide Citie, Suburbes... which have been so infected'. Attempting to limit the spread of 'greate Plague and mortality', the proclamation adopts a diseased rhetoric similar to that of the play—yet explicitly emphasizes 'mortality' over sexual commerce; neither brothels nor sexual practices are mentioned. When this privileged document finally refers to the razing of houses, moreover, it cites this practice not as an intervention but as an extension of previous edicts: 'the said Roomes, Houses, or places as by *any Proclamation heretofore published*, are ordered or appointed to be rased or pulled down' (emphasis added). Such predecessors include not only the contemporary—Elizabeth I issued a similar edict on 22 June 1602—but also the historical: nearly forty Royal Proclamations attending to these and related issues published between 1487 and 1603.[25] If early modern playgoers associated Pompey's claim with the Stuart proclamation, the reference likely stimulated memories not simply of suppression but also of persistence: an authoritarian failure to extirpate that which was seen as dissolute and diseased.

[25] *Tudor Royal Proclamations*, 2 vols., and *Stuart Royal Proclamations*, V1. Citations from *SRP* 25.

Pompey's allusion likely stimulated two further memories, both of which significantly alter the play's representation of prostitution: first, the 1546 abolition of state-sanctioned prostitution by royal proclamation under Henry VIII, and second, its perceived persistence throughout the remainder of the sixteenth century. As the Stow account suggests, when writers of the period remembered the official suppression of sexual commerce, they spoke not of 1603, but of 1546. These memories allude to another proclamation—Tudor Royal Proclamation (TRP) 265, 'Ordering London Brothels Closed', issued 14 April 1546—that resonates more precisely with the world of Shakespeare's Vienna, and one that also situates itself within an extended legacy of authoritarian failures to suppress the London sex trade. The document remains, to this day, an extant, material mnemonic of English sexual practice in the sixteenth century.

In 1546, the 'King's most excellent majesty, considering how by toleration of such dissolute and miserable persons...have been suffered to dwell beside London and elsewhere in common, open places called the stews, and there without punishment or correction exercise their abominable and detestable sin...thought [it] requisite utterly to extinct such abominable license'.[26] If the playwrights, actors, and playgoers of 1603–1604 likely did not have direct access to this text, TRP 265 and *Measure for Measure*'s Duke nonetheless describe state prostitution in strikingly similar language. Closer akin to one another than to the favoured Stuart proclamation, the two in tandem—as well as in combination with other textual traces spanning the century—reveal an array of complex cultural, sexual, and political memories swirling at the site of sexual commerce. Focused specifically on the London suburbs, the Tudor proclamation decries the 'abominable and detestable sin' of 'persons as have accustomed most abominably to abuse their bodies contrary to God's law and honesty'—sentiments quite similar to those of a Duke who castigates the 'abominable and beastly touches' of those who 'believe thy living is a life, / So stinkingly depending' (3.1.291–294). The proclamation also implies the trade's 'abominable license' by state authority. This brief reference, easily overlooked amidst an invective-filled opening paragraph, could indicate a general licentiousness. Yet given the long-standing practice of officially sanctioned prostitution in medieval and early modern London,

[26] *Tudor Royal Proclamations*, I.365.

dating at least as far back as 1276,[27] the allusion possesses further resonances: as in Shakespeare's play, an official proclamation suppressing prostitution simultaneously encodes—and memorializes—state involvement ('license') in sexual commerce. Indeed, *Measure for Measure*'s proclamation itself stimulates memories of past Viennese sexual practices: 'Why,' Mistress Overdone notes, 'here's a change indeed in the commonwealth!' (1.2.113–114).

The Henrician suppression appears to have succeeded, at least on one level: following the 1546 proclamation, prostitution disappears from the royal record.[28] The document thus memorializes a pivotal moment, or transition, in the histories of London prostitution: the date upon which the Tudor monarchy formally revoked its 'abominable license' of London sex work. Yet the cultural memories associated with this suppression, including those potentially stimulated and produced in and by *Measure for Measure*, offer an alternative narrative, one that posits the proclamation not as an end but a beginning, not as an erasure but as the inauguration of an official forgetting, an ongoing memory practice that actively enabled the unofficial toleration of sexual commerce. Silenced within one medium of cultural memory (Tudor records), the proclamation took on new life in other discursive fields,[29] including the London stage.

While such memories enrich *Measure for Measure*'s second scene, they also raise important conceptual and epistemological concerns. Slotted between the Duke's narrative deferral (1.1) and the acknowledgement of his complicity (1.3), this scene provides the essential content of Viennese sexual memory, touching upon issues of fornication, prostitution, venereal disease, sexual geography, bawdy language, marriage, lechery, desire, religion, and authority. Yet, just as the scene progresses towards the potentially fatal significance of Juliet's (absent) pregnant body, it simultaneously questions whether sexual practices signify—and if so, where and how they might be remembered.

The scene begins by exploring the materiality of memory. In a humorous if seemingly trivial exchange, Lucio opens by discussing a prospective war with Hungary, arguing that his hawkish counterparts—like

27 Karras, *Common Women*.

28 *Tudor Royal Proclamations* and *Stuart Royal Proclamations*, V1, *passim*.

29 See for example Latimer, 'The Third Sermon of M. Hugh Latimer'; Taylor, '*A Common Whore*'.

'sanctimonious' pirates who head out 'to sea with the ten commandments'—conveniently ignore injunctions that counter their material or martial desires. In so doing, pirate and soldier alike symbolically raze the letter of divine law, scraping undesirable prohibitions from the surface 'of the table' (1.2.7–9). The intense materiality of this image—an audacious sinner chiselling commandments from Moses's tablet—emphasizes the labour necessary to banish unwanted edicts into absentia. Adopting the languages of *ars memoria*, the exchange speaks to a central legal, ethical, and memorial concern raised in several Shakespearean works: can one effectively raze or erase that which exists in memory?[30] Macbeth hopes to 'Pluck' the 'rooted sorrow' from his wife's 'memory', yet can find no 'antidote' to 'Raze out the written troubles' plaguing her conscience (*Macbeth*, 5.3.43–45). Upon his father's death, Prince Hal declares his intention to 'raze out' the memory of his former 'vanity' in *2 Henry IV* (5.2.126–129), yet the Dauphin attests to its clear persistence in *Henry V*, noting that 'as matching to his youth and vanity, / I did present him with the Paris balls' (2.4.130–131). Gloucester, shocked to hear of the king's marriage to Margaret in *2 Henry VI*, argues that this marital alliance will blot their 'names from books of memory, / Razing the characters of [their] renown'—only to find himself razed from their presence (1.1.96–97). And, perhaps most famously, the speaker of Sonnet 122 ('Thy gift, thy tables, are within my brain') argues that one's internal memory far outlasts the external mnemonic.[31]

Throughout Shakespeare's works, memories persist 'Beyond all date, even to eternity', even in the face of external forces seeking 'razed oblivion'. Only death, the Sonnet speaker implies, can defeat memory: 'so long as brain and heart / Have faculty by nature to subsist…thy record never can be missed' (*Sonnets* 122.4–8). From such a perspective, Lucio's suggestions of erasure encode as well the possibilities—indeed, the likelihood—of remembrance and return: not only of Viennese sexual law, whose 'enrolled penalties' have 'like unscoured armour, hung by the wall / So long that nineteen zodiacs have gone round' (1.2.164–166), but also, and paradoxically, the practices of prostitution that demanded such penalties in the first place. His comments, moreover, suggest that practices

[30] For a fascinating study that connect these questions to the material histories of Renaissance writing tables, see Stallybrass et al., 'Hamlet's Tables and the Technologies of Writing in Renaissance England'.

[31] All citations in this paragraph come from *The Norton Shakespeare* (2008).

of forgetting themselves depend upon, and may well solidify, the very memories they seek to suppress. To forget divine law, he argues, the sinner must scrape the table itself; analogously, when Angelo attempts to erase the places and practices of prostitution from the face of the city, he recognizes their presence. Indeed, the very authority he draws upon to suppress prostitution derives from two mnemonics that testify to its presence and ensure its memorial persistence: the original edict outlawing fornication and the subsequent proclamation suppressing sexual commerce.

Focused upon official statutes, whether material or ethereal, this humorous exchange moreover highlights relations of the individual and the collective: what happens when the pirate simply ignores or reconfigures a mandate from above? Given the play's religious allusions, especially conceptions of justice rooted in the biblical phrase 'measure for measure', the Gentlemen's philosophy appears foolish. Yet the episode pointedly distinguishes between human and divine law: just as Lucio opens the scene by defending the authority of divine law, he closes it by decrying the application of a pointedly human law—absent from the Ten Commandments—that erroneously equates human 'life' with a 'game of tick-tack' (1.2.187–189). The double entendre proves especially significant: in their semiotic imprecision, such metaphors posit the scene's central dramatic, political, and epistemological questions: to what, exactly, does Lucio refer? How does 'tick-tack' signify sex? Does it? How might these exchanges remember and forget Viennese sexual practice? How, ultimately, does one know the sexual practices of another?

In addition to official edicts, whether divine commandment or state proclamation, this early scene also introduces an array of sexual mnemonics that enclose their own polymorphous narratives. Centred upon the conspicuous visibility of Juliet and Claudio's sexual relations—their 'most mutual entertainment / With character too gross is writ' upon her swelling womb—the scene locates the body itself as one memorial register (1.2.152–153). This exemplary case foregrounds gender as a critically operative category, yet exactly what Juliet's pregnant body signifies remains in question.[32] Indeed, where 'pregnant' in the play indicates both a parturient condition and the possession of knowledge—as

[32] DiGangi, 'Pleasure and Danger'.

noted, the Duke opens by praising Escalus's 'pregnant...art and practice'—Juliet's mnemonic body proves both symbolically rich and polyvalent: whereas Angelo reads it as the sign of abhorrent fornication (2.2.23), Claudio cites it as a reminder of their most mutual enjoyment (1.2.152). Speaking to Isabella, Lucio remembers Juliet's womb as the expression of natural growth and fecundity (1.4.40-44)—a construction the pious Isabella immediately associates with marriage (1.4.48).

Acknowledging the polyvalent possibilities of the parturient woman, the scene further complicates its sexual hermeneutics by considering other bodies and practices. Following their opening repartee, Lucio and the gentlemen debate just how and if their (male) bodies bear the traces of past sexual practices—whether they 'art tainted or free' (1.2.41–42). When the first Gentleman claims he can read syphilis in Lucio's absent hair—or, more specifically, in the velvet used to cover his bald spots—his counterpart responds by detecting the signs of disease in their symptomatic absence: the Gentleman is 'sound as things that are hollow. Thy bones are hollow; impiety has made a feast of thee' (1.2.53–55). This dialogue soon incorporates Mistress Overdone, whose sciatic hips the men attempt to read as indicators of venereal disease (1.2.56–57).

The scene's constant punning and double entendres foreground the play's epistemological and memorial politics; just as the gentlemen appear to speak of and about sex, sexuality, fornication, prostitution, whoredom, syphilis, brothels, and desire, these terms are conspicuously absent from their dialogue: they are never voiced in the exchange. Instead, sexual memories assume alternative shapes and forms, appearing opaquely in bodies, bawdy allusions, clothing, proclamations, taverns, and even names themselves: Mistress Overdone bears the traces of her marital and sexual past in an infamous appellation, one further supplemented by the moniker 'Madam Mitigation' (1.2.43). Through such polymorphous traces and polyvalent mnemonics, Viennese sexual practices surface everywhere and nowhere at once. Like Lucio's Ten Commandments, the state may scrape commercial sexuality from the face of the city table, yet its practices and languages persist in this scene, as ethereal as they are material. When Pompey introduces the proclamation, he famously notes that the brothels inside the city 'shall stand for seed', but also suggests that those of the suburbs will survive by adopting new forms, names, or locales: 'Come: fear you not; good counsellors lack no clients. Though you change your place, you need not change your trade' (1.2.98–107). By suppressing the visible sites and standard mnemonics of illicit sexuality, he argues, state authorities have merely catalysed the evolution and adaptation of sexual commerce in the early modern city. 'I'll be your tapster still' (1.2.107), he claims, inferring that Viennese prostitution will be re-membered—quite literally, will be put back together—under the guise of tavern keeping.[33]

Pompey's suggestion, neither contested nor negated by the citizens of Vienna, explicates a curious sidenote in TRP 265: bawds must 'leave off their victualing and forbear to retain any guest or stranger into their house either to eat and drink or lodge'. In a pointed effort to divorce food and housing from sites of sexual commerce, the proclamation reveals an anxiety that, once the 'houses white and painted with signs on the front for a token' are removed, all houses will prove sexually suspect. From this perspective, Pompey's comments can be seen to participate in the vast conceptual distribution of urban prostitution in late Elizabethan and early Jacobean literature: even if working brothels were generally restricted to a few select areas in early modern London, often along or outside the city walls (Southwark, Aldgate, Cock Lane, Ram Alley, Smithfield, Clerkenwell, Whitefriars), they could be imagined anywhere. One thus finds dozens of city spaces associated with sexual commerce in the literature and drama of the period, including such prominent locations as Bishopsgate, Cheapside, Eastcheap, Fleet Street, Guildhall, Holborn, Lambeth Marsh, Paris Garden, the Royal Exchange, Shoreditch, Spitalfields, Saint Thomas Hospital, Tabard Street, Westminster, and even Saint Paul's Cathedral.[34] *Measure for Measure*'s proclamation participates in this memorial tradition: far from restricting or razing sexual spaces, the Viennese proclamation catalyses their literal and conceptual distribution throughout the city. In the attempt to elide its own explicit relations to sexual commerce, the play suggests, the state further relinquishes its capacity to identify, control, and/or contain practices of illicit sexuality. Arguing that prostitution will not only persist but permeate Vienna, *Measure for Measure*

[33] On the association of brothels and taverns in early modern England, see especially Howard, *Theater of a City*, and Bray, *Homosexuality in Renaissance England*.

[34] On the role played by contemporary 'whore plays' in this conceptual and geographic distribution, see especially Howard, 'Sex and the Early Modern City'.

encourages readers and playgoers to consider just how sex will be remembered: not only recollected, that is, but also assume new shapes and relations ('re-membered'[35]) in the early modern city.

Notorious Bodies

Like *Pericles* and *Troilus and Cressida*, discourses of prostitution in *Measure for Measure* conspicuously associate sexual commerce with death and disease. Yet even as Lucio claims that he has 'purchased' multiple 'diseases' from Mistress Overdone (1.2.43–44), he and his fellow citizens do not seem particularly concerned about their physical health; it is the interventions of the state, not their own sexual practices, that threaten their well-being. The men joke about syphilis and mock one another's potential contagion, and while the play's sexual discourses are infused with a diseased rhetoric, not a single character articulates pain or suffering associated with venereal infections—even as the play explicitly recognizes that illicit sexual activities have occurred, not only between Juliet and Claudio, but Angelo and Mariana as well as Lucio and Kate Keepdown. Instead, the gravity of the play's sexual politics derives not from, in Angelo's words, a 'stained' body, but rather a condemned one (2.4.54). As Claudio is paraded through the streets, his shackled body exemplifies state intercession in the sexual practices of its citizens. Witness to such punitive and capricious sexual politics, Lucio decries authoritarian hypocrisy—as well as, in his terms, an unhealthy, puritanical approach to human sexual practices.

While Lucio playfully debates his own potentially diseased status, he also derides Angelo as 'a man whose blood / Is very snow-broth, one who never feels / The wanton stings, and motions of the sense' (1.3.57–59). Speaking to the disguised Duke later in the play, he draws on contemporary humoral discourses to construct the deputy as an unnatural, almost inhuman figure: 'They say this Angelo was not made by man and woman.... Some report, a sea-maid spawned him. Some, that he was begot between two stockfishes. But it is certain that when he makes water his urine is congealed ice, that I know to be true' (3.1.366–373). It is an opinion ratified by the Duke and even, albeit implicitly, Angelo

[35] 'Re-member, *V. (2).*', *Oxford English Dictionary Online.*

himself: 'Lord Angelo is precise', the Duke informs the Friar, he 'stands at a guard with envy, scarce confesses / That his blood flows, or that his appetite / Is more to bread than stone' (1.4.50–53). In contrast to the porous body of early medical discourses, one whose health depends upon the steady flow or movement of bodily humours, Angelo is stopped, frozen, and unnatural. If coldness could indicate the healthy moderation of unruly desires,[36] Angelo represents not moderation but extremism. Once stirred by desires, Angelo's erotic subjectivity shifts dramatically from an almost inhuman abstemiousness ('his appetite / is more bread than stone') to an uncontrolled and rapacious gluttony: 'And now I give my sensual race the rein', he tells Isabella, 'Fit thy consent to my sharp appetite' (2.4.161–162).

In this immoderate rejection of sexual desire and practice, Angelo again substitutes for the Viennese Duke: both fashion themselves as possessors of a 'complete bosom' impermeable to desire. Yet as they do so, an array of Viennese subjects—Lucio, Pompey, and Overdone, but also Escalus, Isabella, and the Provost—openly critique such extreme views, especially from those empowered to police others; in their manifold rejoinders, these figures allege that to 'measure' the practices or desires of another, one must first remember sex, both on an individual and cultural scale. While the Duke and Angelo actively attempt to forget sex, Isabella and the Provost frame Claudio's punishment in direct relation to Viennese sexual history: 'All sects, all ages smack of this vice', the Provost decries, yet Claudio will 'die for't' (2.2.5–6). Isabella soon echoes this sentiment, imploring Angelo to remember 'who is it that hath died for this offence? / There's many have committed it' (2.2.88–89). Such recollections foreground notions of justice and equity—as Lucio notes, 'for the rebellion of a codpiece to take away the life of a man!' (3.1.376–377)—but also of empathy: an ability to see oneself in the actions of another. Even Escalus, who invariably supports the Duke's positions and policies, encourages Angelo to remember his own temptations when judging Claudio, to envision himself in the place of the man he condemns (2.1.8–16). When Angelo disregards the entreaty, he sets the stage for his fall from grace and power.

To remember sex in *Measure for Measure* is neither to celebrate nor recuperate prostitution as a cultural institution, but rather to examine

[36] Schoenfeldt, *Bodies and Selves in Early Modern England.*

how cultures and institutions recall, identify, enable, suppress, forget, and overlook sexual commerce. Moreover, to position Lucio as a figure of memory seeks not to valorize his actions—including his notorious denigration and abandonment of Kate Keepdown—but to adopt an alternative framework through which audiences might perceive the sexual politics of Shakespeare's Vienna. From such a perspective, Lucio can be seen as a libertine Antigone: a figure of counter-memory who conspicuously challenges the state's proclaimed disinterest in sexual desire and commerce, an incessant voice—'not bid to speak'—who speaks precisely that which state authority seeks to silence and suppress. A peripatetic figure, Lucio traverses the many sexual spaces of Vienna, interacts with characters across the social spectrum, and lays claim to an alternative understanding of 'The nature of our people, / Our city's institutions, and the terms / For common justice'. Arguing on behalf of sexual practice as a natural human condition, as common as 'eating and drinking' (3.1.366), he conspicuously remembers the sex that the state seeks to forget. Crossing the many sites of sexual memory, debating the sexually mnemonic body, and playing with bawdily imprecise yet evocative language, he embodies desires, practices, and memories that the Duke seeks to 'extirp' (3.1.366). Proclaiming that the state itself possesses desire, he links sex and state—a union later concretized in the Duke's abrupt marriage to Isabella (5.1.495). Disregarding inferences of syphilis, he challenges constructions of sex as corrupt or diseased. Hailing Mistress Overdone as Madam Mitigation, he infers that prostitution may serve a healthy body politic.[37] Surmising that the Duke himself has patronized prostitutes, he locates Viennese authority at the very centre of the city's sex trade, foreshadowing the play's final acts of bawdry.

To restore order in the play's final scene, the Duke must reveal himself: he has to return from absence to author his preferred narrative. Threatened with torture for articulating (as the Friar) the corruptions of his state, faced with inferences of his own licentiousness, and responsible for the sexual liaison of Angelo and Mariana, he depends upon the authority of his office to enforce his memories—and, significantly, to

[37] See also Elbow's famous malapropism construing Pompey and Froth as 'notorious benefactors' (2.1.49), a sobriquet that alludes to the long-standing construction, discussed in Chapter 3, of prostitution as a necessary evil.

silence Lucio. As is well known, the Duke concludes the play by ordering the monetary and marital relations of Vienna: he aligns Claudio with Juliet, Angelo with Mariana, and himself with Isabella. Yet while marriage serves as his privileged mechanism of social reconciliation, it simultaneously conjoins sexual commerce with state authority. Indeed, Lucio's enforced marriage to Kate Keepdown metonymically aligns such unions with the absent prostitutions of the Viennese state: the prostitute becomes the wife, the client a husband. Gesturing towards a 'palace' offstage, the Duke promises that the narrative will continue: 'we'll show / What's yet behind, that's meet you all should know' (5.1.541–542). As memory work persists beyond the world of the play, playgoers are left to wonder just how the prostitutions of past and present will be remembered—and forgotten—in the future.

Shakespeare and the Making of English Whoredom. Stephen Spiess, Oxford University Press.
 DOI: 10.1093/9780191851223.003.0006

Epilogue

Undoing Whoredom

Scholars often seek conceptual clarity only to find that it confounds us every time. John Taylor's *A Common Whore With all these Graces Grac'd: Shee's very honest, beautifull and chaste* (1622), seems especially well suited to delivering this desideratum, collating as it does seemingly every conceivable name, narrative, trope, *topos*, history, body, and relation that one might associate with, or ascribe to, the early modern English whore.[1] Across eight hundred lines set in heroic couplets, readers are introduced to '*Whores* and *Whore-masters*' historical, mythological, biblical, royal, public, private, male, female, and gender non-conforming (sig. B2v). They hear of 'Stewes' in Belgium, Bohemia, Italy, and England (sig. A6v); of Catholic toleration for sexual commerce; of the suppression of licit sex work in London by Henry VIII; and of the 'damned crew of priuate *whores*' who emerged in its wake (sig. B3r). They encounter some of the many names under which a whore might travel, from the seemingly conventional (*Concubine*, *Doxy*, *Queane*, *Punke*) to the affectionate (*Paramore*, *Love*, *Sweethart*) to the euphemistic (*Dove*, *Ducke*, *Lambe*, *Squall*) to the ironic or paradoxical (*Prudence*, *Temp'rance*, *Faith*, *Grace*).[2] They are told that whores

[1] Printed three times in quarto (1622, 1625, 1635), the pamphlet also appeared in the 1630 folio edition of Taylor's complete works, *All the Workes of Iohn Taylor The Water Poet* (1630), sigs Kk1r–Kk5r.

[2] *A Common Whore* (1622), sigs A5r, B6r–v.

are marked by disease but also masters of disguise, able to cloak their iniquity and thereby deceive even the most perceptive of observers. They learn that a whore's life inevitably ends in a ditch or hospital, where they will die alone, decrepit, and despised—but also that such figures can perform 'Pennance', prove 'honest', and thereby undo this fixed trajectory (sig. B7v). They are immersed, in other words, in some of the many discursive relations and quandaries explored in *Shakespeare and the Making of English Whoredom*. But these labours, it must be stressed, have delivered neither the definitional clarity that I once desired nor even a coherent understanding of *A Common Whore*. To this day, rather, I find the pamphlet to be a bewildering text: one whose sheer copiousness—not to mention its satirical timbre, metaphorical ambition, conceptual elasticity, and textual self-reflexivity—animates such a dizzying array of terms, tropes, histories, and paradoxes that I inevitably lose track of who or what is being described therein.[3] Far from shoring up the 'whore' as a fixed or coherent object of socio-sexual knowledge, the pamphlet undoes the very premise that its surplus meanings can be distilled into a single or defining essence. To engage Taylor's discursive 'Treasurie' (sig. A3r), therefore, is to navigate an epistemological paradox wherein the more I know about early modern whoredom, the less I know the early modern whore. What I now appreciate is that this condition itself encodes important insights about the meanings and makings of English whoredom, if not early modern culture more broadly and the methods that scholars employ to make sense of cultures past. Put differently, I understand that the confusions that animate—and are animated by—*A Common Whore* are not simply problems to be puzzled out but part and parcel of what 'makes' whoredom such a vital category of early modern life and thought.

Where does this leave us? In the broadest sense, *Shakespeare and the Making of English Whoredom* has endeavoured a three-tiered intervention: historical, methodological, and epistemological. First, and at the level of history, I have not only revealed whoredom to be yet another 'utterly confused category' in early modern England but foregrounded the extraordinary—and ongoing—discursive labour necessary to

[3] See 'Bewilder, *V.*', *Oxford English Dictionary Online*: '(1) *literal.* "To lose in pathless place, to confound for want of a plain road" (Johnson). *archaic*; (2) *figurative*. To confuse in mental perception, to perplex, confound; to cause mental aberration.'

produce and sustain the fiction of its conceptual stability and ready intelligibility in that historical culture.[4] This cultural work, I have shown, unfolds across a variety of historically situated social, textual, and linguistic processes, from the writing of dictionary entries, character sketches, lyric poems, and stage dramas to public proclamations, conversion rituals, coercive legal manoeuvres, and more. It extends into the present era, where scholars continue to shore up whoredom's incoherences and to reproduce moralized distinctions between 'real' prostitutes and 'discursive' whores. Second, and at the level of methodology, I have modelled an epistemological approach that—by shifting the analytical lens away from questions of representational verisimilitude, social discipline, and authorial perspective to those of signification and knowledge—channels critical attention to the roles played by ignorance, ambiguity, and opacity in the making of a prominent category of socio-sexual knowledge, as well as to the material practices, cultural logics, and social affects that emerge to negotiate them. As we have seen, this methodology encourages us to linger with, rather than bypass or foreclose, the various semantic, evidentiary, historiographic, and hermeneutic problems that stymie our efforts to make sense of cultures past, and to scrutinize the knowledge relations and material processes that underpin their 'resolution' in specific historical contexts. In so doing, this methodology connects our literary and cultural analyses to broader epistemological concerns, both in early modern England and present-day scholarship. Third, and at the level of epistemology, I have contributed to a queer critical tradition that advances a deconstructive understanding of ignorance and opacity as essential to, and constitutive of, what passes as knowledge and clarity, and therefore as sites of meaning and analysis in their own right, rather than obstacles or impediments that scholars must overcome in order to apprehend 'knowledge' as it is constituted and operates within a given historical culture. Understood thus, 'queer epistemology' not only 'queers' epistemology—i.e. casts in relief that discipline's own normative definitions, histories, practices, and procedures—but also repositions the (semantic, textual, historical, hermeneutical, political) aporia as a critical *locus* that can be leveraged

[4] Foucault famously describes sodomy as 'that utterly confused category' in *The History of Sexuality*, Vol. 1, 101.

to illuminate epistemic assumptions, relations of power-knowledge, and the cultural work necessary to set the terms by which such impasses are mediated, animated, or elided.

In *Shakespeare and the Making of English Whoredom*, I have demonstrated how this critical praxis can be brought to bear on a problem of sexual knowledge as it emerges and is mediated at the often-intersecting levels of semantics, evidence, and archive; criticism and politics; language and textuality; discourse and embodiment; sexual and narrative time; history and memory. Undoubtedly, the epistemology of the early modern whore incorporates far more texts, knowledge relations, and material processes than have been analysed here. This book thus advances a call for yet more expansive thinking about the meanings and makings of English whoredom. But might it point in other directions as well? Given that the interventions detailed above are clearly intertwined, it is fair to ask how and whether the praxis developed here is unique to the problem at hand—i.e. the making of early modern whoredom, if not sexual knowledge making more broadly—or if it bears resonance for issues and topics that extend beyond these specific concerns. I return to Taylor's pamphlet.

Among its many provocations, *A Common Whore* advances two prominent conceits that explicitly link whoredom to language, textuality, and knowledge, and thereby encourage readers to do the same. The first, which both inaugurates and concludes the poem that comprises the majority of the pamphlet,[5] collapses any fixed distinction between Taylor's 'Booke' and its nominal subject matter:

> My Booke, an honest *Whore*, I fitly call,
> Because it treats of *whores* in generall:
> Then though this Pamphlet I doe name a *whore*,
> Let no man shun her company therefore,
> For if ten thousand with her lodge and lye,
> No reputation they shall lose thereby.

[5] *A Common Whore* (1622), sig. A3v. While I focus here on the first six lines of the poem, it is worth noting that the conceit is already operative in the pamphlet's title: *A Common Whore With all these Graces Grac'd: Shee's very honest, beautifull and chaste.* This title is extended in 1630 folio edition, where it concludes '*With a comparison between a* Whore *and a* Booke'.

Witty, sardonic, dehumanizing, provocative: Taylor's opening gambit both establishes the conspicuous metaphoricity that characterizes his broader account and prompts readers to contemplate the textual and conceptual affinities by which he conjoins whores and books. Like the former, he argues, his pamphlet is 'common vnto all men', available for purchase, and ready to be 'turn'd and tost' by 'Readers' across the social spectrum.[6] Like the latter, he claims, whores circulate widely, 'waxe olde & stale', then are 'painted new': cloaking '[o]bsceane and beastly' interiors under 'gaudy coate[s]...and silken strings' (sigs C2v–C3r). Grafting whore tropes onto books and book tropes onto whores, Taylor animates a play of language that is also a play of mind, encouraging readers to re-envision the seemingly familiar by way of these figurative splices. Developed throughout the pamphlet, the conceit reaches its apogee in an aphoristic couplet that pairs these privileged entities as repositories of knowledge stored: '[e]xperience shewes that *Bookes* much knowledge brin[gs] / And by experience *Whores* know *many Thinges*' (sig. C3v).[7] To procure either, readers are led to believe, is to acquire 'knowledge'. It is an audacious premise, if not also a savvy marketing technique.

Yet just as *A Common Whore* brings whoredom, textuality, and knowledge into intimate proximity, the pamphlet unravels these metonymic bonds by curating an ironic sense that undercuts the veracity of Taylor's language and, as such, channels readerly attention to their own reception of it. As we have seen, this meta-rhetorical consciousness is cultivated from the outset, where Taylor's emphasis on the 'honest[y]' that characterizes his '*Whore*[-Booke]' activates a presiding irony that unsettles the very relationship this opening conceit aims to establish: to the extent that honesty is precisely what distinguishes Taylor's 'Booke' from '*whores* in generall' (sig. A3r), the more *A Common Whore* delivers an accurate or true account of its subject matter, the more it proves the lie of this governing conceit. It is a paradox which places readers in an epistemological bind, denying a stable interpretive viewpoint from which to ascertain the text's knowledge claims: if readers accept Taylor's

[6] *A Common Whore* (1622) sig. A3v. In the dedicatory note, Taylor pointedly delineates a broad readership, identifying 'Lord, Master, Goodman, Gaffer, *or* Knave; Lady, Mistresse, Good-wive, Gammer, *or Whore*', as presumed or potential 'Readers' (sig. A2r).

[7] See also Taylor's inference that books and whores are both 'full of words' and designed 'to be examin'd' (sig. A3v).

claim—that his 'Booke-[*Whore*]' is an 'honest' account that, as such, discloses the truth of whoredom—at face value, i.e. unironically, the conceit itself is proven to be a lie. Conversely, if readers interpret the claim ironically, i.e. as playing on the common presumption that whores are defined in part by their capacity to feign 'honesty' and thereby deliver lies that masquerade as truth, then all subsequent knowledge claims are rendered (potentially) counterfeit.

This epistemological impasse is amplified by the pamphlet's second conceit, which prompts readers to consider how whoredom might operate like a (broken) language. Significantly, Taylor introduces the trope by professing ignorance of the very linguistic system that structures it: 'Yet though I have no learning to my share, / A *whore* to broken Latine Ile compare' (sig. A3v). Distinguishing his own (lack of) 'learning' from that of the presumed reader (whose familiarity with Latin grammar is the conceit's enabling condition), Taylor ironizes his rhetorical ploy and presses readers to query their own linguistic competencies. Having curated this interpretive self-consciousness, he begins the comparison proper by exploring the various ways in which whores—like Latin nouns, pronouns, and adjectives—can be seen to 'decline' (sig. A3v): change shape or form depending upon the contexts in which they are situated.[8] It is a grammar, he suggests, which explains the whore's gender variability as well as their openness to a variety of sexual pairings:

> And with small teaching she will soone decline
> *Mulier* [Latin: woman] into the Gender Masculine.
> By her Attire, of which sex she should be,
> She seemes the *doubtfull Gender* vnto me,
> To either side her habit seemes to leane,
> And may be taken for the *Epicene*.
> Vnto the *Newter* I compare her can,
> For she's for thee, or me, or any man. (Sig. A3v)

Extending the conceit, Taylor turns from gender and number to mood ('Her *Mood* commands like the *Imp[e]rative*'), tense ('Her goodnesse

[8] Characteristically, Taylor's selected term here also encodes a pun, i.e. 'decline' as indexing the whore's presumed teleological regression. On this chronologic, see especially Chapter 3.

all is in the *Future tense*'), and voice ('And he shall finde, that takes her for his choyce / An *Interiection*, or *Imperfect voyce*'), all while deploying a variety of puns that—to the extent that they require a basic understanding of Latin grammar to signify 'properly'—further cultivate readerly awareness of the knowledge and ignorance that they bring to this textual encounter.[9] As before, however, Taylor conspicuously undercuts the veracity of his conceit even as he discloses its conceptual fecundity: 'For mine owne part I dare to sweare and vow, / I ne'r us'd *Accidence* [sic] so much as now, / Nor all these Latine words here enterlac'd, / I doe not know if they with sense are place'd, / I in the Booke did finde them, and conclude / At rando[m] to a *Whore* I them allude.' Reiterating his unfamiliarity with the Latin tongue, Taylor suggests that the entire conceit is an accident, a fancy, a whim: he simply happened upon these 'Latine words' in an unnamed book, does not know how they signify, and thus only haphazardly has affixed them to the '*Whore*'. Any 'sense[s]' that emerge by way of this linguistic work, he therefore implies, are the products of 'random'—rather than motivated or referential—linguistic relations. Or, as we might put it today, arbitrary.

Surely, it is a playful moment: a tongue-in-cheek *apologia* that, as throughout the pamphlet, activates an ironic sense that forces readers to contemplate the truth or falsehood of the relations proposed therein. Do we take Taylor at his word and dismiss the conceit—indeed, the entire pamphlet—as meaningless play? Can we find meaning in his words, even and perhaps especially if they exceed his intended use? Can any such words bespeak the truth or essence of whoredom, if we understand the relations that subtend them to be random or arbitrary? But it is also an epistemological moment: at the precise moment in which *A Common Whore* proposes that language can be leveraged to hammer out the instabilities of whoredom, it prompts readers to contemplate how language is itself a system of unstable and shifting relations; how its figurative capacities enable meanings and possibilities that slip the moorings of grammar, structure, and logic; and how, therefore, an epistemology of the early modern whore—or any conceptual category, for that matter—is also and concurrently an epistemology of

[9] *A Common Whore* (1622), sig. A4r. See, instance, lines 63–64: 'Not *lapis* [i.e. stone] singularly, her can please, / She loves the plurall number *lapides* [i.e. testicles]'. As this example reminds us, such puns draw upon readerly knowledge of Latin, of contemporary sexual slang, of male anatomy, and/or specific erotic desires or practices.

the language(s) and textualities through which it is constructed and materialized.[10]

What we encounter in *A Common Whore* is neither a stable definition nor a coherent category but rather an early modern writer leveraging the instabilities of whoredom to think with and through the instabilities of language, of gender, of the book, and ultimately of the 'knowledge' that each helps to shape and materialize in his world. In its conspicuous irony and self-conscious rhetoricity, Taylor's cornucopia reveals that early moderns were well acquainted with what we would today identify as the deconstructive capacities of language and the epistemological problems which derive thereof, and that while it may require modern methodologies—such as the queer epistemological approach modelled here—to illuminate how and where such knowledge relations emerge and are mediated, it is historically accurate to identify them as such.[11] In so doing, *A Common Whore* prompts us to recognize that the full potential of 'undoing whoredom' lies not only in harnessing that category's capacity to undo itself—i.e. to disclose its own instabilities and incoherences, and thereby to allow scrutiny of the knowledge relations and material processes that contribute to its making and unmaking in specific historical contexts—but to reveal and animate the undoing of other conceptual categories and systems of meaning-making in early modern England. We encounter a modest form of this categorical-deconstructive expansion in *ALL THE WORKES OF IOHN TAYLOR THE WATER-POET* (1630), published some eight years after *A Common Whore*, wherein the poet grafts the textual and linguistic

[10] It also, we might note, suggests how irony operates as a privileged rhetorical figure for illuminating the knowledge relations at play in any act of reading. Embedded within this striking disclaimer is yet another meta-textual allusion—'I in the Booke did finde them'—that not only revisits the pamphlet's other governing conceit, thereby conjoining the two, but places readers in the precise position that Taylor has just ironized: like him, we find ourselves encountering words and ideas and relations in the 'Booke' at hand, and must soon 'conclude' how and whether these bear any meaningful relationship to the '*Whore*' with which they have been connected.

[11] Put differently, the pamphlet demonstrates that whoredom's capacity to undo itself, as well as other categories and systems, is not a characteristic which requires an anachronistic application of poststructuralist methodologies to reveal. Rather, and as I have demonstrated throughout *Shakespeare and the Making of English Whoredom*, the terms and texts that come to us from that historical culture are already suffused by a multiplicity of knowledge relations, and while it may take deconstructive, materialist, and epistemological approaches to render these visible, it is historically accurate to describe them as such.

conceits detailed above onto the figures of 'A Bawd' and 'A Thiefe', respectively.[12] Small steps, to be sure, but ones which nevertheless underscore the fact that early modern textual and lexical undoing is not exclusive to the whore per se, and that these deconstructive capacities are as intrinsic to language and textuality as they are to the category central to this project. What is at stake in the making of English whoredom, therefore, is not simply a reckoning with the instabilities that attend and animate a particular socio-sexual category, or an emergent lexicographic project, or strategies of gendered embodiment, or acts of conversion, or interpretive logics of sex, or theories of sexual time, or depictions of English sexual history and memory on the London stage, but with the making of knowledge itself and the unique capacities of literary and dramatic texts to disclose this epistemological work, the knowledge relations that it incorporates, and the material processes through which it is puzzled out. To reckon with these insights may transform not only how we read, write, and claim to know the histories of early modern sex, but our understanding of how culture 'works', including in and through figures such as the early modern whore.

Shakespeare and the Making of English Whoredom. Stephen Spiess, Oxford University Press.
 DOI: 10.1093/9780191851223.003.0007

[12] See, for instance, Taylor's figuration of a Bawd as a (potentially) deceptive 'grammarian': 'for her knowledges in the Arts and Sciences, she hath the grounds of a *Grammar*, whereby she can speake and write *Amorously, fainedly, merrily, lamentably, crastily, purposely, Bawdily*: these words all ending in Lye (doe make her true dealing questionable) yet her ayme is to liue *profitably*, though her fate is to dye *miserably*' (sig. Ii2r). Closely modelled on *A Common Whore*, which directly precedes it in Taylor's omnia opera, *An arrant Thiefe, whom euery Man may trust: in Word and Deed exceeding true and iust* echoes it predecessor by unfolding, as a second subtitle reveals, an extended '*Comparison between a* Thiefe *and a* Booke' (sig. Kk5r).

BIBLIOGRAPHY

Primary Sources

Aquinas, Saint Thomas. *De Perfectione (The Perfection of the Spiritual Life)*, trans. John Proctor (Westminster: Newman Press, 1950). Available online at https://isidore.co/aquinas/PerfectVitaeSpir.htm

Aquinas, Saint Thomas. *The Summa Theologiae of St. Thomas Aquinas*, 2nd and revised edition, trans. Fathers of the Dominican Province (2017). Available online at https://www.newadvent.org/summa/.

Ambrose, Saint. *Saint Ambrose: Letters*, trans. Sister Mary Melchior Beyenka (Washington, DC: Catholic University of America Press, 1954).

Aristotles Masterpiece (London: for J. How, 1684).

Augustine, Saint. *S^T. AVGVSTINE, OF THE CITIE OF GOD: WITH THE LEARNED COMMENTS OF Io. Lod. Vives* (London: George Eld, 1610).

Augustine, Saint. *Contra Faustum (Reply to Faustus the Manichaean)*, trans. Richard Stothert, in *Nicene and Post-Nicene Fathers*, Vol. 4, ed. Philip Schaff, 1st series (Buffalo: Christian Literature Publishing, 1887), 155–345.

Augustine, Saint. *On Order [De Ordine]*, trans. Silvano Borruso (South Bend: St. Augustine's Press, 2007).

Bacon, Francis. *Valerius Terminus of the Interpretation of Nature*. Project Gutenberg (2002). Available online at https://www.gutenberg.org/files/3290/3290-h/3290-h.htm.

Bale, John. *The Actes of Englyshe votaries comprehendynge their vnchast practyses and examples by all ages, from the worldes begynnynge to thys present yeare, collected out of their owne legendes and chronycles by Iohan Bale* (Wesel: S. Mierdman, 1546).

Bale, John. *THE IMAGE of both Churches after the most wonderfull and heauenly Reuelation of sainct Iohn the Euangelist, contayning a very fruitfull exposition or paraphrase vpon the same. Wherin it is conferred with the other scriptures, and most auctorised histories* (London: Thomas East, 1570).

Baret, John. *AN ALVEARIE or Triple Dictionarie in Englishe, Latin, and French: Very profitable for all such as be desirous of any of those three languages* (London: Henry Denham, 1574).

Becon, Thomas. *The Worckes of Thomas Becon whiche he hath hitherto made and published, with diverse other newe bookes added to the same, heretofore neuer set forth in print, diuided into thre tomes or parts and amended this present [sic] of our Lord 1564; perused and allowed, accordyng to thorder appointed in the Quenes maiesties iniunctions* (London: John Day, 1564).

The Bible and Holy Scriptvres Conteyned in the Olde and Newe Testament (Geneva: Rouland Hall, 1560).

Blount, Thomas. *Glossographia: or a Dictionary, Interpreting all such hard words, whether Hebrew, Greek, Latin, Italian, Spanish, French, Teutonick, Belgick, British or Saxon, as are now used in our refined English tongue also the terms of divinity, law, physick, mathematicks, heraldry, anatomy, war, musick, architecture, and of several other arts and sciences explicated* (London: Tho. Newcomb, 1656).

Brathwaite, Richard. *The English Gentlewoman, drawne out to the full body expressing, what habilliments doe best attire her, what ornaments doe best adorne her, what complements doe best accomplish her* (London: B. Alsop and T. Fauucet, for Michaell Sparke, 1631).

Breton, Nicholas. *The Good and the Badde, or Descriptions of the Worthies and Vnworthies of this Age. Where the best may see their graces, and the worst discerne their basenesse* (London: George Purslowe, for Iohn Budge, 1616).

Bullokar, John. *An English Expositor teaching the interpretation of the hardest words vsed in our language. With sundry explications, descriptions, and discourses* (London: Iohn Legatt, 1616).

Burton, Robert. *The Anatomy of Melancholy* (Oxford: John Lichfield for Henry Cripps, 1628).

Camden, William. *Camdens Britannia, Newly Translated into English: with large Additions and Improvements* (London: F. Collins for A. Swalle and A. & J. Churchil, 1695).

Cary, Elizabeth. *The Tragedy of Mariam, The Fair Queen of Jewry*, ed. Barry Weller and Margaret W. Ferguson (Berkeley: University of California Press, 1984).

Case, Thomas. *Spiritual Whoredome Discovered in a Sermon preach'd before the Honourable House of Commons assembled in Parliament, upon the solemn day of humiliation, May 26. 1647* (London: J. Macock, for Luke Fawne, 1647).

Cawdrey, Robert. A *Table Alphabeticall, conteyning and teaching the true writing, and vnderstanding of hard usuall English wordes, borrowed from the Hebrew, Greeke, Latine, or French. &c.* (London: I. R. for Edmund Weauer, 1604).

Cawdrey, Robert. *A Treasvrie or Store-Hovse of Similes: Both pleasaunt, delightfull, and profitable, for all estates of men in generall* (London: Tho. Creede, 1600).

Chamberlayne, Thomas. *The Complete Midwifes Practice, In the most weighty and high Concernments of the Birth of Man* (London: for Nathaniel Brooke, 1656).

Cockeram, Henry. *The English Dictionarie: or, An Interpreter of hard English Words* (London: for Nathaniel Butter, 1623).

Cooke, Richard. *A White Sheete, Or A Warning for Whoremongers* (London: Iohn Dawson, for Henry Overton, 1629).

Cooper, Thomas. *THESAURUS LINGUÆ Romanæ & Britannicæ* (London: Henry Denham, 1578).

Coote, Edmund. *THE ENGLISH SCHOOLE-MASTER: Teaching all his Schollers, of what age soever, the most easie, short, and perfect order of distinct Reading, and true Writing our English-tongue, that hath euer yet beene knowne or Published by any* (London: for the Company of Stationers, 1630).

Coryate, Thomas. *CORYATS CRUDITIES hastily gobled vp in five moneths trauells in France, Sauoy, Italy, Rhetia co[m]monly called the Grisons country, Heluetia aliàs Switzerland, some parts of high Germany, and the Netherlands; newly digested in the hungry aire of Odcombe in the county of Somerset, & now dispersed to the nourishment of the trauelling members of this kingdome* (London: W.S. for the author, 1611).

THE COSTLIE WHORE. A COMICALL HISTORIE Acted by the companie of the Revels (London: Augustine Mathewes, for William Sheares, 1633).

Cotgrave, Randle. *A DICTIONARIE OF THE FRENCH AND ENGLISH TONGVES* (London: Adam Islip, 1611).

Cranley, Thomas. *AMANDA: OR, THE REFORMED WHORE* (London: John Norton, 1635).

Cranley, Thomas. *THE CONVERTED COURTEZAN, OR THE REFORMED WHORE* (London: for Bernard Langford, 1639).

Daborne, Robert. *A Christian Turned Turk* (1612), in *Three Turk Plays from Early Modern England*, ed. Daniel Vitkus (New York: Columbia University Press, 2000), 149–239.

Dekker, Thomas. *The Belman of London. BRINGING TO LIGHT THE MOST NOTORIOVS villanies that are now practised in the kingdome. Profitable for gentlemen, lawyers, merchants, citizens, farmers, masters of housholdes, and all sorts of seruants to mark, and delightfull for all men to reade* (London: for Nathaniell Butter, 1608).

Dekker, Thomas. *The Converted Curtezan, with the Humours of the Patient Man, and the Longing Wife* (London: V. Simmes for J. Hodgets. 1604), Q2.

Dekker, Thomas. *THE Honest Whore, With, The Humours of the Patient Man, and the Longing Wife* (London: V.S. for Iohn Hodgets, 1604), Q1. Available online at http://digitalrenaissance.uvic.ca/Library/Texts/1HW/, ed. Joost Daalder.

Dekker, Thomas. *The Honest Whore, Part I*, in *The Dramatic Works of Thomas Dekker*, Vol. II, ed. Fredson Bowers (Cambridge: Cambridge University Press, 1955), 1–130.

Dekker, Thomas. *The Honest Whore, Part II*, in *The Dramatic Works of Thomas Dekker*, Vol. II, ed. Fredson Bowers (Cambridge: Cambridge University Press, 1955), 131–227.

Dekker, Thomas. *LANTHORNE and Candle-Light. Or The bell-mans second nights-walke In which hee brings to light, a broode of more strange villanies, than euer were till this yeare discouered* (London: for Iohn Busby, 1608).

Dekker, Thomas. *The Second Part of the Honest Whore, with the Hvmors of the Patient Men, the Impatient wife: the Honest Whore, perswaded by strong Arguments to turne Curtizan again. her braue refuting those Arguments* (London: Elizabeth All-de, for Nathaniel Butter, 1630).

Dekker, Thomas and Thomas Middleton. *The Patient Man and the Honest Whore*, ed. Paul Mulholland, in *Thomas Middleton: The Collected Works*, ed. Gary Taylor and John Lavagnino (Oxford: Oxford University Press, 2007), 280–327.

Dekker, Thomas and Thomas Middleton. *The Honest Whore, Part I (Modern)*, ed. Joost Daalder. *Digital Renaissance Editions*. Internet Shakespeare. University of Victoria, 4 Apr. 2015. Web. 4 Apr. 2015. <https://digitalrenaissance.uvic.ca/Library/Texts/2HW/M/default/>.

Dekker, Thomas and John Webster. *Northward Ho*, ed. Fredson Bowers, in *The Dramatic Works of Thomas Dekker*, Vol. II (Cambridge: Cambridge University Press, 1955), 405–490.

Donne, John. '2 (XVIII) Show me, dear Christ, Thy spouse, so bright and clear', in *John Donne's Poetry*, ed. Arthur L. Clements, 2nd edition (New York: W. W. Norton & Company, 1992), 119.

Downame, Iohn. *A Treatise Against Fornication and Adulterie*, in *Fovr Treatises tending to dis-swade all Christians from foure no lesse hainous then common sinnes; namely, the abuses of swearing, drunkennesse, whoredome, and briberie* (London: Felix Kyngston, for William Welby, 1608).

Earle, John. *Micro-cosmographie, or, a peece of the world discovered: in essayes and characters* (London: for William Stansby, for Robert Allot, 1628).

Elyot, Sir Thomas. *The Dictionary of Syr Thomas Elyot knight* (London: Thomas Berthelet, 1538).

Erasmus, Desiderius. *A modest meane to mariage, pleasauntly set foorth by that famous clarke Erasmus Roterodamus, and translated into Englishe by N.L.* (London: Henrie Denham, 1568).

Erasmus, Desiderius. *Seven Dialogves Both Pithie and profitable* (London: W.B. for Nicholas Ling, 1606).

Florio, John. *A Worlde of wordes, or Most copious, and exact dictionarie in Italian and English* (London: Arnold Hatfield for Edw. Blount, 1598).

Florio, John. *Queen Anna's New World of Words, or Dictionarie of the Italian and English tongues* (London: Melch. Bradwood for Edw. Blount and William Barret, 1611).

Fuller, Thomas. *The Church-History of Britain* (London: for Iohn Williams, 1655).

Gainsford, Thomas. *The Rich Cabinet Furnished with varietie Of excellent discriptions, exquisite Characters, witty discourses, and delightfull Histories, Deuine and Morrall* (London: I.B. for Roger Iackson, 1616).

Greene, Robert. 'The conuersion of an English Courtizan', in *A* Dispvtation, *betweene a hee conny-catcher, and a shee conny-catcher whether a theefe or a whoore, is most hurtfull in cousonage, to the common-wealth. Discouering the secret villanies of alluring strumpets. With the conuersion of an English courtizen, reformed this present yeare, 1592* (London: A.I. for T.G., 1592), sigs D1r–D2v.

Greene, Robert. *A Dispvtation, betweene a hee conny-catcher, and a shee conny-catcher whether a theefe or a whoore, is most hurtfull in cousonage, to the common-wealth. Discouering the secret villanies of alluring strumpets. With the conuersion of an English courtizen, reformed this present yeare, 1592* (London: A.I. for T.G., 1592).

Greene, Robert. *A notable discouery of coosnage, now daily practised by sundry lewd persons, called connie-catchers, and crosse-biters. Plainely laying open those pernitious sleights that hath brought many ignorant men to confusion* (London: Iohn Wolfe for T.N., 1591).

Greene, Robert. *Selimus, Emperor of the Turks* (1594), in *Three Turk Plays From Early Modern England*, ed. Daniel J. Vitkus (New York: Columbia University Press, 2000), 55–148.

Hall, Edward. *The vnion of the two noble and illustrious famelies of Lancastre & Yorke* (London: Richard Grafton, 1548).

Hall, Edward. *Hall's Chronicle; Containing the History of England, during the Reign of Henry the Fourth, and the Succeeding Monarchs, to the End of the Reign of Henry the Eighth, in which are particularly described the manners and customs of those periods* (London: for J. Johnson et al., 1809).

Harman, Thomas. *A caueat or warening* For Common Cvrsetors vulgarely called *uagabones, set forth by Thomas Harman, esquiere, for the vtilite and proffyt of his naturall cuntrey* (London: 1567).

Herbert, George. 'Church-Music', in *The Complete English Poems* (London: Penguin, 2005), 59.

Heywood, Thomas. *Γυναικειον: or,* Nine Bookes *of Various History Concerninge Women* (London: Adam Islip, 1624).

Hollyband, Claude. *The Treasurie of the French Tong: Teaching the waye to vaerie all sortes of Verbes: Enriched so plentifully with Wordes and Phrases (for the benefit of the studious in that language) as the like hath not before bin published* (London: Henrie Bynneman, 1580).

The Holy Bible, conteyning the Old Testament, and the *New* (London: Robert Barker, printer to the Kings most excellent Maiestie, 1611).

Huberinus, Caspar. *A riche storehouse, or treasurie, for the sicke, full of Christian counsels, holesome doctrines, comfortable persuasions, and godly meditations, meete for all Christians, both in sicknesse and in health* (London: H. Middleton, for Ralph Newberrie, 1578).

Huloet, Richard. *Abcedarium Anglico Latinum* (London: 1552).

Hyspanus, Petrus. *The Treasury of Health conteynyng many profitable medycines, gathered out of Hypocrates, Galen and Auycen* (London: Willam Copland, 1550).

I.C., SAINT MARIE MAGDALENS CONVERSION (Printed with License, 1603).

Jewel, John. *An Apologie, or aunswer in defence of the Church of England, concerninge the state of Religion vsed in the same* (London: Reginald Wolf, 1562).

Jonson, Ben. *The Alchemist*, in *English Renaissance Drama. A Norton Anthology*, ed. David Bevington, Lars Engle, Katherine Eisaman Maus, and Eric Rasmussen (New York: W. W. Norton, 2002), 861–960.

Kid, Thomas. *The Spanish Tragedy*, ed. Clara Calvo and Jesús Tronch. Arden Early Modern Drama (London: Bloomsbury, 2013).

Latimer, Hugh. 'The Third Sermon of M. Hugh Latimer, Preached before King Edward (1549)', in *Sermons by Hugh Latimer Sometime Bishop of Worcester* (London: J. M. Dent & Co., 1906).

Lenton, Francis. *Characterismi:* OR, LENTONS LEASVRES. *Expressed* IN ESSAYS AND CHARACTERS, *Neuer before written on* (London: I.B. for Roger Michell, 1631).

Lodowyk, Francis. *THE GROUND-WORK, OR FOUNDATION LAID (or so intended) For the Framing of a New Perfect LANGUAGE* (London: 1652).

Luther, Martin. *Luther on Women: A Sourcebook*, ed. Susan C. Karant-Nunn and Merry E. Wiesner-Hanks (Cambridge: Cambridge University Press, 2003).

Luther, Martin. 'The Estate of Marriage, 1522', trans. Walter I. Brandt, in *Luther's Works*, Vol. 45 (Philadelphia: Muhlenberg Press, 1962), 11–51.

Markham, Gervase. *THE FAMOVS Whore, or Noble Curtizan* (London: Nicholas Okes for Iohn Budge, 1609).

Marlowe, Christopher. *Doctor Faustus*, ed. David Scott Kastan (New York: W. W. Norton & Company, 2005).

Marlowe, Christopher. *Edward the Second*, ed. Charles R. Forker. The Revels Plays (Manchester: Manchester University Press, 1988).

Marston, John. *The Dutch Courtesan*, ed. David Crane. New Mermaids (London; New York: W. W. Norton, 1997).

Meres, Francis. *Palladis Tamia. WITS TREASVRIE Being the Second part of Wits Commonwealth* (London: P. Short for Cuthbert Burbie, 1598).

Middleton, Thomas. *MICHAELMAS Terme. AS IT HATH BEEN SVN-dry times acted by the Children of Paules* (London: A.I., 1607).

Minsheu, John. *Ductor in Linguas, THE GVIDE INTO TONGVES* (London: for Ioannem Browne, 1617).

Montaigne, Michel de. *ESSAIES WRITTEN IN French by MICHAEL Lord of Montaigne, Knight of the Order of S. Michael, gentleman of the French Kings chamber: DONE INTO ENGLISH, according to the last French edition, by IOHN FLORIO reader of the Italian tongue vnto the Soueraigne Maiestie of Anna, Queene of England, Scotland, France and Ireland, &c. And one of the gentlemen of hir royall priuie chamber* (London: Melch. Bradwood for Edward Blount and William Barret, 1613).

Mulcaster, William. *THE FIRST PART OF THE ELEMENTARIE WHICH ENTREATETH CHEFELIE OF THE right writing of our English tung* (London: Thomas Vautroullier, 1582).

Munday, Anthony et al. *Sir Thomas More*, ed. John Jowett. The Arden Shakespeare, 3rd series (London: Thomson Learning, 2011).

Nashe, Thomas. *CHRISTS TEARES OVER IERVSALEM. WHEREVNTO IS AN-nexed, a comparatiue admonition to London* (London: for Andrew Wise, 1594).

Nashe, Thomas. *Pierce Penileffe HIS SVPPLICATION to the Diuell* (London: Abell Ieffes, for I.B., 1592).

Ouerburie, Thomas. *NEW AND CHOISE CHARACTERS, of seuerall Authors: Together with that exquisite and unmatcht poeme, The wife/written by Syr Thomas Ouerburie* (London: Thomas Creede, for Laurence L'isle, 1615).

Paré, Ambrose. *The Workes of that famous Chirurgion Ambrose Parey* (London: Th. Cotes and R. Young, 1634).

Partridge, John. *The treasurie of commodious conceits, & hidden secrets and may be called, the huswiues closet, of healthfull prouision* (London: Richarde Iones, 1573).

A Pepysian Garland: Black-Letter Broadside Ballads of the Years 1595–1639, ed. Hyder E. Rollins (Cambridge: Cambridge University Press, 1922).

Ptolemy of Lucca, with portions attributed to Thomas Aquinas. *On the Government of Rulers: De Regimine Principum*, trans. James M. Blythe (Philadelphia: University of Pennsylvania Press, 1997).

Raleigh, Sir Walter. *The Poems of Sir Walter Raleigh: Collected and Authenticated with those of Sir Henry Wotton and Other Courtly Poets from 1540 to 1650*, ed. J. Hannah (Juniper Grove, 2007).

Rich, Barnabie. *THE EXCELLENCY of good women The honour and estimation that belongeth vnto them. The infallible markes whereby to know them* (London: Thomas Dawson, 1613).

Rider, John. *BIBLIOTHECA SCHOLASTICA. A DOVBLE DICTIONARIE, Penned for all those that would haue within short space the vse of the Latin tongue, either to speake, or write* (Oxford: Ioseph. Barnes, 1589).

Rogers, Daniel. *MATRIMONIAL HONOUR: OR, The mutuall Crowne and comfort of godly, loyall, and chaste MARRIAGE* (London: Th. Harper for Philip Nevil, 1642).

Salesbury, William. *A DICTIONARY of Englyshe and Welshe moche necessary to all suche Welshemen as wil spedly learne the englyshe to[n]gue thought vnto the kynges maiestie very mete to be sette forthe to the vse of his graces subiectes in Wales: wherevnto is p[re]fixed a litle treatyse of the englyshe pronu[n]ciacion of the letters, by Wyllyam Salesbury* (London: N. Hill, 1547).

Shakespeare, William. *Antony and Cleopatra*, ed. Walten Cohen, in *The Norton Shakespeare Based on the Oxford Edition*, ed. Stephen Greenblatt, Walter Cohen, Jean E. Howard, and Katharine Eisaman Maus, 2nd edition (New York: W. W. Norton, 2008), 2633–2721.

Shakespeare, William. *The Complete Works of Shakespeare*, ed. David Bevington (New York: Harper Collins, 1992).

Shakespeare, William. *The Complete Works of William Shakespeare*. Available from: https://shakespeare.mit.edu. Accessed on 15 October 2025.

Shakespeare, William. *The first Part of Henry the Sixt[h]*, in MR. WILLIAM SHAKESPEARES COMEDIES, HISTORIES, & TRAGEDIES (London: Isaac Iaggard, for Ed. Blount, 1623). Reprinted in *The Norton Facsimile: The First Folio of Shakespeare*, ed. Charles Hinman (New York: Norton, 1996).

Shakespeare, William. *Hamlet* (Quarto 2, 1604). *Internet Shakespeare Editions*. University of Victoria, NaN. [Accessed 15 Apr. 2026]. Available from: https://internetshakespeare.uvic.ca/doc/Ham_Q2/complete/index.html.

Shakespeare, William. *King Henry VI, Part 1*, ed. Edward Burns. The Arden Shakespeare, 3rd series (London: Thomson Learning, 2000).

Shakespeare, William. *King Lear*, ed. R.A. Foakes. The Arden Shakespeare, 3rd series (London: Thomson Learning, 1997).

Shakespeare, William. *Love's Labor's Lost* (Quarto 1, 1598). *Internet Shakespeare Editions*. University of Victoria, NaN. [Accessed 15 Apr. 2026]. Available from: https://internetshakespeare.uvic.ca/doc/LLL_Q1/complete/index.html.

Shakespeare, William. *Measure for Measure*, ed. J. W. Lever. The Arden Shakespeare, 2nd series (London: Thomson Learning, 1965).

Shakespeare, William. *Measure for Measure*, ed. N. W. Bawcutt. Oxford World Classics (Oxford: Oxford University Press, 1991).

Shakespeare, William. *Measure for Measure*, ed. A. R. Braunmuller and Robert N. Watson. The Arden Shakespeare, 3rd series (London: Bloombury, 2020).

Shakespeare, William. *The Merchant of Venice*, ed. John Russell Brown. The Arden Shakespeare, 2nd series (London: Thomson Learning, 2005).

Shakespeare, William. *The Merchant of Venice* (Folio 1, 1623). *Internet Shakespeare Editions*. University of Victoria, NaN. [Accessed 15 Apr. 2026]. Available from: https://internetshakespeare.uvic.ca/doc/MV_F1/complete/index.html.

Shakespeare, William. *THE MOST EX-cellent and Lamentable Tragedie, of Romeo and Iuliet* (London: Thomas Creede, for Cuthbert Burby, 1599).

Shakespeare, William. *MR. WILLIAM SHAKESPEARES COMEDIES, HISTORIES, & TRAGEDIES* (London: 1623). *Proquest*. Web. Available from: https://www.proquest.com/docview/2240890297/99846615/7702FD91FF194F0APQ/1?. Accessed on 15 October 2025.

Shakespeare, William. *The Norton Shakespeare Based on the Oxford Edition*, ed. Stephen Greenblatt, Walter Cohen, Jean E. Howard, and Katharine Eisaman Maus, 2nd edition (New York: W.W. Norton, 2008).

Shakespeare, William. *OpenSource Shakespeare*, based on the 1864 Globe Edition of the complete works. Published on 5 April 2012. Available from: http://www.opensourceshakespeare.org/. Accessed on 15 October 2025.

Shakespeare, William. *Othello*, ed. Walten Cohen. In *The Norton Shakespeare Based on the Oxford Edition*, ed. Stephen Greenblatt, Walter Cohen, Jean E. Howard, and Katharine Eisaman Maus, 2nd edition (New York: W. W. Norton), 2109–2191.

Shakespeare, William. *The Oxford Shakespeare: The Complete Works*, ed. John Jowett, William Montgomery, Stanley Wells, and Gary Taylor, 2nd edition (Oxford: Oxford University Press, 2005).

Shakespeare, William. *Richard II* (Quarto 1, 1597). *Internet Shakespeare Editions*. University of Victoria, NaN. [Accessed 15 Apr. 2026]. Available from: https://internetshakespeare.uvic.ca/doc/R2_Q1/complete/index.html.

Shakespeare, William. *Romeo and Juliet* (Quarto 2, 1599). *Internet Shakespeare Editions*. University of Victoria, NaN. [Accessed 15 Apr. 2026]. Available from: https://internetshakespeare.uvic.ca/doc/Rom_Q2/complete/index.html.

Shakespeare, William. *Romeo and Juliet*, ed. Jill L. Levenson. Oxford World's Classics (Oxford: Oxford University Press, 2000).

Shakespeare, William. *Romeo and Juliet*, ed. René Weis. The Arden Shakespeare, 3rd series (London: Thomson Learning, 2002).

Shakespeare, William. *Romeo and Juliet*, ed. Stephen Greenblatt. In *The Norton Shakespeare Based on the Oxford Edition*, ed. Stephen Greenblatt, Walter Cohen, Jean E. Howard, and Katharine Eisaman Maus, 2nd edition (New York: W.W. Norton, 2008).

Shakespeare, William. *Romeo and Juliet*, ed. Brian Gibbons. The Arden Shakespeare, 2nd series (London: Bloomsbury Publishing, 2012).

Shakespeare, William. *Romeo and Juliet*, ed. Peter Holland. The Pelican Shakespeare (New York: Penguin Books, 2016).

Shakespeare, William. *Romeo and Juliet: Texts and Contexts*, ed. Dympna Callaghan (Boston: Bedford/St. Martin's, 2003).

Shakespeare, William. *The Riverside Shakespeare*, ed. G. Blakemore Evans and J. J. M. Tobin, 2nd edition (Boston: Houghton Mifflin, 1997), digitized edition. Access provided by University of Michigan Libraries.

Shakespeare, William. *The Taming of the Shrew* (Folio, 1623). *Internet Shakespeare Editions*. University of Victoria, NaN. [Accessed 15 Apr. 2026].

Available from: https://internetshakespeare.uvic.ca/doc/Shr_F1/index.html

Shakespeare, William. *Titus Andronicus* (Quarto 1, 1594). *Internet Shakespeare Editions.* University of Victoria, NaN. [Accessed 15 Apr. 2026]. Available from: https://internetshakespeare.uvic.ca/doc/Tit_Q1/index.html

Shakespeare, William. *The Tragedy of Hamlet, Prince of Denmark*, in *The Norton Shakespeare Based on the Oxford Edition*, ed. Stephen Greenblatt, Walter Cohen, Jean E. Howard, and Katharine Eisaman Maus, 2nd edition (New York: W. W. Norton, 2008), 1683–1784.

Shakespeare, William. *Troilus and Cressida* (Quarto 1, 1609). *Internet Shakespeare Editions.* University of Victoria, University of Victoria, NaN. [Accessed 15 Apr. 2026]. Available from: <https://internetshakespeare.uvic.ca/doc/Tro_Q1/complete/index.html>

Sharp, Jane. *The Midwives Book* (London: for Simon Miller, 1671).

Sharpham, Edward. *The Fleire. As it hath beene often played in the Blacke-Fryers by the Children of the Reuells* (London: to be sold by F.B., 1607).

Sheldon, Richard. *The Motives of* Richard Sheldon, *Pr. for his iust, voluntary, and free renouncing of communion with the Bishop of Rome* (London: for Nathaniel Butter, 1612).

Sidney, Sir Philip. *An Apology for Poetry*, in *Sir Philip Sidney's An Apology for Poetry and Astrophil and Stella: Texts and Contexts*, ed. Peter C. Herman (Glen Allen: College Publishing, 2001), 55–126.

Stow, John. *A Svrvay of London* (London: Iohn Wolf, 1598).

Stuart Royal Proclamations, Vol. I: *Royal Proclamations of King James I, 1603–1625*, ed. Paul L. Hughes and James F. Larkin (Oxford: Clarendon Press, 1973).

Swetnam, Joseph. *The araignment of leuud, idle, froward, and vnconstant women or the vanitie of them, choose you whether: with a commendation of wise, vertuous and honest women: pleasant for married men, profitable for young men, and hurtfull to none* (London: George Purslowe for Thomas Archer, 1615).

Taylor, Iohn. *A Common Whore, With all these Graces Grac'd: shee's very honest, beautifull and chaste* (London: for Henry Gosson, 1622).

Taylor, Iohn. *All the Workes of Iohn Taylor The Water-Poet Being 63 in number Collected into one Volum[e] By the Author With Sundry new Additions, Corrected, Reuised, and Newly imprinted* (London: J.B. for James Boler, 1630).

Thomas, Thomas. *Dictionarivm Lingvae Latinae et Anglicanae* (London: for Richard Boyle, 1587).

Tilney, Edmund. *The Flower of Friendship: A Renaissance Dialogue Contesting Marriage*, ed. Valerie Wayne (Ithaca: Cornell University Press, 1992).

The Trotula: An English Translation of the Medieval Compendium of Women's Medicine, ed. and trans. Monica H. Green (Philadelphia: University of Pennsylvania Press, 2002).

Tudor Royal Proclamations, ed. Paul L. Hughes and James F. Larkin, 2 Vols. (New Haven: Yale University Press, 1964–1969).

Tuke, Thomas. *A Discovrse Against Painting and Tincturing of Women* (London: for Edward Marchant, 1616).

Tyndale, William. *The newe testament of oure sauioure Jesu Christ, newly and diligently translated in to Englysshe by Thomas Mathew with annotations in y[e] mergent to helpe the reader to the vndersta[n]ding of ye texte* (London: Thomas Gybson, 1538).

Vaughan, William. *The Golden-Groue, moralized in three Bookes* (London: Simon Stafford, 1608).

Vele, Abraham. *The deceyte of women, to the instruction and ensample of all men yonge and olde, newly corrected* (London: W. Copland for Abraham Vele, 1557).

Vives, Juan Luis. *A very frutefull and pleasant boke called the Instructio[n] of a Christen woma[n]/made fyrst in Laten/and dedicated vnto the quenes good grace/by the right famous clerke mayster Lewes Viues/and turned out of Laten in to Enlgysshe by Rycharde Hyrd* (London: in the house of Thomas Berthelet, 1529).

Wager, Lewis. *A new enterlude, neuer before this tyme imprinted, entreating of the life and repentaunce of Marie Magdalene not only godlie, learned and fruitefull, but also well furnished with pleasaunt myrth and pastime, very delectable for those which shall heare or reade the same. Made by the learned clarke Lewis Wager. The names of the players. Infidelitie the vice. Marie Magdalene. Pride of life. Cupiditie. Carnall concupiscence. Simon the Pharisie. Malicious iudgement. The lawe. Knowledge of sinne. Christ Iesus. Fayth. Repentaunce. Iustification. Loue. Foure may easely play this enterlude* (London: Iohn Charlewood, 1566).

White, Harim. *The Ready Way to Trve Repentance* (London: G.E. for T.B., 1618).

Willett, Andrew. *An Antilogue or Counterplea to an Apologicall (he should haue said) Apologeticall Epistle published by a fauorite of the Romane separation, and (as is supposed) one of the Ignatian faction* (London: for Thomas Man, 1603).

Wilson, Thomas. *The Arte of Rhetorique, for the vse of all suche as are studious of Eloquence* (London: Richard Grafton, 1553).

Secondary Sources

Adelman, Janet. *Suffocating Mothers: Fantasies of Maternal Origin in Shakespeare's Plays, Hamlet to The Tempest* (New York: Routledge, 1992).

Akhimie, Patricia. *Shakespeare and the Cultivation of Difference: Race and Conduct in the Early Modern World* (New York: Routledge, 2018).

Alfar, Cristina León. *Women and Shakespeare's Cuckoldry Plays: Shifting Narratives of Marital Betrayal* (London: Routledge, 2017).

Amussen, Susan Dwyer. *An Ordered Society: Gender and Class in Early Modern England* (New York: Columbia University Press, 1988).

Amussen, Susan Dwyer. 'Elizabeth I and Alice Balstone: Gender, Class, and the Exceptional Woman in Early Modern England', in *Attending to Women in Early Modern England*, ed. Betty S. Travitsky and Adele F. Seeff (Newark: University of Delaware Press, 1994), 219–240.

Andreadis, Harriette. *Sappho in Early Modern England: Female Same-Sex Literary Erotics, 1550–1714* (Chicago: University of Chicago Press, 2001).

Archer, Ian. *The Pursuit of Stability: Social Relations in Elizabethan London* (Cambridge: Cambridge University Press, 1991).

Arondekar, Anjali. *For the Record: On Sexuality and the Colonial Archive in India* (Durham: Duke University Press, 2009).

Arvas, Abdulhamit. *Boys Abducted: The Homoerotics of Empire and Race in Early Modernity* (Durham: Duke University Press, 2025).

Atkinson, Clarissa W. '"Precious Balsam in a Fragile Glass": The Ideology of Virginity in the Later Middle Ages', *Journal of Family History* 8 (1983), 131–143.

Bailey, Derrick. *Sexual Relation in Christian Thought* (New York: Harper & Brothers, 1959).

Bailey, Amanda and Roze Hentschell. *Masculinity and the Metropolis of Vice, 1550–1650* (New York: Palgrave MacMillan, 2010).

Baldo, Jonathan. 'Wars of Memory in Henry V', *Shakespeare Quarterly* 47.2 (1996), 132–159.

Barish, Jonas. *The Antitheatrical Prejudice* (Berkeley: University of California Press, 1981).

Barkan, Leonard. *Transuming Passion: Ganymede and the Erotics of Humanism* (Stanford: Stanford University Press, 1991).

Bartels, Emily C. *Spectacles of Strangeness: Imperialism, Alienation, and Marlowe* (Philadelphia: University of Pennsylvania Press, 1993).

Bate, Jonathan. *How the Classics Made Shakespeare* (Princeton: Princeton University Press, 2019).

Beattie, Cordelia. *Medieval Single Women: The Politics of Social Classification in Late Medieval England* (Oxford: Oxford University Press, 2007).

Ben-Amos, Ilana Krausman. *Adolescence and Youth in Early Modern England* (New Haven: Yale University Press, 1994).

Berlin, Normand. *The Base String: The Underworld in Elizabethan Drama* (Rutherford: Farleigh Dickinson University Press, 1968).

Berry, Philippa. *Of Chastity and Power: Elizabethan Literature and the Unmarried Queen* (London: Routledge, 1989).

Bevington, David. 'The Domineering Female in *1 Henry VI*', *Shakespeare Studies* 2 (1966), 51–58.
Blake, Liza, Simone Chess, Catherine Clifford, and Ashley 'Aley' O'Mara. 'A Bibliography for Early Modern Asexualities.' October 2020; updated March 2022. Available online at https://tinyurl.com/earlymodacebib.
Blank, Paula. 'The Babel of Renaissance English', in *The Oxford History of English*, ed. Lynda Mugglestone (Oxford: Oxford University Press, 2006), 212–239.
Blank, Paula. *Broken English: Dialects and the Politics of Language in Renaissance Writings* (London: Routledge, 1996).
Blank, Paula. 'The Proverbial "Lesbian": Queering Etymology in Contemporary Critical Practice', *Modern Philology* 109.1 (2011), 108–134.
Bloom, Harold. *Shakespeare: The Invention of the Human* (New York: Riverhead Books, 1998).
Bly, Mary. 'Carnal Geographies: Mocking and Mapping the Religious Body', in *Masculinity and the Metropolis of Vice, 1550–1650*, ed. Amanda Bailey and Roze Hentschell (New York: Palgrave MacMillan, 2010), 89-114.
Bly, Mary. *Queer Virgins and Virgin Queans on the Early Modern Stage* (Oxford: Oxford University Press, 2000).
Bonheim, H. 'Shakespeare's "Goose of Winchester"', in *Philological Quarterly* 51.4 (1972), 940–941.
Boose, Lynda E. 'The Family in Shakespeare Studies; or—Studies in the Family of Shakespeareans; or—The Politics of Politics.' *Renaissance Quarterly* 40.4 (1987), 707–742.
Boose, Lynda E. 'The Priest, the Slanderer, the Historian, and the Feminist', *ELR* 3 (1995), 320–340.
Boose, Lynda E. 'Scolding Brides and Bridling Scolds: Taming the Woman's "Unruly Member"', *Shakespeare Quarterly* 42.2 (1991), 179–213.
Bovilsky, Lara. *Barbarous Play: Race on the English Renaissance Stage* (Minneapolis: University of Minnesota Press, 2008).
Bray, Alan. *Homosexuality in Renaissance England* (New York: Columbia University Press, 1982).
Bray, Alan. *The Friend* (Chicago: University of Chicago Press, 2006).
Bredbeck, Gregory W. *Sodomy and Interpretation: Marlowe to Milton* (Ithaca: Cornell University Press, 1991).
Britton, Dennis Austin. *Becoming Christian: Race, Reformation, and Early Modern English Romance* (New York: Fordham University Press, 2014).
Bromley, James and Will Stockton, eds. *Sex before Sex: Figuring the Act in Early Modern England* (Minneapolis: University of Minnesota Press, 2013).
Brown, Carolyn E. 'The Homoeroticism of Duke Vincentio: "Some Feeling of the Sport"', *Studies in Philology* 94 (1997), 187–220.
Brown, Peter. *The Body and Society* (New York: Columbia University Press, 1988).

Brownlee, Victoria. 'Imagining the Enemy: Protestant Readings of the Whore of Babylon in Early Modern England, c.1580–1625', in *Biblical Women in Early Modern Literary Culture, 1550–1700*, ed. Victoria Brownlee and Laura Gallagher (Manchester: Manchester University Press, 2015), 213–233.

Brunning, Alizon. '"Thou Art Damned for Alt'ring Thy Religion": The Double Coding of Conversion in City Comedy', in *Plotting Early Modern London: New Essays on Jacobean City Comedy*, ed. Dieter Mehl, Angela Stock, and Anne-Julia Zwierlein (London: Routledge, 2004), 145–162.

Bullough, Vern L. 'The Prostitute in the Early Middle Ages', in *Sexual Practices & the Medieval Church*, ed. Vern L. Bullough and James Brundage (Buffalo: Prometheus Books, 1982), 34–42.

Bullough, Vern L. and James Brundage. *Sexual Practices & the Medieval Church* (Buffalo: Prometheus Books, 1982).

Burton, Jonathan and Ania Loomba. *Race in Early Modern England: A Documentary Companion* (New York: Palgrave MacMillan, 2007).

Bush, M. L. 'The Act of Proclamations: A Reinterpretation', *American Journal of Legal History* 27.1 (1983), 33–53.

Butler, Judith. *Bodies That Matter: On the Discursive Limits of 'Sex'* (New York: Routledge, 1993).

Butler, Judith. *Excitable Speech: A Politics of the Performative* (New York: Routledge, 1997).

Cadden, Joan. 'Medieval Scientific and Medical Views of Sexuality: Questions of Propriety', in *Medievalia et Humanistica: Studies in Medieval & Renaissance Culture*, ed. Paul Maurice Clogan (Rowman & Littlefield, 1986), 157–171.

Cady, Diane. 'Linguistic Dis-ease: Foreign Language as Sexual Disease in EM England', in *Sins of the Flesh: Responding to Sexual Disease in Early Modern Europe*, ed. Kevin Siena (Toronto: Centre for Reformation and Renaissance Studies, 2005), 159–186.

Capp, Bernard. 'The Double Standard Revisited: Plebeian Women and Male Sexual Reputation in Early Modern England', *Past & Present* 162.1 (1999), 70–100.

Capp, Bernard. *When Gossips Meet: Women, Family, and Neighborhood in Early Modern England* (Oxford: Oxford University Press, 2003).

Carlin, Martha. *Medieval Southwark* (London: Hambledon Press, 1996).

Carroll, William C. 'The Virgin Not: Language and Sexuality in Shakespeare', *Shakespeare Survey* 46 (1994), 107–119.

Carruthers, Mary. *The Book of Memory: A Study of Memory in Medieval Culture* (Cambridge: Cambridge University Press, 1990).

Cave, Terence. *The Cornucopian Text: Problems of Writing in the French Renaissance* (Oxford: Oxford University Press, 1979).

Charnes, Linda. *Notorious Identity: Materializing the Subject in Shakespeare* (Cambridge: Cambridge University Press, 1993).

Chess, Simone. *Male-to-Female Crossdressing in Early Modern English Literature: Gender, Performance, and Queer Relations* (New York: Routledge, 2016).

Chess, Simone. 'Queer Residue: Boy Actors' Adult Careers in Early Modern England', *Journal for Early Modern Cultural Studies* 19.4 (2019), 242–264.

Chess, Simone, Colby Gordon, and Will Fisher, eds. 'Early Modern Trans Studies', *Journal for Early Modern Cultural Studies* 19.4 (2019).

Cohen, Elizabeth S. 'Straying and Led Astray: Roman Maids Become Young Women circa 1600', in *The Youth of Early Modern Women*, ed. Elizabeth S. Cohen and Margaret Reeves (Amsterdam: Amsterdam University Press, 2018), 277–296.

Cohen, Elizabeth S. and Margaret Reeves, eds. *The Youth of Early Modern Women* (Amsterdam: Amsterdam University Press, 2018).

Coleman, Julie. *Love, Sex, and Marriage: A Historical Thesaurus* (Amsterdam-Atlanta: Rodopi, 1999).

Considine, John. *Dictionaries in Early Modern Europe: Lexicography and the Making of Heritage* (Cambridge: Cambridge University Press, 2008).

Cook, Ann Jennalie. '"Bargaines of Incontinencie": Bawdy Behavior in the Playhouses', *Shakespeare Studies* 10 (1997), 271–290.

Cook, Ann Jennalie. *The Privileged Playgoers of Shakespeare's London, 1576–1643* (Princeton, Princeton University Press, 1981).

Cook, Carol. '"The Sign and Semblance of Her Honor": Reading Gender Difference in *Much Ado About Nothing*', *PMLA* 101.2 (1986), 186–202.

Crane, Mary Thomas. '"Players in Your Huswifery, and Huswives in Your Beds": Conflicting Identities of Early Modern English Women', in *Maternal Measures: Figuring Caregiving in the Early Modern Period*, ed. Naomi. J. Miller and Naomi Yavneh (Aldershot: Ashgate, 2000), 212–223.

Crawford, Hannah. *Etymology and the Invention of English in Early Modern Literature* (Cambridge: Cambridge University Press, 2013).

Crawford, Julie. 'Women's Secretaries', in *Queer Renaissance Historiography: Backward Gaze*', ed. Vin Nardizzi, Stephen Guy-Bray, and Will Stockton (London: Routledge, 2009), 111–134.

Cressy, David. *Birth, Marriage, and Death: Ritual, Religion, and the Life-Cycle in Tudor and Stuart England* (Oxford: Oxford University Press, 2002).

Cressy, David. *Bonfires and Bells: National Memory and the Protestant Calendar in Elizabethan and Stuart England* (Berkeley: University of California Press, 1989).

Crewe, Jonathan. *Unredeemed Rhetoric: Thomas Nashe and the Scandal of Authorship* (Baltimore: Johns Hopkins University Press, 1982).

Crowther, Kathleen M. 'Sexual Difference', in *The Oxford Handbook of the Protestant Reformations*, ed. Ulinka Rublack (Oxford: Oxford University Press, 2017), 667–687.

Crystal, David. *Words in Time and Place: Exploring Language Through the Historical Thesaurus of the Oxford English Dictionary* (Oxford: Oxford University Press, 2014).

Crystal, David and Ben Crystal. *Shakespeare's Words: A Glossary & Language Companion* (London: Penguin Books, 2002).

Cvetkovitch, Ann. *An Archive of Feelings: Trauma, Sexuality, and Lesbian Public Cultures* (Durham: Duke University Press, 2003).

Daalder, Joost. 'Dates and Authorship', *Digital Renaissance Editions*. Available online at https://digitalrenaissance.uvic.ca/doc/1HW_Intro/section/.

Dabhoiwala, Faramerz. 'The Pattern of Sexual Immorality in Seventeenth and Eighteenth Century London', in *Londinopolis: Essays in the Cultural and Social History of Early Modern London*, ed. Paul Griffiths and Mark. S. R. Jenner (Manchester: Manchester University Press, 2000), 86–106.

Daileader, Celia R. 'Back Door Sex: Renaissance Gynosodomy, Aretino, and the Exotic', *ELH* 69.2 (2002), 303–334.

Davis, Kingsley. 'The Sociology of Prostitution', *American Sociological Review* 2.5 (1937), 744–755.

Davis, Lloyd, ed. *Sexuality and Gender in the English Renaissance: An Annotated Edition of Contemporary Documents* (New York: Garland Publishing, 1998).

de Grazia, Margreta. 'Homonyms before and after Lexical Standardization', in *Shakespeare Jahrbuch* (1990), 143–156.

Degenhardt, Jane Hwang. *Islamic Conversion and Christian Resistance on the Early Modern Stage* (Edinburgh: Edinburgh University Press, 2010).

Dekker & Middleton's The Honest Whore. The Red Bull Theater. Available online at https://www.redbulltheater.com/the-honest-whore.

Derrida, Jacques. *Archive Fever: A Freudian Impression* (Chicago: University of Chicago Press, 1995).

Derrida, Jacques. *Dissemination*, trans. Barbara Johnson (Chicago: University of Chicago Press, 1981).

Dever, Vincent M. 'Aquinas and the Practice of Prostitution', in *Essays in Medieval Studies: Proceedings of the Illinois Medieval Association* 13 (1996), 39–50.

DiGangi, Mario. 'Early Modern Bodies That Matter', in *Routledge Companion to Women, Sex, and Gender in the Early British Colonial World*, ed. Kimberly Anne Coles and Eve Keller (London: Routledge, 2019), 33–45.

DiGangi, Mario. *The Homoerotics of Early Modern Drama* (Cambridge: Cambridge University Press, 1997).

DiGangi, Mario. 'How Queer Was the Renaissance?', in *Love, Sex, Intimacy, and Friendship Between Men, 1550–1800*, ed. Katherine O'Donnell and Michael. O'Rourke (Houndmills: Palgrave, 2003), 128–147.

DiGangi, Mario. 'Pleasure and Danger: Measuring Female Sexuality in *Measure for Measure*', *ELH* 60.3 (1993), 589–609.
DiGangi, Mario. 'Sexual Slander and Working Women in *The Roaring Girl*', *Renaissance Drama* 32 (2003), 147–176.
DiGangi, Mario. *Sexual Types: Embodiment, Agency, and Dramatic Character from Shakespeare to Shirley* (Philadelphia: University of Pennsylvania Press, 2011).
DiGangi, Mario. 'Shakespeare's "Bawdy"', *Shakespeare Studies* 43 (2015), 131–153.
Dolan, Frances E. *Whores of Babylon: Catholicism, Gender, and Seventeenth-Century Print Culture* (Notre Dame: University of Notre Dame Press, 1999).
Dollimore, Jonathan. *Sexual Dissidence: Augustine to Wilde, Freud to Foucault* (Oxford: Clarendon Press, 1991).
Dollimore, Jonathan. 'Transgression and Surveillance in *Measure for Measure*', in *Political Shakespeare: Essays in Cultural Materialism*, ed. Jonathan Dollimore and Alan Sinfield, 2nd edition (Ithaca: Cornell University Press, 1994), 129–153.
Dollimore, Jonathan. 'Shakespeare Understudies: The Sodomite, the Prostitute, the Transvestite, and Their Critics', in *Political Shakespeare: Essays in Cultural Materialism*, 2nd edition, ed. Jonathan Dollimore and Alan Sinfield (Ithaca: Cornell University Press, 1994b), 129–152.
Douglas, Mary. *Purity and Danger* (London: Routledge Classics, 2002).
Dowd, Michelle. *Women's Work in Early Modern Literature and Culture* (New York: Palgrave MacMillan, 2009).
Duffy, Eamon. *The Stripping of the Altars: Traditional Religion in England, c. 1400–c. 1580* (New Haven: Yale University Press, 1992).
Dursteler, Eric R. *Venetians in Constantinople: Nations, Identity, and Coexistence in the Early Modern Mediterranean* (Baltimore: Johns Hopkins University Press, 2006).
Dusinberre, Juliet. *Shakespeare and the Nature of Women*, 3rd edition (New York: Palgrave Macmillan, 2003).
Eco, Umberto. *The Open Work*, trans. Anna Cancogni (Cambridge, MA: Harvard University Press, 1989).
Eichhorn, Kate. *The Archival Turn in Feminism: Outrage in Order* (Philadelphia: Temple University Press, 2013).
Elton, G. R. 'Henry VIII's Act of Proclamations', *The English Historical Review* 75 (1960), 208–222.
English Broadside Ballad Archive. Available online at http://ebba.english.ucsb.edu.
English Renaissance Drama: A Norton Anthology, ed. David Bevington, Lars Engle, Katherine Eisaman Maus, and Eric Rasmussen (New York: W. W. Norton, 2002).
Erickson, Amy. *Women and Property in Early Modern England* (London: Routledge, 1993).

Erickson, Peter. *Patriarchal Structures in Shakespeare's Drama* (Berkeley: University of California Press, 1985).

Fabian, Johannes. *Time and the Other: How Anthropology Makes Its Object* (New York: Columbia University Press, 1983).

Felperin, Howard. '"Tongue-Tied Our Queen?": The Deconstruction of Presence in *The Winter's Tale*', in *Shakespeare & the Question of Theory*, ed. Patricia Parker and Geoffrey Hartman (New York: Routledge, 1985), 3–18.

Ferguson, Margaret. 'Foreword', in *Menacing Virgins: Representing Virginity in the Middle Ages and Renaissance*, ed. Kathleen Coyne Kelly and Marina Leslie (Newark: University of Delaware Press, 1999), 7–14.

Ferguson, Margaret. 'Hymeneal Instruction', in *Masculinities, Violence, Childhood: Attending to Early Modern Women—and Men*, ed. Amy E. Leonard and Karen L. Nelson (Newark: University of Delaware Press, 2010), 97–129.

Fiedler, Leslie A. *The Stranger in Shakespeare* (New York: Stein and Day, 1972).

Fisher, Will. *Materializing Gender in Early Modern English Literature and Culture* (Cambridge: Cambridge University Press, 2010).

Fisher, Will. 'Queer Money', *ELH* 66.1 (1999), 1–23.

Fisher, Will. 'Thinking Kink.' Unpublished paper.

Fleck, Andrew. 'Exemplarity and Its Discontents in Michael Drayton's *Englands Heroical Epistles*', in *Sexuality and Memory in Early Modern England: Literature and the Erotics of Recolletion*, ed. John S. Garrison and Kyle Pivetti (New York: Routledge, 2016), 66–80.

Fleming, Juliet. 'Dictionary English and the Female Tongue', in *Enclosure Acts: Sexuality, Property, and Culture in Early Modern England*, ed. Richard Burt and John Michael Archer (Ithaca: Cornell University Press, 1994), 290–325.

Fletcher, Anthony. *Gender, Sex and Subordination in England 1500–1800* (New Haven: Yale University Press, 1995).

Floyd-Wilson, Mary, and Garrett A. Sullivan, eds. *Environment and Embodiment in Early Modern England* (Houndmills: Palgrave MacMillan, 2007).

Foucault, Michel. *Discipline and Punish: The Birth of the Prison* (New York: Vintage, 1995).

Foucault, Michel. 'Film and Popular Memory', in *Foucault Live (Interviews, 1961–1984)*, ed. Sylvère Lotringer (NewYork: Semiotext(e), 1996), 122–132.

Foucault, Michel. *The History of Sexuality*, Vol. I (New York: Random House, 1978).

Foucault, Michel. 'Nietzsche, Genealogy, History', in *Language, Counter-Memory, Practice: Selected Essays and Interviews*, ed. Donald F. Bouchard (Ithaca: Cornell University Press, 1977), 139–164.

Foucault, Michel. *The Order of Things: an Archaeology of the Human Sciences* (New York: Random House, 1970).

Fox, Liz. 'Cosmopolitan Desire and Profitable Performance in *The Dutch Courtesan*', *Early Theatre* 21.1 (2020), 145–162.

Freccero, Carla. 'Acts, Identities, and Sexuality's (Pre)Modern Regimes', *Journal of Women's History* 11.2 (1999), 186–192.

Freeman, Elizabeth. 'Introduction', *GLQ* 13.2–3 (2007), 159–176.

French, Marilyn. *Shakespeare's Division of Experience* (New York: Ballantine Books, 1981).

Friedlander, Ari. 'Introduction: Desiring History and Historicizing Desire', *Journal for Early Modern Cultural Studies* 16.2 (2016), 1–20.

Friedlander, Ari. *Rogue Sexuality in Early Modern English Literature* (Oxford: Oxford University Press, 2022).

Froide, Amy. *Never Married: Singlewomen in Early Modern England* (Oxford: Oxford University Press, 2005).

Frye, Susan and Karen Robertson, eds. *Maids and Mistresses, Cousins and Queens: Women's Alliances in Early Modern England* (Oxford: Oxford University Press, 1999).

Gamble, Joseph. 'Please Ask, Please Tell: On Shakespeare's Bawdy', *The Hare* 4.2 (2019).

Gamble, Joseph. *Sex Lives: Intimate Infrastructures in Early Modernity* (Philadelphia: University of Pennsylvania Press, 2023).

Gamble, Joseph and Gillian Knoll, eds. *The Kinky Renaissance* (Tempe: AMCRS Press, 2024).

Garber, Marjorie. *Shakespeare After All* (New York: Anchor Books, 2004).

Garrison, John S. 'Marlowe's Helen and th Erotics of Cultural Memory', in *Sexuality and Memory in Early Modern England: Literature and the Erotics of Recolletion*, ed. John S. Garrison and Kyle Pivetti (New York: Routledge, 2016), 120–8.

Garrison, John S. and Kyle Pivetti, eds. *Sexuality and Memory in Early Modern England: Literature and the Erotics of Recolletion* (New York: Routledge, 2016).

Giffney, Noreen, Michelle M. Sauer, and Diane Watt. *The Lesbian Premodern* (New York: Palgrave, 2011).

Gillen, Katherine. *Chaste Value: Economic Crisis, Female Chastity and the Production of Social Difference on Shakespeare's Stage* (Edinburgh: Edinburgh University Press, 2017).

Gohlke, Madelon. '"I wooed thee with my sword": Shakespeare's Tragic Paradigms', in *The Woman's Part: Feminist Criticism of Shakespeare*, eds. Carolyn Ruth Swift Lenz, Gayle Green, and Carol Thomas Neely (Urbana: University of Illinois Press, 1980), 150–170.

Goldberg, Jonathan. *James I and the Politics of Literature: Jonson, Shakespeare, Donne and Their Contemporaries* (Baltimore: Johns Hopkins University Press, 1983).

Goldberg, Jonathan. *Sodometries: Renaissance Texts, Modern Sexualities* (Stanford: Stanford University Press, 1992).

Goldberg, Jonathan. 'Sodomy and Society: The Case of Christopher Marlowe', *Southwest Review* 69 (1984), 371–378.

Gordon, Colby. *Glorious Bodies: Trans Theology and Renaissance Literature* (Chicago: University of Chicago Press, 2024).

Gowing, Laura. *Domestic Dangers: Women, Words, and Sex in Early Modern London* (Oxford: Clarendon Press, 1996).

Gowing, Laura. 'The Freedom of the Streets: Women and Social Space, 1560–1640', in *Londinopolis: Essays in the Cultural and Social History of Early Modern London*, ed. Paul Griffiths and Mark S. R. Jenner (Manchester: Manchester University Press, 2000), 130–151.

Greenblatt, Stephen. *Hamlet in Purgatory* (Princeton: Princeton University Press, 2001).

Greene, Jody. '"You Must Eat Men": The Sodomitic Economy of Renaissance Patronage', *GLQ* 1.2 (1994), 163–197.

Griffiths, Paul. *Lost Londons: Change, Crime, and Control in the Capital City, 1550–1660* (Cambridge: Cambridge University Press, 2008).

Griffiths, Paul. 'Overlapping Circles: Imagining Criminal Communities in London, 1545–1645', in *Desire and Discipline: Sex and Sexuality in the Premodern West*, ed. Jacqueline Murray and Konrad Eisenbichler (Toronto: University of Toronto Press, 1996), 115–133.

Griffiths, Paul. 'Meanings of Nightwalking in Early Modern London', *Seventeenth Century* 13.2 (1998), 212–238.

Griffiths, Paul. 'The Structure of Prostitution in Elizabethan London', *Continuity and Change* 8.1 (1993), 39–64.

Gutierrez, Nancy A. 'Gender and Value in *1 Henry VI*: The Role of Joan De Pucelle', *Theatre Journal* 42.2 (1990), 183–193.

Hackett, Helen. *Virgin Mother, Virgin Queen: Elizabeth I and the Cult of the Virgin Mary* (New York: St. Martin's Press, 1995).

Hair, Paul, ed. *Before the Bawdy Court: Selections from Church Court and Other Records Relating to the Correction of Moral Offenses in England, Scotland, and New England, 1300–1800* (London: Elek, 1972).

Hall, Kim F. *Things of Darkness: Economies of Race and Gender in Early Modern England* (Ithaca: Cornell University Press, 1995).

Halperin, David. 'The Democratic Body: Prostitution and Citizenship in Classical Athens', in *One Hundred Years of Homosexuality and Other Essays on Greek Love* (New York: Routledge, 1990), 88–112.

Hardwick, Julie. 'In Search of a Remedy: Young Women, their Intimate Partners, and the Challenge of Fertility in Early Modern France', in *The Youth of Early Modern Women*, ed. Elizabeth S. Cohen and Margaret Reeves (Amsterdam: Amsterdam University Press, 2018), 315–332.

Harris, Jonathan Gil. '(Po)X Marks the Spot: How to "Read" "Early Modern" "Syphilis" in *The Three Ladies of London*', in *Sins of the Flesh: Responding to Sexual Disease in Early Modern Europe*, ed. Kevin Siena (Toronto: Centre for Reformation and Renaissance Studies, 2005), 109–132.

Harris, Jonathan Gil. *Untimely Matter in the Time of Shakespeare* (Philadelphia: University of Philadelphia Press, 2009).

Haselkorn. Anne. *Prostitution in Elizabethan and Jacobean Comedy* (Troy: Whitson Publishing Company, 1983).

Healy, Margaret. *Fictions of Disease in Early Modern England: Bodies, Plagues and Politics* (Houndmills: Palgrave, 2001).

Helms, Lorraine. 'The Saint in the Brothel: Or, Eloquence Rewarded', *Shakespeare Quarterly* 41.3 (1990), 319–332.

Henderson, Katherine Usher and Barbara F. McManus, eds. *Half Humankind: Contexts & Texts of the Controversy about Women in England, 1540–1630* (Urbana: University of Illinois Press, 1985).

Hentschell, Rose. 'Luxury and Lechery: Hunting the French Pox in Early Modern England', in *Sins of the Flesh: Responding to Sexual Disease in Early Modern Europe*, ed. Kevin Siena (Toronto: Centre for Reformation and Renaissance Studies, 2005), 133–157.

Higginbotham, Derrick. 'Effete and Elite: The Ambivalence of the Savvy Shopper', in *Insatiable!: Gender, Sexuality and Makeshift Capitalism in England, c.1350–c.1650* (Toronto: University of Toronto Press, forthcoming).

Higginbotham, Jennifer. 'Fair Maids and Golden Girls: The Vocabulary of Female Youth in Early Modern English', *Modern Philology* 109.2 (2011), 171–196.

Higginbotham, Jennifer. 'Girls and Sexuality in Seventeenth-Century Love Lyrics', *SEL* 59 (2019), 153–175.

Higginbotham, Jennifer and Mark Albert Johnson, eds. *Queering Childhood in Early Modern English Drama and Culture* (New York: Palgrave Macmillan, 2018).

Hodgdon, Barbara. *The End Crowns All: Closure and Contradiction in Shakespeare's History* (Princeton: Princeton University Press, 1991).

Hodgdon, Barbara. 'Who Is Performing "in" These Text(s)?; or *Shrew*-ing Around', in *In Arden: Editing Shakespeare:Essays in Honour of Richard Proudfoot*, ed. Ann Thompson and Gordon McMullen (London: Bloomsbury, 2003), 95–108.

Holdsworth, Sir William. *A History of English Law*, Vol. IV (London: Methuen & Co., 1966).

Holland, Peter, ed. *Shakespeare, Memory and Performance* (Cambridge: Cambridge University Press, 2006).

Horbury, Ezra. *Prodigality in Early Modern Drama* (Cambridge: D.S. Brewer, 2019).

Howard, Jean E. 'Civic Institutions and Precarious Masculinity in Dekker's *The Honest Whore*', *Early Modern Culture* 1.1 (2000), 1–15.

Howard, Jean E. 'Mastering Difference in *The Dutch Courtesan*', *Shakespeare Studies* XXIV (1996), 105–117.

Howard, Jean E. 'The New Historicism in Renaissance Studies', *English Literary Renaissance* 16.1 (1986), 13–43.

Howard, Jean E. 'Prostitutes, Shopkeepers, and the Staging of Urban Subjects in *The Honest Whore*', in *The Elizabethan Theatre XV*, ed. C. L McGee and A. L. Magnusson, with Valerie Creelman and Todd Pettirgrew (Waterloo: P. D. Meany, 2002), 161–179.

Howard, Jean E. 'Sex and the Early Modern City: Staging the Bawdy Houses of London', in *The Impact of Feminism in English Renaissance Studies*, ed. Dympna Callaghan (Houndmills: Palgrave MacMillan, 2007), 117–136.

Howard, Jean E. *The Stage and Social Struggle in Early Modern England* (London: Routledge, 1994).

Howard, Jean E. *Theater of a City: The Places of London Comedy, 1598–1642* (Philadelphia: University of Pennsylvania Press, 2007).

Howard, Jean E. 'Women as Spectators, Spectacles, and Paying Customers', in *Staging the Renaissance: Reinterpretations of Elizabethan and Jacobean Drama*, eds. David Scott Kastan and Peter Stallybrass (New York: Routledge, 1991), 68–74.

Howard, Jean E. and Phyllis Rackin. *Engendering a Nation: A Feminist Account of Shakespeare's English Histories* (London: Routledge, 1997).

Hoy, Cyrus. *Introductions, Notes, and Commentaries to texts in 'The Dramatic Works of Thomas Dekker' Edited by Fredson Bowers*, 4 vols (Cambridge: Cambridge University Press, 1980).

Hubbard, Eleanor. 'A Room of Their Own: Young Women, Courtship, and the Night in Early Modern England', in *The Youth of Early Modern Women*, ed. Elizabeth S. Cohen and Margaret Reeves (Amsterdam: Amsterdam University Press, 2018), 297–314.

Hubbard, Eleanor. *City Women: Money, Sex, & Social Order in Early Modern London* (Oxford: Oxford University Press, 2012).

Hull, Isabel. *Sexuality, State, and Civil Society in Germany* (Ithaca: Cornell University Press, 1996).

Hull, Suzanne W. *Chaste, Silent, and Obedient: English Books for Women, 1475–1640* (San Marino: Huntington Library, 1982).

Hyman, Wendy Beth. *Impossible Desires and the Limits of Knowledge in Renaissance Poetry* (Oxford: Oxford University Press, 2019).

Ingram, Martin. *Carnal Knowledge: Regulating Sex in England, 1470–1600* (Cambridge: Cambridge University Press, 2017).

Ingram, Martin. *Church Courts, Sex, and Marriage in England, 1570–1640* (Cambridge: Cambridge University Press, 1987).

Ingram, Martin. 'The Reformation of Manners in Early Modern England', in *The Experience of Authority in Early Modern England*, ed. Paul Griffiths, Adam Fox, and Steve Hindle (New York: Palgrave, 1996), 47–88.

Jackson, Gabriele Bernhard. 'Topical Ideology: Witches, Amazons, and Shakespeare's Joan of Arc', in R. J. C. Watt, ed., *Shakespeare's History Plays* (London: Pearson Education, 2002), 20–41.

James, Heather. *Ovid and the Library of Speech in Shakespeare's England* (Cambridge: Cambridge University Press, 2023).

Jameson, Anna Brownell. *Shakespeare's Heroines* [1832] (London: George Bell & Sons, 1897).

Jankowski, Theodora. *Pure Resistance: Queer Virginity in Early Modern English Drama* (Philadelphia: University of Pennsylvania Press, 2000).

Jardine, Lisa. *Still Harping on Daughters: Women and Drama in the Age of Shakespeare* (New York: Columbia University Press, 1989).

Jardine, Lisa. '"Why Should He Call Her Whore?": Defamation and Desdemona's Case', in *Addressing Frank Kermode: Essays in Criticism and Interpretation*, ed. Margaret Tudeau-Clayton and Martin Warner (Urbana: University of Illinois Press, 1991), 124–153.

Johnson, David J. *Southwark and the City* (Oxford: Oxford University Press, 1969).

Johnston, Mark Albert. '"To What Bawdy House Doth Your Maister Belong?": Barbers, Bawds, and Vice in the Early Modern London Barbershop', in *Masculinity and the Metropolis of Vice, 1550–1650*, ed. Amanda Bailey and Roze Hentschell (New York: Palgrave MacMillan, 2010), 115–135.

Jones, Ann Rosalind and Peter Stallybrass. *Renaissance Clothing and the Materials of Memory* (Cambridge: Cambridge University Press, 2000).

Kahn, Coppélia. *Man's Estate: Masculine Identity in Shakespeare* (Berkeley: University of California Press, 1981).

Kahn, Coppélia. 'Whores and Wives in Jacobean Drama', in *In Another Country: Feminist Perspectives on Renaissance Drama*, ed. Dorothea Keller and Susan Baker (Metuchen: Scarecrow Press, 1991), 246–260.

Karim-Cooper, Farah. *Cosmetics in Shakesperean and Renaissance Drama* (Edinburgh: Edinburgh University Press, 2006).

Karras, Ruth Mazo. *Common Women: Prostitution and Sexuality in Medieval England* (New York: Oxford University Press, 1996).

Karras, Ruth Mazo. 'Prostitution and the Question of Sexual Identity in Medieval Europe', *Journal of Women's History* 11.2 (1999), 159–177.

Karras, Ruth Mazo. 'Prostitution in Medieval Europe', in *Handbook of Medieval Sexuality*, ed. Vern L. Bullough and James A. Brundage (New York: Garland, 1996), 243–260.

Karras, Ruth Mazo. 'The Regulation of Brothels in Later Medieval England', *Signs* 14.2 (1989), 399–433.

Karras, Ruth Mazo. *Sexuality in Medieval Europe: Doing unto Others* (New York: Routledge, 2005).

Kelly, Henry Ansgar. 'The Right to Remain Silent: Before and after Joan of Arc', *Speculum* 68.4 (1993), 992–1026.

Kelly, Henry Ansgar. 'Bishop, Prioress, and Bawd in the Stews of Southwark', *Speculum* 75.2 (2000), 342–388.

Kelly, Kathleen Coyne. *Performing Virginity and Testing Chastity in the Middle Ages* (New York: Routledge, 2002).

Kelly, Kathleen Coyne and Marina Leslie, eds. *Menacing Virgins: Representing Virginity in the Middle Ages and Renaissance* (Newark: University of Delaware Press, 1999).

Kiernan, Pauline. *Filthy Shakespeare: Shakespeare's Most Outrageous Sexual Puns* (New York: Gotham Books, 2006).

Kiernan, Pauline. 'The Honest Whore', Shakespeare's Globe Archives. Available online at https://archive.shakespearesglobe.com/CalmView/GetMultimedia.ashx?db=Catalog&type=default&fname=9b%5C0c48b7-d73d-4224-844b-a7c52b3ab776.pdf.

King, Margaret L. *Women of the Renaissance* (Chicago: University of Chicago Press, 1991).

Klein, Joan Larsen. *Daughters, Wives, and Widows: Writings by Men about Women and Marriage in England, 1500–1640* (Urbana: University of Illinois Press, 1992).

Korda, Natasha. 'Singlewomen and the Properties of Poverty in *Measure for Measure*', in *Money and the Age of Shakespeare: Essays in New Economic Criticism*, ed. Linda Woodbridge (New York: Palgrave MacMillan, 2003), 237–250.

Kozusko, Matt. 'Taking Liberties', *Early Theatre* 9.1 (2006), 37–60.

Kuhn, Thomas S. *The Structure of Scientific Revolutions* (Chicago: University of Chicago Press, 1962).

Kyle, Chris R. 'Monarch and Marketplace: Proclamations as News in Early Modern England', *Huntington Library Quarterly* 78.4 (2015), 771.87.

Lacan, Jacques. *Ecrits*, trans. Bruce Fink (New York: W. W. Norton, 2006).

Leggatt, Alexander. *Citizen Comedy in the Age of Shakespeare* (Toronto: University of Toronto Press, 1974).

Leggatt, Alexander. *Shakespeare's Political Drama: the History Plays and the Roman Plays* (London: Routledge, 1988).

Leinwand, Theodore. *The City Staged: Jacobean Comedy, 1603–1613* (Madison: University of Wisconsin Press, 1986).

Lenz, Joseph. 'Base Trade: Theater as Prostitution', *ELH* 60.4 (1993), 833–855.

Lenz, Carolyn, Gayle Green, and Carol Thomas Neely. *The Woman's Part: Feminist Criticism of Shakespeare* (Urbana: University of Illinois Press, 1980).

Levin, Carole. *The Heart and Stomach of a King: Elizabeth I and the Politics of Sex and Power* (Philadelphia: University of Pennsylvania Press, 1994).

Lexicons of Early Modern English (LEME). Available online at http://leme.library.utoronto.ca.

Little, Arthur L., Jr. 'Re-Historicizing Race, White Melancholia, and the Shakespearean Property', *Shakespeare Quarterly* 67 (2016), 84–103.

Lochrie, Karma. *Heterosyncrasies: Female Sexuality When Normal Wasn't* (Minneapolis: University of Minnesota Press, 2005).

Loomba, Ania. '"Break her will, and bruise no bone, sir": Colonial and Sexual Mastery in Fletcher's *The Island Princess*', *Journal for Early Modern Cultural Studies* 2.1 (Spring/Summer, 2002), 68–108.

Loomba, Ania. '"Delicious Traffick": Alterity and Exchange on Early Modern Stages', *Shakespeare Survey* 52 (1999), 201–214.

Loughlin, Marie H. *Hymeneutics: Interpreting Virginity on the Early Modern Stage* (Lewisburg: Bucknell University Press, 1997).

Love, Heather. *Feeling Backward: Loss and the Politics of Queer History* (Cambridge, MA: Harvard University Press, 2007).

Lupton, Julia Reinhardt. *Citizen-Saints: Shakespeare and Political Theology* (Chicago: University of Chicago Press, 2005).

Mallin, E. S. 'Charity and Whoredom in *Timon of Athens*', *Shakespeare Quarterly* 69 (2018), 75–100.

Manzione, Carol. 'Sex in Tudor London: Abusing Their Bodies with Each Other', in *Desire and Discipline: Sex and Sexuality in the Premodern West*, ed. Jacqueline Murray and Konrad Eisenbichler (Toronto: University of Toronto Press, 1996), 87–100.

Marcus, Leah. *Puzzling Shakespeare: Local Reading and Its Discontents* (Berkeley: University of California Press, 1988).

Marshall, Peter. *Beliefs and the Dead in Reformation England* (Oxford: Oxford University Press, 2002).

Masten, Jeffrey. *Queer Philologies: Sex, Language, and Affect in Shakespeare's Time* (Philadelphia: University of Pennsylvania Press, 2016).

McEachern, Claire. '"A Whore at the First Blush Seemeth Only a Woman": John Bale's *Image of Both Churches* and the Terms of Religious Difference in the Early English Reformation', *Journal of Medieval and Renaissance Studies* 25.2 (1995), 245–269.

McLuskie, Kathleen. 'The Patriarchal Bard: Feminist Criticism and Shakespeare', in *Political Shakespeare: Essays in Cultural Materialism*, 2nd edition, ed. Jonathan Dollimore and Alan Sinfield (Ithaca: Cornell University Press, 1994), 88–108.

McMullen, John L. *The Canting Crew: London's Criminal Underworld, 1550–1700* (New Brunswick: Rutgers University Press, 1984).

Meltzer, François. *For Fear of the Fire: Joan of Arc and the Limits of Subjectivity* (Chicago: University of Chicago Press, 2001).

Menchi, Silvana Seidel. 'The Girl and the Hourglass', in *Time, Space, and Women's Lives in Early Modern Europe*, ed. Anne Jacobson Schutte, Thomas Kuehn, and Silvana Seidel Menchi (Kirksville: Truman State University, 2000), 41–74.

Mendelson, Sara and Patricia Crawford. *Women in Early Modern England, 1550–1720* (Oxford: Clarendon Press, 1984).

Menon, Madhavi. *Wanton Words: Rhetoric and Sexuality in English Renaissance Drama*. (Toronto: University of Toronto Press, 2004).

Miller, J. Hillis. *Speech Acts in Literature* (Stanford: Stanford University Press, 2001).

Mowry, Melissa M. *The Bawdy Politic in Stuart England, 1660–1714: Radical Pornography and Prostitution* (Aldershot: Ashgate, 2004).

Mowry, Melissa M. 'London's Bridewell: Violence, Prostitution, and Questions of Evidence', in *Violence, Politics, and Gender in Early Modern England*, ed. Joseph P. Ward (New York: Palgrave Macmillan, 2008), 207–222.

Mullaney, Steven. *The Place of the Stage: License, Play, and Power in Renaissance England* (Chicago: University of Chicago Press, 1988).

Mullaney, Steven. *The Reformation of Emotions in the Age of Shakespeare* (Chicago: University of Chicago Press, 2015).

Murray, Molly. *The Poetics of Conversion in Early Modern English Literature: Verse and Change from Donne to Dryden* (Cambridge: Cambridge University Press, 2009).

Neely, Carol Thomas. *Broken Nuptials in Shakespeare's Plays* (Urbana: University of Illinois Press, 1993).

Newman, Karen. *Fashioning Femininity and English Renaissance Drama* (Chicago: University of Chicago Press, 1991), 129–144.

Newman, Karen. 'Sex in the City', in *Cultural Capitals: Early Modern London and Paris* (Princeton: Princeton University Press, 2007), 134–146.

Nocentelli, Carmen. *Empires of Love: Europe, Asia, and the Making of Early Modern Identity*. (Philadelphia: University of Pennsylvania Press, 2013).

Norberg, Kathryn. 'The Body of the Prostitute: Medieval to Modern', in *The Routledge History of Sex and the Body: 1500–Present*, ed. Sarah Toulalan and Kate Fisher (New York: Routledge, 2013), 393–408.

Orgel, Stephen. 'The Further Adventures of Ganymede', in *Childhood, Education and the Stage in Early Modern England*, ed. Deanne Williams and Richard Preiss (Cambridge: Cambridge University Press, 2017), 141–163.

Orgel, Stephen. *Impersonations: The Performance of Gender in Shakespeare's England* (Cambridge: Cambridge University Press, 1996).

Orgel, Stephen. *The Reader in the Book: A Study of Spaces and Traces* (Oxford: Oxford University Press, 2015).

Orlin, Lena Cowen. 'Women on the Threshold', *Shakespeare Studies* XXV (1997), 50–58.

Oxford English Dictionary Online. Available online at http://oed.com.

Oxford Latin Dictionary, 2nd edition, Vols I–II, ed. P. G. W. Clare (Oxford: Oxford University Press, 2012).

Panek, Jennifer. '"This Base Stallion Trade": He-Whores and Male Sexuality on the Early Modern Stage', *ELR* 40.3 (2010), 357–392.

Panek, Jennifer. *Widows and Suitors in Early Modern English Comedy* (Cambridge: Cambridge University Press, 2004).

Park, Katherine. 'The Rediscovery of the Clitoris: French Medicine and the Tribade, 1570–1620', in *The Body in Parts: Fantasies of Corporeality in Early Modern Europe*, ed. David Hilman and Carla Mazzio (New York: Routledge, 1997), 171–193.

Parker, Patricia. *Literary Fat Ladies: Rhetoric, Gender, and Property* (London: Methuen, 1987).

Parker, Patricia. *Shakespeare from the Margins: Language, Culture, Context* (Chicago: University of Chicago Press, 1996).

Parker, Patricia. *Shakespearean Intersections: Language, Contexts, Critical Keywords* (Philadelphia: University of Pennsylvania Press, 2018).

Partridge, Eric. *Shakespeare's Bawdy* (New York: E. P. Dutton & Co., 1948).

Paster, Gail Kern. *The Body Embarrassed: Drama and the Disciplines of Shame in Early Modern England* (Ithaca: Cornell University Press, 1993).

Paster, Gail Kern. *Humoring the Body: Emotions and the Shakespearean Stage* (Chicago: University of Chicago Press, 2004).

Patterson, Mary Hampson. *Domesticating the Reformation: Protestant Best Sellers, Private Devotion, and the Revolution of English Piety* (Madison: Fairleigh Dickinson University Press, 2007).

Payer, Pierre. *The Bridling of Desire: View of Sex in the Later Middle Ages* (Toronto: University of Toronto Press, 1993).

Peterson, Kaara L. 'Elizabeth I's Virginity and the Body of Evidence: Jonson's Notorious Crux', *Renaissance Quarterly* 68.3 (2025), 840–871.

Peterson, Kaara L. 'The Ring's the Thing: Elizabeth I's Virgin Knot and *All's Well That Ends Well*', *Studies in Philology* 113.1 (2016), 101–131.

Phillips, Susan E. 'Schoolmasters, Seduction, and Slavery: Polyglot Dictionaries in Pre-Modern England', *Medievalia et Humanistica* 34 (2008), 129–158.

Polkinghorne, Donald E. *Narrative Knowing and the Human Sciences* (Albany: SUNY Press, 1988).

Porter, Roy. *London: A Social History* (Cambridge, MA: Harvard University Press, 1994).

Preiss, Richard and Deanne Williams, eds. *Childhood, Education, and the Stage in Early Modern England* (Cambridge: Cambridge University Press, 2017).

Rackin, Phyllis. 'Androgyny, Mimesis, and the Marriage of the Boy Heroine on the English Renaissance Stage', *PMLA* 102.1 (1987), 29–41.

Rackin, Phyllis. *Shakespeare and Women* (Oxford: Oxford University Press, 2005).

Rackin, Phyllis. *Stages of History: Shakespeare's History Chronicles* (Ithaca: Cornell University Press, 1990).

Rambuss, Richard. *Closet Devotions* (Durham: Duke University Press, 1998).

Riggs, David. *Shakespeare's Heroical Histories: Henry VI and Its Literary Tradition* (Cambridge, MA: Harvard University Press, 1971).

Roof, Judith. *Come As You Are: Sexuality and Narrative* (New York: Columbia University Press, 1996).

Roper, Lyndal. 'Discipline and Respectability: Prostitution and the Reformation in Augsburg', in *Feminism and History*, ed. Joan Wallace Scott (Oxford: Oxford University Press, 1996), 333–365.

Roper, Lyndal. *The Holy Household: Women and Morals in Reformation Augsburg* (Oxford: Clarendon Press, 1991).

Rose, Jacqueline. 'Sexuality in the Reading of Shakespeare: *Hamlet* and *Measure for Measure*', in *Alternative Shakespeares*, ed. John Drakakis (London: Routledge, 1985), 95–118.

Rossiaud, Jacques. *Medieval Prostitution* (New York: Barnes & Noble, 1984).

Rubright, Marjorie. 'Becoming Scattered: The Case of Iphis's Trans*version and the Archipelogic of John Florio's *Worlde of Wordes*', in *Ovidian Transversions: 'Iphis and Ianthe', 1300–1650*, ed. Valerie Traub, Patricia Badir, and Peggy McCracken (Edinburgh: Edinburgh University Press, 2019), 118–149.

Rubright, Marjorie. *Doppelgänger Dilemmas: Anglo-Dutch Relations in Early Modern English Literature and Culture* (Philadelphia: University of Pennsylvania Press, 2014).

Rubright, Marjorie. 'Going Dutch in London City Comedy: Economies of Sexual and Sacred Exchange in John Marston's *The Dutch Courtesan* (1605)', *ELR* 40.1 (2010), 88–112.

Rubright, Marjorie. 'Incorporating Kate: The Myth of Monolingualism in William Shakespeare's *Henry the Fifth*', in *The Oxford Handbook of Shakespeare and Embodiment: Gender, Sexuality, and Race*, ed. Valerie Traub (Oxford: Oxford University Press, 2016), 468–490

Rubright, Marjorie. 'Shakespeare's Albion: The Racecraft of White Happiness.' Unpublished paper.

Rubright, Marjorie and Stephen Spiess, eds. *Logomotives: Words that Change the World, 1400–1700* (Edinburgh: Edinburgh University Press, 2025).

Rust, Jennifer R. 'Political Theology and Shakespeare Studies', *Literature Compass* 6.1 (2009), 175–190.

Saccio, Peter. *Shakespeare's English Kings: History, Chronicle, and Drama* (London: Oxford University Press, 1977).

Salgado, Gemini. *The Elizabethan Underworld* (Totowa: J.M. Dent & Sons, 1977).
Salkeld, Duncan. *Shakespeare among the Courtesans: Prostitution, Literature, and Drama, 1500–1650* (Burlington: Ashgate, 2012).
Salkeld, Duncan. 'Shakespeare, Theatre and Transgression', in *The Routledge Companion to Shakespeare and Politics*, ed. Chris Fitter (London: Routledge, 2025), 205–218.
Sanchez, Melissa E. *Erotic Subjects: The Sexuality of Politics in Early Modern English Literature* (Philadelphia: University of Pennsylvania Press, 2011).
Sanchez, Melissa E. *Queer Faith: Reading Promiscuity and Race in the Secular Love Tradition* (New York: NYU Press, 2019).
Sanchez, Melissa E. *Shakespeare and Queer Theory* (London: Bloomsbury, 2019).
Saussure, Ferdinand de. *Course in General Linguistics*, ed. Charles Balley and Albert Sechehaye, trans. Roy Harris (Chicago: Open Court, 2016).
Schafer, Jurgen. *Early Modern English Lexicography: A Survey of Monolingual Printed Glossaries and Dictionaries, 1475–1640* (Oxford: Clarendon Press, 1989).
Schmidt, Alexander. *Shakespeare Lexicon and Quotation Dictionary*, 2 vols (New York: Dover Press, 1971).
Schoenbaum, Samuel. *William Shakespeare: A Compact Documentary Life* (Oxford: Oxford University Press, 1977).
Schoenfeldt, Michael C. *Bodies and Selves in Early Modern England: Physiology and Inwardness in Spenser, Shakespeare, Herbert, and Milton* (Cambridge: Cambridge University Press, 1999).
Schwarz, Kathryn. *Tough Love: Amazon Encounters in the English Renaissance* (Durham: Duke University Press, 2000).
Schwarz, Kathryn. 'The Wrong Question: Thinking through Virginity', *Differences: A Journal of Feminist Cultural Studies* 13.2 (2002), 1–34.
Sedgwick, Eve Kosofsky. *Epistemology of the Closet* (Berkeley: University of California Press, 1990).
Sedgwick, Eve Kosofsky. *Tendencies* (Durham: Duke University Press, 1993).
Serjeantson, Richard. 'Francis Bacon's *Valerius Terminus* and the Voyage to the "Great Instauration"', *Journal of the History of Ideas* 78.3 (2017), 341–368.
Shannon, Laurie. *Sovereign Amity: Figures of Friendship in Shakespearean Contexts* (Chicago: Unversity of Chicago Press, 2002).
Shapiro, James. *Shakespeare and the Jews* (New York: Columbia University Press, 1996).
Shepard, Alexandra. *Meanings of Manhood in Early Modern England* (Oxford: Oxford University Press, 2003).
Shuger, Deborah. *Political Theologies in Shakespeare's England: The Sacred and the State in Measure for Measure* (Houndmills: Palgrave, 2001).
Shugg, Wallace. 'Prostitution in Shakespeare's London', *Shakespeare Studies* X (1977), 291–313.

Singh, Jyotsna. 'The Interventions of History: Narratives of Sexuality', in *The Weyward Sisters: Shakespeare and Feminist Politics*, ed. Dympna Callaghan, Lorraine Helms, and Jyotsna Singh (Oxford: Blackwell, 1994), 7–58.

Soltan, Margaret. 'Night Errantry: The Epistemology of the Wandering Woman', *New Formations* 5.2 (1988), 108–119.

Smalley, Baryl. *English Friars and Antiquity in the Early Fourteenth Century* (Oxford: Basil Blackwell, 1960).

Smith, Bruce R. *Homosexual Desire in Shakespeare's England: A Cultural Poetics* (Chicago: University of Chicago Press, 1992).

Smith, Ian. 'The Queer Moor: Bodies, Borders, and Barbary Inns', in *A Companion to the Global Renaissance: English Liiterature and Culture in the Era of Expansion*, ed. Jyotsna Singh (Malden: Wiley Blackwell, 2009), 190–204.

Somerset, Alan. 'Cultural Poetics, or Historical Prose? The Places of the State', *Medieval & Renaissance Drama in England* 11 (1999), 34–59.

Spevack, Marvin. *A Complete and Systematic Concordance to the Works of Shakespeare*, 5 vols (Hildesheim: Georg Olms Verlagsbuchhandlung, 1970).

Spiess, Stephen. 'The Confounding Gloss: Reading the Lowne in *Pericles* and *Edward II*', *Modern Philology* 121.3 (2024), 296–325.

Stallybrass, Peter. 'Books and Scrolls: Navigating the Bible', in *Books and Readers in EM England: Material Studies*, ed. Jennifer Anderson and Elizabeth Sauer (Philadelphia: University of Pennsylvania Press, 2001), 42–77.

Stallybrass, Peter. 'Patriarchal Territories: The Body Enclosed Text', in *Rewriting the Renaissance: The Discourses of Sexual Difference in Early Modern Europe*, eds. Margaret W. Ferguson, Maureen Quilligan, and Nancy J. Vickers (Chicago, University of Chicago Press (1986), 123–142

Stallybrass, Peter. 'Shakespeare, the Individual, and the Text', in *Cultural Studies*, ed. Lawrence Grossberg, Cary Nelson, and Paula A. Treichler (New York: Routledge, 1992), 593–612.

Stallybrass, Peter. 'The World Turned Upside Down: Inversion, Gender, and the State', in *The Matter of Difference: Materialist Feminist Criticism of Shakespeare*, ed. Valerie Wayne (Ithaca: Cornell University Press, 1991), 202–220.

Stallybrass, Peter, Roger J. Chartier, Franklin Mowery, and Heather Wolfe. 'Hamlet's Tables and the Technologies of Writing in Renaissance England', *Shakespeare Quarterly* 55.4 (1996), 379–419.

Stanton, Kay. 'A Presentist Analysis of Joan, La Pucelle: "What's Past and What's to Come She Can Descry"', in Evelyn Gajowski, ed., *Presentism, Gender, and Sexuality in Shakespeare* (New York: Palgrave MacMillan, 2009), 103–121.

Stanton, Kay. *Shakespeare's 'Whores': Erotics, Politics, and Poetics* (Houndmills: Palgrave Macmillan, 2014).

Steedman, Carolyn. *Dust: The Archive and Cultural History* (New Brunswick: Rutgers University Press, 2002).

Stein, Gabriele. *The English Dictionary before Cawdrey* (Tubingen: Max Niemeyer Verlag, 1985).

Stern, Tiffany. *Documents of Performance in Early Modern England* (Cambridge: Cambridge University Press, 2009).

Stewart, Alan. *Close Readers: Humanism and Sodomy in EM England* (Princeton, Princeton University Press, 1997).

Stockton, Will. 'Chasing Chastity: The Case of Desdemona', in *Rethinking Feminism: Gender, Race, and Sexuality in the Early Modern World*, ed. Ania Loomba and Melissa Sanchez (New York: Ashgate, 2016), 195–212.

Stoler, Laura Ann. *Along the Archival Grain: Epistemic Anxieties and Colonial Common Sense* (Princeton: Princeton University Press, 2009).

Stoler, Laura Anne. *Race and the Education of Desire: Foucault and the Colonial Order of Things* (Durham: Duke University Press, 1995).

Storey, Tessa. *Carnal Commerce in Counter-Reformation Rome* (Cambridge: Cambridge University Press, 2008).

Sullivan, Garrett. *Memory and Forgetting in English Renaissance Drama: Shakespeare, Marlowe, Webster* (Cambridge: Cambridge University Press, 2005).

Taylor, Craig, ed. and trans. *Joan of Arc: La Pucelle* (Manchester: Manchester University Press, 2006).

Taylor, Larissa Juliet. *The Virgin Warrior: The Life and Death of Joan of Arc* (New Haven: Yale University Press, 2009).

Thompson, E. P. *The Making of the English Working Class* (New York: Vintage, 1963).

Tisdale, Catherine. 'Stranger Compass of the Stage: Difference and Desire in Early Modern City Comedy' (PhD dissertation, University of Massachusetts-Amherst, 2022).

Todd, Barbara J. 'The Remarrying Widow: A Stereotype Reconsidered', in *Women in English Society, 1500–1800*, ed. Mary Prior (London: Routledge, 1985), 25–52.

Toulalan, Sarah. '"Age to Great, or to Little, Doeth Let Conception": Bodies, Sex, and Life Cycle, 1500–1700', in *The Routledge History of Sex and the Body: 1500–Present*, ed. Sarah Toulalan and Kate Fisher (New York: Routledge, 2013), 279–295.

Traub, Valerie. *Desire and Anxiety: Circulations of Sexual Energy in Shakespearean Drama* (London: Routledge, 1992).

Traub, Valerie. 'The Perversion of Lesbian Desire', *History Workshop Journal* 41.1 (1996), 23–49.

Traub, Valerie. *The Renaissance of Lesbianism in Early Modern England* (Cambridge: Cambridge University Press, 2002).

Traub, Valerie. *Thinking Sex with the Early Moderns* (Philadelphia: University of Philadelphia Press, 2016).

Tricomi, Albert H. 'Joan La Pucelle and the Inverted Saints Play in *1 Henry VI*', *Renaissance and Reformation* XXV.2 (2001), 5–31.

Twyning, John. *London Dispossessed: Literature and Social Space in the Early Modern City* (New York: St. Martin's Press, 1988).

Ungerer, Gustav. 'Prostitution in Late Elizabethan London: The Case of Mary Newborough', *Medieval and Renaissance Drama in England* 15 (2002), 138–223.

Ure, Peter. 'Patient Madman and Honest Whore: The Middleton-Dekker Oxymoron', *Essays and Studies* 19.1 (1966), 18–40.

van der Meer, Theo. 'Medieval Prostitution and the Case of a (Mistaken?) Sexual Identity', *Journal of Women's History* 11.2 (1999), 178–185.

Varholy, Christine M. '"But She Woulde Not Consent": Women's Narratives of Sexual Assaults and Compulsion in Early Modern London', in *Violence, Politics, and Gender in Early Modern England*, ed. Joseph P. Ward (New York: Palgrave MacMillan, 2008), 41–66.

Varholy, Christine M. '"Rich Like a Lady": Cross-Class Dressing in the Brothels and Theaters of Early Modern England', *Journal for Early Modern Cultural Studies* 8.1 (2008), 4–34.

Varnado, Christine. '"Invisible Sex!": What Looks Like the Act in Early Modern Drama?', in *Sex before Sex: Figuring the Act in EM England*, ed. James Bromley and Will Stockton (Minneapolis: University of Minnesota Press, 2013), 25–52.

Vitkus, Daniel J. *Turning Turk: English Theater and the Multicultural Mediterranean, 1570–1630* (New York: Palgrave MacMillan, 2003).

Walker, Garthine. *Crime, Gender, and Social Order in Early Modern England* (Cambridge: Cambridge University Press, 2003).

Walkowitz, Judith R. *Prostitution and Victorian Society: Women, Class, and the State* (Cambridge: Cambridge University Press, 1980).

Walkowitz, Judith R. *City of Dreadful Delight: Narratives of Sexual Danger in Late-Victorian London* (Chicago: University of Chicago Press, 1992).

Wall, Wendy. *The Imprint of Gender: Authorship and Publication in the English Renaissance* (Ithaca: Cornell University Press, 1993).

Warhol, Robyn L. and Susan S. Lanser. *Narrative Theory Unbound: Queer and Feminist Interventions* (Columbus: Ohio State University Press, 2015).

Warner, Marina. *Joan of Arc: The Image of Female Heroism* (Berkeley: University of California Press, 1981).

White, Hayden. 'The Value of Narrativity in the Representation of Reality', *Critical Inquiry* 7.1 (1980), 5–27.

Wiesner-Hanks, Merry E., ed. *Gendered Temporalities in the Early Modern World* (Amsterdam: Amsterdam University Press, 2018).
Wilder, Lina Perkins. *Shakespeare's Memory Theater* (Cambridge: Cambridge University Press, 2010).
Williams, Gordon. *A Glossary of Shakespeare's Sexual Language* (London: Athlone, 1997).
Williams, Raymond. *Keywords: A Vocabulary of Culture and Society*, revised edition (New York: Oxford University Press, 1983).
Woodbridge, Linda. *Women and the English Renaissance: Literature and the Nature of Womankind, 1540–1620* (Urbana: University of Illinois Press, 1986).
Yates, Frances. *The Art of Memory* (Chicago: University of Chicago Press, 1966).
Ziegler, Georgianna, with Frances E. Dolan and Jeanne Addison Roberts. *Shakespeare's Unruly Women* (Seattle: University of Washington Press, 1997).

INDEX

For the benefit of digital users, indexed terms that span two pages (e.g., 52–53) may, on occasion, appear on only one of those pages.

The manufacturer's authorised representative in the EU for product safety is Oxford University Press España S.A. of El Parque Empresarial San Fernando de Henares, Avenida de Castilla, 2 - 28830 Madrid (www.oup.es/en or product.safety@oup.com). OUP España S.A. also acts as importer into Spain of products made by the manufacturer.
Printed and bound by CPI Group (UK) Ltd, Croydon, CR0 4YY
30/09/2026
02225518-0003